# STATUS UPDATE

———

# STATUS UPDATE

CELEBRITY, PUBLICITY,

AND BRANDING IN

THE SOCIAL MEDIA AGE

ALICE E. MARWICK

Yale
UNIVERSITY PRESS

New Haven & London

Yale University Press books may be purchased in quantity for
educational, business, or promotional use. For information,
please e-mail sales.press@yale.edu (U.S. office) or
sales@yaleup.co.uk (U.K. office).

Set in Caslon Pro and Whitney types by Westchester Book Group.
Printed in the United States of America.

Library of Congress Cataloging-in-Publication Data

Marwick, Alice Emily.
Status update : celebrity, publicity, and branding in the social
media age / Alice E. Marwick.
pages cm
Includes bibliographical references and index.
ISBN 978-0-300-17672-8 (cloth : alkaline paper)
1. Web 2.0.   2. Social media.   3. Social status.
4. Celebrities.   5. Publicity.   6. Branding (Marketing)
I. Title.
TK5105.88817.M36 2013
305.5'2—dc23
2013017042

A catalogue record for this book is available from the British Library.

This paper meets the requirements of ANSI/NISO Z39.48–1992
(Permanence of Paper).

10 9 8 7 6 5 4 3 2

To my family

# CONTENTS

———

Introduction
1

1
A Cultural History of Web 2.0
21

2
Leaders and Followers: Status in the Tech Scene
73

3
The Fabulous Lives of Micro-Celebrities
112

4
Self-Branding: The (Safe for Work) Self
163

5

Lifestreaming: We Live in Public

205


6

Designed in California: Entrepreneurship and the Myths
of Web 2.0

245


Conclusion

273


Appendix: Cast of Characters

283


Acknowledgments

287


Notes

293


Bibliography

317


Index

347

# INTRODUCTION

———

A few months after I arrived in San Francisco, a friend invited me to the Facebook company Christmas party. The theme was the 1940s, so I put on a flowered dress, pinned my hair in victory rolls, and painted on red lipstick. The first stop was a pre-party in a luxury apartment complex in San Francisco's South of Market district, where a group of twenty-somethings, the men in suits and fedoras and the women in BCBG cocktail dresses and gladiator heels, were mixing drinks and playing beer pong. The apartment was sparsely furnished, containing only a futon, a ping-pong table, and a giant flat-screen TV. The Facebook employees were raucous and excited. They loved their jobs, loved Facebook, and loved working with lots of other young people. It was common, they told me, to share, even "overshare," details of their personal life at work. But the line between personal and work was hard to find; they worked and socialized together.

Once my compatriots were sufficiently buzzed, we cabbed to an opulent, hilltop event space set between ritzy Nob Hill and the run-down Tenderloin. The main room featured dueling pianos, karaoke, and an elaborate buffet of sushi, mashed potatoes served in martini glasses, cooked-to-order steak, and a chocolate fountain. Downstairs, M. C. Hammer danced with an attractive date, employees played blackjack and roulette for a chance to win snowboarding gear, and girls crowded into a digital photo booth, mugging for the camera. At my table we were all in our mid-thirties, and by far the oldest guests there. The exuberant Facebook employees all seemed to be around twenty-four. Life was good: they worked at one of the hot-test companies in America, and their youthful founder, Mark Zuckerberg, was an icon of the new tech boom. As the night went on, attendees became increasingly drunk, the dancing increasingly dirty, and the karaoke increasingly off-key. I spotted one girl fall off her heels as other inebriated coworkers attempted to lift her. I left at 1:00 A.M. The party was still in full swing.

The week before, Yahoo! had laid off 10 percent of its staff, includ-ing employees of formerly hot startups such as Flickr and Last.fm.[1] Two months previously, the stock market had suffered its worst drop in two decades.[2] By the winter of 2009, many companies were canceling their holiday parties in the wake of the worsening eco-nomic crisis.[3] Facebook appeared to be fine. Its user base increased from about 12 million in 2006 to 150 million in 2008 and would grow to almost a billion by the middle of 2012, when the company's initial public offering (IPO) launched to great fanfare and a $104 billion valuation.[4] Facebook was the crown jewel of the new social media startups that had emerged, mostly in San Francisco, in the wake of the dot-com bust of the late 1990s.

Social media has had a huge impact on life in the past decade. Fifty percent of all Americans now use social media sites like Face-book. Among teenagers, 76 percent use social media, and 93 per-cent of those use Facebook.[5] What was once a niche pastime called "computer-mediated communication" is now central to many people's social lives. Social media is also a powerful symbol that has come to represent, at different times, American entrepreneurialism and in-novation, freedom and participation, and revolution and change. *Time* magazine famously named "You" the 2006 person of the year, echo-ing claims that the popular video-sharing site YouTube would revo-lutionize the stranglehold that highly consolidated media companies had over video content, allowing more space for unconventional and marginalized voices.[6] The U.S. State Department believed Twitter to be so integral to the Arab Spring uprisings in Iran, Tunisia, Libya, and Egypt that it forbade the company to undertake planned downtime, regardless of the actual impact of Twitter on these pop-ular movements.[7] Academics like Yochai Benkler, Clay Shirky, and Henry Jenkins linked social media to new models of organization and by proxy to radical social change.[8]

The U.S. technology industry also remained a bright spot in an otherwise dim national economy. While high unemployment num-bers plagued industries like construction and manufacturing, engi-neers were in such demand in Silicon Valley that Google paid six figures to computer science graduates fresh out of college. Keith Ra-bois of Square, the smartphone credit-card-reader startup, described high-tech recruiting in San Francisco as "more competitive and in-tense and furious than college football recruiting of high school athletes."[9] Venture capital funding in the Bay Area increased be-tween 2007 and 2011 despite the economic downturn.[10] Facebook's young, wealthy, and entitled employees were reaping the benefits.

The excitement around social media and the immense wealth of young technologists glamorized entrepreneurs as the rock stars of twenty-first-century capitalism. Technology workers, media, and businesspeople valorized Steve Jobs, Mark Zuckerberg, and Ev Williams as visionary leaders. Prestigious universities launched en-trepreneurship programs, cities from New York to Waterloo invested significant public money into encouraging technology startups, and incubators popped up to nurture potential young entrepreneurs.[11] Indeed, 77 percent of fifth- to twelfth-graders stated in a 2011 Gallup poll that they wished to own their own business.[12] Entrepreneurs were thought to embody bravery, gumption, self-promotion, and creativity, the predictors of contemporary success. Indeed, the ideal of entrepreneurship expanded beyond the technology industry into other aspects of life, including our most personal understandings of selfhood, relationships, and the body.

This book is about the center of the social media world, San Francisco, where I conducted ethnographic fieldwork from 2006 to 2010.[13] It is about how "the tech scene" functions, what it values, and what it produces: technology that used to be called "Web 2.0" and is now roughly encapsulated by the term "social media." I first moved to San Francisco the summer after my first year of my Ph.D. program to work as a researcher at a startup. Although I studied internet community, I had never heard of many of the sites and slang terms that were de rigueur among my new friends who worked at companies like Digg, Get Satisfaction, and Yelp. Their social lives revolved around company-sponsored parties, where hundreds of twenty- and thirty-year-olds drank, danced, and talked shop. My friends and I went to meetups and concerts and watched *Snakes on a Plane* in a theater with dozens of other meme-inspired nerds. At the time, the predominant discourse about Web 2.0 was its potential for liberation and participation, or its ability to empower regular people to garner as much attention as big companies and huge brands.

But my interactions made clear that the tech scene had, in fact, a strict social hierarchy. It mattered what company you worked for, whether you were an entrepreneur, and how much attention you received online. I hypothesized that studying the status structure of this community—the people who built virtually all the popular social media applications of the time—would reveal a great deal about how status was built into Web 2.0, and thus illuminate how popular social software may promote inequality rather than counter it.

The history of the Northern California tech industry and San Francisco's roots in radical counterculture have created an ideology of Web 2.0 that ascribes both enormous power and profitability to social technologies. This ideology is a peculiar mix of entrepreneurial capitalism, technological determinism, and digital exceptionalism, which frames everything from photo-sharing websites to casual gaming as potential "game-changers." In studying this world closely, I found that, far from the revolutionary and progressive participation flaunted by entrepreneurs and pundits, social media applications encourage people to compete for social benefits by gaining visibility and attention. To boost social status, young professionals adopt self-consciously constructed personas and market themselves, like brands or celebrities, to an audience or fan base. These personas are highly edited, controlled, and monitored, conforming to commercial ideals that dictate "safe-for-work" self-presentation. The technical mechanisms of social media reflect the values of where they were produced: a culture dominated by commercial interest. Although freewheeling creativity, rebellion, and non-hierarchical communality still exist online, they are dwarfed by social media applications that transform "social graphs," the web of digital connections around a single user, into networks of personal brands contending for the very real benefits of high online status.[14] These changes are deeply rooted in contemporary consumer capitalism, specifically the philosophy of deregulation and privatization known as "neoliberalism."

The focus of this book is how, and why, social media—or Web 2.0—produces subjects. In other words, what types of selves are people encouraged to create and promote while using popular technologies like Facebook, Twitter, and YouTube? Strategic online self-presentation plays an enormous role in increasing one's social status, how one is viewed both online and off. What factors influence these online selves? What do we hope to be like online? What is the relationship between our online and offline selves? What is the relationship between our ideals of our selves, and the political and economic philosophies of the technology we use? For neoliberal market policies to operate properly, people must adopt actions, ways of thinking, and discourses that are congruent with neoliberalism. Neoliberalism, or the infiltration of market logic into everyday social relations, requires a willing subject and is far more effective when consensual and dispersed through micro-interactions than when imposed from the top down. This book argues that Web 2.0 models ideal neoliberal selves, and rewards those who adopt such subjectivities.

### What Was Web 2.0?

Web 2.0 was a moment in technology innovation sandwiched between the dot-com bust and the App store. It wasn't just a set of technologies (APIs, Ajax, client-side browser-based software, mash-ups), or a group of websites (Flickr, del.icio.us, Twitter, MySpace, YouTube), but a collection of ideals (transparency, participation, and openness) as well. It was also an opportunity to make some money. The "2.0" appellation, borrowed from software version numbers, differentiated the websites of 2006–2009 from those of 1997–2001. It supposedly marked a break from the failures of the past and a radically new shift in the internet, from the web to "Web 2.0." In this book, I treat Web 2.0 both as a historical moment and an ongoing discourse—one that combines technological progressivism (technology always makes things better) and technological determinism (technology determines social effects). The result is a set of characters, mythologies, and actions drawn from familiar American themes, like the rags-to-riches entrepreneur, and repositioned within startup culture.

While the term Web 2.0 seems dated, many of its guiding principles are more important today than they were in 2005. Others have virtually disappeared. Web 2.0 celebrated developments like open-source software and "interoperability," the ability to port data from one site to another. These ideals seem quaint in the context of closed networks like Facebook, proprietary formats like the Apple App Store, and highly regulated environments like mobile carriers.[15] Even sites like Twitter, which once encouraged third-party development, now limit access to their data. But entrepreneurship, along with self-presentation techniques like micro-celebrity, self-quantification, and self-promotion, are more salient today than they were in the mid-2000s. "People in San Francisco," one of my interviewees noted in 2009, "it's like they're from the future."

"Web 2.0" is also a kind of social, economic, technological, and intellectual "imaginary" in Benedict Anderson's sense of an "imagined community."[16] It describes and opens up for consideration a world in which technology creates greater cultural participation, where creativity and control are disseminated throughout the population rather than concentrated in the hands of a few large corporations. Web 2.0 suggests that technology can be used to bring about positive political changes and new relationships between citizens and governments, individuals and movements, and customers and businesses. It also articulates a world of wealth in which regular people, without Ivy League educations or family connections, can use the tools of web and application development to become very rich. In addition, it allows one to imagine a work environment unfettered by hierarchy or boredom. These ideals provide a way to make sense of a rapidly changing technological and economic landscape.

Social media is intrinsically focused on individuals—the "profile" being the key unit of Web 2.0—who produce and consume content. Thus this book deals with self-presentation strategies. Individuals tend to adopt a neoliberal subjectivity that applies market principles to how they think about themselves, interact with others, and display their identity. People present themselves online based on a host of factors including their physical environment; social context; race, ethnicity, gender, sexuality, and economic background; the availability of technical infrastructure; the technical affordances of different applications; and the norms of those with whom they interact online. But the organizing principles of Web 2.0 technologies are deeply influenced by the context in which they were created: the venture-backed startup scene of San Francisco.

### I'm Updating My Status . . .

In 2008, Twitter was the hottest technology in San Francisco. One night, a friend organized a girl's dinner for four. We had pizza at Little Star on Divisadero and drinks afterward at a bar across the street. My friends spent most of the night tweeting about what we were doing, @replying to each other's tweets, posting pictures on-line, and sharing things they had posted to Tumblr. Their iPhones rarely left their hands, even as they ate. At the time, I was a broke graduate student with a Sidekick phone.[17] I had joined Twitter at the conference South by Southwest the previous year, but had barely tweeted since. My initial reaction to Twitter was suspicion and jealousy (what techies call FOMO, or "fear of missing out"). I felt left out and frustrated by my friends' fascination with a service that seemed trivial. While I slowly learned to use, and eventually like, the service, I still found the technology scene's obsession with Twitter startling.

San Francisco is an unusual place for many reasons, including its famed liberalism, GLBTQ community, and rich history of activism. It is also the center of technology development for the United States, and in some sense the world. The Bay Area of Northern California, including San Francisco and its southern suburbs of Silicon Valley, is home to the majority of name-brand social media startups, including Google, Facebook, Twitter, Instagram, Pinterest, and Flickr. Silicon Valley has been ground zero for boom-and-bust cycles of technological development since the 1960s, and it boasts a rich infrastructure that supports engineering, venture capital, and technological innovation. Around this industry has grown up a lively community of social media enthusiasts who socialize in person and online. This "tech scene" is comprised of people working at venture-backed technology startups, employees at big companies like Google, freelancers, social media "gurus," engineers, academics, fanboys, and designers, many of whom move to San Francisco to participate in the community. People in the scene write software, start companies, collaborate, and use each other's products. Their interactions are chronicled and publicized by blogs like *TechCrunch* and *Mashable* and followed vicariously by people all over the world. This scene is in some respects a subset of the much larger Silicon Valley technological infrastructure and thus reflects many of its values, but it is distinct in crucial ways from the cultures of immigrant engineers, old-school computer geeks, and businesspeople that predominate in the southern suburbs.[18] New York has since become a secondary social media destination, boasting Etsy, Kickstarter, Tumblr, Foursquare, and other hot startups, but it was not when I began this project.

I spent nine months in San Francisco from 2008 to 2009 conducting fieldwork and returned several times to do follow-up interviews. During this time, I conducted about fifty interviews with prominent and obscure members of the scene and talked to hundreds of people informally. I attended between two and five tech events a week, sometimes several on the same night. I went to meetups about mobile technology, virtual currency, and using Web 2.0 to improve the urban environment. I went to *Mashable* parties, *TechCrunch* parties, and South by Southwest (four times); I attended Women 2.0 events, Girls in Tech events, lectures, roundtables, panels, book parties, tweetups, drinkups, and conferences.[19] I followed insiders to social events such as rock shows, birthday parties, picnics, dinners, and gatherings in bars. I learned which coffee shops were the most popular places to work (Sugarlump, Ritual Roasters, and Coffee Bar) and spent hours there, sometimes joining other people for "co-working" sessions, and I co-worked at spaces formally set up for this purpose, such as CitizenSpace and PariSoma.[20] I took regular fieldnotes on these excursions, scribbling in my notebook on the sidelines of various events, to the extent that I was asked several times if I was a journalist. Twice I was mistaken for a reporter for *Valleywag,* a notorious tech gossip blog. People in the tech scene spend a lot of time talking to each other online as well as in person, and I began to check Twitter throughout the day, although I did not really "get it" until I bought an iPhone halfway through my fieldwork, and subsequently switched to the sophisticated Twitter client TweetDeck on my laptop. (Both changes were more or less precipitated by peer pressure from my informant group.)[21] While Twitter was by far the most popular place for interaction within the scene, I observed interactions on Facebook and Flickr and read tech blogs, particularly *Valleywag, TechCrunch,* and *Mashable,* every day.[22]

This project could be considered a "multi-sited ethnography," in that I collected data from more than one "site," but it was difficult to determine where these sites began or ended. Unlike discrete, bounded online communities like Usenet or Second Life, the rambling online tech scene includes comments, links, and aggregators that mix and mash up information. I asked informants for good resources, followed links posted on Twitter, learned about sites and tools at conferences, and frequently Googled key people.[23] For the most part, this project is more a traditional ethnography than a "digital" or "virtual" one, since I myself witnessed most of the anecdotes and descriptions in this book. But the firm division between "online" and "offline" is immensely complicated in places like San Francisco with high rates of technology use. What happens in person affects what happens on the internet, and vice versa. In the tech scene, social media is a part of everyday life, not apart from it.[24] As a result, the way people seek status online has tangible effects on face-to-face interactions. High online status opens doors, and the lines between cultural, social, and financial capital are blurred.

## Why Study Status?

I chose to investigate status in the tech scene so that I could analyze inequality from a perspective that incorporated more than any singular point of view, such as class, race, gender, or sexuality. As I delved into modern conceptions of status, I found that social media's broadcasting ability has transformed social status, encouraging people to prioritize attention and visibility. Social media tools like Twitter, Facebook, and YouTube teach users strategies and practices to achieve "micro-celebrity"; these strategies combine the entrepreneurialism fetishized by techies and businesspeople with marketing and advertising techniques drawn from commercials and celebrity culture. Social media has brought the attention economy into the everyday lives and relationships of millions of people worldwide, and popularized attention-getting techniques like self-branding and lifestreaming. To provide an example of just how far this has gone,

I recently conducted a study with Nicole Ellison that found that people who maintain Facebook pages memorializing deceased individuals brag about the number of "Likes" they have received.[25]

Borrowing from the French theorist Michel Foucault, I argue that these techniques constitute technologies of subjectivity; that is, social media has become a way that people govern themselves. Moreover, this self-governance ties into modern neoliberal market capitalism. The self-presentation techniques so valued by technology workers are intimately connected to the tech industry's strong faith in deregulated capitalism and entrepreneurship.

## Life in a Free Market

*Neoliberalism* describes an economic philosophy that privileges the unfettered functioning of the free market. Neoliberal policies advocate corporate deregulation, privatization, competition, entrepreneurialism, and open markets to achieve both financial success and individual self-actualization. According to neoliberal ideologies, the logic of the market can be used both to understand human behavior and to regulate it. Stemming from the economic philosophies of Chicago school economists like Milton Friedman and Friedrich Hayek, neoliberal economics came to prominence in the 1980s under politicians like Ronald Reagan, Margaret Thatcher, and later, Bill Clinton, all of whom advocated globalization and minimal government regulation.[26] While these policies have met with global protests, they have become the predominant paradigm of the twenty-first century.[27]

The term "neoliberalism" is rarely used by free-market proponents, who prefer the terms "neoclassical" or "globalization." In fact, the term "neoliberalism" holds an implicit critique of market capitalism. This use of the word is rooted in the Marxist tradition, which holds that industry alienates people from the fruits of their labor and benefits the wealthy rather than the workers. As a result, you are most likely to hear "neoliberalism" used by leftist academics and activists, often as a shorthand for the worst excesses of capitalism or as a general criticism of market economics. For example, in the introduction to Noam Chomsky's *Profits over People*, Robert McChesney defines neoliberalism as "the policies and processes whereby a relative handful of private interests are permitted to control as much as possible of social life in order to maximize their personal profit."[28] This wide application has made the term frustratingly vague and difficult to use analytically.[29]

Regardless of my personal feelings about late capitalism, using "neoliberalism" as a critique is counterproductive given its contentiousness. So I use "neoliberalism" to indicate a form of governmentality, specifically the theory that the free market has become an organizing principle of society.[30] Governmentality, as defined by Foucault, includes "the totality of practices, by which one can constitute, define, organize, [and] instrumentalize the strategies which individuals in their liberty can have in regard to each other."[31] In other words, governmentality is a way to govern people, a technique that determines the strategies available for people to use in interpersonal relationships and self-expression.[32] Political power becomes intertwined with our ideals of our selves, and the very idea of what it means to be human.[33] This governance takes place through the creation and popularization of technologies that encourage people to regulate their own behavior along business ideals. In the early twentieth century, the technology of public schooling was designed to regulate children to work in factories: children were trained to respond to bells, walk in lines, and perform repetitive tasks.[34] This book argues that Web 2.0 technologies function similarly, teaching their users to be good corporate citizens in the postindustrial, post-union world by harnessing marketing techniques to boost attention and visibility.

In the past forty years, unionized industrial capitalism has declined in the United States and the Western world at large. The rise of neoliberalism is concurrent with a shift from factory and agricultural labor to service work, such as retail, customer service, and fast food. While in 1955 a significant 28 percent of the workforce was unionized, in 2011 only 11 percent of Americans held union jobs.[35] Real wages have stagnated since the 1980s.[36] Large corporations have moved many manufacturing jobs overseas, and replaced other positions with automated machinery.[37] In this environment, a worker trained for repetitive tasks, manual labor, and Pavlovian-style responses is at a disadvantage. A different set of skills is needed to succeed in a neoliberal environment, both as a worker and consumer.

Neoliberalism contains a discursively embedded ideal subject. In an uncertain economic climate, successful workers must be active, entrepreneurial risk-takers. Given corporate deregulation and the de-emphasis on government-provided social services, neoliberal citizens should be self-sufficient and responsible. The rapid pace of information technology and global labor requires a flexible workforce that learns quickly. An effective neoliberal subject attends to fashions, is focused on self-improvement, and purchases goods and services to achieve "self-realization." He or she is comfortable integrating market logics into many aspects of life, including education, parenting, and relationships. In other words, the ideal neoliberal citizen is an entrepreneur.

This ideal subject appears in many locations. She is present in makeover shows like *What Not to Wear* and *Queer Eye for the Straight Guy*, which contrast an undesirable "before" with a consumer-friendly "after."[38] He can be seen in reality television, which presents individuals as products (celebrities) and normalizes corporate and government surveillance.[39] And she is apparent in Web 2.0 technologies, which idealize and reward a particular persona: highly visible, entrepreneurial, and self-configured to be watched and consumed by others. These technologies make it possible for the neoliberal subject to come into being through individual self-regulation, rather than through top-down governance. The integration of market logics into social media and the effect of these logics on those who practice neoliberal subjectivity are together the focus of this book.

### Learning Who to Be

Foucault's concept of "technology of the self" refers to anything that helps people alter themselves to best fit an ideal, including therapy, plastic surgery, and self-help books. These technologies of the self intrinsically demonstrate how to be a proper modern person, be it one who is centered, thin, pretty, or productive. Since these ideals collude with the dominant political perspective, "technologies of the self" also function as a mode of governance, or governmentality. Rather than regulating people to fit into an ideal directly, technologies of subjectivity result in self-regulation. Foucault argued that neoliberalism places homo economicus at the center of politics, promoting a model of people as rational, competitive, self-interested subjects rather than civic-minded citizens.[40] This "subjectivity," or way of thinking about the self, is furthered by media and discourse, and is achieved through technologies of the self. For instance, the anthropologist Aiwa Ong identifies citizenship as a neoliberal technology of subjectivity because it rewards the benefits of citizenship—understood here as being a recognized member of a nationality—to those who best meet the definition of global, mobile subjects, rather than to people living in a particular territory. People thus regulate and modify themselves along neoliberal principles to receive these benefits.[41]

Web 2.0 is a neoliberal technology of subjectivity that teaches users how to succeed in postmodern American consumer capitalism. Social media not only demonstrates the lessons of white-collar business success by rewarding flexibility, entrepreneurialism, and risk-taking; it also provides a blueprint of how to prosper in a society where status is predicated on the cultural logic of celebrity, according to which the highest value is given to mediation, visibility, and attention. That is, the technical affordances of social media reward with higher social status the use of behaviors and self-presentation strategies that make people look.

This increased status, reputation, or popularity motivates online engagement, since successful internet content is modeled by others. Teen idol Justin Bieber, who rose to prominence on YouTube, has inspired a gaggle of other young musicians. The teen singers Grayson Chance (who appeared on *Ellen* after the talk show host saw a YouTube video of his performance of "Paparazzi" by Lady Gaga),

Rebecca Black (who appeared in a Katy Perry video after her song "Friday" became an internet sensation), Charice (who was cast in a recurring role on *Glee* based on her viral video of trying out for a Filipino reality show), and Maria Aragon (who sang with Lady Gaga in concert after the pop star saw her version of "Born This Way" online), operate as living instruction manuals for aspiring young pop stars. (Specifically, they demonstrate the value of posting content to YouTube.) Highly followed Twitter users encourage others to re-tweet, @reply, and self-promote with the goal of becoming the next @aplusk (actor Ashton Kutcher) or @garyvee (entrepreneur Gary Vaynerchuk). Successful food bloggers, fashion bloggers, and "mommy bloggers" inspire thousands of imitators hoping to achieve similar success. Web 2.0 sites instruct wannabes in the art of entrepreneurialism, self-promotion, and careful self-editing.

## Status Update

I begin by exploring Web 2.0 as a discourse, a set of technologies, and a history. Web 2.0 ideology is not simply a reworking of Silicon Valley beliefs, but rather incorporates threads of West Coast countercultural movements that argued that institutions like politics and media were on the brink of failure and proposed new technologies as solutions. This combination of radical activism and business culture created a strain of idealistic techno-determinism that, rather than rejecting mainstream capitalism, embraces it. As a way of explaining this scene in more detail, I focus in Chapter 2 on what Web 2.0 insiders consider high status, and how social media replicates these priorities.

In the next three chapters of the book, I look at three strategies for self-presentation and self-promotion that I saw people adopt during my time in San Francisco, and introduce characters who epitomize the pitfalls and possibilities of each. Chapter 3 focuses on microcelebrity, a mindset and set of techniques in which the subject views his or her friends or followers as an audience or fan base, maintains popularity through ongoing fan management, and carefully constructs and alters his or her online self-presentation to appeal to others. The fourth chapter delves into self-branding, a strategy of success in which one thinks of oneself as a "brand" and uses social media to promote it, through creating, presenting, and maintaining a strictly "edited self." In Chapter 5 I draw from theories of privacy and publicity to analyze lifestreaming, the ongoing sharing of personal information with others through technology as a way of maintaining affective ties. Next I analyze three ideals that appear throughout the book: authenticity, meritocracy, and entrepreneurship, and use gender to show that these ideals are really myths, stories that justify practices used to systematically exclude women from the highest echelons of the tech scene. The book finishes with a discussion of digital elitism, developments in the scene since the end of my fieldwork, and what this project implies about the future of social technology. Throughout, any quotations not given their own endnote are from my own interviews.

This book is not a rejection of social media, a desire to see Facebook disappear, an attempt to blame users for any negative outcomes they may encounter, or nostalgia for earlier forms of sociable technologies. In fact, I am a technological enthusiast, like many of my informants. (I'm not sure what I would do without Twitter or Tumblr, although the world would be spared my musings on the Oscars and Britney Spears.) Instead, in this book I aim to carefully describe and analyze how Web 2.0, or social media, technologies are used by a particular group of people—what Ilana Gershon calls their "idiom of practice"— and so explore an alternate hypothesis: that Web 2.0 makes it possible for people to fully integrate advertising and marketing practices into the ways that they view their friends and themselves.[42] Obviously, the logics of celebrity culture, pervasive advertising, and reality television predate social media. But their values, priorities, and cultural logics have trickled down to mass culture to the point where when tools come along that allow people to copy the ways in which Kim Kardashian or Kanye West pursue status, they do so—avidly.

I briefly considered titling this book "NSFW," a slang term that warns web surfers that a link contains nudity, crude language, or violence, rendering it "not safe for work." While this book is quite SFW, NSFW reflects how business norms affect technology workers' self-presentation strategies. An online self-presentation must quite literally be "safe for work" to accrue status and benefit its creator. Whether this entails promoting one's image as a company would promote a brand or celebrity, or adhering to a single verifiable identity so that status can persist across sites, people follow online norms that will increase their status. But what is high status in social media is often that which benefits technology companies and sustains neoliberal discourse. A verifiable identity makes it possible to leverage status across websites, but it also makes it simple to track people as they move around the web. A strong self-brand is a self-regulating mechanism that functions as a response to economic uncertainties. And while the social information created and shared through social media strengthens social ties, it does so in a limited way. "Authenticity" and "being yourself," advice that is emphasized over and over again in social media discourse, have become marketing strategies that encourage instrumental emotional labor. For all of these reasons, social media has come to promote an individualistic, competitive notion of identity that prioritizes individual status-seeking over collective action or openness.

The social norms of the tech scene are, in many ways, the social context of social media. Many of the loudest voices in public discourse around technology belong to this group: they appear on television and radio to discuss new technology, meet at South by Southwest and Foo Camp, write op-eds and bestselling nonfiction books, and read each other's blogs. The whirlwind of hype around social media, both positive and negative, comes from the people most acquainted with these technologies, with the most to gain from their use. It is also the people who create Web 2.0 technologies who share these norms and values. While social media is used in a dizzying variety of ways around the world, many of the presumptions about use and users follow from Silicon Valley and San Francisco culture.[43] This book sheds some light on these taken-for-granted assumptions. Understanding the presumptions and discursive notions of self, other, friendships, and status promoted within the technology scene helps us to uncover some larger notions embedded in social media applications themselves, even if users do not receive or act on these notions in the same way that the technology scene does.

The leaders in this culture are the same people that technology discourse has celebrated for fifty years: young, white, rich men. The communicative infrastructure of the Valley rewards quantifiable metrics, like venture capital raised, number of Twitter followers, company valuation, employee number, and stock options. While the technology scene couches this hierarchy in arguments about "meritocracy" that are identical to those used by Web 2.0 celebrants, those deemed successful at social media usually fit into a narrow mold, and, as we will see, those who don't are criticized. The techniques that are required to achieve status in the tech scene do not celebrate, for instance, outspoken women, discussion of race in technology, or openly gay entrepreneurs. To get the kind and amount of attention that is so valued in the tech industry, it is best to fit a limited set of social norms.

When I started this project in July 2007, the economy was vastly different than it is now. Like the dot-com boom before it, Web 2.0 was hyped as a revolutionary schism with the past that would transform the world for the better. Those claims are heard less frequently today. People who spoke lovingly of a new age of participation and equality facilitated by Web 2.0 have begun to contribute to nuanced critiques of social software, critiques that involve visual culture analysis, the commercial contexts of user interaction, and larger cultural impacts.[44] (Even Facebook's IPO did not turn out to be as lucrative as promised.) This project was conceived as a response to a celebratory rhetoric that has, to a certain extent, diminished.

But these new concerns do not mean that this book's critique of social media is irrelevant. The techniques that people use to gain status in the scene—lifestreaming, self-branding, and microcelebrity—are deeply embedded in American society. They reflect a fragmented economy that celebrates individualism as it eliminates job security; a popular culture that is based on celebrity, publicity, and attention; and an incredible rise in the number of social technologies available to the average American. When looking at the great potential positive effects of social media, the promises of participation and egalitarianism, we need to weigh them against Web 2.0's reinforcement of hierarchy. Huge populations of people who are marginalized in the world at large—non-Westerners, women, people of color, and queer populations, for instance—are de-emphasized or ignored. Moreover, there are consequences for moving our social lives into realms that are so focused on the free market. Social media has changed the way we broadcast and share personal information, creating a cultural shift with long-term implications for social interactions, privacy, social status, and social hierarchies.

1

# A CULTURAL HISTORY OF WEB 2.0

———

In 2006, the cover of *Time* magazine's annual "Person of the Year" issue depicted a computer with a shiny mirrored Mylar screen, intended to reflect the face of the viewer. The person of the year: You. The author of the piece, Lev Grossman, wrote:

> 2006 . . . [is] a story about community and collaboration on a scale never seen before. It's about the cosmic compendium of knowledge Wikipedia and the million-channel people's network YouTube and the online metropolis MySpace. It's about the many wresting power from the few and helping one another for nothing and how that will not only change the world, but also change the way the world changes. The tool that makes this possible is the World Wide Web . . . not even the overhyped dotcom Web of the late 1990s. The new Web is a very different thing. It's a tool for bringing

together the small contributions of millions of people and making them matter. Silicon Valley consultants call it Web 2.0, as if it were a new version of some old software. But it's really a revolution.

This cover has become a cliché of technological utopianism, but *Time*'s breathless excitement over user-generated content was reflected in revolutionary rhetoric that appeared throughout the mainstream media as well as in hundreds of conferences and TED talks. To quote the *Investor's Business Daily*, "User-contributed content will forever change online media—and the entire media business."[1] A writer for the *Los Angeles Times* claimed that Google's acquisition of YouTube was about "the triumph of radical left-wing politics— which means it's just as likely to subvert business as to support its reinvention."[2] And a commentator for *Wired*, reliably, wrote that "Web 2.0 . . . is about democratizing digital technology. There's never been a better time to tap that technological ethic to re-democratize our democracy."[3] Utopian rhetoric also appeared in academia, where scholars investigated the new democratized web, discussed the participatory potential of crowdsourcing, and coined terms like "folksonomy," "smart mobs," and "free culture." It seemed that the intellectual, media, and technological elite had converged on a single idea. The time was ripe for a revolution, and the mish-mash of technologies collected under the umbrella "Web 2.0" was there to provide it.

Technologists and pundits liberally applied the Web 2.0 label to wikis, blogs, social network sites, tagging, and user-generated content sites like Wikipedia, MySpace, Facebook, YouTube, del.icio.us, Flickr, Digg, and Twitter. These technologies purportedly foretold freedom from traditional media sources, or "Big Media." They promised the democratization of celebrity and entertainment, new forms of activism, and the potential for open, transparent information of all kinds. Web 2.0 celebrated the adoption of social technologies as a precursor to a better, freer society, and framed the collection and sharing of information as the bedrock of revolution. Any institution that prevented people from accessing information and using cultural products as raw materials for creativity became an obstacle to overcome, through collective action if necessary. The political arm of Web 2.0, such as it is, is focused on net neutrality, copyright reform, peer-to-peer advocacy, and government reform; Larry Lessig, the founder of Creative Commons and the Free Culture movement, launched "Change Congress," a campaign against government corruption and the influence of special interests in the Senate, with Howard Dean's former campaign manager Joe Trippi.[4] Cory Doctorow, the science-fiction writer and co-author of the popular blog *Boing Boing*, moonlights as a copyright activist whose scope includes proprietary technologies of all kinds, from genetically engineered seeds that last only a season to printer cartridges that automatically stop working after a certain period of time.[5] These beliefs, which draw heavily from hacker and free and open-source software (FOSS) development, are on their face antithetical to the libertarian, free-market ethos of entrepreneurial capitalism that also characterizes Web 2.0.

What's important to remember is that Web 2.0 originated in San Francisco. Northern California has a long history of generating wealth from innovative technologies: transistors, micro-electronics, video games, and dot-com companies. This history begat the "Californian Ideology," a set of widely held beliefs that increasing the adoption of computer technologies brings positive social consequences, that the technology industry is where the best and brightest thrive, and that an unfettered free market is the best way to ensure prosperity for all.[6] Web 2.0 discourse incorporates both shifts from and continuities with the Californian Ideology. The tech scene assigned the highest status to venture-backed startups: capitalism was considered an agent of political change rather than something to be questioned. The web made possible genuinely innovative and potentially disruptive cultural products, but the San Francisco tech scene more often focused on the wealth and fame accrued by the founders of successful companies like Twitter, Digg, and Facebook (replace with "Instagram, Pinterest, and Quora," or whatever startups are in fashion as you read this). Even as the mainstream media celebrated the presumed upheaval of the establishment, they made cover stars of tech founders and newly minted social media millionaires like Digg's Kevin Rose, Twitter's Ev Williams, and Facebook's Mark Zuckerberg.

These developments seemed doubly exciting because popular wisdom had all but written off the web after the 2001 dot-com crash. Investors and journalists claimed that people would never again pay for online content, that Amazon was the victor in the e-commerce wars, and that money, funding, and attention had left the internet, possibly for good. Web 2.0 shone a spotlight back on the young entrepreneurs and "thought leaders" of Silicon Valley. In the process, it brought utopianism back to the front lines and created new investments and personal fortunes.

While the Californian Ideology is still widespread in Silicon Valley, the Bay Area's strong countercultural influence has also, and in equal measure, shaped the contemporary technology scene. Web 2.0 ideology is the child of both Silicon Valley entrepreneurial capitalism and activist subcultures like independent publishing, anti-globalization activism, Burning Man, cyberdelic rave culture, and free and open-source software. These countercultural movements can be hard to detangle. Many anti-corporate activists believed that the consolidation of media companies during the Reagan and Clinton eras created a homogenized, profit-led mass media, resulting in toothless journalism that lacked the muscle to check corporate or government power. During the early web era, dot-com workers built personal homepages in their free time to provide an alternative to mainstream entertainment. In the Web 2.0 age, blogs and Twitter facilitated "citizen journalism," a bottom-up form of media that was thought to be able to compensate for the shortcomings of mainstream media. Web 2.0 situated itself in allegiance with the countercultural critique of mainstream media, but positioned social technology, rather than protest or political participation, as the solution. The preexisting affinity between West Coast anti-establishment activism and the homebrew ethos of technology culture created a fertile environment for these ideologies to intermingle. This combination of radical activism and business culture created a strain of idealistic techno-determinism that, rather than rejecting mainstream capitalism, embraces it.

## Talking 'Bout a (Technological) Revolution?

What do I mean by the "discourse" of Web 2.0? I mean that when everyday people, popular media, and scholars discuss Web 2.0, they often abstract real events, technologies, and people into an all-encompassing metanarrative. Talk about Web 2.0 is a part of social life in the tech community, and is itself reflected in social media, blog posts, popular books, and presentations. These texts have far-reaching effects on how people think about themselves and their actions, on which technologies are attended to and which are ignored, and on how financial resources circulate. Web 2.0 discourse is, ultimately, embedded in the everyday life and conversations of people.[7]

Web 2.0 discourse demonstrates what is called "digital exceptionalism," the idea that the internet is different from other forms of communication and therefore not bound by the same legal and market forces. Obviously, internet communication has different properties than mass or face-to-face communication (Microsoft Research scientist danah boyd summarizes these properties as persistence, replicability, scalability, and searchability).[8] These differences have been extrapolated into a series of discredited claims: the internet cannot be regulated, it is intrinsically democratizing, and so forth. During the mid-1990s, "cyberspace" was frequently conceptualized as a sphere separate from daily life. This "disembodiment hypothesis" suggested that internet communication freed people from their earthly bodies, allowing for pure communication unfettered from discrimination.[9] Theorists like Sherry Turkle and Sandy Stone hypothesized that digital communication could transcend structural power relations like sexism and racism.[10] (Research instead indicated that internet communication reflects the power relations of the people communicating.) Web 2.0 again places exceptionalism front and center. This illusion is nothing new. As legal scholar Tim Wu points out, "Again and again in the past hundred years, the radical change promised by new ways to receive information has seemed, if anything, more dramatic than it does today."[11] Excitement over the newest of the new media is an endless historical cycle.

Web 2.0 narratives also frequently assume that simply introducing social technology to a community will result in greater participation and democracy, while disrupting those institutions and industries that do not adapt. The idea that the adoption of technology causes behavioral changes and social effects, regardless of context, is false.[12] Historical analyses of science and technology show that this technological determinism is a fiction, because political, economic, and social differences in places and times affect the deployment and use of technology. The printing press and the Gutenberg Bible did not cause the Protestant Reformation. To say so would ignore factors such as the rise of anti-clericalism, the breakdown of feudalism, the rise of urbanism and the merchant class, and the Renaissance.[13] Likewise, when we introduce new technologies into different social settings, they find different uses. American teenagers, Japanese teenagers, West African entrepreneurs, and Egyptian activists, for instance, demonstrate different patterns of mobile phone use, and understand the use of technology differently.[14]

While much work on Web 2.0 tends to stress its positive aspects, an increasing number of popular books take the opposite approach. Andrew Carr's *The Shallows* argues that social media, text messaging, and web browsing are distracting people and making it difficult to concentrate.[15] Former cyberutopian Jaron Lanier claims in *You Are Not a Gadget* that values "baked in" to social media technologies emphasize robotic conformity over expressive individualism.[16] Andrew Keen's *Cult of the Amateur* contends that user-generated culture is dreck that crowds out expertise.[17] While these books can be provocative and engaging, they often make the same rhetorical moves as Web 2.0 supporters. In other words, they fall into both digital exceptionalist and technologically determinist traps, the difference being that for these authors, the effects of social technologies are uniformly bad (Keen especially goes off the rails, blaming Web 2.0 for child pornography and online poker). Rather than drawing from empirical data, both techno-optimists and techno-pessimists extrapolate grand, singular theories about technology.[18]

To unravel the complex assumptions within Web 2.0 ideology, it is necessary to understand its origins. The term began as a marketing ploy to differentiate a new crop of tech companies from their failed dot-com counterparts. Web 2.0 is firmly grounded in a history of labor that emphasizes creative capitalism, personal fulfillment through work, and entrepreneurialism. These traditions combined with grassroots initiatives to engender a Web 2.0 "scene" of San Francisco technology workers. This scene was predominantly young, white, and male, and favored developers who were simultaneously committed to venture-backed startups and core Web 2.0 principles like openness and transparency. That is, Web 2.0 emerged from a geographically rooted history, dragging its baggage into a new era. Social media thus has to be understood as a continuation of preexisting cultural forces rather than as deterministically transformative.

### Not One Origin, but Many

As hinted previously, Web 2.0 culture has a variety of influences. In the 1980s and 1990s, a mesh of social movements criticized the increasingly international structures of corporations, governments, and media. To groups of people as diverse as hackers and anti-globalization activists, these systems were stifling, monopolistic, and working against the public interest. Anti-globalization activists bemoaned the abuses of multinational corporations. Grassroots media activists argued that consolidated mainstream journalism had failed to provide a check on government or corporate power, and turned to alternatives like independent media centers and weblogs. The homogenization of corporate entertainment inspired "zine" and "e-zine" publishers to create bootstrapped, independent, photocopied magazines and emphasize "doing it yourself." Following the hacker ethos, free and open-source software developers critiqued the political and economic implications of proprietary software and, by proxy, intellectual property. Many participants in these social movements believed that internet technologies could be a literal instantiation of their political ideals. By designing open, participatory technologies, activists could encourage cooperation and coordination rather than top-down hierarchies. The intrinsic decentralization of the internet could potentially break down information asymmetry and give equal access to broadcast and distribution technologies, ending monopolistic media practices.

Many (but by no means all) of these philosophies emphasized the fundamental deficits of corporate capitalism, calling for "dropping out" and creating alternatives outside the mainstream. In Northern California, for example, an explicitly countercultural movement grew up in tandem with dot-com internet technologies—a movement that claimed online communication could build community and open minds. This utopian "cyberdelic" mindset relied on self-organizing communities and volunteerism. Rather than rejecting capitalism, however, Web 2.0 ideology fully embraced it. Northern California has a long history as both a center for technical innovation and counterculture, and the anti-capitalist ethos of hacker culture and print zines became overshadowed by a new ethic of Silicon Valley in which the free market became the purveyor of choice and creativity. Web 2.0 discourse positioned the entrepreneur as the mythic hero and venture-backed startups as the epitome of high status. In other words, social media positioned capitalism to be an agent of social change without challenging underlying inequalities. And while many of the preceding social movements were diverse, Web 2.0 was primarily white, male, and technologically determinist. Web 2.0 thus selectively drew from elements of San Franciscan counterculture while embracing Silicon Valley's technologically fueled economic success. The tense relationship between these two ideals has been evident throughout its history.

## Coding Freedom: Hacker and Open-Source Culture

On the one hand information wants to be expensive, because it's so valuable. The right information in the right place just changes your life. On the other hand, information wants to be free, because the cost of getting it out is getting lower and lower all the time. So you have these two fighting against each other.

—Stewart Brand, 1984[19]

The hacker's information sharing and "do it yourself" (DIY) ethic is the core of social media ideology and deeply woven into the free and open-source movement. The hacker appears in popular culture like *Hackers* and *Wargames* as a talented technological aficionado, or, more typically, an antisocial young man hunched over a laptop, wreaking havoc.[20] In actuality, hacking is a philosophy and a diverse, varied global subculture of programming enthusiasts devoted to openness and transparency.[21] The term "hack" refers to a clever and elegant solution to a complicated problem. Originally applied only in technical contexts, the concept was broadened, leading to terms like "lifehacking," which involves solving everyday problems to increase productivity.[22] Although hackers are often maligned and grouped with spammers, phishers, "cyber-terrorists," or malware distributors, the liberal ideals embodied in the hacker ethic are still evident in technologically mediated cultures, and are intimately tied to the philosophy and culture of social media and its affiliated projects.[23]

Hacking has a long and arguably noble history; many computer pioneers began their careers as hackers.[24] The first groups of hackers inhabited the hallowed halls of MIT. By the early 1970s, the center of hacking culture had moved to the Stanford Artificial Intelligence Lab, the Stanford Research Institute, Xerox PARC and the burgeoning microcomputer DIY culture in Silicon Valley: in other words, Northern California.[25] Apple Computer emerged from the Bay Area homebrew computer culture, which was composed of groups of enthusiasts who hand-built computers and traded tips and ideas with each other. This scene included hobbyists, hippies influenced by the antiwar movement, phone phreakers, engineers, and programmers, and it drew from "technologically politicized" community projects like the Berkeley People's Computer Club, which made computers available for everyday people to use. Another such project, the Homebrew Computer Club, was organized around principles of information sharing, exploration, decentralization, and meritocracy—precisely the values of hacker culture, and later the ideals of Web 2.0.[26] These early microcomputing groups molded the complex sociotechnical geography of the Bay Area, and profoundly influenced the development of software as an industry.

The political philosophy of hackers is often summarized as "information wants to be free," a phrase that emphasizes openness and transparency. In other words, anyone should be able to understand how things work, and use this information to tinker with technologies, political systems, the workings of city governments, and so on.[27] Steven Levy summarizes the Hacker Ethic as:

> A common philosophy that seemed tied to the elegantly flowing logic of the computer itself. It was a philosophy of sharing, openness, decentralization, and getting your hands on machines at any cost—to improve the machines and to improve the world. This Hacker Ethic is their gift to us: something with value even to those of us with no interest at all in computers.[28]

This ethic is not espoused by all hackers, who love to debate and argue the meaning of their own actions.[29] But taking the hacker ethic as an ideal, intrinsic within it is the idea that information is supposed to benefit everyone. This concept of freely circulating information was especially valuable to those collaborating on iterative hardware and software improvements in the early days, when there was no possibility of proprietary profit.[30]

The first microcomputer available for home use, the Altair 8800, illustrates how this hacker ethic influenced the development of new technologies. It appeared on the cover of *Popular Mechanics* in 1975, and unlike today's home computers, came as a bundle of circuit boards and transistors that had to be soldered together by hand. The company manufacturing the hardware, MITS, could barely keep up with the demand and worked directly with hardware hackers to improve the product, giving out data sheets on the chips and encouraging hobbyists to write code for the machine and build devices like input-output boards and joysticks.[31] In 1976, two college students surmised that MITS would need some sort of operating system; they called the company and proposed a version of BASIC for the Altair. BASIC is a programming language appropriate for a computer like the Altair, which doesn't have a lot of storage space. One of the students hacked a version of BASIC together in eight weeks. The other flew to Albuquerque to pitch it to MITS, who bought it. The two students were Bill Gates and Paul Allen, who promptly quit school to found Microsoft.

Gates and Allen soon realized that many homebrew hobbyists were using their version of BASIC without paying for it. Gates addressed this issue in an "Open Letter to Hobbyists" that was printed in the Altair newsletter, the Homebrew Computer Club newsletter, and various other publications. It read, in part: "As the majority of hobbyists must be aware, most of you steal your software. Hardware must be paid for, but software is something to share. Who cares if the people who worked on it get paid?"[32] The bitingly sarcastic letter caused a commotion in the hobbyist community and codified an explicit conflict between the ideals of the Hacker Ethic and the realities of proprietary software. Ideally, the BASIC source code should be distributed so anyone could use it. But according to Gates and Allen, BASIC was their project and they deserved compensation. In response to the hubbub, hobbyists proposed several alternatives. Some members wrote their own versions of BASIC. One created what he considered to be a superior version and sold it for five dollars, while another member, Jim Warren, founded a journal about "free and very inexpensive software" saying that "there is a viable alternative to the problems raised by Bill Gates . . . when software is free, or so inexpensive that it's easier to pay for it than duplicate it, then it won't be 'stolen.'"[33] But the lines between the collaborative hacker ethic and the proprietary, paid ownership model of software had been drawn. Levy's book chronicling the conflict inspired *Whole Earth Catalog* founder Stewart Brand to hold a hacker's conference in 1984, where one session focused exclusively on maintaining the hacker ethic in the face of proprietary software. The participants concluded that being a hacker was a set of personality traits, and that, while open information access was an excellent ideal, it was ultimately "only an ideal."[34]

The idealism of the hacker ethic was most fully realized in the free software movement, founded in 1983 by MIT student Richard Stallman, who deeply regretted missing the golden age of MIT hacking. Stallman was (rightly) concerned with the prospect of large software companies dominating the computer industry and crowding out hobbyists. Most of Stallman's hacker friends at MIT had left to form software companies, and he was disgusted with monopolistic software practices, nondisclosure agreements, and locked-down source code, which he considered a betrayal of his principles.[35] Biella Coleman and Alex Golub write: "In 1984, [Stallman] founded the Free Software Foundation in order to further the values of reciprocity, pedagogy and scientific openness he had learned among the MIT hackers and to halt the intrusion of copyrights and patents in software. Stallman was a hacker, and so he *realized his liberal ideals in a technological idiom* and he linked his political goals to one of the most popular operating systems among the technical community, UNIX."[36] Stallman founded the GNU project ("Gnu is Not Unix"), a free, non-commercial operating system with shared source code available to anyone who wanted it.[37] GNU was a technological instantiation of Stallman's commitment to "a liberal version of freedom that invoked the virtues of sharing and pedagogy."[38] In other words, Stallman wrote software that embodied his ideals. Along with the software, he wrote the GNU manifesto, which outlined the "four freedoms" of software: "The right to use, distribute, mod-ify and redistribute derivative versions." This ideal became an inte-gral part of free/open-source philosophy, which notes that "it is the right of every user to use, modify, and distribute computer software for any purpose."[39] Freely available source code not only encouraged learning and tinkering; it also actively discouraged monopolistic, proprietary software practice. It was a technological solution to an institutional problem.

Stallman's model of "free as in speech" (rather than "free as in beer") software was challenged by Eric Raymond and Bruce Peren's model of "open-source" software. This model, which Raymond and Perens thought sounded more professional and pro-business, caused various conflicts with Stallman and other members of the commu-nity.[40] Ultimately both terms were adopted, and free and open-source software evolved into both a culture and a community. Anthropologist Chris Kelty identifies five aspects of FOSS: "creat-ing a movement, sharing source code, conceptualizing openness or open systems, writing copyright (and copyleft) licenses, and coordi-nating collaborations."[41] Today Google, Microsoft, and other stolid software companies release free and open-source software, and inde-pendently developed programs like Apache, Mozilla, and Linux are used by millions, presenting a significant alternative to proprietary software.

Equally significantly, the philosophy of free/open-source has been extended to nontechnical projects.[42] Kelty writes that "free software is about making things *public*."[43] This liberal commitment to publicness can be seen in a variety of efforts. User-contributed content leverages the community aspect of open source to solve complicated problems, culminating in projects like Wikipedia, the "free encyclopedia that 'anyone can edit.'"[44] The OpenCourseWare initiative provides free, searchable online access to course materials from schools like MIT and Tufts.[45] Similarly, the Open Access movement advocates that peer-reviewed academic articles be freely available to anyone, not just people affiliated with institutions that hold expensive journal subscriptions.[46] These projects openly draw from the ideals of FOSS to make information accessible for the benefit of all.

Legal scholar Yochai Benkler chronicled these developments in his 2006 book *The Wealth of Networks*. Benkler claimed that new models of commons-based peer production pioneered by FOSS would bring about advancements in individual autonomy, democracy, freedom, and justice, unless they were threatened by preexisting industrial actors determined to continue exclusive rights-based models, such as drug companies and the entertainment industry. Benkler argued that the internet allowed for a shift from an "industrial information economy" to a "networked information economy" focused on non-market, individual, decentralized production using nonproprietary strategies.[47] Benkler's work echoes that of another legal scholar, Larry Lessig, who named Stallman as the major influence for his beliefs in the introduction to his book *Free Culture*.[48] *Free Culture* applied the ideals of the free software movement to all creative, cultural works and became popular with students and technologists, inspiring collegiate Free Culture clubs, protests, and blogs. Free culture advocates assert that people should be able to critically comment on mainstream culture, employ cultural raw material for their own uses, and create "transformative works" such as fan fiction or mashups without fear of litigation or punitive damages from the entertainment industry. Free culture is linked to a variety of other activist movements such as copyleft and Creative Commons, which provide alternatives to current U.S. copyright law. Older organizations like the Electronic Frontier Foundation echo these principles, stating that "innovation is inextricably tied to freedom of speech, and innovators need to be protected from established businesses that use the law to stifle creativity and kill competition."[49] This bundle of activism, theory, and philosophy is the primary driving force behind much of Web 2.0's idealism. The internet is positioned as an innovative force that opposes—and revolutionizes—failing cultural institutions.

The ideals of the hacker culture are the foundations of internet culture. Dissatisfaction with mainstream culture, however, was felt deeply by people other than hackers. Zine creators shared the belief that mainstream media was stultifying and, like hackers, idealized the creation of alternatives to traditional mass culture. These independent publishers, however, drew not just from the hacker ethic, but also from feminism, punk rock, and DIY culture.

## The Personal Is Published: Zines and E-Zines

In 1995, John Katz wrote in *Wired* magazine that "net culture, as it happens, is an even greater medium for individual expression than the pamphlets cranked by hand presses in colonial America."[50] Katz wasn't referring to blogs; the term "weblog" was coined two years later. He wasn't referring to social network sites or online newspapers. Instead, he was talking about a sprawling network of textual internet communication that included Usenet, listservs, and personal homepages, which existed years before the dot-com boom, and which were often described using the familiar rhetoric of self-expression, participation, and democratization. This rich digital culture gave rise to personal homepages and independent e-zines, online magazines positioned as alternatives to mainstream media. Often written and designed by dot-com workers at their day jobs, e-zines espoused points of view not found in magazines or television shows. Many were run by women and emphasized detailed personal stories and experiences, or focused on communities of color. Some of these e-zine creators would go on to be deeply influential in the technology scene. But to properly contextualize e-zines, we must begin with their predecessors: paper zines.

Zines are photocopied magazines written by individuals and passed around by mail and through independent bookstores. Zines originated in science fiction fandom, but by the 1990s ran the gamut from obscure topics like *The Brady Bunch* to autobiographical accounts of personal experiences.[51] Zines are sold for small amounts of money or are exchanged through a barter system, and they often emphasize the futility of wage-slave labor and lower-middle-class existence. Stephen Duncombe, in his academic book about zines, writes:

In an era marked by the rapid centralization of corporate media, zines are independent and localized, coming out of cities, suburbs, and small towns across the USA, assembled on kitchen tables. They celebrate the everyperson in a world of celebrity, losers in a society that rewards the best and the brightest. Rejecting the corporate dream of an atomized population broken down into discrete and instrumental target markets, zine writers form networks and forge communities around diverse identities and interests. Employed within the grim new economy of service, temporary, and "flexible" work, they redefine work, setting out their creative labor done on zines as a protest against the drudgery of working for another's profit. And defining themselves against a society predicated on consumption, zinesters privilege the ethic of DIY, do-it-yourself: make your own culture and stop consuming that which is made for you.[52]

Notably, many claims about zines—small, independent, self-expressive, user-created, alternatives to Big Media—are identical to those made about YouTube videos and blogs. Also notable is the strong political ethos that Duncombe highlights. While some zine writers overtly write about politics, the process of writing and distributing a zine itself requires certain elements that palpably reject corporate capitalism, like "borrowing" photocopies and computer time from an employer, corresponding with like-minded zinesters and fans through the mail, and utilizing a barter system.

The DIY ethic of print zines is rooted in American punk rock. In the 1980s, punk rock bands, most of which were either label-less or signed to small, independent record labels, created an alternative set of institutions to facilitate the sharing and spreading of music ignored by mainstream radio and MTV. These included "Book Your Own Fucking Life," photocopied pages of information about different venues where an independent band could set up a tour; mail-order record and zine distributors; small music venues, which were often the houses of punk fans; print zines like *Maximumrocknroll* and *Punk Planet;* silk-screen and sticker companies; and instructional information on everything from building an amp to cooking a vegan breakfast.[53] The idea of "doing it yourself" became a key element of American punk rock. Daniel Sinker, former editor of *Punk Planet,* writes: "Punk has always been about asking 'why' and then doing something about it. It's about picking up a guitar and asking 'Why can't I play this?' It's about picking up a typewriter and saying 'Why don't my opinions count?' It's about looking at the world around you and asking 'Why are things as fucked up as they are?' and then it's about looking inwards at yourself and saying 'Why aren't I doing anything about this?' "[54]

DIY cultural production of music, writing, or art was an explicit act of political resistance.[55] Listening to bands on independent labels was an overt rejection of corporate media.[56] Writing a zine was a way to express viewpoints absent from majority culture. This dichotomy of independent versus mainstream meant that "selling out," whether by signing to a major label or putting a bar code on the cover of a zine, was strictly policed. While not all zinesters were involved in punk rock, the two shared an emphasis on "wage slavery" and independence from mainstream, capitalist media.

Hackers also enthusiastically embraced zines, but from within the burgeoning personal computer culture rather than punk rock. "Textfiles," plain text documents spread through dial-up bulletin boards, emerged as an indigenous online literature during the 1980s. Jason Scott, an internet historian, manages an online archive of textfiles. He writes that a textfile, or t-file, is an ASCII file "written to explain in detail an important new computer discovery, a great new concept, or an old piece of knowledge that needed to be passed on. It included stories, poems, songs, ramblings, and long treatises on theories that the writer couldn't possibly have known."[57] Since longer files were more likely to be downloaded, textfile creators who wanted to increase their readership compiled multiple t-files into a single newsletter-like format, known as an "e-zine."[58] Other independent hacker magazines were published both online and in print. For instance, two prominent hacker zines, *2600* and *Phrack,* were founded in 1984. *Phrack* referred to itself as a "newsletter-type project" that appeared only online, while *2600: The Hacker Quarterly* was published both in print and online.

Many print zinesters adopted e-mail, BBSs (bulletin board systems), and other early forms of electronic communication. The first issue of the germinal zine catalog *Factsheet Five,* released in 1982, listed electronic bulletin boards alongside print zines; its founder, Mike Gunderloy, started a zine-focused BBS in 1987, which he kept up until 1995.[59] In 1992, the Usenet newsgroup alt.zines was created for print zinesters to chat about their activities. At the same time, ASCII e-zines expanded in topic beyond hacking and computer culture. A message on alt.zines from 1993 titled "e-zine list of electronic zines" listed twenty-six ASCII e-zines, ranging in focus from the goth group Sisters of Mercy to "free play-by-electronic-mail wargames."[60]

With the invention of the World Wide Web, e-zines could incorporate pictures, audio, and graphic design rather than simply ASCII text; these were dubbed "webzines" to distinguish them from their plain text counterparts. Caterina Fake relates, "We were calling things 'zines' in the classic way that new tech adopts the names of old tech, i.e. 'horseless carriage,' thus 'zine.'" Some e-zines were direct translations of print zine culture. *Boing Boing,* one of the most popular blogs on the web, started off as a print zine. Cory Doctorow published a print zine called *Craphound,* which is still the name of his personal site. Caterina Fake moved from print zines to a webzine, *Wench.com.* Feminist zines like *Bust* and *Bitch* had significant early online presences. While it seemed logical for independent personal publishing to move wholly to the web, there were significant cultural and practical differences between print zine culture and webzine culture. While some print zinesters published issues of their zines online, others used the web solely to advertise their print zines, and still others created new projects designed specifically for the internet.[61] Yet other print zinesters disliked the internet medium, seeing it as static and impersonal compared to the lively epistolary community of zine writers.[62]

Many webzine creators had no connection to print zines. Molly Steenson, co-founder of Maximag.com, points out that many e-zine creators were employed in the dot-com boom, and used their free time and employer's resources to create their e-zines. (This is similar to print zinesters who "borrowed" copy paper and photocopiers to publish their zines.) To create a webzine, publishers needed to know HTML and have rudimentary graphic design skills. In contrast to the cut-and-paste aesthetic of zines, e-zine producers often emulated the professional design of mainstream magazines. This was viewed with suspicion by some print zinesters as "selling out." Michelle Comstock, in her study of grrrl zines, sniffed that "unlike their print zine colleagues, [e-zine editors] seem more committed to making a name in the commercial end of technology as professional writers, Web designers, or computer technicians."[63]

San Francisco's dot-com boom created a place for e-zine publishers to congregate. A group of dot-com workers including Eddie Codel and Ryan Junell founded the Webzine conference, "a forum, exhibition, and party for those who create non-commercial creative projects for the Internet."[64] Over the years, speakers included Web 2.0 luminaries like Caterina Fake (Flickr), Tantek Çelik (Technorati, microformats), Evan Williams (Blogger, Twitter), Chris Pirillo (GnomeDex), Matt Mullenweg (WordPress) and Owen Thomas (*Valleywag*). Webzine brought together zinesters, dot-com professionals, and early web publishers like Fray, Suck, Bust, and Maxi in a celebration of independent publishing that helped connect those involved in e-zines and personal homepages. Ryan Junell, one of the founders, writes:

The WEBZINE event happened in San Francisco because of the environment's dynamic blend of technology geeks, experimental artists, radical writers and advanced partiers. Dozens of other unique cultural movements, such as the Gold Rush, the Beat poets, the Haight/Ashbury hippies, the UC Berkeley protests, Silicon Valley, underground raving, Burning Man and the over-zealous dot.com industry, have flourished in the Bay Area. The WEBZINE event drew directly from this hub of attitude, perspective, experience, and vibe to identify and unify a community of geeks interested in independent publishing on the web.[65]

For Junell, Webzine was a reaction to the "gold rush" of the dot-com era, which turned an "open, non-commercial medium of free expression" into "a huge, greedy strip mall."[66] Like zinesters, many independent web publishers saw themselves as taking a stand against homogenized corporate content, and as exercising their right to free speech as citizens of a democracy. E-zines were a way for dot-commers to express themselves creatively and celebrate the potential of the web, rather than working day jobs that were often boring and frustrating.

Both print and webzines had a significant feminist presence. Print zines spawned the Riot Grrrl feminist punk scene of the 1990s, and continue to be a significant part of the young feminist community.[67] In zines, young women wrote about their experiences with everything from eating disorders and sexual assault to school and parents. Creators of these zines corresponded via the postal service and created dense, tight-knit communities of zinesters. Espousing straightforwardly feminist values, zines took the "personal is political" into print. Like many forms of female community building, zines were a way for women to share personal stories within a community context, much like book clubs and fan forums. Zines like *Bamboo Girl* and *Slant,* written by young women of color, provided an anti-imperialist analysis of whiteness in punk rock and Riot Grrrl, complicating the idea of a unified "zine culture."[68] This work was directly influenced by critical race theory, postcolonial theory, and feminist theory, and contributed sophisticated self-reflexivity and critique to young women's understanding of feminism.

A collection of women's webzines also popped up in the mid- to late 1990s. Rather than competing with each other, the most successful of these sites formed alliances in "webrings" to promote each other's content. Estronet was made up of *Wench, Maxi, Bust, gUrl, Hue,* and the *Tripod Women's Room,* while ChickClick included *Disgruntled Housewife, RiotGrrl, GrrlGamer,* and *Bimbionic.* These sites primarily focused on edgy, personal content, and were maintained on shoestring budgets by a handful of people. They combined the Riot Grrrl aesthetic of reclaimed girl culture like Hello Kitty and plastic barrettes with ironic 1950s clip art, which Michelle Comstock calls the "kitten-with-whip" look.[69] Many of these zinesters saw themselves as providing an empowering alternative to mainstream women's content, but not necessarily as radically feminist. ChickClick founder Heidi Swanson said in a 1998 interview, "Most women's on-line sites assume women just want their horoscopes, recipes and tips on losing weight and getting a boyfriend. But that's not reality. Women between 13 and 35 are hungry for information about what really impacts their lives—getting jobs, music, dating, even snowboarding."[70] Women's webzines were inspired by a drive for self-expression and a frustration with the shallow content of women's magazines, rather than a more esoteric interest in the theoretical intricacies present in many print zines.

At first, these sites were successful. Estronet and ChickClick merged in 1998; ChickClick sponsored the 1999 Lillith Fair. But the dot-com bust led to a steep decline in such sites, which because of their "edgy" content were a difficult draw for advertisers. Mainstream women's sites like iVillage and Oxygen hired several webzine veterans to write and produce their content, probably due to their early adopter status and comfort with the web medium.[71] Eventually, the early independent webzines petered out, or turned into blogs, and the most popular sites for women remained those about "online horoscopes, sex tips, celebrities and parenting advice."[72] The anti-capitalist, multicultural perspectives disappeared entirely from mainstream women's sites.

The ethic of "doing it yourself," of learning from others without a profit motive, of self-expression, and of focusing on obscure interests and sharing personal experiences, became part of the creative fabric of Web 2.0 at the same time that it was depoliticized. The shift to content that was less likely to offend the mainstream culture was no accident. As Barnard College librarian Jenna Freedman writes:

> While blogs can be a very empowering medium, there aren't many people out there capable of fully hosting their own blogs. Therefore, there is usually an Internet service provider that has the power to pull the plug on something it deems offensive, be it because of politics, sex, religion, copyright, or anything else. It's also much more difficult for the average blogger to be truly anonymous than it is for a zinester. Being able to violate copyright and readers' ethics or sensibilities [has its] good and bad points. Part of what makes zines what they are and what makes them so great is the total freedom not afforded to, but taken by the zinesters.[73]

Blogs and e-zines lacked the anti-capitalist ethos and rhetoric around "selling out" that characterized punk and zine culture. As Freeman points out, hosting a blog on a commercial server makes one vulnerable to the whims of a service provider. Moreover, the explicit feminist ethos found in abundance in paper and webzine culture is a marginal part of blog culture, and almost entirely absent from Web 2.0. (The most popular women's blogs are about food, fashion, or parenting, while the "feminist blogosphere" focuses almost entirely on traditional politics and feminist theory.) Although zines and DIY culture celebrated the individual and rejected Big Media, they did so within a critique of labor and the service industry. Not so with Web 2.0.

Other activists focused on different elements of the media industry. While zinesters generally criticized the homogeneity of mainstream media, their alternatives often focused on personal storytelling and niche topics ignored by the media. Critics of the news media, by contrast, examined the political implications of media consolidation. Often drawing from similar inspirations as zinesters, people interested in international news and politics positioned weblogs as a viable alternative.

### From Battles to Blogs: Anti-Corporate Activism and Independent Media

In 1999, the World Trade Organization met in Seattle and was greeted by what came to be called "The Battle in Seattle" or the "WTO riots." Huge coalitions of activist groups came together in largely peaceful marches and rallies to protest a common enemy. While a few black-clad students smashed the windows of Niketown and Starbucks, the term "riot" was a misnomer. The police response—tear gassing the crowd, firing rubber bullets at protesters, and assaulting civilians—would set a brutal baseline for the treatment of people at future protests like the GTO Summit in Vancouver, the 2004 Republican Convention in New York City, and the nationwide Occupy protests of 2011.[74]

The anti-corporate movement protested the rise of multinational corporations, their environmental impact, the homogenization of mass culture, media consolidation, and the pervasiveness of advertising. These criticisms were brought to popular attention in Naomi Klein's *No Logo,* Eric Schlosser's *Fast Food Nation,* the films *The Corporation* and *Super Size Me,* and the magazines *Adbusters, Stay Free!* and *The Baffler.*[75] Anti-corporate activists advocated ethical consumption, supporting small businesses, and boycotting major multinational corporations, and they organized events like "Buy Nothing Day" and "Turn Off Your TV Week." These organizations used networked, distributed structures and technologies to create nonoppressive collaborative strategies and principles. Jeff Juris writes that anti-globalization practices enact a "dual politics" by "intervening within dominant publics while generating decentralized network forms that prefigure the utopian worlds they are struggling to create."[76] Like open-source software, the movements themselves are instantiations of political principles.

The first Independent Media Center (IMC, usually referred to as "Indymedia") was set up in Seattle during the WTO protests as a central space to disseminate information.[77] The Seattle IMC served as an organizing model for other groups and by 2006, there were 150 IMC groups in fifty countries, with about five thousand members.[78] Indymedia's slogan "be the media" referred to its foundational commitment to participatory media as a core component of radical democracy. As Victor Pickard writes: "Indymedia's radical democratic practice entails an active renegotiation of all power relationships by democratizating the media (exemplified by an interactive web-based interface), leveling power hierarchies (exemplified by consensus-based decision-making), and countering proprietary logic (exemplified by open-source software)."[79] The WTO protesters adopted techniques from activist history, such as affinity groups—small groups of activists with personal ties networked together in a rhizome-like structure for collective action—which have been used by anarchists since the Spanish Civil War.[80] Indymedia centers also drew from the tactics and philosophies of other radical groups to create a non-hierarchical, anti-authoritarian model for organizing that involved decentralization and consensus-based decision making. Specifically, the IMC borrowed from free and open-source software philosophy, manifesting the principles of radical democracy in its technological infrastructure, which, as Pickard writes, was oriented toward "de-privatizing technology, increasing and de-centralizing participation in news production, and leveling bureaucratic hierarchies."[81] In fact, the second principle of IMC's ten "principles of unity" maintains that "open exchange of and open access to information [is] a prerequisite to the building of a more free and just society" and the ninth reads "All IMCs shall be committed to the use of free source code, whenever possible, in order to develop the digital infrastructure, and to increase the independence of the network by not relying on proprietary software."[82] IMCs were committed to free/open-source principles as a way to spread freedom and equality.

Even though Indymedia's global affiliates worked together to formulate the principles of unity, Indymedia's Seattle origins are important. Seattle was a major center for dot-com activity and is the home of multinational technology corporations Microsoft, Nintendo, and Amazon.com, as well as a top-ten computer science school, the University of Washington. Just as in San Francisco, this technology culture influenced the choices of activist groups. Seattle Indymedia and the IMC as a whole were technologically driven, using e-mail lists to organize members and a web interface to publish news stories. IMCs considered FOSS principles to be just as important as their activist commitments for the pursuit of equality and democracy. Pickard writes, "In the case of Indymedia, the technology and institutional structure are mutually constitutive. Undoing one would disable the other . . . the radical openness of Indymedia's technology is predicated on a radical democratic institutional structure; this structure could not exist without internet communications, especially on the global network level."[83] Participatory publishing software and FOSS allowed IMC members to live the principles of anti-globalization activism in day-to-day life.

That anyone could use the IMC newswires to publish a news story was the IMC's challenge to corporate media coverage of radical politics. Participants in the WTO protests were disgusted by what they saw as sensational and inaccurate coverage of their activism, which they attributed to media consolidation. In 1996, the Telecommunications Act dissolved a number of laws that regulated the number of media outlets a company could own. The resulting mergers concentrated media ownership in six huge companies, including Disney and Viacom, that now control virtually all mainstream media. Scholars like Lance Bennett, Robert McChesney, and Eric Klinenberg have thoroughly documented the effects of media consolidation on the corporate news media. These include a decline in the coverage of foreign and local news, a reliance on mainstream sources, a decrease in minority viewpoints, a reduction in substantive educational content, an increase in cross-promotion and sponsor-driven content, and a pro-government, pro-capitalist bias.[84] These problems were especially relevant during the post–September 11 Bush administration, when progressives criticized corporate media for cheerleading the war effort and for failing to investigate policies carefully or provide historical context for government decisions.[85] In contrast, online publishing provided a platform for people with views outside the mainstream to voice opinions and practice amateur investigative journalism.

Blogs were heralded as the new frontier of this participatory journalism. During the beginning of the second Iraq War, "warblogging" spread "trustworthy alternative views concerning the objectives of the Bush Administration and Pentagon and the corporate media spin surrounding them."[86] And in 2002, then-senator Trent Lott made a pro-segregationist remark at a birthday dinner for venerable former Dixiecrat senator Strom Thurmond. While it was largely ignored by the mainstream media, which treated it as a minor tidbit, it was picked up by two major liberal blogs: *Talking Points Memo* and *Eschaton*. A few days later, the *New York Times* began covering the story, and two weeks later, Lott stepped down.[87] Blogs exemplified the FOSS maxim "given enough eyeballs, all bugs are shallow," though in this case, inadequate reporting by the mainstream media, not a computer programming "bug," was what was being overcome by a helpful group of citizens.[88]

The term "weblog," coined by *Robot Wisdom* editor Jorn Barger, originally described technology-focused "filter blogs," which contained links to external content and were primarily written by men in the technology industry.[89] But "blog" was essentially a new name for online journals or link lists, which had existed on personal homepages for years.[90] Early bloggers like Barger, Justin Hall, and David Winer were active on Usenet, personal homepages, and e-mail newsletters, respectively. Moreover, bloggers constructed their activities in opposition to the mostly female users of online journaling sites like LiveJournal and Diaryland. Feminist technology scholar Susan Herring has argued that this delineation of "weblogs" as a genre positioned filter blogging, primarily done by men, as a more serious political activity than women's online writing.[91] Online communities of color, such as AsianAve, BlackPlanet, and MiGente, also offered different interpretations of current events than those normally represented in the mainstream media, but they were similarly excluded from the excitement over blogging. Eventually, "blog" broadened to include diary writing and personal publishing, at least partially through the popularization of the San Francisco–based personal publishing platform Blogger.[92]

The media fervor over weblogs did not go uncriticized. Geert Lovink argued that far from being revolutionary, blogs were a form of "creative nihilism" that tore down the institutional structures of mass media without providing an alternative, that merely created unpaid replacements for journalists while furthering libertarian political beliefs.[93] Blogs are usually hosted in heavily commercial, privatized spaces, which diminishes their democratic potential and according to critics hinders their "objectivity."[94] In *Republic.com,* Cass Sunstein claimed that the blogosphere would result in "echo chambers" where people with similar political beliefs would talk only to each other, creating political isolationism.[95] This proposition has been fiercely debated, with some scholars finding the ideological divide between right- and left-wing bloggers widening over time, and others observing the opposite effect.[96] Still other researchers find weblogs a poor substitute for professional political content, arguing that amateur production produces substandard writing and cannot make up for investigative reporting or foreign news coverage.[97] Bart Cammaerts lists several other criticisms of blogs' participatory potential, including government censorship, appropriation by elites, and the possibility of encouraging anti-democratic publics.[98]

Indymedia's struggles with the professionalization of online content demonstrate some of the problems involved in positioning user-contributed content as an alternative to professional journalism. Pickard writes: "As an institution, Indymedia is torn between aspiring to become a credible news institution able to challenge corporate mainstream representations, and wanting to be inclusive so as to not repel large numbers of people who may not be able—due to lack of privilege and education—to produce content according to mainstream news quality standards."[99] Grassroots media activists positioned blogs and IMCs as an accessible way for everyone to participate in democratic journalism, but Indymedia found it difficult to separate itself from the norms of Big Media. It was tricky to find untrained contributors who could create coverage of the same quality as that provided by mainstream newspapers. The legitimacy of online journalism was often measured by whether or not Big Media picked up a story, as in the Lott case. Although blogs and independent media were positioned as an anti-institutional alternative, the realities of dealing with capitalist structures were more complex.

Hacker culture and various forms of independent publishing and activism upheld the belief that social technology could be a direct instantiation of political ideals and could succeed where established institutions had failed. One of the reasons "Web 2.0" was so discursively prevalent is that it appealed to multiple, disparate audiences. But rather than accepting the full radicalism of these ideals, Web 2.0 ideology was dampened in its transformative potential by Silicon Valley orthodoxy. Network sociologist Manuel Castells argues that internet culture has four elements: "the techno-meritocratic culture, the hacker culture, the virtual communitarian culture, and the entrepreneurial culture."[100] These historical influences are not intrinsically compatible; as we have seen, they conflict in complex ways, some of which stem from the Web 2.0's geographic origins. Thus, to trace further the history of Web 2.0, from the "Californian Ideology" of Silicon Valley, through the utopian days of mid-1990s digital culture, to the flexible, entrepreneurial work cultures of the dot-com boom, requires a return to Northern California.

### The Californian Ideology and Cyber-Libertarianism

Web 2.0's symbolic center, the technology culture of San Francisco, is inextricably intertwined with Silicon Valley, only a few miles south. The term "Silicon Valley" was coined by Don Hoefler in *Microelectronics News* in 1971 to describe the prevalence of micro-electronics companies headquartered in the South Bay, including Intel, Hewlett-Packard, and IBM.[101] Until the 1970s, this area was primarily agricultural, with only a few scattered radio machinists and engineers. But a massive boom in the production of semiconductors and other electronic components led to an international concentration of technical resources and infrastructure in the cities of Palo Alto, Mountain View, and San Jose.[102] This enormous expansion in micro-electronics was due to an extensive history of defense contracts, the intellectual power of Palo Alto's Stanford University, and innovative manufacturing and business processes pioneered by the radio and machinist industries, including stock options and profit-sharing.[103]

In the decades since, the Valley has been marked by boom-and-bust cycles centering on personal computing, video games, multimedia, and internet startups. These cycles have left deep traces. Po Bronson, writing about the dot-com boom, explained:

> What those often-cited "Silicon Valley advantage" theories don't convey is how evolved this place has become just from being on the high heat for years. The competition has bred electronics stores the size of eight football fields, electronics stores open all night, electronics stores where you can do your laundry while shopping. There are [VCs, or venture capitalists] who invest only in video chips, VCs who funnel only foreign money, VCs who write books, VCs who are professors of sociology. There are headhunters who handle only Cobol programmers from Singapore, headhunters who specialize in luring toy company executives, and, I've recently learned, a headhunting firm that helps other headhunting firms hunt for headhunters.[104]

More prosaically, Silicon Valley has venture capitalists, consultants, lawyers, manufacturers, marketers, professional associations, technical expertise, and above all, as anthropologist Jan English-Lueck writes, "social capital embodied in Silicon Valley's knowledge workers."[105] These factors create a fertile space for technological entrepreneurs. Stowe Boyd, a blogger and consultant, explained:

> At any given moment in time, there's a big infrastructure here of people, venture capitalists, smart technical people, all the peripheral stuff, the media marketing, all that. So,

people who are interested in this, and are tired of living in Iowa, they'll move here. So it's a mecca, in that sense. People literally make the pilgrimage, in order to do their new idea or whatever it is . . . People self-select, and as a result, you have all these honestly self-motivated, upward striving, overachievers. You get all these people . . . motivated to go do the best they can.

The Web 2.0 boom took place in Northern California partly because the infrastructure, social capital, and human resources were already there.

The boom-and-bust cycles in the technology industry also left strong ideological traces in the Valley. The political sensibility of Silicon Valley tends to be of a decidedly libertarian bent, espousing self-improvement, meritocracy, and "work-life balance."[106] Of course, what passes for libertarianism in Northern California is distinct from the conservative right-wing version. Silicon Valley libertarian beliefs are rooted in a strong belief that intelligence and drive are indicators of success, an almost mythological trust in entrepreneurialism, the "do it yourself" ethic, and an idealized view of the internet as utopian space—à la Castells's layers of internet culture. Silicon Valley encourages a faith in technological solutions, and imagines that widespread adoption of computer technologies will lead to positive social change (in the case of Web 2.0, increased participation, democracy, and community).[107] This almost contradictory combination of "technological determinism and libertarian individualism" is, as discussed earlier, what Richard Barbrook and Andy Cameron labeled the "Californian Ideology."[108]

Barbrook and Cameron formulated their theory in response to the mid-1990s *Wired* magazine enthusiasm about "the information superhighway." They criticized the libertarian belief system espoused by such digital elites as Kevin Kelly (editor of *Wired* and former editor of *The Whole Earth Catalog*), Nicholas Negroponte (founder of MIT's Media Lab and the One Laptop Per Child Association), Esther Dyson (venture capitalist and author of *Release 2.0*), and

Louis Rossetto (former *Wired* editor). Skeptics pointed out that this libertarianism overlooks basic social inequalities that make entrepreneurial capitalism possible, and discounts the influence of government on the development of internet technologies and Silicon Valley, while it simultaneously counsels against raising taxes to pay for public education or welfare.[109] Barbrook and Cameron claim that the democratic emancipation fantasized about by "hi-tech artisans" excludes the mostly nonwhite underclass who cannot afford computers and internet access. It is well known that the Silicon Valley culture depends on undocumented labor to build microchips, clean offices, and mow the lawns of technology workers relocated from Bangalore, Shanghai, Dublin, and Des Moines—even though these undocumented workers rarely appear in rapturous press descriptions of the area.[110] The authors of *The Silicon Valley of Dreams* note that while one narrative of Silicon Valley focuses on wealth, egalitarianism, and brilliant ideas, the other describes "a place of considerable human suffering, preventable illness and premature death, the exploitation of thousands of workers, widespread ecological devastation, and increasing social inequality."[111] Many of these jobs have since moved overseas, but the misery associated with them continues; the labor conditions in Chinese technology factories like Foxconn are so extreme that they provoked widespread protest from American consumers when brought to light in 2012.

Overwhelmingly, the Californian Ideology is neoliberal, meaning that it adheres to a political philosophy that advocates deregulated, free-market economic policies as a means to freedom and prosperity.[112] Silicon Valley has become a model of neoliberal economic development and a fantasy about the possibilities of space. The success of the Californian Ideology has encouraged other governments to promote their own "siliconia" in the hope that it would offer a universal solution to localized problems; a Wikipedia page lists Silicon Gulf in the Philippines, Silicon Wadi in Israel, Silicon Saxony, Cwm Silicon in Wales, Silicon Beach, Silicon Corridor, Silicon Prairie, and so forth.[113] The varying degrees of success of these other initiatives underscore the importance of geography and history to Silicon Valley's own story.

Naturally, when Barbook and Cameron's critique of the Californian Ideology was published in *Mute* magazine, it garnered a number of indignant reactions. Louis Rossetto sputtered that it descended "into the kind of completely stupid comments on race in America that only smug Europeans can even attempt" while espousing "utterly laughable Marxist/Fabian kneejerk that there is such a thing as the info-haves and have-nots."[114] (His complete dismissal of structural inequality is telling.) A more even-handed critique was given by game designer and Georgia Tech professor Celia Pearce, who pointed out that many members of this elite "virtual class" had been deeply influenced by the autodidactic hacker culture, in which learning, information-sharing, and nonhierarchical bartering of services and products are normative: "In this model, cooperation and a sense of community is said to benefit all."[115] Others criticized Barbook and Cameron's linkage between the New Left of the 1960s and *Wired*'s techno-utopianism; as meticulously researched by Fred Turner, the founders of *Wired* were grounded more in the New Communalist movement of 1970s back-to-the-land hippies and the *Whole Earth Catalog* than the New Left.[116]

By the early 1990s, however, digital counterculture was drawing from an entirely different set of influences.

### The PC as LSD: Netravers, Cyborganic, and Burning Man

Before the dot-com boom, cutting-edge San Francisco technoculture had focused on the revolutionary potential of raising consciousness and building community through computer networks. This utopian ideal was strongly influenced by Marshall McLuhan, rave culture, psychedelic drugs, and the possibility of tribal, collective organization. In his book *Cyberia,* Douglas Rushkoff describes the denizens of this "cyberdelic" culture:

> The people I met at my first rave in early 1990s San Francisco claimed they could experience this same boundless, hypertext universe without the use of a computer at all. For

them, cyberspace can be accessed through drugs, dance, spiritual techniques, chaos math, and pagan rituals. They move into a state of consciousness where, as if logged onto a computer, the limitations of time, distance, and the body are perceived as meaningless. People believe that they move through these regions as they might move through computer programs or video games—unlimited by the rules of a linear, physical reality. Moreover, they say that our reality itself, aided by technology, is about to make a wholesale leap into this new, hypertextual dimension.[117]

Cyberdelic subculture was a mishmash of electronic music, "neo-paganism," ecstasy and LSD, "smart drugs," online communities, computer hacking, and freewheeling theories about universal consciousness linked together by fractals and memetic theory. It advocated a do-it-yourself approach to altering consciousness and reality, using immersion in "cyberspace" to achieve psychedelic bliss. Many of the shamans of this culture were former hippies: Timothy Leary, Stewart Brand, Terrence McKenna, and John Barlow (founder of the Electronic Frontier Foundation and former Grateful Dead lyricist) appeared at raves, gave lectures, and were quoted in magazines like *Mondo 2000* and *Extropy;* Leary famously stated, "The PC is the LSD of the 1990s."[118] Radical theorists surmised that the internet would allow participants to tap into a cyber-consciousness, creating a post-human body that was stronger, better, and more evolved than the meat-space self. While these theories ran the gamut from William Gibson–esque extremism to the more practical "virtual homesteading" accounts of Howard Rheingold, they shared an ideal of the internet as a utopian space where people could overcome the difficulties of everyday life. Cyberdelic culture rejected the mainstream in favor of this cybersphere. Rudy Rucker, one of the *Mondo 2000* founders, describes the audience for one of his talks as:

Reality hackers, nuts, flakes, entrepreneurs, trippers, conmen, students, artists, mad engineers—Californians with the naïve belief that a) There is a Better Way and b) I Can Do It Myself. To put it in a clear gelatin capsule for you, I'd say that (a) and (b) are the two beliefs that underlie every single entry in the "Mondo 2000 User's Guide." The way that Big Business or The Pig does things is obviously not the best way; it's intrusive, kludgy, unkind, and not at all what you really want . . . Now, thanks to high-tech and the breakdown of society, you're free to turn your back on the way "they" do it, whatever it might be, and do it yourself.[119]

This combination of hacker ethics, rave culture, and "virtual communitarianism" was very attractive to early net users.

In 1993, the first popular web browser, Mosaic, was released. San Francisco's SOMA neighborhood emerged as a center of the new, exciting internet boom. Cyber-utopian culture was widely embraced by the software developers who flocked to San Francisco in the mid- to late 1990s to establish dot-com companies. For geeks, rave culture epitomized open-source community, since it was collectively organized by members and emphasized a better way that was solidly outside the mainstream. In 1992, UC Berkeley freshman Brian Behlendorf started an e-mail list called sfraves that made the connection to the nascent internet culture. Behlendorf was one of the first developers of the Apache open-source server software, and he went on to co-found the Apache Software Foundation and serve on the Mozilla board of directors. Sfraves quickly grew to more than five hundred members, who began to hang out together. They were dubbed "netravers"—people enthusiastic about both raves and the newly invented internet.[120] Behlendorf wrote to the list in 1993, "Our method of communication could be a model, a basis for something bigger . . . SFRaves became a channeler for memes, for emotions, for expressions on what house culture is and how San Francisco is/could be the center of it all."[121] To netravers, internet communication had the potential to actualize and spread a spirit of community and trust.

Some of the first subscribers to sfrave were a group of roommates who lived on Ramona Avenue in San Francisco; their apartment quickly became a center for pre-parties and digital events. One of these roommates was Jonathan Steuer, a doctoral student in communication at Stanford. He was intensely interested in the potentials of internet community and an early employee at *Wired*. Steuer founded a startup, Cyborganic, with the goal of leveraging New Communalist principles to create community, both face-to-face and online. Jennifer Cool, one of the first employees of Cyborganic and an anthropologist who wrote a lengthy dissertation about it, summarizes:

> Cyborganic's central premise was that online and face-to-face interaction are mutually sustaining and can be used together to build uniquely robust communities. The project was to use computer-mediated communication, not to transcend geographical place, but to build a local, networked community. Those who led the project wanted to create such a community in their own lives. But they also wanted to demonstrate the possibilities of using technology in this way out of a sense that others, too, would benefit from Cyborganic's example and its project to spread the gospel of networked, local community. The project was pursued as a business startup and though that enterprise provided the impetus and framework (both technical and imaginative) for the community, the two were symbiotic aspects of a whole that can only be understood holistically and within the context of the Web industry that emerged in San Francisco in the 1990s.[122]

Steuer made a conscious decision to use the entrepreneurial culture of dot-com-era San Francisco to accomplish his goal of spreading the gospel of "networked, local community." Steuer and Cool envisioned a multi-sited community: an online bulletin board, a hosting platform for personal publishing, and a cyber café that would teach classes and serve as a meeting place for like-minded web devotees. To this end, they wrote up a business plan, incorporated as Cyborganic Corporation, and sought funding. They eventually moved into a commercial office space in the SOMA neighborhood. Jenny Cool wrote the first Cyborganic manifesto in 1995, which concluded, "We must use [new technologies] to serve our own ends, not as ends in themselves, and we must work together to build a future we want, in our imaginations and in our lives."[123] The founders of Cyborganic recognized that although internet technologies had immense potential, they were not intrinsically positive. Instead, improving community and connection required hard work.

In some ways, the project succeeded. The Cyborganic apartments on Ramona hosted weekly Thursday night dinners and became a central meeting space for up-and-coming digerati. Cool estimates that the extended Cyborganic community at the time comprised 100 to 150 people, with a disproportionately significant influence on San Francisco's technology scene. Cyborganic members worked at *Wired* and its online offshoot *HotWired;* founded Organic.com, C|Net, ChickClick, and a variety of other startups; and contributed to high-profile open-source projects like Apache. Justin Hall of links.net, often cited as the first blogger, was a member. Cyborganic was written up in *Wired* and *Rolling Stone,* which described the community as "ground zero in the information revolution. This is the spawning ground for Webheads, geeks, pagan rituals and creative anarchy. This is where the future is being born, mutating and replicating in every pixeled-out, sugar-fueled twenty-something brain."[124]

Cyborganic was deeply embedded within previous iterations of San Franciscan technology culture. The slightly older generation of digerati like Howard Rheingold and Kevin Kelly, members of the WELL online community, served as mentors to the group. Cyborganic drew inspiration from the early homebrew computer scene and identified strongly with Apple products and Jobs's and Wozniak's garage startup origins, as many social media aficionados do today. Some Cyborganics supported Apple because they worked there, but others detested Microsoft's proprietary model and viewed Macintosh computers as ideologically aligned with openness and self-expression.[125]

Because Cyborganic attempted to meld the principles of community and open-source living with the very different values of venture-backed entrepreneurialism, it ultimately failed. As Cool relates, "Relationships that had been informal and voluntary were formalized in job descriptions, reporting structures, and legal contracts. While this was a practical necessity, it also involved ceding to the Corporation claims on intellectual property created in a community context on a volunteer basis, signing non-disclosure agreements, and apportioning stock options."[126] People who were happy to donate volunteer time and labor were less likely to give to a for-profit corporation. Once Cyborganic got funding, its slick office space made members homesick for the ramshackle hominess of Ramona Avenue. Thursday night dinners were ordered in rather than potluck, and petered out after 1997. To drum up revenue, Cyborganic began charging members to host their personal sites on the Cyborganic domain, but the business model was unsustainable. Gradually, employees left the company and funding dried up. Ultimately, conflicts between what was best for Cyborganic as a business and Cyborganic as a community contributed to its demise.

The Burning Man festival was a meeting point for the Cyborganic community, as it has been for several generations of San Francisco digerati. While it took a completely different approach to achieving community, it drew from many of the same cultural influences. Burning Man was a product of San Francisco 1980s countercultural groups like the Cacophony Society, the Suicide Club, and Survival Research Laboratories.[127] In 1986, Larry Harvey and Jerry James burned a wooden figure on Baker Beach to celebrate the summer solstice, in an example of what Burners now call "radical self-expression."[128] Burning Man became an annual event attracting hundreds of people, until the burning of a four-story wooden figure in a public place became impossible for authorities to overlook and the event was moved in 1990 to Nevada's Black Rock Desert. Today Burning Man is a city, built from scratch every year for the week, that celebrates artistry and individual self-expression in ways set out in the "Ten Principles" of Burning Man, which include radical inclusion, participation, communal effort, gifting, decommodification, and leaving no trace.[129]

From the beginning, technology workers were an integral part of Burning Man.[130] As Scott Beale, founder of the art and technology blog *Laughing Squid,* stated, "It used to be that everyone went [to Burning Man] and that you could actually put that into your contract, 'I'm gonna be gone this week in August.' I remember LinuxWorld happened one year during Burning Man—asinine! So, all these like Linux sysadmins and geeks are out there at Burning Man . . . all these things happening." Google's first "Google Doodle," an illustrative representation of the Google logo, included the Man and, according to Google, "was intended as a comical message to Google users that the founders were 'out of office.'"[131]

In many ways, Burning Man is a physical representation of Web 2.0 principles of openness, collaboration, and self-expression. Co-founder Larry Harvey told personal homepager Jessica Barron that "this environment we've created is a physical analog of the Internet. It's radically democratic. It allows people to conjure up entire worlds—like websites—voila! Out of nothing!"[132] Brewster Kahle, the founder of the Internet Archive and long-time Burner, told C|Net that "The communities are very interchangeable . . . There's a great deal of overlap; the open aspects of the Internet and Burning Man come from the same place. Burning Man and the Internet . . . disproved the 1980s myth that people will only do something if they're paid for it."[133]

Fred Turner argues that Burning Man provides a cultural infrastructure for new media labor, modeling commons-based peer production, gift economies, community participation, and the potential of "vocational ecstasy": self-fulfillment through creative work and radical self-expression.[134] Turner links the social structure of Burning Man to Google's company culture, which emphasizes collaboration, a relatively flat corporate hierarchy, and the pursuit of individual passion projects through "20 percent time." He maintains that for Bay Area technologists, Burning Man represents a week where the idealistic principles of new media production are brought to life, cementing the rich social networks that flexible labor models make necessary, and "work[ing] through the contradictions" of locating these ideals in a corporate setting.[135] Burning Man demonstrates a commitment to the same values that Web 2.0 idealizes, and allows technologists to affirm the validity, importance, and presence of these ideals in their lives. Just as Burning Man is a blueprint for creating a community that runs on gifts, bartering, and volunteerism, the rhetoric of Web 2.0 suggests that technology as a business can embody the same values.

Burning Man has become part of the lifecycle of Bay Area technologists; as such, it demonstrates the conflicts intrinsic to for-profit corporations holding up non-commodification as an ideal. Google is a large company, but its corporate culture mirrors many principles of creative labor epitomized by both today's venture-backed startups and the dot-com boom of the 1990s. While Google can create and maintain infrastructures like YouTube that facilitate commons-based peer production, ultimately it is responsible to its shareholders and cannot operate on an economy of gift exchange. The belief that creative expression through technical labor is the path to self-actualization often results in long hours at work and the integration of personal and corporate life. Cyborganic demonstrates how difficult it can be to maintain the ideals of community and connection while attempting to play by the rules of entrepreneurialism. And while in some ways Burning Man is a radical space, it is also primarily inhabited by the wealthy, white people who run the technology industry: further, the values of Burning Man have been transformed by the technical enterprise into business practices that justify unstable labor models and valorize neoliberalism. Burning Man itself remains a nonprofit, but it struggles with its growing popularity and can no longer offer entrance to all who wish to attend.

## Webheads and Dot-Communists: The Boom

The excitement surrounding the internet experienced by early San Francisco netizens spread like a fever across the United States.

During the height of the dot-com boom in 1999 and 2000, millions of dollars in venture capital were pumped into internet companies, hundreds of which went public at high valuations, sending the stock market soaring. Young people flocked to the centers of the boom: San Francisco, Seattle, New York, and Austin. Dot-commers emphasized the "five c's"—content, commerce, community, context, and connectivity—and extolled the massive changes that the "New Economy" would bring about. The New Economy, a buzzword popularized in 1997 by a series of articles in *BusinessWeek,* referred to the massive changes that the technology industry would bring to the economic climate of the United States, specifically low unemployment rates, fast growth, low inflation, and increased productivity.[136] L. John Doerr, a Silicon Valley venture capitalist, called the internet "the largest legal creation of wealth in history."[137] *Wired* magazine put "The Long Boom" on the cover and claimed, "We are watching the beginnings of a global economic boom on a scale never experienced before. We have entered a period of sustained growth that could eventually double the world's economy every dozen years and bring increasing prosperity for . . . billions of people on the planet. We are riding the early waves of a 25-year run of a greatly expanding economy that will do much to solve seemingly intractable problems like poverty and to ease tensions throughout the world. And we'll do it without blowing the lid off the environment."[138]

Despite these predictions, the stock market reached a peak in March of 2000 and then dropped 34.2 percent in five weeks, causing massive job loss in the technology sector and something like a collective hangover.[139] Today, the dot-com boom is mostly remembered for wretched excess, inflated company valuations, and the stereotype of the "ultracool, twenty-something cyberhead with a tattoo and a skateboard, plotting the overthrow of Microsoft from a fifth-floor walk-up on East 10th Street," as the *New York Times* characterized the industry in 1997.[140]

While there are several key differences between the type of companies involved in the dot-com boom and those dubbed Web 2.0, dot-com companies served as a template for the way that creative, technically savvy labor functioned in urban centers from the 1990s onward. The emphasis on self-actualization through work was drawn directly from boomtime philosophy. The philosophy of self-branding, or promoting oneself like a corporate entity, appeared during the boom, as did the lofty idealism and wild rhetoric of changing the world that permeated the time period.[141] Although the realities of the dot-com work experience differed from city to city, company to company, and industry to industry, two major shifts in the nature of work pioneered during the dot-com era remain key parts of the social media experience today. First, "entrepreneurial labor" became a major product of this new economy, as identified in sociologist Gina Neff's ethnographic studies of New York City's Silicon Alley. This labor model encourages flexibility but normalizes high-risk working environments where freelance and contract positions are common. Individuals have the glittering possibility of wealth through profit-sharing, but simultaneously bear the risk of market failure (layoffs, lack of health insurance, unemployment), a trade-off that is much easier for the economically privileged to bear. Workers are encouraged to adopt an enterprising attitude toward business and take responsibility for their own skill development, career progression, successes, and failures.[142] Neff points out that part of the symbolic capital for workers in such industries is the glamour of working in a "cool" job in a "hot" field, which becomes a form of nonmonetary compensation typical to commons-based peer production.[143] Andrew Ross compares what he calls the "no-collar" labor model, bohemian workers in ultimately unstable work environments, with the work ethic of Silicon Valley; both share an emphasis on personal growth, optimism, and idealism, mixed with libertarian politics.[144] Ross claims that as this model moved from the sterile suburbia of the South Bay to chic urban environments like Seattle and New York, it drifted left and mixed with an artistic, non-conformist Generation X ethic, like that found in zine culture, to create "industry with an indie pedigree."[145]

The second major change concerned the working conditions under which new media professionals labored. Richard Florida's influential *The Rise of the Creative Class* chronicled the increase in creative labor, "people in design, education, arts, music and entertainment, whose economic function is to create new ideas, new technology and/or creative content."[146] New Economy rhetoric rejected the hierarchical, buttoned-down company organization of large, traditional business, which was derided as *Dilbert*-ish cubicle culture. Instead, dot-com companies were supposedly structured to indulge and reward skilled artisans by emphasizing self-actualization, creativity, and autonomy. Workers could wear what they wanted, show up at noon, play foosball and video games on break, pursue creative interests outside of work, freely voice their opinions and concerns, and collaborate with others in intellectually stimulating environments. Ross writes that "in such a workplace, the zeal of employees was more like a quest for personal and existential stimulation, closer in spirit to extreme sport or adventure travel than to the sobriety of the self-dependent man who saw himself as a pious and productive member of society."[147] Inculcating this passion in workers, particularly young workers willing to work sixty or even eighty hour weeks without overtime, was of course more advantageous to companies than to their employees.

In San Francisco proper, the dot-com crash had a devastating effect. The Bay Area lost 450,000 jobs in the bust, the equivalent of the entire working population of today's San Francisco.[148] Nationwide, the economic crash put a damper on techno-utopianism and prematurely dulled the enthusiasm surrounding the internet; John Cassidy, a financial writer for the *New Yorker*, wrote in his book *dot.con* that the internet "was not a 'disruptive technology' . . . bookstores, newspaper companies, and brokerage houses are still in business, and most of them are doing fine."[149] Despite this dismissal, many survivors of the dot-com era, made wealthy by Amazon.com, eBay, PayPal, and Netscape, founded or invested in Web 2.0 companies. Furthermore, entrepreneurs who bucked conventional wisdom and started internet companies in the post-bust era— Wikipedia in 2001, Friendster in 2002, MySpace and LinkedIn in 2003, and Flickr and Digg in 2004—became some of the stars of the Web 2.0 boom.[150] These stories were widely circulated in Silicon Valley after the economic downturn in 2008, serving as inspiration to hopeful CEOs attempting to move forward with their own companies as venture capital diminished. Finally, much of the culture pioneered by dot-com companies, itself massively influenced by the history of Silicon Valley, persisted into the social media era: flexibility, entrepreneurial labor models, creativity, self-actualization through work, and the bootstrapped startup are all common to both.

## Where Did Web 2.0 Come From?

While the dot-com bust seemingly decimated the San Francisco technology scene, it in fact only restructured it. The next iteration of Northern California technology excitement was precipitated by a strategic marketing ploy to leave "dot-com" behind and move forward. Web 2.0's transformation from a buzzword to a scene was geographic; even post-boom, large numbers of people interested and inspired by technology remained in the Bay Area.

While there are scattered references to "Web 2.0" in the late 1990s and early 2000s, the term was first used in its current sense by publisher Tim O'Reilly in 2004.[151] O'Reilly was promoting his company's Web 2.0 conference, which cost $2,800 to attend, featured sessions like "The Architecture of Participation" and "So, Is This a Bubble Yet?" and boasted A-list tech speakers like *Boing Boing* blogger Cory Doctorow, Creative Commons founder Larry Lessig, Amazon CEO Jeff Bezos, entrepreneur Mark Cuban, and tech blogger Om Malik.[152] The conference came at a time when Silicon Valley was cautiously optimistic. In June 2004 the *New York Times* had reported that "'Silicon Valley is back' is on the lips of eager entrepreneurs and venture capitalists, who are rejoicing over the success of Google."[153] O'Reilly, his partner John Batelle, and marketing company MediaLive International batted around the moniker "Web 2.0" as a way to highlight afresh the web as a destination for investment and a locus of innovation. The term described companies that embraced "the web as platform," "collective intelligence," data openness, iterative software development, rich user experience, and "software as a service" as integral to the next generation of internet technology.[154]

O'Reilly and Battelle chose "2.0," the language of "versioning," to describe their conference. They did so more to distance themselves from the failures of the dot-com boom than to describe a paradigm shift in technological innovation. Indeed, "the web as platform"—the vague explanation of the term used by O'Reilly and Battelle—did not describe a singular technological innovation, nor did it mark the beginning of "social software" or "social media."[155] Paul Graham, an attendee and future founder of Y Combinator, an incubator for young entrepreneurs, wrote: "I don't think there was any deliberate plan to suggest there was a new *version* of the web. They just wanted to make the point that the web mattered again. It was a kind of semantic deficit spending: they knew new things were coming, and the "2.0" referred to whatever those might turn out to be."[156] In fact, most of the technologies described as "Web 2.0" existed before the term was coined, including wikis, online journals, blogs, user-generated content, and online community.

In addition to entrepreneurs and technologists, the conference boasted the activist triumvirate of Lawrence Lessig, Cory Doctorow, and Mitch Kapor, who spoke passionately about the political and social implications of the internet. Lessig's *Free Culture*, published in 2004, popularized the notion that the internet was enabling new forms of creativity and user-generated content that were threatened by the legal potency of Big Media.[157] He gave a fiery speech in which he advocated for "a right to remix without permission from anyone . . . a right to take these words and remix and spread them to build and to spread ideas."[158] Mitch Kapor, the cofounder of the Electronic Frontier Foundation, discussed technology's ability to increase transparency and stated, "If Thomas Paine was writing 'Common Sense' today, he would be doing so on a Linux laptop."[159] Tim O'Reilly expressed admiration for the speakers' zest and fire and exclaimed, "We can't let the past use legal means to prevent the future from happening!"[160]

"Web 2.0" represented a "reboot" back to the ideals of the early web, the "five c's."[161] One of the reasons Web 2.0 was so successful is because it both revived and revitalized long-held techno-utopian beliefs held by dot-com survivors, activists, and old-school geeks, as well as presenting another opportunity for wealth generation. The appellation "2.0" suggested a return to the early web as an exciting space of creativity and innovation, rather than the crass, carpet-bagger gold rush of the dot-com boom. From the start, Web 2.0 encompassed both financial and idealistic motivations for techno-logical innovation.

While O'Reilly's event was expensive and marketed toward high-level professionals, the excitement sparked by wikis, blogs, mashups, and the cutting-edge of 2004 participatory culture was palpable in the blog posts and comments that followed each talk. While the mainstream media largely ignored the conference (even the *San Francisco Chronicle* dismissed it as an "online lovefest"), it was embraced by West Coast technologists.[162] Entrepreneur Jason Calacanis live-blogged the conference, while venture capitalist Esther Dyson snapped photos and instantly posted them to Flickr, the photo-sharing site that served as a centerpiece to the conference. Evan Williams (founder of Blogger and Twitter) enthusiastically blogged, "Seems like perfect timing for such a conference. The feeling of doing things again, but newer and better is in the air—and *lots* of folks are ready to play."[163] Richard MacManus at *ReadWriteWeb* began a Web 2.0 column and interviewed Tim O'Reilly about the "web as platform."[164] Steven Levy, writing for *Newsweek*, summarized:

> Are you ready for the new Web? It's getting ready for you. It turns out that bidding on eBay, gathering with Meetup and Googling on, um, Google are only the opening scenes in a play whose running time will top "Mahabharata." While we've been happily browsing, buying and blogging, the tech set has been forging clever new tools and implementing powerful standards that boost the value of information stored on and generated by the Net. Things may look the

same as the old Web, but under the hood there's been some serious tinkering, and after years of hype among propeller-heads, some of the effects are finally arriving.[165]

The prospect of another bubble, however, had others on edge. A C|Net journalist wrote, "This was billed as a coming-out party for the new Web, and the Internet executives and venture capitalists in attendance would much rather forget the excesses of the old."[166] A writer for *PC Magazine* noted that the "familiar faces" of the web's "glitterati" were in attendance, but seemed "slightly less breathless about the Web than they were during the dot-com boom," even as "they still characterized the Web as full of innovation and promise."[167]

The importance of conferences and social interactions to technologically mediated cultures has been well documented.[168] From MIT's Model Railroad club and Stewart Brand's original hacker conference to today's free and open-source software "cons," these events not only allow for face-to-face interactions between people who share common interests, but also create "scenes" of people who become friends, work together, and support each other. Despite near-constant discussion and chit-chat through the online communication tool du jour, it is often in-person socialization and collaboration that bring to bear the geographical importance of a scene. While O'Reilly's conferences, including Emerging Technology (eTech), Where 2.0, and the Web 2.0 Expo popularized the concepts identified with Web 2.0, it was a number of more grassroots, in-person events that facilitated this collaboration, openness, and participation and helped to solidify the vibrant scene around social media in the mid- to late 2000s.

Perhaps the most important of these grassroots happenings was the South by Southwest festival held yearly in Austin, Texas. Founded as "SXSW Multimedia" to celebrate Austin's burgeoning new media industry, SXSW had steadily grown since its inception in 1995 and emerged in the mid-2000s as a destination for the same digerati excited by Web 2.0. The 2005 festival, for instance, featured keynotes from Malcolm Gladwell, *Wonkette* blogger Ana Marie Cox, and science-fiction author Bruce Sterling. For Web 2.0, "South By" represented what Burning Man did for an earlier generation of geeks. It helped to constitute a social world, providing an annual touchstone for people to reconnect and revive their passion for technology. It allowed hard-working geeks to blow off steam and eat barbeque in the sun while nattering about RSS feeds and trading business cards. SXSW could kickstart careers; Twitter broke into the mainstream during SXSW 2007 and Foursquare was launched there in 2009. Scott Beale, the founder of *Laughing Squid,* relates, "I really look at 2005 as the first year for so many things . . . Eddie [Codel] and I went to South By together and we're like, 'Holy crap! This is like a really big version of Webzine!' We got totally inspired. At the event, Eddie revived Webzine for one more time and we did it in 2005." Webzine 2005 brought together older and wiser dot-com veterans and newcomers to the scene to celebrate the participatory potential of online publishing.

The year 2005 was also the first for two largely ad-hoc gatherings, SuperHappyDevHouse and BarCamp, which attracted social media enthusiasts primarily working at venture-backed startups. Scott Beale, who began blogging on New Year's Day 2005, relates one of the first meetings between himself, WordPress founder Matt Mullenweg, open source activist Chris Messina, and blogger Om Malik. Beale was using WordPress software and learned from Mullenweg's Flickr stream that Mullenweg had just relocated to the Bay Area and was hosting a meetup. Beale was eager to meet the man behind the software: "This is so hard to conceive of now but I'm like, 'Wow! I could actually meet the guy who made the script that I use for my blog.'" At the meetup, Beale suggested to Mullenweg that he throw a public party for WordPress. The party successfully brought together many other technologists.

Such face-to-face meetups are important within the San Francisco social media scene. Informal chats, parties, and conferences allow people working on disparate but similar projects to network, share inspiration, and generally help each other out. SuperHappy-DevHouse, for example, was a semi-regular series of overnight hackathons where developers worked on personal projects simultaneously. The invitation to the second SuperHappyDevHouse reads:

> You could think of SuperHappyDevHouse as an all-night hackfest. Come work on your personal projects; this is an excuse to do it. Maybe you'll learn about new technologies or methodoligies [*sic*]. Maybe you'll find people interested in working on that project with you. Maybe you and others will form an idea for something that you could easily prototype together that night. If not, the environment is fun and productive, just what you need to get your work done solo.[169]

SuperHappyDevHouse drew from the hacker ethic to bring together programmers to share information and collaborate in a mutually beneficial effort. While the attendees were not necessarily working on social media projects, they were drawing from the collaborative ethic of social media, itself directly influenced by FOSS.

Technorati employees Tantek Çelik and Ryan King were driving back from an around-the-clock hacking session at the second Super-HappyDevHouse when the idea for BarCamp was born. Çelik was complaining about being excluded from the second Foo Camp, an invite-only hacker camp run by O'Reilly media. He wrote in his blog:

> Knowing that the focus and content of FooCamp were mostly attendee driven, armed with a plethora of photos from previous FooCamps, and inspired by the scrappy can-do attitude of events like SuperHappyDevHouse and Web-zine2005 which were both openly or at least semi-openly organized by volunteers, I asked the rhetorical question: "Why don't we do our own FooCamp?" followed shortly

thereafter with something like "We could call it BarCamp and make it open."[170]

"Bar" was a joke: "foo" and "bar" are both metasyntactic variables that programmers use for placeholders. A few weeks later, Çelik, King, Chris Messina, Andy Smith, Matt Mullenweg, and Eris Free met at Ritual Roasters to plan the first BarCamp, which was held six days later. Scott Beale recalls the importance of BarCamp in bringing together key figures of Web 2.0, including Robert Scoble and Michael Arrington, two of the most influential Web 2.0 bloggers: "BarCamp is seminal. This is like the most important thing of all of this . . . Scoble came by, and he was really into it. It was actually the very first public demo of Flock and Pandora. It was a really big deal, those things coming out of it, and the funny thing that we always think about is Arrington was there. None of us knew him." BarCamp became a template for "open-source," "unconference" organizing. It has been described as "an ad-hoc gathering born from the desire for people to share and learn in an open environment. It is an intense event with discussions, demos and interaction from participants who are the main actors of the event."[171] In other words, BarCamps are participant driven, allowing attendees to facilitate sessions and decide on discussion topics. The "camp" metaphor suggests rugged informality and collectiveness, a back-to-basics approach that contrasts with the modernity of technology. BarCamp is constructed as an authentic space where the ideals of collectivity can flourish without the infiltration of profit motives. The BarCamp format has proven immensely popular and has been used for hundreds of conferences worldwide; in 2009, there were more than 450 BarCamps in sixty-seven countries.[172] Like Indymedia and Burning Man, BarCamp is an instantiation of Web 2.0 principles that emphasizes participation, openness, transparency, and information-sharing.

By the second Web 2.0 conference in late 2005, the mainstream media had caught up with the West Coast. "Web 2.0" appeared frequently in technology columns and financial news and became a legitimate buzzword. Partly this was due to the emergence of exciting, trendy technologies that journalists could hang a hook on; it was easier to point to Flickr, tagging, and mashups as concrete examples of newness rather than the clumsy buzzwords "software as a service" and "client-side applications." By the end of that year, journalist Mathew Ingram could sigh that "2005 was—for better or worse—the year of 'Web 2.0.'"[173]

By 2006, the technology industry was bubbling over with enthusiasm for social-network-site success stories, YouTube celebrities, user-created content, and exciting young entrepreneurs like Mark Zuckerberg of Facebook and Kevin Rose of Digg. Fox bought MySpace for $770 million and Google bought YouTube for $1.65 billion.[174] The enormous valuations of these companies made the financial aspects of interactive technology as attractive as they had been during the late 1990s. In intellectual circles, the ideas of Lessig, Doctorow, Kapor, and academics like Henry Jenkins and Yochai Benkler became mainstream. "Free culture," "participatory culture," and the "networked information economy" were hot. "The Long Tail," a theory formulated by Chris Anderson, editor-in-chief of *Wired* magazine, postulated that the internet and fragmented mainstream culture created infinite niche audiences for cultural products, while *The Wisdom of Crowds* put forth the idea that collective intelligence could surpass individual smarts.[175] Blogs like *TechCrunch, BoingBoing,* and *Mashable* fueled readers with a steady diet of stories and gossip about the possibilities of these new, liberating technologies. The scene had blown up. Scott Beale described it as "this ultimate scaling thing, nothing can even be how it originally was. That's 2006."

"Web 2.0" stayed hot for several years (luckily, while I was doing research for this book). Ultimately, though, the ideals of Web 2.0 gave way to the same disillusionment as the dot-com bust. While the economic downturn of 2008 turned out to be merely a blip rather than a bubble bursting, the term "Web 2.0" became passé by the early 2010s. The idea of openness and participation seemed naïve in the face of walled-garden App Stores and Facebook. While many of the first set of Web 2.0 companies failed, others succeeded spectacularly. The preferred term became "social media" and Northern California reemerged as a center for venture capital investment and enormous acquisitions. By 2012, even small companies like Instagram and OMGPOP were valued at millions, even billions, of dollars. The dearth of engineers to feed this ravaging juggernaut led to intense competition over recruitment and a steady stream of get-rich-quick wannabes flocking to Silicon Valley once again. A friend referred to them derisively as "Web 2.0 carpetbaggers"—people who don't care about the technology, only the profits.

Caterina Fake told me over IM:

> It's always that way, with new technology . . . the [people] who first get into, say, radio, love the medium for what it is. the second wave of [people] come because they sense a gold rush. it is the way of things. nobody will love the medium as much as the [people] who first found it, and invented it. you can sit around lamenting its demise, and drink cocktails and get misty-eyed about the golden age, but it's not coming back.

Regardless of how the current technological boom ends, the San Francisco technological elite will be present for whatever the next round of technological achievement happens to be, because the beliefs of this scene are so deeply immersed in cyber-utopian rhetoric and vice versa. As Jaron Lanier writes,

> The ascendant tribe is composed of folks from the open culture / Creative Commons world, the Linux community, folks associated with the artificial intelligence approach to computer science, the Web 2.0 people, the anticontext file sharers and remashers, and a variety of others. Their capital is Silicon Valley, but they have power bases all over the world, wherever digital culture is being created. Their favorite blogs

include Boing Boing, TechCrunch and Slashdot, and their embassy in the old country is *Wired*.[176]

While the techno-activist, techno-utopian rhetoric existed long before the buzzword "Web 2.0," and will continue after it has long disappeared, its peak marked a dramatic period characterized by intensive financial investment, a rapid proliferation of startups, and the ready adoption of social technologies. But who were the people who thrived in this period, and how did this peculiar combination of factors affect how they saw themselves, and each other?

# 2

## LEADERS AND FOLLOWERS

———

### Status in the Tech Scene

I wait, somewhat impatiently, in a long line outside a club in the South of Mission. It is September 2008, and I am in San Francisco to attend TechCrunch's annual conference, a massive event that brings people from all over the country to hear about the latest startups and social technologies. This particular party is sponsored by Seesmic, a video-sharing startup. A velvet rope, with muscled bouncers on both sides, bars the door. Behind that rope, a passel of attractive twenty-something women—in cocktail dresses, sparkly jewelry, and lots of makeup—are checking names off a guest list. As I wait to get in, a shiny black Town Car pulls up to the curb. A British man, wearing a collection of conference badges around his neck and accompanied by a photographer and a well-preserved woman in her fifties, emerges from the car. The British man shows his badge to the bouncer and says officiously that he is TechCrunch staff. The bouncer points to the end of the line, which is now winding around the block. The man shakes his head and repeats himself, emphasizing the word "staff." The bouncer again indicates the line. Increasingly agitated, the man insists as his companions wait awkwardly behind him. The bouncer shakes his head. Finally, I'm at the front of the line; I drop the name of my roommate, who is a co-organizer, and the women give me a wristband and a drink ticket and whisk me inside.

Every social group has a pecking order, and those higher on the ladder reap the benefits of respect, money, and freedom.[1] Alain de Botton, in his book *Status Anxiety,* defines status as "one's value and importance in the eyes of the world."[2] Status is what your peers think of you, whether they hold you in esteem or contempt, and the privileges that accord from this position. Status is a powerful tool that reveals the values and assumptions shared by a group; it shows power dynamics and the limits of egalitarian ideals. Yet what's considered high status differs from context to context: an individual can have high status in one context and low status in another.[3] The TechCrunch employee believed that his job granted him high status, but this meant nothing to the bouncer, a hired hand who was not a member of the tech community and thus did not share this opinion. I was virtually unknown in the scene, but my roommate was popular and well connected. In this case, the social capital accrued by being "in the know" garnered more weight than self-important blustering.

While sociologists, economists, and anthropologists agree that status is a fundamental part of social life, scholars know little about how status operates online. Status is present in virtually every human interaction: hierarchies exist in all social groups—even among animals—and status-seeking is a primary motivator for human action.[4] In American society at large, higher social status has been linked to longevity, wealth, deference, respect, and influence.[5] As a result, people at all levels of society devote considerable time to status-seeking activities.[6] Status is a similarly powerful impetus for online participation; one study found that a desire to be more popular was a major reason why undergraduates used Facebook.[7] The importance of status is borne out by the fact that practically every online community has developed a way to mark social status. While it is rarely remarked on, many popular social media technologies have what I call "status affordances," technical mechanisms that signal greater social status. For example, Twitter has followers, Facebook has "Likes," and Slashdot has "karma," all metrics that provide comparable measures of importance. (The startup Klout, which measures online "influence," is entirely a status affordance.) But even in technologies without these built-in mechanisms for demonstrating status, people come up with other ways to signal hierarchy. For instance, although the simple textual software of Usenet has no status affordances, within the soap opera Usenet groups studied by communication scholar Nancy Baym, the highest status was ascribed to long-term group members who had contributed valuable knowledge. People signaled deference to high-status members through linguistic cues like "our friend so-and-so," by citing them in the Frequently Asked Questions, and by regularly quoting their posts.[8] Individual newsgroups developed status signals based on group norms and ongoing interaction.

Given that communities without built-in status signals create them anyway, the prevalence of online status hierarchies calls into question the mid-2000s belief that sites like Wikipedia and YouTube demonstrate open and democratic online participation. In reality, a close examination of practically any online group will reveal tightly wound status hierarchies that often serve to limit participation, sometimes by following timeworn lines of power. A survey of Wikipedia participants, for instance, found that only 13 percent of contributors and editors are women.[9] Wikipedia researcher Joseph Reagle argues that the values of openness and transparency found in hacker and free and open-source software culture may actually serve to limit women's involvement by giving priority to small groups of argumentative or misogynistic men while labeling concerns about sexism as "censorship."[10] That is, although the culture pays lip service to "an online encyclopedia that anyone can edit," this "anyone" is circumscribed by the status hierarchy of the community.

Reputation and trust, which many others have written about, are not the same as status. Online reputation and trust both refer to systemized ranking systems, or slightly more ineffable qualities that are roughly "what people say about you online" and "whether this website will steal your money." Status incorporates and reveals more—the contextual nature of status means that a person's status can ebb and flow not only throughout their life, but also in the course of a day, making it impossible to pin down with a single metric. Status is reflected in a wide range of characteristics, from personality type to accent to fashion, but the same trait can signal different levels of status depending on the context. For example, within a group of friends, having a deep knowledge of *Star Trek* may be deeply admired. But in the broader, popularity-driven world of high school, that knowledge can brand one as a nerd. Status can either be ascribed or achieved, in that it can encompass characteristics like gender and race as well as accomplishments, like education or material possessions. Ascribed status comes from what one is recognized to inherently have, whereas achieved status comes from what one is recognized as having done.[11] For instance, "ascribed" status might include one's family owning a cabin in the popular ski destination of Lake Tahoe, whereas speaking at an exclusive conference is an accomplishment that grants "achieved" status.

The technology scene outwardly values openness, transparency, and creativity, maintaining a vestige of meritocracy. But Silicon Valley has long prioritized entrepreneurship, technical knowledge, and wealth. The mixture of these two sets of ideals peculiar to Web 2.0 creates a climate in which participating in the culture of techno-business, sharing personal information online, and commanding and maintaining a large audience have become modern status symbols. The highest status is still wrapped up in engineering culture and technology-fueled wealth, but the popularity of social media has given rise to an equivalent hierarchy based on attention and visibility. Since this shared set of values and beliefs is the context that fuels the creation of social software, unpacking it helps us to understand the assumptions that technology creators make about "users" and "social behavior."

Like any community, especially one with wealth and power involved, the tech scene has a closely striated social hierarchy and commonly understood status symbols, although many participants have denied that the tech scene is at all interested in "status." Some of these symbols are internet-related. For instance, having a two-letter Twitter handle signals that its possessor was an early adopter (someone in-the-know, or someone with a certain prescience about emerging technologies), or at least someone with connections to Twitter, both of which mark insiderness and social significance. Likewise, having a huge blog readership implies importance (since it means that people like to read what you have to say), high visibility, and the ability to command an audience. Other status symbols are more universal, such as owning an amazing house in Pacific Heights (especially if it was paid for with money earned from a wildly successful startup) or taking exotic vacations (particularly to attend exclusive conferences). Status symbols are determined by what the community values, which in these examples means technical knowledge, attention, being part of an exclusive network, and business success. Because these are the values of the people who create social software, the assumptions that reflect these values often find their way into social media—that is, how technologies like Klout or Twitter are used to display and manipulate social status hierarchies reflects the technology scene's cultural beliefs about how the world is ordered and organized.[12] In other words, social media technologies illuminate and reward status-seeking practices that reflect the values of the technology scene: idealism, privilege, business acumen, and geek masculinity.

Business and work are central. In Jan English-Lueck's *Cultures@ SiliconValley* project, an ethnography of 1990s Silicon Valley technology workers, she describes the centrality of modern work practices to Silicon Valley techno-culture and identifies the discrepancy between its discourse of egalitarianism and the realities of social hierarchy. She writes, "This [Silicon Valley] identity, in which work defines worth, is based on producing technology, and embracing a fast pace and open attitude. In theory, it embodies the ultimate expression of personal achievement beyond the restrictions of one's birth. People assert that opportunity is not affected by national origin, class, or gender. However, differences are detectable. The culture of opportunity looks different to a janitor, an admin, an engineer, and a high-tech executive."[13] The San Francisco technology scene prides itself on being open to those seeking to break in, but social position definitely affects how others treat you; your access to people, conferences, and technologies; your job and relationship prospects; your ability to command an audience; and many other privileges.

Many of these status symbols are types of knowledge. Neoliberal economies are ones in which the production and circulation of knowledge predominates, and where knowledge as a product is emphasized. The technology sector is a place where knowledge—of topics, of industries, of players within the industry—often governs possibilities. Possession of such knowledge indicates that the owner has succeeded in an ostensibly merit-based social order. The Marxist theorist Antonio Gramsci used the concept of the "organic intellectual" to distinguish individuals emanating from the working classes, who gain social power through expertise, from those whose status comes from their association with state-sanctioned bodies like universities. Like Gramsci's organic intellectuals, high-status technology workers believe that their status is achieved through their own actions, rather than ascribed by circumstances.

The technology scene ascribes high value to wealth, risk-taking, entrepreneurship, visibility, access to others, technical know-how, and intelligence. The conflicts between some of these status symbols and practices reveal the inherent tension in Web 2.0 culture. For instance, it's cool to be rich, but not in a flashy way, only in a way appropriate to a smart, idealistic rich person. The idealism of Web 2.0's countercultural roots, the belief in meritocracy embedded in engineering culture, and the neoliberal ethic of work-life integration and relentless self-marketing have created a strange mishmash of wealth and privilege framed as pious self-improvement, all taking place in public. Although it is not easy to achieve the highest status in the tech scene, which requires being a successful entrepreneur, boosting one's status requires full participation in both the attention economy of social media and the more traditional economy of technology.

### Talking, Working, Doing

The technology scene has a well understood and clear social hierarchy, notwithstanding proclamations of its inclusiveness or openness. Despite frequent claims by technologists that the scene was egalitarian, during my period of study insiders were happy to describe divisions in great detail. Blogger and marketing entrepreneur Tara Hunt, for example, explained her perceptions of the community to me this way: the "lower rungs of the hierarchy," she said, are "those who are talking about it." These are the people who follow the happenings of the community and network in hopes that their plans for a startup might one day come true. Hunt then described the "middle class" as those who are "working on it"—actually creating a startup. (Note her use of "on it" as a universally understood synonym for "founding a startup," indicating a shared knowledge and priorities.) The lowest in that stratum are those "just doing it for money" or pursuing projects with dubious prospects for success; those who are working on something promising lead that class. "The top, the upper crust, are the people that have done it," Hunt said. "They had a company people loved. They sold it. They are now doing whatever the hell they please."

Talking, working, doing—Hunt describes a hierarchy in which the majority of people milling around at technology events exchanging business cards are at the bottom, while successful, wealthy entrepreneurs are at the top. What's clear in her description is that status level is conferred through one's position in the business of technology. Work is conflated with value, morality, personality, and character. When Hunt talks about "having done it," she explains that this first means having "a company that people loved," which speaks to the centrality of technology to daily life. Creating something that people use, and emotionally connect with, is high status in and of itself. The second step, "selling it," is exemplified by Instagram's sale to Facebook ($1 billion), OMGPOP's acquisition by Zynga ($180 million) or YouTube's purchase by Google ($1.65 billion). Naturally, the combination of both is the highest status of all; the prevalent conception of success, and the dream many people in the tech scene are chasing, is to found a successful technology company and get rich from its acquisition or IPO (initial public offering). As Hunt's taxonomy demonstrates, people's position on the social hierarchy of the scene is determined by how close they are to this goal. But as we will also see, attention can be a way to jump the queue and boost popularity without an enormous company valuation.

The highest position on the status hierarchy is reserved for entrepreneurs. As one high-ranking social media executive who preferred to remain anonymous explained: "Even if you're not going to make money it's like other people will give you more respect if you've started a company than if you're an employee. A lot of the employees are really important and they, a lot of [the] time, add more value to the world as an employee than they would as a founder of a company that isn't going to go anywhere." Even founding an unsuccessful company can lead to higher status than working at a successful company. This may seem peculiar, since rank-and-file engineers often have more stable jobs and make more money in the long run than do failed entrepreneurs. But entrepreneurship represents the lauded qualities of independence and risk-taking, not to mention the possibility of creating what some refer to as "fuck you money"—the type of money where, if you have it, you don't have to do anything you don't want to, ever again. The success of many young entrepreneurs and the prevalence of funding for technology startups have created a climate ripe for wannabe founders. As Jeremy Stoppelman, the founder of Yelp, said, "In 2005, it was not necessarily cool to have a start-up. It was cooler to work for a great company or have a job that was layoff free. And so now, the pendulum [has] shifted back to you're uncool unless you're a founder of a company." Being "safe" isn't cool, and brands you as a fuddy-duddy tied down to someone else's dream. If you are a rank-and-file employee, it is better to be one at a hot startup than a large company; there's more risk, but more chance of getting rich by proxy. While the chance for massive wealth rarely pans out—something like 85 percent of start-ups fail—it is this hope that fuels entrepreneurs and workers alike.

Another demonstration of how business ideals are integrated with social values is the extent to which one's work for a particular company defines one's self. English-Lueck describes work as "the lodestone of SV life," an emphasis that has characterized Silicon Valley for decades.[14] The anonymous executive elaborated, "The companies are almost like a cult, right?" He described a startup as a "clan" with t-shirts, membership in which requires workers to spend all of their time at "weird events like Hackathons" that isolate them from their families and discourage outside interests. Unlike in other parts of the world, he said, "here [work is] woven into people's life more."

The San Francisco tech scene does pride itself on an ostensible sheen of work-life balance. In San Francisco, I was told, people love to snowboard, ride bikes, and go to concerts, as opposed to their boring suburban counterparts who just work all the time. But during fieldwork, when I asked people what they did, they answered with a list of work projects. When I first met someone, she often gave me an elevator pitch for her latest project. In their free time, people pursued personal projects that looked remarkably similar to their paid work, such as building a personal website rather than coding one for a client. Social occasions were frequently sponsored by companies or held at startup headquarters. People wore t-shirts and hats with company logos, and roomed and socialized with their co-workers. Work was a source of satisfaction, fulfillment, and personal worth, both literally and figuratively. When asked about work-life balance in a speech to Girls in Tech, Leah Culver, founder of the now defunct micro-blogging site Pownce, said, "Pick one or the other, make your choices, whatever makes you happy."[15] The "life" in "work-life balance" is often a gendered euphemism for family and children. The prioritization of work implied that these things were unimportant; I did not hear any young men discussing their concerns in this area. The common attitude was that one could not have both; the underlying implication was that one should pick work.

This hierarchy also demonstrates the technology scene's idealism. When Hunt refers to "working on it" or "doing it," she means engaging in what the community thinks is important. This isn't just creating technology, but following your passion, in the sense of popular Web 2.0 motivational speaker Gary Vaynerchuk, whose book bears the tagline "Cash In on Your Passion." Status is linked not just to job title, but also to creative output. Moreover, I frequently encountered the rhetoric that social media entrepreneurs were "changing the world." As Jeremy Stoppelman states:

> It does feel like a bit of a unique place, because there really are people that are trying to change the world. It sounds kind of silly or idealistic to say that. But some places, it might be competing for fame or competing for cash, and there are those elements here, too. It's not like they don't exist. But there is a bit of a competition if the guy on top is probably changing the world more than the next guy. That's really the competition, whose startup is more revolutionary and impactful in driving the industry forward, is more interesting than just who has the most money or who has the fancy corporate jets or who drives the fancy cars.

Tristan Walker, an alum of both Twitter and Foursquare, said wistfully, "There are other folks—if you think about Ev [Williams] and Jack [Dorsey] and Dennis [Crowley] and Mark Zuckerberg—like fundamentally changing lives, and doing important things in the world. So I'm jealous . . . that's actually I think what a lot of folks aspire to." Status is not simply conferred by getting rich, but through creating something with a significant impact. Tristan concluded, "I think you can aspire to getting wealthy. But you can also have that wealth come as a result of your changing the world fundamentally." The tech scene believed strongly that changing the world through social media was possible, but it's arguable whether building a better local search, for instance, is really world-changing. In my interviews with tech industry leaders, I found that they consistently ascribed not only high status, but also extreme importance, to the industry's own trends and achievements. If one is truly "changing the world," then one probably deserves the millions of dollars that may come with achieving that goal. Those who chase wealth for its own sake, though, seem much less deserving.

### Symbolizing Status

This uneasy prioritization of work and social change played out in the tech community's definition of status symbols. The San Francisco technology scene adhered to an ethos of visible consumption focused on "functional" goods, experiences, and travel. Certain expenses were deemed acceptable if they could be linked to pursuits with a larger purpose, but anything that couldn't be linked to either work or self-improvement was frowned on. For instance, it was totally acceptable to carry a Chrome messenger bag filled with the latest gadgets and ride a fancy bike, but spending on clothes or luxury brand names for everyday goods was terribly gauche. (Apple products were an exception, since electronics were considered necessary work tools.) The most popular sports in the tech scene—rock climbing, biking, and yoga—can be practiced cheaply, but usually are not. It is important to note that this is not an ethic of anti-consumption. Tech people had no problem spending large, even exorbitant, sums of money on personal possessions or travel as long as they could be framed as part of their work life.

Justifying expensive experiences as part of a creative project or as essential to self-improvement is typical in Silicon Valley. As English-Lueck writes:

> Our informants saw money as a way of keeping track of relative status—nothing startling there. More interesting

was the way in which money was recast instrumentally. It was viewed repeatedly as a way of sustaining what was truly important, supporting a comfortable lifestyle that enabled people to engage in creative work, not an end in itself. Of course, those with enough money to be comfortable can afford to engage in other obsessions—a high median income disguises the reality of living at the lower range.[16]

While wealth was necessary to maintain the comfortable lifestyle of San Francisco tech workers, the idealism of the technology scene emphasized passion and framed money in itself as unimportant. But even if the idea of wealth is wrapped in a discourse of self-actualization, the potential to get extremely rich is a major motivator for many to enter the technology scene. Although most people never earn millions of dollars, there is a presumed income level among San Francisco technology workers that might best be characterized as "bohemian yuppie," or artsy upper-middle class. Flying off to Austin for SXSW, buying a tiny digital video camera or a brand-new MacBook Pro, joining a rock-climbing gym, renting a house in Tahoe for the winter—these things are considered typical without acknowledging that they require a high level of economic privilege. Nobody complains about overdrafts or wages on Facebook or Twitter, but many are willing to talk about their vacations to exotic places (the winter I lived in San Francisco, four different friends visited Thailand) or about obtaining tickets to the Inaugural Ball.[17] I only met a few people during fieldwork who admitted that they had difficulty paying for a group sailing trip or the latest gadget. Around this time Leah Culver began selling advertising on her laptop case in order to pay for her new computer, but this explicitness about money was rare among people I met in the tech scene, which speaks to a larger attitude of entitlement and privilege: tech professionals are used to having money, and because they view the scene as egalitarian, they assume others have money too. My informants echoed Jan English-Lueck's observation of Silicon Valley workers that money was valuable insofar as it facilitated what was "truly important." When I told a friend that I couldn't go to the full ten days of SXSW music and interactive, she scoffed that she always prioritized it. As a graduate student, I simply did not have the money to go, but she framed my reluctance as a lack of desire to share an experience—according to her mindset, time, not money, was the truly limited commodity. While people may privately recognize financial differences, in general economic disparity is hardly ever discussed.

Even so, extremely rich people in the scene are expected to avoid flaunting their wealth. Technology writer Kara Swisher explains: "They're a better class of rich people. They do mingle. Bill Gates does mingle with the hoi polloi, kind of thing. He doesn't really have to. He can go to a little island by himself as far as I'm concerned, but I think there is a lot more equality in mingling . . . They don't have Hamptons houses and they don't exclude themselves and you can run into them in Palo Alto . . . There's not a lot of limousines and that kind of stuff. But there is status related to their wealth." The first dot-com boom abounded with tales of newly minted millionaires living in studio apartments and wearing torn t-shirts.[18] Flaunting one's wealth is considered tacky, because it defies the scene's emphasis on intelligence and technological savvy; a focus on looks or superfluous material possessions is viewed somewhat suspiciously as non-techie or at least non-nerdy. There is a certain anti-fashion ethos in some geek cultures: focusing too much effort on appearance or status goods is seen as "mainstream," feminine, or otherwise unimportant compared with what really matters.[19] Men in the tech scene, whether twenty or fifty, wore jeans, sneakers, and t-shirts or button-downs. San Francisco is a low-key city with a casual aesthetic, but looks and appearance were still consistently deemphasized, as a way of supposedly demonstrating that tech workers prioritized intelligence and creativity over such irrelevancies as fancy clothes. At a *Mashable* party, I was accosted by a woman from New York who had recently moved to San Francisco. She bemoaned the lack of style in the room. "You'd never wear those boots in New York!" she said, pointing to my button-up knee boots. (She was wrong.) Her fashionable studded sheath dress, trendy haircut, and high heels clearly marked her as an outsider; I suspected that given enough time in San Francisco, she would be wearing jeans and flats like most of the other women in the room.

Rational, justifiable consumption was invariably contrasted against the popular image of the wasteful, frivolous luxury consumer. Technology workers unconsciously labored to ensure that they were not seen as superficial consumers, a subject position that has historically and consistently been assigned to women. In the mass culture of post-Depression America, there was widespread social anxiety that the newly founded mass media would inculcate unbridled consumption among passive audiences, leading to excess, indulgence, and madness. This archetype was, as historian Alison Clarke writes, "a self-indulgent woman, freed from household drudgery by labor-saving devices to wile away her time in non-productive pursuits, [who] shopped as an act of pleasure, self-fulfillment, and autonomy rather than household provisioning."[20] By contrast, technology workers in the late 2000s, whether male or female, adhered to a supposedly masculine ethos of spending in which consumerism was justifiable only if it could be linked to more worthy pursuits: self-improvement or work.

### Meeting Up, Tweeting Up

Another perfectly acceptable expense was conference travel. Tech workers frequently flew to expensive, exclusive events like TED, Sundance, Coachella, South by Southwest, New York Internet Week, and technology conferences all over the world. Frequent travel, and the subsequent accumulation of frequent flier miles, showed that one was lucky enough to have a flexible work schedule, plenty of money, and worldliness. Meeting up with peers in airport lounges and hotel rooms created a sense of a far-flung diaspora, in which members were connected through wealth, travel, and technology—while also making it clear that this style of meeting required immense privilege. A technology executive told me, "Everyone's at

Burning Man this week and it's like you're saying, 'I can afford to do this really inconvenient thing and take a week off of work and not do any work and pretend I'm from the desert, from the earth,' right? But it costs a lot of money to go and you have to buy tickets . . . [it] shows that you were able to go and do this wasteful thing." Burning Man, as described in the last chapter, was considered to be an important opportunity for self-exploration and actualization. But even more humdrum technology conferences contributed to a sense of global cosmopolitanism. One New York tech insider tweeted: "Declining 80%-90% of speaking invites, trying to minimize travel+blur. But they're also the only way to connect with Global Intercity Peeps." This tweet was somewhat of a "humblebrag," a complaint that also reinforced that its writer was important enough to be asked to speak frequently. While travel can be stressful and time-consuming, it was necessary to keep up one's access and connections to other members of the international tech scene.

In part, this constant conference travel solidified membership in the tech elite. Gabriella Coleman talks about the role of the "con" in hacker culture; conferences "reconfigure the relation between time, space and persons; allow for a series of personal transformations; and, perhaps most importantly, reinforce group solidarity."[21] Conferences have been similarly instrumental in creating a community around Web 2.0, because they provide an opportunity for people to meet, brainstorm, learn, and socialize in a way that maintains the primacy of business and work. Kara Swisher, who runs the All Things Digital conference, describes their role:

Tech people are very social and like to get together in an analog fashion in a way that is kind of antiquated [compared] to their obsession with Twitter and all that stuff . . . That's why the conferences succeed so much, and why there's so much of that kind of stuff going on, because they're very successful. You can make a lot of money doing them. [People] like to chat with each other in person, in real-life style, which is kind of funny if you think about it.

Conferences in the tech scene create new friendships and cement older ones, produce stories to retell later, and foster a sense of intimacy and inclusion among participants. Many of these interactions are public, and conference attendees post pictures from events, tweet about sessions, and write blog posts about their experiences. This conspicuousness marks conference consumption as a way to display one's access and connections to others, not to mention the status of being invited in the first place. As a graduate student, I experienced waves of jealousy when I saw my Twitter followers talking about Foo Camp and the Microsoft Social Software Symposium, both invite-only events with very limited guest lists. The prevalence of social media made conference attendance obvious and made it clear to anyone paying attention that those attending were part of the "in crowd."

The most significant conference in the tech scene is still considered South by Southwest Interactive, held yearly in Austin, Texas. This "spring break for geeks," familiarly referred to as "South By," is a five-day event with myriad panels and lectures and an abundance of parties, concerts, dinners, and drinkups spun off from the long-running music festival; die-hard music fans in the scene spend several thousand dollars on hotel and registration fees to stay for both. It is considered a breakout site for new technology launches, and it served that purpose for Twitter and Foursquare. Get Satisfaction founder Thor Muller told me: "The thing about South by Southwest is that first and foremost, it's a music festival. It's where the rock stars, or the budding rock stars, go. So, as an interactive festival, in my opinion, it always had an element of that rock and roll mystique to it. It was a different kind of birthplace for a new kind of ethos around what we were building." Indeed, the conference reached almost mythical proportions among members of the tech scene. Hillary Hartley explains that the conference "kind of changed my life." "I think everybody who has gone at least once says the same thing," she says, "which is it's not necessarily the conference; it's just the people that you meet . . . We're all sort of like conference geeks. We see each other two or three times a year, but we have a great time and great conversations when we do." Social media consultant Laura "Pistachio" Fitton explains, "South By Southwest, all the years I've gone, has been a huge point of acceleration, so there's something also very interesting about, not only social media that leads to face to face, but face to face that persists more effectively and more connectedly because of a social media connection." Meeting at SXSW often leads to following people on Twitter or reading their blogs, further cementing social ties. A number of informants told me they had moved to San Francisco after SXSW.

South by Southwest has also solidified the scene's reputation for cliquishness. The conference is so significant to group membership that missing the yearly party is an obstacle for newcomers who want to become insiders. But as Kevin Cheng, co-founder of Incredible Labs and former Twitter employee, said, "The first year I went, I was like, 'This is a really annoying conference. It's very cliquish, and it's actually really hard to meet people and there's all these like quote unquote celebrities,' and then the next year, I was friends with most of those people already." While at South By, it is clear who the "celebrities" are, because people constantly gossip about them, they appear on panels and give keynotes, and they all seem to know each other. This inclusivity is compounded by the practice of waiving the registration fee for SXSW if an attendee organizes or speaks on a panel: many repeat attendees arrange to speak on their friends' panels not only to obtain speaker status, but also to save money.

SXSW has rock stars just like its musical counterpart. The blog *ReadWriteWeb* noted, "Don't lie—we know you get butterflies at the thought of bumping into iJustine or Robert Scoble at a tech conference" and published a "SXSW 2010 for Web Celeb Stalkers" guide that included tips on meeting Leah Culver, Kevin Rose, and Evan Williams.[22] At one South By, I received a pack of "Internet ALL STARS" trading cards as a promo for a software company. They featured people like Robert Scoble and Gary Vaynerchuk, and included their websites and Twitter handles. The importance of Web

2.0 celebrities is frequently reinforced, meaning that even if you don't know who they are at your first SXSW, you will afterward. Although Cheng became friends with the "celebrities" after he returned to SXSW as a "veteran," making these social connections can be difficult. While repeat attendees aren't necessarily averse to meeting those who are new, Cheng says, they won't "go out of their way to meet new people . . . So the newcomers have to make an effort to that break that barrier." Without this bridge, the barrier between "insiders" and "outsiders" remains solid, reinforcing the "specialness" of the San Francisco elite who interact with internet all-stars as a matter of course.

In the mid-2000s, SXSW felt like the geeky offshoot of the main music festival, but it is now bigger than its predecessor. In 2007, just 6,500 people attended the interactive portion, but by 2012 this number had jumped to 25,000.[23] The conference is now rife with PR firms, overcrowded parties, and international brands like Pepsi putting up giant booths that have little connection to social media. The possibility of becoming an insider inspires thousands of people worldwide to make the trip to Austin, but the likelihood of getting to know these insiders becomes more and more remote every year. SXSW thus reinforces the tech scene's sense of self-importance and broadcasts the significance of the San Francisco Bay Area to those unlucky enough to live outside of it.

## Accessing the Elite

The tech scene is very much a publicly articulated social network, in that social media like Twitter makes it easy to see who is connected to whom. Databases like CrunchBase extend informal social connections to funding and investment, as tech insiders attempt to drum up "angel investment" for their projects from wealthy friends. (Angel investors are affluent individuals, almost always men, who provide capital for startups in exchange for equity.)[24] Social technologies both reveal connections and offer ways for relationships to be acknowledged and reinforced publicly. People strategically publicize their connections to high-status people, whether by Instagramming a digital snapshot of themselves posing with a company founder or by having a conversation via @replies on Twitter.[25] Status hierarchies are partially maintained through erecting and reinforcing boundaries between insiders and outsiders, as we saw in the discussion of internet celebrities at South by Southwest. Breaching these boundaries requires a sophisticated knowledge of the social sphere and its practices.[26] In other words, to achieve elite status in the tech scene requires acceptance from and connections to those high in the social hierarchy. As Tristan Walker explained, "I've been fortunate that I've been immersed in that network, and it's a very, very small network, but it's hard to get in that small network." Those with these connections are often careful to make them public.

Access is most obvious to those who do not have it, particularly newcomers with an outsider's perspective. Kevin Cheng's earlier assessment of South by Southwest as "cliquish" and Tara Hunt's description of the "overly eager, desperately hungry" wannabes demonstrate the low status ascribed to people attempting to enter the scene. While the tech community emphasizes networking as a necessary skill for business success, people attending large tech parties who aggressively pitch their company to people whom they don't know are considered somewhat pathetic. Technology journalist and former C|Net blogger Caroline McCarthy explained this hierarchy when describing the New York Tech Meetup, a very large-scale event: "That's the sort of thing where afterwards . . . you're going to be getting like business cards passed to you left and right, you don't know who's legit, you don't know this, that, and the other thing. I don't want to call it the bottom of the pecking order, but that's like the most open-entry, and still is. And to the point where I don't even really go to it anymore, because if there are companies presenting, I've heard about them already." Implicit in this quote is that some people are "legit" and others are not, a distinction that is primarily determined through social relationships. For example, at a Digg meetup in November 2008, I was talking to *Valleywag* blogger Nick Douglas when a woman came up to us, took our picture, and immediately handed us cards promoting her "Smart Mom's Network." Her business card had three different product links on it, an e-mail address, and a cell phone number. Neither of us knew her and we were not employed in a field related to her business, so this networking seemed both aggressive and meaningless. Indiscriminately blanketing an event with business cards shows a lack of access to those networks necessary to make a business a success, and demonstrates a limited understanding of who is or is not considered important (Nick and I were not important). Networking only works if you are already somewhat inside the network.

Success in the technology scene is thus at least partially dependent on the ability to access a preexisting social network. Melissa Gira Grant, activist and former *Valleywag* blogger, describes the difference between people integral to this network and those outside of it: those outside "have no perspective or scale. They have this thing that they heard somewhere in some marketing article in like, *Fast Company*, that everybody you talk to is important and then they don't really know how to weigh the human reality in front of them against these tips that they got for how to succeed, which I see all the time." At the time, the trendiness of Web 2.0 was attracting outsiders to the tech scene hoping to share in its wealth (the previously mentioned term "Web 2.0 carpetbaggers" fits here, because it implied outsiders rushing to San Francisco with no "authentic" interest in tech besides the possibility of getting rich quick). But social connections and knowledge of the scene functioned as gatekeeping mechanisms to maintain boundaries between scene insiders and outsiders. That is, while people already in the tech scene viewed it as open to all and easy to access, they themselves were often dismissive of outsiders, who often described the scene as a "high school." The insiders' claims of meritocracy, then, were undermined by the fact that in order to succeed, newcomers had to have already accessed preexisting, elite networks.

## Making it Visible: Social Media

Social media plays a key role in maintaining inequalities between high- and low-status people by reducing complex relationships to visual displays of quantity and quality. As we have seen, while the values of engineering and geek culture play into what is considered high status, so does the attention one garners within most popular social media sites, which often rank users based on how large an audience they can command. Technologies like Twitter, Facebook, and blogs encourage status-seeking behaviors that blur the lines between work and play and promote the infiltration of marketing and advertising techniques into relationships and social behavior. The emphasis on metrics, which track attention and visibility, shows how significant these values are in the Web 2.0 scene.

Twitter was the most popular technology while I was in San Francisco; it is still very popular among tech people, but the frenzy with which people embraced it in 2008–2009 has diminished as it has mainstreamed and become less novel. Twitter asks users, "What are you doing?" and the result is an almost constantly updated stream of 140-character "tweets," messages ranging from the mundane to breaking news, shared links, and thoughts on life. In Twitter's directed model of friendship, users choose others to "follow" in their stream, and each user has his or her own group of "followers." There is neither a technical requirement nor a social expectation of reciprocity, which typically means that people have more followers than people they follow. Tweets can be posted and read from the web, smartphone apps, text messages, or third-party clients for desktop computers and tablets. This integration allows for instant postings of photos, on-the-ground reports, and quick replies to other users.

The site launched in 2006 and broke into the mainstream in 2008–2009, when user accounts and media attention increased exponentially. For the first two years of its existence, Twitter was used almost exclusively by San Francisco tech workers. By 2009, the bloggers, technologists, and company founders who were its most frequent users had been replaced by musicians, actors, television shows, and news organizations. When I began conducting interviews in 2007, it was possible to have two hundred followers and rank among the top users: the technology had a clubby, insider feel. Popular video blogger Veronica Belmont summed it up:

> Twitter was very much in the Valley and very much in San Francisco in its early days. So of course, you know, people like me and people like Kevin Rose and Leo [Laporte], who were covering it on their shows and podcasts very early[,] got a lot of followers very quickly, and now that it's gaining more mainstream success, and the general public are becoming more aware of it, and the people in the limelight in the general public are starting to get more followers as well. And it's interesting to see how the tech clique is now suddenly mashing up against the mainstream media, the mainstream actors and politicians who are picking up on Twitter and realizing its potential, it's definitely "times they are a changing."

My fieldwork took place during a period when Twitter was transitioning from an early adopter user base to a mainstream social media tool. During this time, Twitter was omnipresent. I missed out on social events and gossip because I didn't check Twitter. The service was discussed at conferences, at dinner, and in almost every conversation I had, about technology or otherwise. Interviews were peppered with references to Twitter: how it was used, how people thought it should be used, its benefits and drawbacks, and where people believed it would go in the future. When I asked interview subjects what technology they thought was hot, virtually everyone answered, "Twitter." Not only was Twitter a San Francisco company whose early adopters were members of the tech scene, its founders, Evan Williams and Jack Dorsey, were held up as model entrepreneurs because the site had achieved rapid success, remained independent, and would presumably make the founders very wealthy.

Twitter provided an overlay of important social information that informed all my interactions with the scene. After attending an event, I went home and read all the tweets about that event, which helped me map out often obscure social connections and made me feel up-to-date. One evening early in my fieldwork, I was at a big tech party waiting at the bar for a drink and heard a man introduce himself to one of my friends: "Did you post a tweet about Hollywood being so over? I recognized you from your Twitter picture." (He was half joking, but it was hard to tell which half.) People wrote their Twitter handles on conference nametags. It permeated the social, technical, and business life of the scene. Twitter was a piece of software, a social practice, and something that facilitated meta-discussions of events, as well as an overall discourse about information-sharing and status.

Twitter displays one's status in three different ways: follower numbers, re-tweets, and @replies. On Twitter, the number of followers, shown on each individual profile, displays one's "worth" in terms of quantity, while retweets and @replies display one's worth in terms of the number and (implicit) status of users who publically acknowledge one's existence. Most interviewees knew their follower number exactly, and could often identify how many followers close friends and associates had as well. Sites like Twitterrank and Twitterholic aggregate and display these numbers in a strict ranking, and people are continually comparing follower numbers. Evan Williams, Twitter founder and former CEO, explained:

> I think Twitter absolutely is part of that [status] . . . it rewards popularity above pretty much all else. And we try to build in things that can break out of the popularity. Like the way we built retweet which was for the purpose of trying to get good information spread most efficiently to where it wanted to go. But still, in general, what's rewarded is popularity. You could argue [that] you can get popular by creating really good stuff. Or you can get popular by doing sensationalistic crap.

Not only does follower number literally measure popularity; it also implies a level of influence, visibility, and attention. Veronica Belmont can tweet something like "For future reference, a vodka tonic before cardio kickboxing is probably not the best course of action" and have it read by more than half a million people—more than the reach of some television shows. Because number of followers connotes such status, some people actively court new followers by cultivating an audience, frequently replying to followers, and tailoring tweets to their followers' interests.[27]

When I asked Derek Overby, a social media strategist for the real estate site Roost.com, why people were concerned with their Twitter numbers, he responded:

> I think they have to. If they weren't at the level where they were, they would want to be there. Because it's like, and maybe it's not an ego driven thing, maybe it's a purely business thought, but I think if you're not being followed by a lot of people, you're just kind of—I wouldn't say you're insignificant because you're significant to your group of followers. But to be able to touch 25,000 or 75,000 or 150,000 people with one push of a button—specifically to Twitter—is very powerful.

The broadcasting capabilities of social media make it possible to command enormous audiences, reinforcing the self-importance of people with large numbers of followers. While Overby claims that it's "not an ego thing," I've certainly experienced a frisson of pride knowing that three thousand people may have read my natterings about a lowbrow television show. Perhaps ordinary people are now checking their rising status in so-called attention economies not because they are delusional or narcissistic, but because they have unconsciously absorbed a set of economic ideals belonging to the people who have designed the software we use to socialize each day. As the quote illustrates, if you only have 150 followers while your peers have 150,000 followers, you are considered, by those in the tech scene, to be less important.

Overby told me a story about venture capitalist Guy Kawasaki (who at the time of this writing had nearly 250,000 followers), who decided to discard follower count in favor of number of re-tweets (RTs) in order to measure his "success" at Twitter. Re-tweets are "the Twitter-equivalent of e-mail forwarding where users post messages originally posted by others."[28] For example:

Kevinrose: RT: Facebook is cool but Twitter is the sh*t! (via @mrskutcher) haha Demi Moore speaks the truth :) (3/9/09)

Kevin Rose RTs @mrskutcher (actor Demi Moore) and adds his own commentary: "haha Demi Moore speaks the truth :)." People re-tweet for many reasons; as social media researcher danah boyd and her colleagues write, "Retweeting can be understood both as a form of information diffusion and as a structure within which people can be part of a conversation. The spread of tweets is not simply about getting messages out to new audiences, but also about validating and engaging with others."[29] Re-tweets usually imply that the original message was funny, clever, useful, or otherwise worth repeating. Kawasaki implies that follower count is less useful than re-tweets as a metric because one's number of followers does not indicate the usefulness of one's tweets—but he still relies on a metric to determine whether or not his account is helpful to others. Metrics, whether automatically or algorithmically generated, are socially interpreted as measures of self-worth. Kawasaki wants to be useful to others, echoing an instrumental, business-like approach to social media use, but he also uses metrics to determine how he himself measures up.

The @reply, consisting of the @ sign and username, lets users target a particular conversation or reference a particular user, but these tweets can be viewed by anyone through search.twitter.com, the public timeline, or the sender's Twitter page.[30] For instance:

Kevinrose: @tjsimmons I'm getting a kindle 2, I'll let you know how it is (2/9/09)

brianhart22: @garyvee listening to a keynote speaker he is talking ab working brand while at wk but not to forget your brand at home-Thought u would like (6/21/10)

The @reply feature is designed to get the attention of a particular user, so fans frequently @reply celebrities or highly followed people in the hope that they will answer. In their discussion of Twitter conversations, information science scholars Courtenay Honeycutt and Susan Herring refer to this practice as "addressivity."[31] Boyd and her colleagues point out that "the function of such messages is also attention-seeking; it is specifically intended to alert the mentioned person that they are being talked about."[32]

Using @replies to indicate a close relationship with others often similarly signals status:

ArielWaldman: @samovartea with @cjmartin @verbiee @laurensays @lauraglu @timoni (12/21/08)

Leahculver: Just left @alembicbar. Delicious dinner with @arielwaldman and friends. (2/1/09)

Aubs: At the Rev3 Holiday party with @veronica lamenting that @ryanblock & @kevinrose are nerdily playing chess. Getting shots now. (12/17/08)

In these tweets, @replies are used to notify others that the people referenced are geographically proximate. In the tech scene, Twitter was presumed to be reciprocal, a true technology of the networked audience rather than a broadcast mechanism. As a result, it was considered proper to include someone in an @reply if they were in attendance at an event, or were part of an ongoing conversation. Re-tweets were attribution, so rebroadcasting someone's tweet without crediting them was akin to plagiarism. People who continually tweeted without acknowledging anyone else, responding to @replies, or re-tweeting their friends were derided. Interaction designer Adrian Chan called these frequent references to others a way to delineate a tribe, a form of "social inclusion."

Since being mentioned frequently on Twitter confers status, referring to a friend in a tweet is an act of politeness. This is particularly true if the friend doing the referring has high status, as Garrett Camp, founder of StumbleUpon, explained: "Sometimes [I search for] my own nickname because I see this huge spike in followers. And I'm like, 'Why is this happening?' Then I realize Guy Kawasaki retweeted me." Being mentioned by a highly followed person can increase followers, the most important status metric on Twitter. Referencing high-status people like @kevinrose or @ryanblock also demonstrated connectedness to people admired by the community, reinforcing the high value that was placed on access. Technology journalist Megan McCarthy dismissed this approach: "You're sending out like 'I'm with this person, this person, this person.' Right. It's more of like the display thing, a whole bunch of peacocks running around and fluffing their feathers and broadcasting it to the world." That is, @replies are a way of showing connectedness and access that boosts the status of the tweet's originator. This is particularly true when @replies demonstrate that a relationship beyond the virtual exists between the tweet's originator and the person sending the @reply. This distinction implies that face-to-face interactions signal deeper social ties than online discussions.

Although @replies originated as an informal convention, Twitter incorporated them into the site in May 2008.[33] Clicking on an @ reply brings you to that user's profile, and on the Twitter.com home page, clicking on the "@username" reveals a list of tweets by others that include one's username. Frequent @replies imply popularity, an engaged and active audience, or a Twitter stream that is interesting enough to encourage audience engagement. The ability to attract and command attention is highly valued because it demonstrates significance and information quality; informants assumed that people with very high follower numbers were "good at Twitter," which entails attracting a wide audience through interesting content and ongoing interactions with the audience.

For my informants, Twitter was the primary way in which they immersed themselves in the current concerns of the tech scene. They used it to follow real-life friends and acquaintances in the field as well as high-status tech people and celebrities. Further, because individual tweets are typically viewed within a Twitter stream comprised of other people's tweets, the roles of follower and broadcaster blend, forming an aggregate social context. Then as today, this context is rich with social information about relationships, mores, customs, and trends, and thus provides more information than the sum of its parts. For instance, looking at how the tech scene defined acceptable Twitter use reveals the key role that Twitter followers played in determining status in the community.

### Learning to Tweet

While virtually everyone I met in the tech scene used Twitter, a set of norms governed how information was shared and how the service was used. These norms were not universal to all Twitter users. Since Twitter is open-ended, it is used in many different ways; among fan groups, for example, there is a lot of direct tweeting to celebrities, while teenagers often participate in #hashtag games that show up on the trending topics. Neither were these norms implicit. People had very particular ideas about how Twitter should be used, which were debated in person, on Twitter, at conferences, and on blogs. Sites like Twitctionary and Twittonary attempted to formalize the emerging rules of the medium, but norms were often reinforced through micro-interaction. For example:

kazaroth: @Rhipadmore ooh, why have you protected your updates? Dont do that! See this: http://tinyurl.com/5fwbvy (02/03/09)

Kazaroth tells rhipadmore that she should not protect her updates and includes a link to an article called "The Ten Commandments of Twitter" by James Dickey. She clearly feels that Twitter "should" be public, in line with social expectations that private accounts are "wrong" (90 percent of Twitter accounts are public). Because Twitter is considered a broadcast medium, and because it is used so frequently for self-promotion, making accounts private defeats this purpose. Dickey's article advises new users on the "best" use of Twitter. He writes:

> Now for the most controversial option—locking your Tweets. Unless you're a minor (in which case I'm not sure you should be on Twitter at all), DON'T. It's the Twitter equivalent of walking into a room and asking everyone else who's already there to put on earplugs while you talk to the 3 people you like the most. Mostly it just makes you look like you don't understand Twitter. If someone's a bore, or a spammer, or a creep, block them. Assume everyone else is just another nice person like yourself looking for a new outlet to reach whatever goal they selected.[34]

Such normative statements are subjective. Some people argued vociferously that Twitter users should follow everyone who followed them, implying that people like Kevin Rose who had very high follower counts but followed only a few in return were "Twitter snobs" who were misusing the service.[35] Others considered it impossible to follow more than a few hundred people. The author of *The 4-Hour Body*, Tim Ferriss, weighed in:

> I follow mostly close friends and celebrities, both of whom are unlikely to send me many direct messages, as the former knows I prefer phone and the latter doesn't know I exist. The other approach, which bruises fewer egos, is to follow friends and strangers alike but make it clear that you don't read any DMs, a la Gary Vaynerchuk. Based on attempts to

do the latter on Facebook and LinkedIn, I've concluded that most of the world doesn't read directions or alerts, so I opted for the friend and celeb option.[36]

Ferriss discusses two competing norms and explains why he chose one of them. It is through these types of public discussions and micro-interactions that the norms of an emerging technology are worked out within a social group.[37] Eventually some controversies were settled by the technology; the emerging practice of re-tweeting was incorporated into Twitter's software and people no longer argued that it was an illegitimate use of the site.

I found wide agreement among members of the tech scene on certain normative uses of Twitter. First, people had to be interesting. In interviews, many people talked about dropping boring Twitter users by unfollowing them. They mentioned people who tweeted too frequently about their pets or kids, tweeted too much, or provided repetitive information. Thor Muller told me:

> There is a guy who I know who has decided that he wants to be a philosopher king and he is kind of isolated. He just moved into town. And now he just emits this constant stream of philosophy aphorisms that he's coined, many of which are half-baked, the way that I think he speaks is mostly self-important. But, you know, I don't have to follow him. And he actually, on his own, noted that "nobody is really responding, replying to my philosophy tweets. So maybe I should not do these as much." So silence in a space does eventually communicate to somebody about whether their thought is working. I know other people who would tweet many times in a row. They would have one long thought that would be a good blog post and break it into 140 character pieces. And people told them, "You know what? That's not what Twitter is for." Right? So there is some self-direction in there.

Muller's observation that "silence in a space does eventually communicate to somebody about whether their thought is *working*" indicates the importance of Twitter as a communicative medium. Not receiving replies to a tweet or, at worst, being unfollowed, signaled to a user that they were not using Twitter correctly. Successful users tracked how many people followed them and altered their tweets accordingly. For example, Annalee Newitz told me, "I have to moderate . . . I notice if I do too many tweets people leave, stop following me." Like many members of the scene, Newitz actively monitored her follower count and noticed if it fell. Adam Jackson established an "algorithm" of frequency and interestingness that he used to maximize his follower count. Because a low follower number implied that the user was not "good at" Twitter, people could immediately judge their success. Active attention to Twitter's status metric thus affects how people share information, and how they frame themselves in particular ways to attract attention.

The follower count is such a crucial display of status on Twitter that unfollowing someone becomes the ultimate act of protest, sending a message about the acceptability of a behavior:

> Adactio: Concurring with @briansuda. I think I may trim the number of people I'm following on Twitter by dropping anybody who retweets.

Adactio is so incensed over re-tweeting that he invokes the nuclear option of unfollowing, somewhat similar to un-friending on Facebook or LiveJournal, which signals intense social disapproval or dislike.[38] When I unfollowed Stowe Boyd because of how frequently he tweeted, he not only noticed but also confronted me in person at a crowded WordPress party, shouting through the room, "I'm not speaking to you anymore—you stopped following me on Twitter!" He may have been joking (although I don't think so), but he clearly paid close attention to his follower numbers. I did not refollow him.

### Metrics and Measurement

The internet has facilitated the decentralized production of content that can be easily distributed to a networked audience.[39] The possibility of one's blog, online videos, or digital pictures reaching millions of people worldwide was impossible before the World Wide Web, and its potential today means that attention and visibility are highly valued, because larger audiences translate into more influence and more recognition. One's audience, too, can be easily quantified due to the metrics built into most social media that measure readers or followers, which provide a way, however clunky, to compare people to each other that does not require an understanding of their subtle personal interactions. Metrics are thus used not only to measure a website's success, traffic, or profitability, but also as a way of determining personal status. Megan McCarthy explains: "A lot of people around here are engineers, they're not very good with subtleties and cues and the numbers are easy . . . Numbers don't change on you." Knowing this, many social media applications incorporate "leaderboards," the term for a videogame scoreboard, which allow direct comparisons based on specific numbers. People track different metrics based on whichever technology is trendy, but the underlying principles are constant. Glenda Bautista, a business strategist and blogger since the late 1990s, explains how bloggers used to compare number visits to one's website, but now compare Twitter followers:

> I'll pull up the life cycle of bloggers. Status. It's definitely the same concept, only repeated over Twitter. Where status is—who's linking to you at all times. Get linked by Kottke! Get lots of hits. It's all like reincarnations of the same thing to me. It's like Memepool is like Digg.

Adam Jackson compares Technorati, a blog ranking site, to number of Twitter followers:

> I'd say a year ago the big thing was you want your blog to be in the Technorati Top 5000 or 1000, and Scott Beale was always talking, "I'm the top 200 blogs," and that was a big deal to him. Then it shifted to, did you reach the 5000 Facebook

friend count, with the maximum Facebook Friends. The latest thing is of course Twitter followers.

Owen Thomas goes even further back, to quantifiable metrics in traditional media:

> I think that in the old days it would be clips, right? How many column mentions did you get in the newspaper? The heads of Wall Street brokerages compare their column inches and "heard on the street." Nowadays everyone has a Google Alert on their own name. The frequency with which that pings; the frequency [with] which those alerts come is also a measuring status. @replies on Twitter. These guys, they're engineers by and large. They think if you can't count it, then it's not [relevant].

Bautista, Jackson, and Thomas draw lines of connection between earlier metrics and those related to Twitter. Unsurprisingly, these metrics all measure visibility and attention. In the days of newspaper clippings, only celebrities and CEOs could expect frequent news stories about themselves. Today, the prevalence of social media, and the ability to promote oneself indiscriminately, mean that anyone in the tech scene can track their online presence and boost it if necessary.

In 2008 the startup Klout began aggregating data from multiple social sites to see how often individuals are "liked," re-blogged, @replied, and so forth, claiming that they measure "influence based on your ability to drive action."[40] If your algorithmically generated "Klout Score" is high enough, you might qualify for perks such as free Essie nail polish or a visit to the set of *Dallas*. (My Klout score hovers around fifty, making me eligible for nothing.) Klout never uses the term status, but it measures influence in three vectors: the number of people you reach, how likely those people are to act on your content (for example, by commenting on it or re-tweeting it), and how influential your network is. Klout rewards people precisely for achieving the status metrics of Web 2.0. Klout was widely mocked upon its launch; one friend said, "Your Klout score should go down every time you check your Klout score." This cynicism seems misplaced given the obsession that most tech workers have with metrics, but Klout's putting it front and center violates an unspoken social pact that one should not be seen taking this so seriously. Web 2.0 workers would often claim that they didn't pay attention to follower count, while simultaneously being able to recite their own follower numbers, almost to the digit.

Despite skepticism, this type of measure of influence is extremely valuable to brands and marketing firms. By 2012 Klout had $40 million in venture capital investment and a score of competitors, including PROSkore, Twitter Grader, and Peer Index. Word-of-mouth marketing is a huge buzzword, with advertisers salivating over the possibility of getting "authentic" person-to-person recommendations cheaply. (*Adweek* reported that Adidas was amazed when "some random user" made an animated .gif of one of their television ads, which garnered 90,000 reblogs on Tumblr without any money involved.)[41] Klout is the ultimate status affordance, an entire business model based around the quantifiability of importance.

This obsession with metrics extends beyond technology insiders. Marianne Masculino, a "Happiness Engineer" for the blog company WordPress, told me that to her customers, "readership is a huge thing, a lot of people love the SEO [search engine optimization], love to get their numbers and love looking at their stats hourly, daily kind of things." This same quest for attention leads people to tailor content to their perceived audience. C|Net blogger Andrew Mager told me:

> You have a sense of power when you're updating 1900 people. If it also goes to Facebook, there's another couple thousand people on there that get it. So, you also have to craft your message a little bit better, too. It's funny. If you send a text message to your friend, you don't think about it,

you're just typing . . . but if you're going to send a text message to a thousand people, it has got to be a good one.

This can lead to a sense of life as an ongoing performance. Megan McCarthy scoffed, "If nobody was watching I think half the people in Web 2.0 would not know what to do with themselves." People who attract attention without any sense of accomplishment or skill, however, are derided as "famewhores," which suggests that visibility itself is not enough. Just as Kawasaki distinguished between followers and number of re-tweets, visibility based on merit—achieved status—is what people admire.

Technology bloggers like Om Malik (*GigaOm*), Michael Arrington (*TechCrunch*) and Robert Scoble (*Scobleizer*), who have audiences in the tens of millions, are good examples of status based on visibility versus merit as the tech scene defines it. Kara Swisher explains, "You have these people who have bustled their way into that space, not based on being successful, per se, as a captain of industry or venture capitalist, but because they've become A-listers. There's a very small list of people like that who have a ridiculous impact, but there really aren't very many of them. Arrington, Scoble, people like that, the kind of people who have hundreds of thousands of people stumbling over their words." Although a tech blogger's ability to command huge audiences is a status symbol, his perceived lack of technical or entrepreneurial skill may be a mark against him.[42] Technical knowledge functions as cultural capital and it is a primary status symbol that trumps attention in this instance. This shows the complexity of status in the tech scene: whereas engineering and programming norms and mores are built into the fabric of the Northern California tech scene, the affordances of social media create a parallel track of highly valued practices. Tantek Çelik described this conflict: "There's another example. Robert Scoble. He's got a lot of status. But he hasn't built any websites, he is not a programmer, he's not technical, and he'd be the first to tell you all those things. Right, but he has a lot of status. So what's going on there?" Malik, Arrington, and Scoble are able to reach large numbers of people, understand the players and technologies that matter to the community, and access high-status people as a result of their own status. This is especially impressive to other bloggers and people aspiring to join the community who read *TechCrunch* and *GigaOm* to learn about the technology scene. While their high status may seem inexplicable to programmers, these bloggers are central to a larger network of social media enthusiasts who understand audience and visibility as primary markers of status.

Jeremy Stoppelman pointed out that engineers have their own status hierarchy in which the coolest companies are the ones solving hard engineering problems: "You can draw a Venn diagram, a brand and then engineering hardcoreness. And the really hot ones are the ones that are perceived as engineering hardcore." A company like Groupon, which at the time of our interview had a high valuation and was considered very "hot," did not require solving hard problems and so was lower status for engineers, whereas the scaling issues involved with rapidly growing startups like Facebook and Twitter presented interesting technical problems for programmers to solve. While obviously not everyone in the tech scene is an engineer, for those who are, technical skill often trumps any other marker of status.

Twitter illuminates the importance of quantifiable metrics, influence, attention, and visibility to the San Francisco social media scene. Status is afforded through public connections and follower numbers, @replies, and re-tweets. These social values are embodied in the technology and thus encourage status-seeking behaviors that privilege audience and performance. Notably, there is a cottage industry of Twitter tools like TweetDeck, HootSuite, and Twitterfall that monitor usernames, hashtags, and topics as they are mentioned on Twitter. These tools are used widely not only by companies and brands, but also by individuals to track their @replies, re-tweets, and references to their friends, partner, band, and so forth. These applications reveal the expectation that individuals will want to monitor and manage their Twitter handle. And as we will see, users have come to use the same tactics for self-surveillance that companies use for brand management.

## Status, Online and Off

In social contexts like the tech scene where applications like Facebook, Foursquare, Flickr, and Twitter are part of daily life, status is signaled using both emergent status signals and status affordances. On Twitter, follower count is the primary metric, somewhat to Evan Williams's discomfort. @replies and RTs began as informal ways to communicate on Twitter (and incidentally display access, connection, and status). These conventions, which became accepted more widely through their use by early adopters in the tech scene, were implemented by Twitter itself and integrated into the software, becoming status affordances.

Offline status affects how people are seen online, and vice versa. A famous person with an infrequently updated or mundane Twitter feed might have hundreds of thousands of followers, while an unknown person with sparkling wit could come to prominence on the service. Those who use and talk about Twitter like to promote the idea that good content is rewarded most, but it is clear that often sensationalism or celebrity is more likely to boost follower numbers. Another social media executive compared Twitter to Quora, a question-and-answer site founded in 2009 that encourages lengthy and detailed replies:

> In the ideal system everyone just does good work, they would do things that they enjoyed or that were going to help their company succeed and no one would spend any time on any of this performance stuff. But if they are going to spend time on performance it's better if that performance is closer to real work. It's like a more honest signal, right? Twitter is like—there's a lot of room for faking and distortion and I think whereas [Quora's] definitely not perfect . . . it's closer

to showing—it's very hard to star yourself too much when you're writing significant answers.

According to this informant, Quora answers, which do tend to be lengthy and informative, make it possible to determine other people's intelligence and knowledge, whereas Twitter popularity can be faked. If people are going to perform publicly for an audience in order to boost their status, this executive believes it is better for them to spend time on a site that rewards depth of content rather than just raw popularity. To a company founder, the end goal is determining who would be a good prospective employee based on a metric. Yet for many of my interviewees, Twitter was more valuable than Quora because on Twitter it was easier to translate one's activity into a commodity that could be measured, rendered into a metric, assigned a value, and ideally, monetized.

For my interviewees, discourses on status helped to naturalize economic hierarchies by framing them instead as social ties. The tech scene idealizes openness, transparency, and creativity, but these ideals are realized as participation in entrepreneurialism, capitalism, work-life integration, heavy social media use, and the inculcation of large audiences. This culture reflects the priorities of the engineers and programmers who launched the industry—who support consumption based on functionalism and practicality rather than "conspicuous consumption," although travel, gadgets, and wealth are still viewed as status symbols. This shared set of values and beliefs about social life helps to explain some of the assumptions about "users" and "social behavior" in social media: in particular, that social networks reveal one's access and connections; that status can be measured through quantifiable metrics for attention and visibility that have been built into social media; and that Twitter facilitates a type of self-presentation and attention to metrics that resembles the highly valued entrepreneurialism of the scene.

There are clearly tensions inherent in Web 2.0's combination of entrepreneurial capitalism and techno-utopianism. To achieve high status, one must be committed to the entrepreneurial startup culture, engage in self-conscious self-marketing, network continually, or do a combination of all three. Yet although the business of technology and social media may value and reward attention and wealth as much as technological knowledge and innovation, it is the knowledge and innovation piece that "really" matters. Status is crucial, but it must be the right kind of status.

3

# THE FABULOUS LIVES OF MICRO-CELEBRITIES

———

At South by Southwest (SXSW), virtually every high-status member of the technology community convenes on Austin for a long weekend. The conference sessions are packed, but busier by far are massive parties sponsored by companies like Foursquare and Twitter. In 2009, the biggest SXSW party was the "Bigg Digg Shindigg" thrown by the social news site Digg. Held at Stubbs, a barbecue restaurant and music venue, indie bands Barcelona and Republic Tigers played as more than two thousand attendees streamed in and out and crowded around the enormous stage. Queuing up for a drink, I met a group of college kids who were dedicated fans of *DiggNation*, the online show starring Digg's founder, Kevin Rose. The students wore homemade shirts that spelled out Digg, and happily posed for pictures with a girl who had hand-painted a tank top to read "I ♥ Kevin." They badly wanted to meet Rose. Later in the party, Rose appeared in front of a step-and-repeat (a logo-covered backdrop for

Figure 1: Digg Fans at SXSW 2009. Photo: Alice Marwick

photos) and was swarmed by fans asking for autographs and snapping digital photos.

Although Rose appeared on the cover of *BusinessWeek* in 2006 under the headline "How This Kid Made $60 Million in 18 Months" (for which he was mercilessly mocked by his colleagues), he had no name recognition outside of the tech scene and his college-aged fan base. But within the scene, Rose was a superstar. Fans stopped him on the street and mobbed him at tech parties; interviewees frequently dropped his name; and admirers attempted to follow in his footsteps. As an entrepreneur of a successful social product that techies used and liked, Rose had the highest status one could have. Naturally a low-key, thoughtful person, Rose was taken by surprise by this rise in status. At the same time, he did not shy away from attention. He appeared weekly on *DiggNation*, was an avid tweeter with 88,000 followers in 2009, dated internet personalities like Shira Lazar and Julia Allison, and hobnobbed with Ashton Kutcher and Tim Ferriss.[1]

Rose exemplifies a type of internet-enabled visibility, the "micro-celebrity." Micro-celebrity is a state of being famous to a niche group of people, but it is also a behavior: the presentation of oneself as a celebrity regardless of who is paying attention. There are two ways of achieving internet fame—by consciously arranging the self to achieve recognition, or by being ascribed fame by others due to one's accomplishments. Kevin was well-known for his entrepreneurial success, for which the scene ascribed him celebrity status. At the same time, he actively courted attention and treated his rabid followers as a fan base to achieve micro-celebrity. Within the scene, both types of micro-celebrities are subject to scrutiny; pursuing attention and visibility for its own sake without commensurate achievement risks having one's personas and activities policed and judged by others.

Becoming a micro-celebrity requires creating a persona, producing content, and strategically appealing to online fans by being "authentic." Authenticity in this context is a quality that takes many forms, from direct interaction with admirers to the public discussion of deeply personal information, and it is tenuous at best.[2] Although micro-celebrity takes the principles of celebrity culture and applies them to online interactions, online celebrities are not traditional celebrities, they do not have teams of agents and managers to protect them from the public, and they lack vast sums of money. Moreover, they are working within a different milieu, that of the internet, which idealizes transparency and thus expects a certain amount of exhibitionism. We may think of movie and rock stars as exhibitionists, but in reality the media business is more guarded, and quite protective of its lucrative properties. Micro-celebrities, by contrast, are generally viewed as fair game for the same vicious criticism that bloggers and audiences give movie stars or musicians, but are expected to be more available and more "real" than stars of the screen or stage. The rewards of achieving micro-celebrity may seem considerable, but the cost is often high.

## What Is Micro-Celebrity?

An Internet celebrity is an unemployed person, often a student,
who is widely known among the members of an e-subculture
or clique. The term itself is a misnomer because people who use the
internet are not popular IRL [in real life]. Most Internet celebrities
have more friends on their LiveJournal friends list than anyone else,
and it is to these vaunted heights of e-fame that all self-respecting
attention or comment whores aspire.

—*The Encyclopedia Dramatica*


Fameballs: individuals whose fame snowballs because
journalists cover what they think other people want them to cover.

—Jakob Lodwick, founder of CollegeHumor.com


Terri Senft, in her book *Camgirls: Celebrity and Community in
the Age of Social Networks,* defines micro-celebrity as "a new style of
online performance in which people employ webcams, video, audio,
blogs, and social networking sites to 'amp up' their popularity among
readers, viewers, and those to whom they are linked online."[3] Celebrity has traditionally been viewed as something someone is,
based on how well known he or she is; micro-celebrity, by contrast,
is something someone does.[4] Regardless of one's actual audience,
micro-celebrity is a way of thinking of oneself as a celebrity, and
treating others accordingly. Micro-celebrity practitioners, be they
professional video gamers, wannabe pop stars, YouTube beauty bloggers, or political activists, strategically construct their presentation
to appeal to others. The people they interact with online are thought
of as fans, rather than friends or strangers, and these relationships
are carefully maintained to sustain popularity. The mindset and
practices of micro-celebrity are made possible by social media technologies, which enable average people to gain the audiences of traditional celebrities.

The technology community is well aware of celebrity's influence.
People with highly visible online personas are dubbed "internet

famous" (Ben Brown, founder of the short-lived geek dating site Consummating, christened himself the "internet rockstar" in 2000, and defined it as "all the fun with none of the pesky pressure to produce another top selling CD or make anybody rich or famous. Except you, Mr. Number One.").[5] *Wired* magazine put Julia Allison on the cover with the headline "Get Internet famous! Even if you're nobody." Like Kevin Rose, many are swamped with attention at conferences: At South by Southwest, I witnessed "mommy blogger" Dooce, a.k.a. Heather Armstrong, backed against a wall by fans. Micro-celebrities are name-dropped on Facebook and Twitter ("At the Rev3 Holiday party with @veronica lamenting that @ryanblock & @kevinrose are nerdily playing chess"). People brag about meeting, hanging out with, and attending parties with the micro-famous; their technologies or accomplishments are followed closely; and their content is read, re-tweeted, and discussed. To many, the distinction between those famous for doing something and those famous for simply being famous is unimportant. What matters is the fame.

But micro-celebrity exists on a continuum, from ascribed to achieved. Micro-celebrity can be *ascribed* to people well-known in certain subcultures, often through the production of celebrity media about them. For example, a tech blog published paparazzi photos of the late Steve Jobs and Google CEO Eric Schmidt drinking coffee in Palo Alto; similar candid shots from Mark Zuckerberg's honeymoon ended up in *Us Weekly*. A paparazzi photo of someone marks them as a celebrity, or at least someone to pay attention to. While micro-celebrity is ascribed to people who are recognizable from online memes, such as the costumed super-fan "Tron Guy" or internet karaoke star "Numa Numa kid," high-status micro-celebrities in the tech scene are those with significant business or technological accomplishments, such as Gary Vaynerchuk and Kevin Rose.[6] An ascribed micro-celebrity is not just someone popular, but someone treated with the celebrity-fan relationship of distance and aggrandizement. In other words, the ascribed micro-celebrity is treated almost as a mainstream celebrity and assigned a high level of status, depending on the source of his or her fame and the community in question. Some ascribed micro-celebrities shun the spotlight, while others use micro-celebrity practices to manage their audience once they reach a certain level of online fame.

*Achieved* micro-celebrity, by contrast, is a self-presentation strategy that includes creating a persona, sharing personal information about oneself, constructing intimate connections to create the illusion of friendship or closeness, acknowledging an audience and identifying them as fans, and strategically revealing information to increase or maintain this audience. Social media technologies are an intrinsic part of this process; for my informants, these activities primarily took place on Twitter, with its stark metrics of follower numbers that invite comparison and competition. Other technologies, particularly blogs, digital photos, and videos, are used to establish an online presence and live a public life. Significantly, micro-celebrity practice uses mediated self-presentation techniques drawn from "traditional" celebrity culture in day-to-day interactions with other people. Thus relationships between individuals become similar to relationships between celebrities and their audiences.[7]

### Creating the Celebrity Self

Becoming a micro-celebrity requires a degree of self-commodification to create a "publicizable personality"; as Ernest Sternberg writes, "performers now intentionally compose their persona for the market, and do so through methods learned from the celebrity world."[8] The micro-celebrity self, like that of celebrities more generally, is carefully constructed and performed to attract attention and publicity. Laura Fitton, a social media marketer who rose to fame as her persona, Pistachio, describes writing her Twitter account as "kind of like being a newspaper columnist": "I get that that's not a hundred percent me . . . But I do think of Pistachio as kind of a separate entity. It doesn't have followers. It has readers. It's a thing." Fitton distinguishes herself from her online persona, which she admits is filtered to show her in a positive way. She thinks of Pistachio as a "thing" that has an audience. Virtually everyone I interviewed was strategic about using social media to reveal or conceal certain aspects of themselves. Owen Thomas, a former *Valleywag* editor, explained, "With social media, we have a sense of the tools to craft those identities. It's almost like when previous programmers had to write in assembly language. And now we got Visual Basic for constructing identities." Profile pictures, likes and dislikes, and subjects chosen to tweet or blog about are calculated to give off a certain impression.[9]

### Interacting with Fans

Micro-celebrity involves closeness and accountability. Micro-celebrity practitioners view their online connections as an audience or fan base, and use communication technologies like Twitter, instant messaging (IM), and e-mail to respond to them. Many people I talked to felt that in order to boost their popularity they were obligated to continue this interaction, which broke down the traditional barriers between audience and performer, spectator and spectacle. The micro-celebrity has direct interaction with fans, while traditional celebrities only give the illusion of interaction and access. As Gabe Beneviste, founder of the music site SonicLiving, explained, "There [have] always been Brad Pitt fan clubs or musicians who have fan clubs." He noted that even mainstream celebrities have traditionally incorporated elements of personal interaction, such as responses to fan letters or public appearances, into their personas, but now all that's required is an @reply message on Twitter. In his view, personal interaction is "not a new phenomenon . . . there's just a much lower barrier to entry." This interaction is crucial to maintaining the micro-celebrity's fame or notoriety. Veronica Belmont, herself a famous video blogger, explains:

> I'm actually super, super lucky with my fans because there's definitely a feeling of a conversation going on, as opposed to me just broadcasting things. On my blog, I respond to comments. I respond to all my email. On Twitter, I reply, not publicly always, but I will always direct message someone if

they have a specific question or comment. I just want to keep the lines of communication open because I feel once you lose that, you lose that relatability, and you lose that ability to converse with your audience. Then, suddenly, you're on this pedestal, and it's just not as fun, and it's not as watchable.

Regularly viewing the cast of a television show in your living room every week creates a feeling of intimacy and familiarity that communication scholars Horton and Wohl have called "para-social interaction."[10] These para-social relationships can be emotionally gratifying, to the point where people tune in to particular programs to check in with their "friends." Micro-celebrity extends this idea to networked webs of direct interaction. As *Wired* founding editor Kevin Kelly told me, "The Tom Hanks or whoever in the world are never going to respond to you really. But even a small percentage of them, if they actually are responding, this is extremely powerful. And it doesn't take very much, a percent of your time, to actually respond to fans, where just seeing this celebrity respond to that fan, you're going to say could it be me? So the fact that it could be me is almost as good." While keeping up these connections is time-consuming, interacting with fans is considered a necessary part of acquiring and maintaining followers.

### Chasing the Authentic

Audiences often expect micro-celebrities to be more "authentic" than traditional celebrities, presumably because they are not subject to the processes of the star-making system.[11] Advice about successful online interaction aimed at brands and marketers frequently emphasizes authenticity. Tara Hunt's book *The Whuffie Factor* ("whuffie" is a synonym for social capital) explores this idea.[12] Hunt writes, "Do not do anything that will destroy your whuffie account. It's really dead simple, if you ask me. It is the most natural thing in the world. It just requires you to build, keep and maintain *authentic* relationships. Customers and potential customers will tune you out if you are not authentic."[13] Despite this constant call for authenticity, authenticity is not an absolute quality, but a social judgment that is always made in distinction to something else.[14] Because authenticity takes many forms, there is not a universal understanding of what makes something "authentic." Rather, authenticity is judged over time, in that people's authenticity is determined by comparing their current actions against their past for consistency. Tristan Walker, the former director of business development for Foursquare and now an entrepreneur-in-residence at Andresson Horowitz, says,

> I think it's very much being unwavering in your understanding of who you are . . . So for me, sure, I'll curse sometimes in public—but if I didn't, folks would think that there's just something wrong with me. Or I might buy these shoes and tweet about them, and they're kind of ridiculous . . . Tristan is Tristan on Twitter, on Facebook, in real life and elsewhere, and I think to me that's authenticity.

To Walker, "authenticity" is not so much about revealing deeply personal information as it is about consistency: "Tristan equals Tristan no matter where you go." He imagines readers judging his authenticity across times and mediums, and coming up with a reliable uniformity of self-presentation. Being "authentic" is a very tenuous definitional frame that can be broken by nearly anything, even something inconsequential. Walker emphasizes a performance of authenticity based on producing and circulating knowledge about himself, which is then measured via informal attributes like "consistency."

In *Sincerity and Authenticity,* Lionel Trilling distinguishes authenticity from sincerity. He conceptualizes authenticity as a display of the hidden inner life, complete with passions and anguish, while sincerity is the opposite of hypocrisy—honesty without pretense.[15] Both senses are used by technology insiders when explaining what authenticity means to them. But it is often this "display of the hidden inner life," the act of revealing intimate information, that creates a bond between micro-celebrity practitioners and their audiences. Proto-mommy-blogger Heather Armstrong, who was fired for her blog *Dooce*, has built a career on speaking frankly about postpartum depression and her marital struggles. And Thor Muller, the founder of customer service site Get Satisfaction, says:

> I'm not an open book all the time . . . I guess I'm sensitive to unforeseen consequences to the stuff I put out there. But [if] I'm out doing something fun with my kid, I'll tweet that. Or if I do something which I feel stupid about, I'll just tweet that. But not constantly. But then again this is me. I do believe that there's something that [philosopher] Xunwu Chen calls the authenticity in our lives. But personally one of the most important things a person could choose is we're aware, we're driven not by business models but by principles within our hearts.

The well-read Muller chooses not to reveal deeply personal things, but believes strongly in the ideal that "principles within our hearts," personal integrity, should dictate one's actions, rather than marketing principles. Both Muller and Walker talk about authenticity in an almost moral sense, adhering to consistency as a driving ethic. This sense of authenticity suggests that it is not about how much one reveals or conceals, but about being measured against an ideal of honesty, in that the information that is revealed has a constancy.

Authenticity is negotiated symbolically; information disclosure is used to determine its presence or absence, but is an incomplete measure at best. Authenticity's slipperiness is part of what makes it useful: it can satisfy many objectives, and can be interpreted widely. Despite this ambiguity, its importance remains strong, not only among members of the tech scene, but to American culture in general.[16]

### Aspirational Production

Micro-celebrity also employs a twist on aspirational consumption, a marketing strategy used by luxury brands like Louis Vuitton and

Chanel. These companies, known for expensive products purchased by the global rich, target middle-class consumers with lower-priced lines of sunglasses and perfumes—the "entry-luxury" consumer base.[17] This lower-level consumer is vitally important: these companies make the bulk of their profits selling $250 sunglasses rather than $10,000 dresses.[18] In social media, "aspirational producers" portray themselves in a high-status light, whether as a beautiful fashionista, a celebrity with thousands of fans, or a cutting-edge comedian. Adam Jackson's thousands of tweets about technology reflect his wish to be a wealthy entrepreneur, just as Julia Allison's glamour shots demonstrate her desire to be the next Carrie Bradshaw. Blogger Rex Sorgatz, himself a skilled self-promoter, called this technique "faux-parazzi" in a *New York Magazine* story on the micro-famous: "taking photos of non-famous people staged to look famous, the gifted microfamer borrows from the paparazzo's handbook by choreographing photos that look accidental but are actually snapped from the perfect angle and with the perfect company."[19]

Aspirational production employs both the types of attention given to celebrities, and celebrities' point of view. Although the micro-celebrity may not be able to get an interview with *Vanity Fair,* she might wrangle an interview by another blogger. If there is no literal paparazzo to follow the Web 2.0 personality around, he can stage a fauxparazzi shoot, have his picture taken by a photoblogger at a party, or pose in front of a "step-and-repeat" (a background covered with logos propped at the entrance to exclusive parties). Caroline McCarthy describes the rise of New York City photobloggers, who used the location-based software Dodgeball to find out where technology workers were gathering:

> Nick McGlynn started this photo site . . . If a bunch of people Dodgeball[ed] into a bar, sometimes he would show up with his camera and take pictures, that sort of thing . . . He, I think, was extremely formative in this crafting of a geek social scene . . . the girl who runs the blog did like a social media yearbook thing. [She] said that I would be the

head cheerleader, which made me a little bit uncomfortable knowing what I thought of cheerleaders when I actually was in high school.

When someone is photographed by a nightlife blogger, they become eligible for possible (ascribed) micro-celebrity status. Although these pictures are published on blogs and sites like Tumblr rather than *Us Weekly*, there is no significant difference in an era where most people scrutinize Oscar outfits on fashion blogs rather than in printed magazines. While social media perhaps enables authentic material "better" than traditional media, aspirational content shared on social media often appears *less* authentic, perhaps because it demonstrates a clear striving toward mainstream celebrity that is somewhat antithetical to the values of the tech community.

Micro-celebrities enable technology workers to see themselves as the types of people who know celebrities. VIP sections, velvet ropes, bouncers, gift bags, and step-and-repeats—all of which mimic the glamorous Hollywood life—are increasingly visible at San Francisco and New York City tech parties. People in the tech scene are interpellated as the audience, dusting the industry with a sheen of glamour. Emulating mainstream celebrity industry creates value: since celebrities represent the top of the status system, ascribing celebrity to high-status people in subcultures allows members of the scene to draw parallels between the highest-status people and the technology world.[20] Clearly, then, people will engage in micro-celebrity practice to gain status—and some, like Adam Jackson, throw themselves into it completely.

### Micro-Celebrity in Practice: Adam Jackson

Scott Beale, founder of the site *Laughing Squid*, referred me to Adam Jackson, telling me that "he embraces every aspect of social media to the 10th degree." Jackson was a self-described young Web 2.0 fanboy from Jacksonville, Florida, who moved to San Francisco after avidly following the latest technological developments on blogs like *TechCrunch* and *Mashable*.[21] I interviewed Jackson eight months after his move, at a coffee shop near the Tenderloin that was almost entirely full of young people with Apple laptops. He wore a t-shirt advertising No Starch Press, which publishes geek and technology books, and a Gary Vaynerchuk terrycloth wristband. While I was impressed with his drive and work ethic, Jackson was very sincere about things like web celebrity and number of Twitter followers, which most of my informants openly mocked (albeit taking them seriously in private). Because Jackson had lived in San Francisco for only a short while, he was still becoming acculturated to the technology scene. Beale related to me that Jackson had arrived in San Francisco wearing a head-mounted webcam attached to a laptop carried in a backpack. Called a "Justin.tv rig," the setup streams live footage to the internet. The site Justin.tv had originated the term "lifestreaming"; by the time Jackson had arrived in San Francisco, however, its founder, Justin Kan, had hung up his camera-equipped baseball hat. "We were like, 'People don't do that anymore,'" Beale said. He continued that Jackson wanted to be associated with the "cool kids" such as Kevin Rose.

When I interviewed Jackson in 2008, he was transforming from someone impressed by micro-celebrities to an insider working at a hot company and gradually attaining micro-celebrity status himself. His attitudes toward micro-celebrity, and the way he viewed himself and his audience, exemplify how engagement with micro-celebrity practice can boost one's status.

Jackson is goal-oriented and a hard worker. At the time of our first interview, he was working full-time at a company called Yoono doing community evangelism; writing a book about Twitter; maintaining a social calendar site, two blogs, and ten Twitter accounts; and finishing up "Adam's Block," which he described as "a project that involved a webcam in the city that documented crime and various activities on my street corner [which] became national news."[22] One of Jackson's main activities was attending tech events;

I frequently saw him out and about at meetups, conferences, and parties. Jackson described his typical schedule: he wakes up at eight, works for two hours, goes to the Yoono office from 10 to 4, attends one or two tech parties, returns home at 11, and works from home until 3 A.M. He saw this as a means to an end:

> I really moved here to really bust butt and make a million dollars by the time I'm 30. That's what my goal is. And I'm 22 now. So I think it's possible. At this rate too, I mean I'm working a lot of hours. I don't sleep two nights a week. And I do tons of work. I'm really focused on my goals. And my goals aren't to complete a specific project. My goals are to do something that inspires someone else.

Jackson believes that when he finally comes up with a winning idea, having a large number of Twitter followers and community connections will make it easier for him to find funding. He explained that networking in the San Francisco scene and becoming known to the community are key to his potential success:

> I just tell people be there. Be at events. Be at places where those things are good. Be at a cafe where you know a lot of Web 2.0 people hang out. Hang out in these circles and then you might get lucky if you have a good idea. But you've got to do both, you gotta have a great idea. I'm not just going to link to you just cause you asked me to. So people really need to work hard, really bust their ass and then also put some time into the community, so that the community knows they're there for them.

Besides in-person networking, Jackson was obsessive about Twitter (he told me "It's really changed the way I live. I think that everyone should deserve to have that chance to use Twitter and really use it to change their lives too"). He used Twitter for everything from weather and traffic reports to finding sponsors for his events. Jackson spent a lot of time perfecting his Twitter technique to keep his audience interested and grow his follower numbers:

> There is a reason why I can post 150 times a day and still have 2,000 followers. People seem really interested in what I am saying. I get more replies than most of the tech experts, because my things . . . make you want to stick to them and reply. I happen to have a knack for it I guess. I spent a year and a half changing the way I tweet, on a monthly basis, to find that algorithm of success.

Jackson tweeted on a variety of subjects:

> Any album that makes me inspired to blog and write and share is an ace in my book. Very few albums hold that title.

> Hello @Starbucks. Thank you for the wonderful Ethiopia Clover Brew that's in stores. Wow.

> I took last week off at the gym and just focused on at home cross fit and cardio. I'm back today going to work upper body. Inhaling Creatine

> My latest post on @TheAppleBlog is up: "The Future of Apple's Retina Display" http://bit.ly/bzOMRB

Jackson saw his Twitter followers and blog readers as an audience, and was very focused on maintaining high follower numbers and producing content to interest and inspire his fans. The persona he presented to the world was carefully crafted to fit his career goals. Many of his actions and choices, like going to tech parties, blogging prolifically, mentoring younger entrepreneurs, inventing hashtags, and sponsoring events, were modeled after people whom he admired, such as gadget blogger Ryan Block, Scott Beale, technology journalist Larry Chiang, microformats pioneer Tantek Çelik, blogger Michael Arrington, and entrepreneur Jason Calacanis. Jackson expressed admiration for their work ethic, community involvement, intelligence, honesty, and initiative, and believed in demonstrating these qualities in his own day-to-day life.

Jackson took micro-celebrity very seriously. He explained the importance of connecting with well-known tech people:

> I went on social networks to find those author's profile pages and connect with them that way . . . When I figured out that most of the guys that are writing about tech live in San Francisco or New York, or most people that are podcasters go to this conference every year, I wouldn't have found that out unless I had been looking at their personal stuff. I don't usually follow Engadget to read Ryan Block's stuff. I follow RyanBlock.com and what he's doing. I use his day to day actions to kind of sculpt my life and that's just one example. So, I associate with the people that these guys are friends with and you'll kind of get in the scene. I could be an expert at certain technology, I could be an expert at memory and ram, and write about it every day but I would never ever catch the eye of the important people unless I was, you know, flocking with those that were already in the know.

He saw little point in socializing without networking; he told me that he was disappointed in a recent social media wine-tasting trip to Napa because the attendees were taking it as an opportunity to unwind and relax.

This enthusiasm made him a figure of fun to some of the more seasoned members of the community. One informant dismissed him as someone "who believes the hype." She told me about a group of high-status people who had invented a social media site called PheltUp, "The Social Site for Thought Leaders," which they were promoting on Twitter as if it were real. (This was clearly meant to poke fun at bombastic "social media gurus" who were considered ego-driven braggarts.) One night, people began to tweet about a fictitious PheltUp party, first saying it was at a popular venue, and then that it had been moved to a secret location. Jackson fell for the joke, and began asking people on Twitter where the party was. My informant clearly thought that Jackson, while not a self-proclaimed "guru," was at least naïve and gullible. But primarily he was a newbie to the community. He openly expressed feelings about the social media scene that marked him as lower status than those who claimed to dismiss the appeal of micro-celebrity culture: in particular, he kept close watch on the constant hype and noise of the blogosphere, which are purportedly ignored by many long-time Silicon Valley residents who have been through multiple boom-and-bust cycles. He represented a young person striving for micro-celebrity status as a way to become successful in a community that he deeply respected.

Jackson demonstrates how micro-celebrity is a learned status-seeking practice that both reflects the values of the technology scene and is intimately integrated with social media tools. He constructed his own Twitter and blog personas based on traits he admired in high-status people like bloggers, venture capitalists, and entrepreneurs—traits that included access to a network, visibility to an audience, work ethic, and community involvement. Jackson used Twitter to strategically seek and inculcate an audience, altering his content production based on what he thought would "inspire" his followers. This reflects both the status structure of the technology community, which prioritizes personal products that illustrate passion and insight, and how social media is used to communicate these values. Jackson also incorporated networking into his personal goals and presentation, viewing it as essential to success in the scene. Notably, this networking took place both in person and using social media tools, indicating the intertwined nature of "online" and "offline" interaction. Micro-celebrity intrinsically reflects the importance to successful self-promotion of access, attention, visibility, and entrepreneurial persistence—all values deeply influenced by Silicon Valley's history of venture-backed capitalism.

In early 2010, Jackson made big changes in his life: he moved to a quieter San Francisco neighborhood, stopped sharing as much personal information online, broke up with his girlfriend, and began working at the mobile startup Brightkite. On his blog, he wrote about Roger Ebert's response to critics: "Resentment is allowing someone to live rent-free in a room in your head."

> I call it "micro-celebrity" . . . because I've been called that a few times. I consider it being famous for not really doing anything. I don't think I've done enough to have 3,000+ Twitter Followers or 30K people reading this blog every month but I do and that comes with some responsibility and, yes, some stalkers. Celebrities have it rough and without a support system, it's easy to let things get to you . . . What wisdom [is] inherited in this quote that truly excites me about one day being able to say this out loud and truly believe it and live it.[23]

By 2012, Jackson had moved to a small town in New Hampshire to work for TomTom, a mapping company. He keeps chickens, ducks, and pigs, brews his own beer, and gardens. In the years since I first interviewed him, Jackson has experienced many of the negative aspects of micro-celebrity and although he still is wholly committed to technology work, he is no longer naïve about the realities of being a micro-celebrity. He e-mailed,

> I miss the instant feedback . . . Call me crazy but there's static and then you tweet, "good morning" and a few dozen people tweet it back to you within seconds. It's addictive and very damaging when it stops happening. . . . It was difficult moving to New Hampshire and losing that almost instantly. The move forced me to make real friends.

Despite the radical shift in his lifestyle, Jackson has grown to love his quiet life in a town of twelve thousand people. He told me, "My chickens are here, I have my river, my best friend and a GF [girlfriend] who is great and now my life doesn't weigh on the positive and negative criticisms of strangers." His story illustrates the tensions intrinsic in adopting micro-celebrity as a status-seeking practice. Jackson got to meet many of his heroes, enjoyed getting immediate responses on his internet musings, and ended up working for a well-known internet company (although not making his million). But he also dealt with public criticism, mockery, and epithets like "asshole" and "fat" in his Twitter stream. Jackson struggled between wanting to participate in a community he loved and realizing that the personal attacks, which often come hand-in-hand with the micro-celebrity persona, were hurting him emotionally. Eventually he decided that the benefits of public living did not outweigh this psychic damage and he drew back, to the point of physically relocating away from the Bay Area.

### Insiders and Outsiders

Jackson's early excitement about the tech scene and its celebrities marked him as an outsider. He attempted to gain insider status by producing content that aspired to the success of his role models, but his very acknowledgment of the importance of micro-celebrity betrayed him as a newcomer. Indeed, the degree to which someone in the tech scene will admit to being impressed by micro-celebrity is a status marker. Many interviewees described moving to San Francisco and being awestruck by "famous" people, only to disclaim quickly that they no longer felt that way. Jackson, who had only been in San Francisco for eight months when I interviewed him, explained:

> I always found tech parties as a way for me to gauge how I'm doing on my projects. I read my Twitter posts from last year. I was meeting people for the first time I'd never met before. I MET KEVIN ROSE—all caps. That kind of crap. And I look back to this year, it's so much different. Everyone that I talk to knows who I am . . . It's a totally different landscape. So that's how I judge how I'm doing. In Web 2.0 not everyone that's successful makes money.

Jackson signals the stages of his improved status by stating not only that has he met Kevin Rose, but that he has moved past the stage where this impresses him. He then gets to the point where he himself is recognized as a micro-celebrity. Derek Overby co-founded the *100 Interviews Project,* which taped and posted quick interviews with "some of the biggest names in social media and technology." I asked him, "What did you learn about the social media community from this project?" He responded:

> They are much more approachable than I thought possible. At the end of the day, they're just average—they may be a little bit smarter, they may be a little bit more connected, but they're still just human beings. I don't think a lot of them take their "celebrity" too seriously. You can really just have fun doing what they're doing.

Overby was moving from outsider to insider, which required familiarity with the tech community's who's who. In a scene obsessed with networking, information, and connections, I got funny looks when I failed to recognize podcaster Leo Laporte or blogger Merlin Mann.[24] The ability to keep up with the projects, relationships, and internet content of important people was a part of participating in the community's public life.

Beyond simply correctly identifying micro-celebrities, an insider must transition from viewing them with awe, to feeling neutrally about them, and, for those with the highest status, to seeing them as peers and friends. Marianne Masculino works directly with WordPress founder Matt Mullenweg, who is well regarded and highly followed. She describes returning home to Texas for a meetup, a company-sponsored event where people using WordPress blogging software are invited to hang out with WordPress employees. "People were lining up to take pictures with him and I was like— it's just Matt!" she said. When she saw her hometown friends reacting to Mullenweg, whom she now viewed as simply a co-worker, Masculino realized that her own status had changed since moving to San Francisco. Yet her purported apathy, which is typical of insiders, is belied by the fact that this closeness to those of high status in the tech scene is also often signaled publicly through Twitter or Facebook.

The outsiders, people deeply impressed by micro-celebrities, are members of what Jackson described as "Web 2.0 fanboys," a global community of people who follow the ins and outs of the San Francisco technology industry without participating directly. Some are involved in their local technology communities, while others hope to gain larger recognition for their online projects. Twitter and blogs like *TechCrunch, Mashable,* and *Silicon Valley Insider* enable fanboys outside of San Francisco to vicariously follow the latest developments in startups and technologies. Scott Beale describes:

> A guy who I met with at dinner in SOMA, I ended up taking him over to some drinkup someone was having. I forget, but it was like, people from Flickr and Digg and all these . . . And he's like, "Holy crap! You just took me to ground zero." Like, "I did?" That was just like any party that we do. This guy lives in Hong Kong and he doesn't see this stuff but he sees these names online. Twitter . . . you see these names repeated and at-replied and, you know, they wanna meet this person. They don't even know who they are or why they want to. I bet all these people were like, who's Robert Scoble and that kind of stuff. But they see his name and they're like, "I should meet him." And if they meet him, they're like, "Oh! I met this person."

The online visibility and name recognition of social media celebrities mark them as people of value or importance, especially to outsiders. And a few of their fans will—like Jackson, Culver, and Rose did—eventually move to San Francisco to pursue their dreams. I had lunch in South Park with a young tech worker who described meeting College Humor co-founder Jakob Lodwick as "one of the highlights of my year—I'm such a tech fanboy." As Charles Kurz-man and his colleagues describe in a discussion of celebrities and status, "When a celebrity deigns to interact with ordinary people, we consider ourselves honored . . . celebrity status may rub off in a small way on the inferior party."[25] This is true both for mainstream celebrities and the micro-famous.

It is not illogical to pay attention to status given that some fans parlay their knowledge of the tech scene into success. Megan Mc-Carthy, editor at the *New York Observer* and former *Valleywag* writer, began her tech journalism career by reading the personal websites of people mentioned on technology blogs. Tristan Walker, too, told me how he got into tech:

> When I got out here, I realized there are like 22-year-olds making millions of dollars. Like "I have some semblance of competence. I can figure this out" . . . And there were 10 blogs that I said I'm going to read every single day for 90 days and become an expert on this stuff . . . *TechCrunch, Mashable,* Scoble's blog, *ReadWriteWeb,* the standard tech stuff. And I literally hunkered down, read them for three months and hustled.

Fitton (Pistachio) said, "I was already kind of oriented around marketing bloggers and startup bloggers right from the get-go, and so I very quickly became aware of Om Malik and Arrington and Tara Hunt and all these people. The 'Alice in Wonderland' sensation of my life has just been them all showing up in my life pretty quickly after I heard about them." It is not uncommon to start in the tech scene this way; Walker and Fitton became insiders at least partially due to their consumption of popular media about the scene. Thor Muller describes this process: "I see this most obvi-ously in people who move here. And, they've been watching it from afar, Twitter or whatever, blogs. They know some of the personali-ties; they know what it's like to have that kind of influence, to be able to have your laptop sponsored, for instance. That's appealing."

Seeing the names of micro-celebrities repeated on blogs and Twitter reinforces the desirability of visibility and motivates outsiders to seek it for themselves. Clearly micro-celebrity is a widely recognized phenomenon in the tech scene that is intimately integrated with status practices. Regardless of how many people claim to dislike micro-celebrity, the existence of tech celebrities is significant, and their importance is reinforced both in person and online.

### Achieved versus Ascribed Micro-Celebrity

The distinction between achieved and ascribed micro-celebrity becomes salient when considering how many people in the tech scene dislike micro-celebrity practitioners. Jeremy Stoppelman, the CEO of Yelp, told me:

> The people that spend more time promoting themselves generally spend less time doing. And so, if you actually look at who are the people that are building the great companies for the next 10 to 20 years, it's probably not people that are spending a lot of time on the conference circuit or spending a lot of time with their millions of followers. Zuckerberg isn't Tweeting much. I'm not sure Steve Jobs has ever Tweeted.

Those who are ascribed micro-celebrity are rewarded in this way for their accomplishments, not their practices. Moreover, there is an assumption that those who are aggressively pursuing internet fame for its own sake have nothing to back it up; the practice is dismissively referred to as "famewhoring" or "fameballing," terms that are usually applied to people without any particular skill or accomplishment that might earn their fame. The very highest status is still reserved for those who are well known for their achievements rather than for just their name recognition. For example, Jakob Lodwick, the co-founder of College Humor, posts deeply personal information and peculiar homemade videos online, but his seeming drive to court attention is forgiven because of his significant accomplishments (and wealth). By contrast, Nick Starr, an out gay man and Apple fanboy who posts constant updates on his sex life and weight loss (even tweeting his liposuction), is considered by many to be desperate for attention. There is a distinction made between "celebrity," or fame for fame's sake, versus fame based on high-status business practice. This distaste means that a successful micro-celebrity practitioner must walk an extremely thin line between maintaining high status in the community through achievements and self-promotion, and going overboard to the point where he or she is mocked or ridiculed. Ascribed and achieved are thus intertwined to the point where achievement that is considered sufficient to rightfully inhabit the micro-celebrity subject position is highly variable and context dependent.

Some people see micro-celebrity as a natural consequence of any social group, particularly one made up largely of former nerds. Derek Overby, a social media strategist for the real estate site Roost .com, mused, "I think geeks have always wanted to be at the center of attention . . . It was always the jocks versus the nerds. But mostly I think there's been a level of respect for being able to sit down and program PHP or whatever, that people are envious they can't do that. So it's just been elevated into a celebrity or at least a fondness for what they've accomplished." Hillary Hartley, who works in Gov 2.0, argued that the need for celebrities is cultural, saying, "I don't think it's any wonder that a specific niche group, like geeky people, techies, need that same sort of celebrity." To Overby and Hartley, micro-celebrity is the logical outgrowth of a scene that values technology workers. While every social group has high-status people, the fact that social media, which encourages broadcasting information about yourself, is the focus of the tech scene means that information about tech celebs travels further than, say, the media of well-known automobile engineers.

But for the most part, internet celebrity was met by those I talked to with ambivalence at best and contemptuousness at worst. Glenda Bautista told me that she was struck by the people "fetishizing geekdom" when she moved to the Bay Area in 2003. "Why are all the nerds like your rock stars?" she asked. Twitter founder Ev Williams's response to someone "young and capable" attempting to achieve internet fame was "A) that's probably not going to work, and B) what a waste of time." When asked about internet celebrity, Annalee Newitz, editor of the *Gawker* science fiction blog *io9*, thought it was "completely repulsive." Newitz perceives people who become famous for something they've done—she referred to popular blogs *I Can Has Cheezburger* and *Cute Overload*—as deserving of their visibility: "You know, sometimes people become popular just because they're doing something cool. And, you know, that's not really their fault." Meanwhile, she perceived people "who pursue [fame] purely just to manipulate the network and manipulate people's responses" as "deeply scary."

Just as mainstream celebrity media treats celebrities as characters to be written into often fabricated plotlines, gossip blogs of the day, like *Valleywag*, fit micro-celebrity personas into preexisting narratives and character arcs that reflected both long-standing tropes about celebrity and the meritocratic mythology of the technology scene. *Valleywag* is one example of how celebrity was ascribed to individuals and how the behavior of people within the tech scene was publicly policed by and judged against the values of Silicon Valley.

### Ascribing Micro-Celebrity: *Valleywag*

*Valleywag*, part of the Gawker Media blog company, ran from 2006 to 2008; in November 2008, it was discontinued, and editor Owen Thomas was given a column on the popular media blog *Gawker* (Gawker Media announced in early 2013 that it is reviving the blog).[26] *Valleywag* alternated stories about company acquisitions and technological developments with dating gossip, affairs, leaked personal e-mails and videos, and sharp take-downs of people like Leah Culver and Kevin Rose. It drew from tropes like the cocky self-made man or the woman sleeping her way to the top to create characters and narratives from the actions of technology workers. Like tabloids, to generate its gossip *Valleywag* depended heavily on un-substantiated rumors, overheard snippets of conversation, and in-sider connections.[27] *Valleywag* reporters monitored content created by micro-celebrities, such as tweets, videos, social network site pro-files, blog entries, and digital photos, highlighting items they found controversial or noteworthy. The blog served to police the actions of micro-celebrities: anyone who violated the standards for normative conduct that had developed was liable to become a target. Posts had titles such as "Kevin Rose, Julia Allison to Date" (2007); "Leah and Brad's Breakup Leaves Gossip Blog Despondent" (2007); "Ariel Waldman, Twitter, and the 'Whore' Algorithm" (2008); "Filthy Rich Matt Mullenweg Calls Rival 'Dirty'" (2008); and "Chris Messina and Tara Hunt: It's Still a Breakup Even if No One Blogs It" (2008).

*Valleywag* reporters lived in San Francisco, went to technology parties and events, and were often friends with the people they covered. I interviewed former editors Owen Thomas and Nick Douglas, and two former reporters, Melissa Gira Grant and Megan McCarthy, to learn why *Valleywag* existed, what it tried to cover, and how the staff justified running some of the nastier stories.

Nick Douglas is a slight, redheaded aspiring comedian who was handpicked by *Gawker* publisher Nick Denton to work for *Valley-wag*. He dropped out a semester before finishing college to move to San Francisco at the age of twenty-one. "When I came out here for a couple of months, I was just blown away," Douglas told me when I interviewed him in 2007. "Goggle-eyed. I was a little star-struck by all these people. Because I had been reading blogs for ages . . . so I was meeting a bunch of people who[m] I'd written about and really built into micro-celebrity status in my mind."

Denton claimed that he chose Douglas precisely for this reason: new to the scene, he would blog about subjects that more seasoned journalists might consider off-limits.[28] Like many San Francisco transplants, Douglas went through a period of enculturation that required him to both recognize and (eventually) feign a blasé atti-tude toward the well-known members of the tech community. He was an incredible source of information about people, and I often interrogated him at parties, where he was an omnipresent figure, to ask him who someone was, or why a certain company was poorly regarded. While Douglas was always friendly and nice to me—to the point of disingenuousness—many people regarded him with, at best, suspicion, viewing him as a hypocrite who curried favor with the Web 2.0 elite while writing poisonous prose about them.

*Valleywag* identified important characters in the tech scene and wrote about them again and again. Its writers aimed to find a chink in the armor or a personal foible of someone with micro-celebrity status, particularly someone whose background and experiences made for good storytelling. Nick Denton, the founder of the blog and head of Gawker Media, emphasized the creation and development of characters that readers could recognize. The coverage of these characters was often tailored to fit archetypes, rather than reality. I talked to a former editor of Gawker.com who said the site only wanted "plot point" stories; they would only write about an event if it fit a character's arc, or plot, which had been predetermined by Gawker. Douglas explained:

> Denton definitely cares about narratives. So there are a few things, constant things, he was always telling the editors about at Gawker, like more contexts . . . So we always try to have [larger] metanarratives and archetypes and we try to find people to fit that. There is the archetype of the young software founder and there is a whole usual story line. Founder finds investor, founder turns down buyout offer, founder gets cocky, and then founder ruins his business.

Thus many people were ascribed micro-celebrity because they were wealthy or interesting enough to fit into a particular narrative that *Valleywag* had assigned them. For example, Leah Culver, the founder of Pownce, was an attractive software developer who was characterized by *Valleywag* as a woman "sleeping her way to the top," and so any story about her dating or sex life was fair game.

Douglas was fired in late 2006 for allegedly covering people whom Denton did not believe were of general interest. In a memo leaked to the *New York Times*, Denton wrote, "Anytime a writer settles in too closely with the subjects he/she's writing about, there comes the inevitable tradeoffs: favor trading, and an elevated sense of one's own importance to the field at hand. Both, to some degree, ended up being the case here."[29] Marketer Tara Hunt and technologist Chris Messina, for example, were well-known in San Francisco but virtually unknown outside of the scene; Douglas covered their breakup on *Valleywag*. Former reporter Megan McCarthy, who worked both for Douglas and Denton, explained:

> The problem was—I think this was why Nick Douglas got let go—the actual billionaires don't really want the press . . . They don't want people to talk about them in stories and stuff that they're not approving. It becomes easier, then, to write about people that want to be in there . . . if you look at the end of Nick's tenure, he was writing about a lot of Web 2.0 people, who didn't matter . . . They have like, a blog. And they've never made any money. They're never going to make any money. They just want to be famous for fame's sake. And it really wasn't interesting to people outside of the scene.

McCarthy highlights a problem with *Valleywag*'s coverage. Legitimate entrepreneurs like Facebook founder Mark Zuckerberg shunned the spotlight and rarely went to parties. So although *Valleywag* attempted to dig up dirt on Zuckerberg, say, or the Google founders, it was easier to write about people like Julia Allison or Tara Hunt, who broadcasted their life online. McCarthy displayed a certain disdain toward these "Web 2.0" people, whom she viewed as meritless attention seekers. After all, there are limitations to micro-celebrity. While some micro-celebrity practitioners are able to translate their fame into a better job or a book deal, very few achieve the financial success or legitimacy given to mainstream celebrities. For the most part, micro-celebrities need further legitimization to reap the benefits of real fame.

While typical celebrity gossip columns write about the traditionally feminine concerns of sex, relationships, parenthood, and fashion, very little of those topics could be found in *Valleywag*.[30] *Valleywag* had to balance stories of interest to tech workers with those of interest to the larger population; in addition, the majority of readers were not San Francisco insiders, but Web 2.0 fanboys. McCarthy explained that *Valleywag* was looking for stories about "sex or money," but mostly money: "There's a hierarchy of stories that we wanted. Yeah, sex and money. Those are the two things. And money was way higher . . . And you always want to know how much . . . A lot of people around here are engineers, they're not very good with subtleties and cues and the numbers are easy." The idea of comparable metrics is an important one in Silicon Valley. Sex is difficult to compare, as are looks; as McCarthy explained, "Everyone is like, 'we're not really good looking out here' so you can't even run pictures of really good looking people, you can't be interested in that." But Owen Thomas saw reporting on sex scandals as a way to bring humanity back into these stories:

> So, I think, you know, the fact that everyone tries to basically pretend that they're disembodied brains and that they're changing the world—I guess that they're not being taken by sex or money. But really, if you look at every social network around, it's about getting laid. Mark Zuckerberg was basically building a system so that he could rate Harvard girls. MySpace Tom was actually running an Asian porn site on the side.[31]

Such over-the-top language, generalizations, and strong moral judgments are typical of *Valleywag*'s approach to gossip.

*Valleywag* also turned its reporters into micro-celebrities. Douglas, Gira, and McCarthy agreed that writing for *Valleywag* had made their personal brand more visible, even as it had encouraged sycophantic behavior from others. McCarthy scoffed, "But, the people who are like, 'Oh, my god. I met someone from *Valleywag*,' I instantly knew that they were kind of naive . . . you could tell they were very, sort of new to the system." People I encountered who were truly high status were not impressed by *Valleywag* or its reporters; instead, they claimed they did not read *Valleywag* or rolled their eyes when it was mentioned. But because *Valleywag* was a blog rather than a newspaper, and did not adhere to any sort of objective standard of journalism, the writers were encouraged to put themselves into the stories. As a result, their opinions and beliefs became part of the story and the brand. Since most of the *Valleywag* staff were freelance writers, they too engaged in micro-celebrity practices such as frequent twittering, maintaining personal blogs, talking to fans, and so on.

Many of the *Valleywag* staff developed a jaded, even contemptuous attitude toward their subjects, which was reflected in their writing. As former reporter Melissa Gira Grant, a long-term feminist activist, told me, "I became really cynical after writing there for like a month. I understand how that happens to people who work for Gawker. People with all this experience, who know what they're doing. Once you are inside of it, you should see the stuff that never makes it. You should see all the conversations that never make it to the public. You should see all the things that we pass on, that are like really crazy." This cynical attitude toward the technology industry helped staffers justify the blog's existence and their own writing.

My interviewees defended *Valleywag* in several ways, claiming variously that the blog revealed hypocrisy; provided investigative journalism on an industry that celebrated its own existence; covered legitimate celebrities with significant influence; and wrote about people who had opened themselves to scrutiny by posting personal information online. Owen Thomas is surprisingly genial and friendly despite his sharp online presence, and I enjoyed talking to him. A big proponent of exposing hypocrisy, he told me: "The fundamentals of hypocrisy in Silicon Valley [are] that everyone says they want to change the world. And that's true. They want to change the world from one in which they're poor into one in which they're rich."

The first two stories posted on *Valleywag* exposed a romantic relationship between Google founder Larry Page and executive Marissa Mayer, and revealed that Google CEO Eric Schmidt was in an open marriage with a mistress. This information was widely known in Silicon Valley, but other technology blogs had avoided writing about it in order to maintain access to Google insiders.[32] Thomas thought that the rest of the business press was toothless and had failed to report on important stories; unlike them, *Valleywag* was not afraid of losing access to high-status tech people. *Valleywag* often poked holes in press releases and puff pieces. Thomas, for example, loathed Elon Musk, the lauded founder of Tesla Motors. He told me Musk had blatantly lied about his last two companies and that in both instances he had been fired by venture capitalists before the companies were sold. Thomas viewed Musk as an egregious liar with a history of founding companies and running them into the ground, and he saw *Valleywag's* reporting as a check on Musk's hubris.[33] He explained that it was *Valleywag's* responsibility to point out when high-status individuals were being outright hypocritical: "Does it matter that Digg was almost out of money and they managed to raise $20 million in the very last minute after the sale [to] Google fell through? I mean in the end, I guess not, because they have the money, you know, and it will last them some years. But, is it important to know that . . . their CEO was looking people in the eye and saying everything's fine and we've got plenty of money and, we're not going to sell the company, even as they're trying to sell? I think you have to know that in order to judge people's character."

Another justification for *Valleywag's* approach was that it critiqued people who were already living public lives. As Kara Swisher told me, "It's just gossip." She pointed out that the New York media scene was covered in-depth by the *New York Post* and *Page Six*. She compared *Valleywag* to *Us Weekly*. "None of that stuff is true about those celebrities. And [people] go, 'Well, they don't know. They sign up for that.' I'm like, 'So do you, kind of, by appearing on all of those magazine covers. Aren't you fabulous? Maybe you need to be taken down.'" Because micro-celebrities like Kevin Rose and Leah Culver courted publicity in certain ways, she argued, they deserved the gossip as well. Owen Thomas similarly saw the people he covered as legitimately famous and so deserving of as much critical press as traditional celebrities received. In his view, people who lived life in public were fair game in a world saturated with celebrity culture:

> This whole argument [is] that these people haven't chosen to live a life of public exposure, that they're just geeks. This is what I hear over and over again and it's kind of tiresome. Of course they're trying to parlay their personality, their intellect, their presence as a thought leader in the industry, into a bigger career to get more success for their business. I mean, they're trying to be . . . public. The thing is they've got this excuse, "Oh! I'm just a geek. I just write code and, therefore, I am somehow off-limits." When you dig into it with just a teaspoon, it falls apart as an artifice.

The attention economy, which treats visibility as status, makes it important for anyone who hopes to succeed in the technology industry to live at least somewhat in the public eye. But by doing this, they open themselves to the type of scrutiny that only entertainment celebrities have traditionally been subject to. Further, while mainstream celebrities are expected to protect their privacy, micro-celebrities cannot or they'll lose this attention. Melissa Gira Grant explained:

> That's really the thing: The more the big deal, I think, that people position themselves as, the more fun it is to watch them fall. I feel like inside people really ask for it themselves. It's a horrible thing to say, but if you do want to be a big player or a scenester, this is part of what comes with that . . . [You] wrap your own personal sense of success up in how much people are talking about you, and you can't control that.

The lack of privacy and ongoing criticism that mainstream celebrities face trickles down to micro-celebrities. While Thomas, and indeed all the writers, seemed sincere in their belief that they were taking down hypocrisy, *Valleywag*'s predilection for reporting on things that have nothing to do with company valuations, shareholders, or anything similar—breakups and the like—makes it difficult to justify the blog's existence from this perspective.

For the most part, *Valleywag* was vilified among people in the tech community. Michael Arrington posted a story on *TechCrunch*, "When will we have our first Valleywag suicide?" and wrote:

> Celebrities have had to live with this kind of nonsense for decades, which explains why some of them pull out of society entirely and become completely anti-social. Perhaps, some argue, they bring it on themselves by seeking fame. But for people in Silicon Valley, who are not celebrities and who have no desire other than to build a great startup, a post on *Valleywag* comes as a huge shock. Seeing [their] marriage woes, DUI or employment termination up on a popular public website (permanently indexed by search engines) is simply more than they can handle. They have not had the ramp up time to build resistance to the attacks.[34]

More mainstream blogs refused to link to *Valleywag* stories, and Nick Douglas was banned from several events, including Arrington's *TechCrunch* parties. (As mentioned earlier, because I often skulked in the corner at parties writing in a notebook, I was mistaken for a *Valleywag* reporter several times, not always in a friendly way.) While many people claimed that they never read it, it was clear by the way stories were discussed and passed around that it had a significant effect on the community.[35] This manifested itself in extreme ambivalence; some hated *Valleywag*, while others enjoyed being covered by it, or even courted coverage. (I was delighted when my SXSW panel discussion on micro-celebrity warranted a paragraph on *Valleywag*.)

Grant told me that it was difficult to get people to submit gossip to *Valleywag* because tech workers didn't want to be disloyal. The Valley is so dependent on networking and flexible labor, and on building and maintaining the relationships that support these practices, that burning bridges is unthinkable. Grant said: "It's harder to get that kind of . . . editorial assistance, sniping, backroom gossip that Gawker gets, because in the Valley, even the lowliest worker thinks that someday they might be a founder . . . But as much as we value outspokenness and transparency, there's a lot more self-censorship and a lot more self-restraint going on here."

*Valleywag* helped to create an audience that sees through the eyes of the self-as-entrepreneur. The view that every tech worker is a potential Mark Zuckerberg propels the rest of the industry, with its long hours, hard work, no unions, no overtime, and no job security. The potential for great wealth makes such sacrifices seem like a reasonable tradeoff, not exploitation. *Valleywag*'s endless promotion of the entrepreneurial narrative feeds this perception. As a result, the negative consequences of participating in social media are usually blamed on naïveté and ignorance. The thought is that people who get fired for something they put online, known as being "dooced" after *Dooce* blogger Heather Armstrong, are responsible; they should have known better. Similarly, cruel gossip is partially justified by public status, although almost everyone puts some sort of content online.

*Valleywag* magnified the "celebrity" part of micro-celebrity practice. Highly read gossip columns covering the lives, loves, outfits, and scandals of tech industry players would inflate the profiles of the people it covered; *Gawker*, for instance, was almost wholly responsible for Julia Allison's rise to fame, and Allison was well aware of this. It, like *Valleywag*, mapped the values of celebrity culture onto the technology scene by publicizing gossip and rumors. *Valleywag* also demonstrated the process by which people were transformed into characters, as it ascribed public personas to regular people and created interconnected, well-worn plots around them. People who had been ascribed micro-celebrity by *Valleywag* were also taken up and written about by other news sources, further inflating their visibility. Kevin Rose was on the cover of *Inc* and *BusinessWeek;* Leah Culver made the cover of *Technology Review;* and Julia Allison was on the cover of *Wired,* while blogs like *Get Off My Internets* analyzed the tweets and personal blogs of many of the *Valleywag* players.

Most importantly, *Valleywag* policed acceptable and unacceptable behavior. Micro-celebrities were held to standards created and maintained by the editors and reporters, standards that reflected the larger values of Silicon Valley culture. These standards were fairly conservative and included monogamy, or at least not promiscuity; a lack of visible "famewhoring"; spending money wisely rather than buying sports cars, mansions, or elaborate vacations; negligible political leanings; and, above all, no hypocrisy (a value that harkens back to the theme of authenticity as consistency). These mores were applied unevenly, particularly in regard to gender; while Thomas painted Leah Culver as promiscuous, he reported on but rarely judged Kevin Rose for his steady flow of attractive girlfriends. *Valleywag* perpetuated the mythology of Silicon Valley, which claims that financial success goes hand-in-hand with intelligence and hard work, and it enforced the anti-conspicuous ethos of consumption that prioritized gadgets and travel over designer clothes or fancy cars. It was okay if people were visible or extremely rich, as long as this was backed up by entrepreneurship, intelligence, hard work, and creativity. Excessive displays of wealth or publicly courting attention undermined the meritocratic myth of Silicon Valley by suggesting that success was not necessarily based on intrinsic personal characteristics.

*Valleywag*'s aggressively negative judgments on those who supposedly violated these unwritten rules served as a reminder of shared social norms. The "Cyprus 20," a group of young New York City tech workers and founders who made a video of themselves lip-synching to "Don't Stop Believing" while on vacation in Cyprus, was called out on *Valleywag* for epitomizing boom-time excess while many companies were conducting highly publicized layoffs. Grant explained:

So they did a lipdub, a private lipdub, to "Don't Stop Believing." And the girls were all in matching bikinis, and the guys were all drinking beer. And they were like in bed together and in the swimming pool frolicking around. At this really expensive house, and it was just when all of these major layoffs had been announced and the stock market was tanking, and it had been leaked from their private Blip account. And Gawker got a copy of it, and it was on *Valleywag* . . . I think this was a great video to be like, that this is that ridiculous level of excess and out-to-lunch mentality. It's really just kids wanting to have a good time, to celebrate the fact that they have a stupid amount of money they don't even know what to do with. But it felt so heartless, considering the state of the economy. I think Sequoia Capital just had a meeting where they said "The fun is over." So, it was really bad timing. It was really, really bad timing.

And then the facetiousness on Owen's part—he knows that people are doing this all the time. He knows there are way more decadent things going on every night of the week, but it seemed that these people were just a good target because of the hubris of making it—and it was a lipdub, and it was perfectly done. It was like one long shot. Nobody screwed up. It was so perfect.

This video was presumably made for personal use, posted on a private social media account, and leaked to *Valleywag*; it was not public (though it is now easily accessible on YouTube). None of the Cyprus 20 was responsible for layoffs, and the lifestyle of wealth and leisure that is shown in the video motivates many young entrepreneurs. *Valleywag* (and *TechCrunch*, which picked up the story), claimed that the participants were "ostentatious" and "tasteless," but that seems a weak justification for repeated public castigation.

Indeed, unlike more traditional celebrities, the people covered in *Valleywag* were mostly technology workers without managers, publicists, agents, or experience dealing with the press. Many found the coverage to be difficult at times, and some found it emotionally devastating. The *Valleywag* editors justified using celebrity gossip, paparazzi, and tabloids to analyze the technology scene by claiming that doing so restrained Silicon Valley hypocrisy. But while it was true that some of the people involved were appearing on the covers of *Wired* and *BusinessWeek* and courting attention, others were not. Ultimately, the idea of using the tools of celebrity culture to analyze the lives of regular people is problematic because the protections available to mainstream celebrities do not exist for micro-celebrities. Further, micro-celebrities depend on attention and visibility to maintain their elevated status, but because most young people put content online, it opens the door for such scrutiny to be applied to almost anyone. And this scrutiny can be very harsh.

## Micro-Celebrity as Experience

She isn't mentally stable enough to handle all the bullshit that comes along with a full-disclosure internet presence.

—Commenter on *Oh No They Didn't* gossip blog, talking about Lindsay Lohan

While there has been a great deal of analysis of celebrity culture from the perspective of fans and celebrity watchers, there has been little attention to how fame is experienced by celebrities, presumably because celebrities are difficult to access. Those celebrities who speak openly about their negative experiences with fame are considered ungrateful if they complain about the consequences of something they presumably wanted to achieve. Here I will describe the experience of micro-celebrity, what it is like for its practitioners, and its positive and negative effects. While we cannot know if this perspective can be extrapolated to the views of mainstream celebrities, we can presume that at least some of these experiences may apply to many other people who live their lives in public.

Most of the micro-celebrity aspirants I interviewed were candid about the strategic nature of their self-promotion. Although some micro-celebrities will claim that they are sharing information for some sort of nebulous social good, marketer and author Tara Hunt questions those people who claim to be "altruistic":

> I mean, if I just wanted to record the moments of my life, I would write a private diary or keep my twitter private or keep my blog totally private . . . you start to write these things because you want people to read them. And why do you want people to read them? Well, maybe sometimes you want your mom to read them and maybe sometimes you want your friends that you've been out of touch with to read this stuff, but . . . mostly you want people to read them because you want people to know who you are and get discovered.

Hunt characterizes those using the tools of micro-celebrity as "external validation junkies" who want attention from a larger audience than just friends and family. This echoes the idea of the social web as an exhibitionist culture where personal blogging and self-portraits encourage an inward focus.[36] The view of oneself as public and of readers as an audience or a fan base is calculated and deliberate. Leah Culver agrees: "I could disappear, I could just quit. Someone else could take my place. So anytime you can quit. That's a nice thing about Internet stuff, though, too, right? You don't have to worry about the paparazzi stalking you." Culver's first experience with internet fame was selling advertisements to be laser-etched on the casing of her laptop for fifty dollars a square inch. She successfully paid for the laptop, the final product made the front page of Digg, and the project became an example of cheap, effective, viral advertising. After that experience, Culver decided that she could handle a greater level of attention, and went on to found her own website, Pownce.

While Culver distinguishes ephemeral internet fame from the permanence of mainstream fame, many informants found micro-celebrity to be a difficult experience. Several micro-celebrities described the hard time they had trusting people and how they wondered whether others were mostly concerned with their public persona. Kevin Rose told me, "I don't know how to handle new people [who] approach me that want to become friends . . . It's a really different experience than it was a few years ago, to go to a party and meet people. Because you have to figure out what their intentions are." Tara Hunt said, "Being a public figure is different . . . I have to always sort of be a little bit more careful about who I date and how I date, and all that sort of stuff."

Micro-celebrity requires the internet famous to police their image and to be watchful of what appears in the public eye, especially with gossip blog minions combing through user-created content. The persistence and searchability of social content like blog entries, photographs, and tweets means that relationships and personas are augmented by a rich context of digital information. For example, Glenda Bautista describes her careful monitoring of digital photography: "I dated someone who's pretty notorious in the community and one day, you know, [his] hand is positioned around the waist, not over the shoulder and I'm like, 'Oh God, that's going to be taken out of context,' you know what I mean? And then pretty soon everybody has commentary on it." Bautista was angry that people's perceptions of her were shaped by local blogs. She described using various tactics to regain control over her image: blogging under an alternate identity, reining in her tendency to comment on personal matters, and shoring up her personal brand. She said, frustrated, "Everyone's perceptions of you are built upon the way in which people have documented you that you really honestly have no control over." Author and business writer Sarah Lacy told me, "I mean everyone, everyone in the scene has had to give up their privacy . . . Even just people covering this scene . . . And so that makes you pull back." While the internet appears to give people control over their self-presentation, this perception is countered by the very real loss of control that happens virtually instantly once information has been released into the ether.[37] While the people I interviewed often talked about this in terms of privacy, what they were really reacting to was the loss of control over their own persona and over their ability to limit the flow of information.

While some of these complaints may serve to enforce the micro-celebrity's own sense of status, it is true that practitioners often quit after a short period due to the scrutiny of public living. Like Adam Jackson, Tara Hunt, whose very public breakup was covered by *Valleywag* and *San Francisco* magazine (sample quote: "In a world not known for its epic romances, Chris and Tara used to be Web 2.0's version of Brangelina"), has pulled back from extreme public disclosure, as has Culver, who sold her microblogging startup and retreated into her true passion, software development.[38]

Many people I talked to spoke of the downsides to micro-celebrity life; namely, that there was constant "drama." Living a public life can be stressful and comes with a lot of gossip and intrigue, partly due to the scrutiny of blogs like *Valleywag*. Lacy explained: "The part that's not fun is . . . the exploitive part . . . people know that if they write certain things about me it'll drive a certain amount of traffic so people will write nasty things." Bautista said, "No one really knew what to do until they had that one instance where too much is like, OK, crossed the line. And you can't tell the difference between the way that the media has spun something versus when what you really honestly know to be true." Micro-celebrities often found that both their online and offline actions were publicized and discussed via social media, creating a fishbowl-like effect that normalized personal scrutiny. The experiences of media personality Julia Allison epitomize this type of scrutiny and illustrate the negative effects it can have on micro-celebrity practitioners.

### Julia Allison

No one knows the object better than the fan.
—Constance Penley, *NASA/Trek*

In 2005, Jonathan Gray coined the term "anti-fan" to describe "those who strongly dislike a given text or genre, consider it inane, stupid, morally bankrupt and/or aesthetic drivel."[39] Instead of avoiding what they dislike, sometimes anti-fans fervently consume the media they "love to hate," in order to discuss it with other like-minded anti-fans.[40] That is certainly the case with a group of anti-fans who are devoted to hating internet celebrity Julia Allison.

Allison is a writer-turned-reality star whose beat is celebrity and relationships. During the mid to late 2000s, she took advantage of the new crop of New York media blogs like *Gawker* and the rise of the New York City technorati to launch herself to prominence. Allison wrote a relationship column, first for the free *Metro* weekly, then for *Time Out New York;* she appeared as a "talking head" for *Star* magazine on various cable news shows; and she wrote intimately about her dalliances with semi-famous men, her love for pretty dresses, and her fluffy white dog. With three of her attractive friends, she founded a "lifecasting" startup called Non-Society that consisted primarily of each woman blogging about her life; the same women starred on a video show called *TMI Weekly*. She wrote a syndicated column about social media for the *Chicago Tribune* that was discontinued after a year. And throughout all of this, she used Tumblr, Twitter, and Facebook to post dozens of self-portraits, muse about what she considered the important things in life, and discuss dates, parties, and Burning Man.

Allison would seem to be a fairly inconsequential figure. The content she writes is not considered very good, but neither is the content of many famous people. She is shameless at courting the press, but she isn't bad at it; again, in her heyday, she made the cover of *Wired* magazine, and her Bravo reality show *Miss Advised* aired in 2012. Certainly, famous-for-being-famous celebrities like Heidi Montag and Spencer Pratt, who have appeared on a series of MTV reality shows and written a book called *How to Be Famous,* are just as brazen. While evidence of Allison's indiscretions, dalliances, and falsehoods abound on the internet, they tend to be fairly lightweight compared to famous celebrity scandals like those of Britney Spears or Charlie Sheen. Moreover, Allison does not get an enormous amount of attention compared to other internet celebrities; she has

115,000 Twitter followers, compared to Kevin Rose's 1.3 million and Ev Williams's 1.5 million, and far fewer mentions on *Gawker* or other blogs than she used to.[41] In fact, by far the outlet giving her the most attention is a "hater blog" called *Reblogging Donk.* What is it about Julia that invites such hatred?

*Reblogging Donk (RBD),* founded as *Reblogging Julia Allison* in January 2009, has three primary bloggers and a lively community that responds almost daily to every piece of content Julia posts.[42] It refers to her as "Donkey," and describes her as an "annoying piece of internet trash" and "another dumb trashy gold digger with a Tumblr."[43] In addition to *RBD, Radar* magazine named Allison the third "most hated person on the Internet," and *Gawker* wrote a vitriolic "Field Guide to Julia Allison" that poked fun at her popularity and sex life. The hatred shown toward Allison seems so out of proportion to her actual activities that *Gawker,* which had spearheaded much of her rise and fall, eventually wrote a series of articles questioning the motives of the individuals behind the *Reblogging* site.[44] Maureen Henderson, after profiling Allison for *Forbes,* found the many negative comments on her story similarly inexplicable: "The idea that someone folks are calling a 'fraud' and an 'awful person' still merits a website focused on bashing her even as readers reiterate that she lacks substance or career success is just so damn weird in a Web 2.0 way."[45]

The vitriol for Allison extends to virtually everything she comes into contact with. My dissertation, for example, included a case study of Allison that included interview quotes. When I proudly made the dissertation available online, *Reblogging Donk* found it and posted the section about Allison. The *RBD* community wrote more than three hundred comments about my stupidity, poor writing, and lack of doctoral qualifications. The community was incensed by the idea that I had believed Allison's "lies" and had failed to uncover the "truth" about her. Only a very stupid person would be taken in by Allison, commenters wrote, and such a person was undeserving of a higher degree.[46]

*Reblogging Donk* is run by three pseudonymous individuals who go by "Juliaspublicist," "Jacy Russiangirl," and "Professor Camping."

The three closely guard their pseudonyms and do not give out personal information.[47] Jacy agreed to be interviewed via e-mail, and wrote lengthy and articulate responses to my queries. She explained, "Our only objective is to point and laugh, like any other audience members of a compelling reality show." To criticize Allison, the rebloggers conduct close readings of the texts she produces. They screenshot tweets, chat logs, and Facebook pages. They pull up Google caches of old blog posts and deleted items. They track down the real names of her boyfriends and post pictures of them on the blog. *Reblogging Donk* features not only a lengthy glossary of Allison-related terms, but also an elaborate timeline that chronicles her life over the last few years that is downloadable in PDF format and titled "The Internet Never Forgets."

The primary driver of the anti-fans is a moral and ethical anger against Allison. Their objections seem similar to those found by Gray in his investigation of anti-fans of the *Apprentice* contestant Omerosa—anti-fans who, in his view, sported a "veneer of moral objection."[48] Omerosa's haters disliked the attention that she got, which they saw as unfairly rewarding talentless, unethical, and immoral behavior. Similarly, the rebloggers' gripes against Allison are summarized by Jacy:

> You see, everyone, she has simply been completely misunderstood! All that psychotic behavior towards exes and their new partners, all the throwing of her friends under the bus to deflect suspicion of criminal harassment, all the years she's spent violating people's privacy, including close family members, all the times she's tried to secretly leak information about her personal life to blogs and websites she claims to despise, all the lying, the boasting, the lunacy—it's all been just a giant misunderstanding![49]

The rebloggers seem to feel that they are "righting a wrong" or "bringing justice to the world" by revealing what they perceive as a series of lies and unethical behavior by Allison.[50] Jacy wrote, "It's hard to tell you what the truth is about JA [Julia Allison], because she is so inherently dishonest with her friends, public and with herself." Juliaspublicist and Jacy, too, both claimed that Julia had lied to me in our interview when she told me that she had lost sponsorships after potential clients found *RBD*. Jacy maintained that this was impossible: Allison lost sponsorships with Sony and other clients due to her own actions, and Bravo had cast her for *Miss Advised* at least partially due to the drama around her online fan base, so "you could argue we helped her get the biggest career opportunity of her life." (This response, however, does not answer Allison's point that *RBD* prevented her from getting other sponsorships.)

A thorough perusal of the comments reveals that the rebloggers define themselves in opposition to Allison. Allison is stupid; they are intelligent. She produces bad content; they produce good content. She is conceited; they are modest. She is insane; they are rational. (Jacy described the *RBD* commenters as "attractive professionals with successful careers and love in their lives.") I was surprised by the vehement objections to my usage of the term "high status markers" to describe Allison's invitations to New York Fashion Week and her (former) friendship with Randi Zuckerberg. It seemed obvious to me that these are indicators of importance to a certain set of people; not everyone can attend a New York Fashion Week show, even a minor one, and Allison has covered this event for ten seasons. Many of the rebloggers, however, claimed that they would never value being on television and being friends with famous people. Instead, they prioritized their friends and family. By suggesting that Allison had high-status accomplishments, I had unknowingly gone against a shared belief system whereby Allison's values were out of whack, and those of the *RBD* bloggers and followers were moral and right.

In her study of *Twilight* anti-fans, Jacqueline M. Pinkowitz remarks that the anti-fans are quick to dismiss their interest. They are not *really* interested in *Twilight;* their hobby does not take much time, and they do not really care. But as Pinkowitz points out, anti-fans "devote the same amount of time and energy to being anti-fans as fans do to being fans."[51] Jacy claimed that she spent "no more than an hour a week, if that" on the site. The commenters maintained that posting about Allison does not mean that they are actually interested or invested in her. But clearly despite all their disavowals, they are as interested in Allison as a text, just as fans would be. The difference is that their engagement is expressed through hatred and contempt rather than admiration or enjoyment.

When I interviewed Allison in April 2010, she gave me more time than any other informant, and we spent three hours discussing her experiences as a micro-celebrity (*RBD* commenters claimed that this showed Allison was desperate to make a good impression). Dressed in a velour sweatsuit and minimal makeup, Allison was extraordinarily open and candid, and I was surprised to find her intelligent and interesting. She told me this is common when she meets someone for the first time, joking that people say, "'You're not a total ditzy retard-slash-asshole.' Um, Yay?" When I asked Allison how she deals with her detractors, she responded, "Hysterical tears, usually. It's not been good for me. And one of my girlfriends who just got her degree . . . said that I reminded her of an abused woman." She elaborated that the negative attention has "crush[ed] me a little bit" and is "beating me down." She said, "It's not even that many people, it's just the relentless nature, and the sense that you're constantly judged . . . It can be literally debilitating, and it's very depressing." Allison told me that she has been dealing with online "haters" since she launched her first website in college, and has never really come to terms with the negative consequences of public living.

Allison gave me a list of protective techniques she said she employs to deal with negative feedback. These included turning off Google Alerts ("the first thing I did"), blocking all "negative people" on Tumblr and Twitter, and deliberately avoiding what is written about her online ("I told my friends, if you see something, don't tell me about it, don't mention it, don't send me a link, do not read it . . . I've asked friends and family, don't read the negative press. I've asked them not to Google"). Allison summarized: "It doesn't always work—but that's the only way I've managed to salvage some semblance of sanity—but even then, people get through with the negative e-mails, it just depends on how I'm feeling at any given time." Allison told me that she had just returned from Los Angeles where she had lunched with *American Pie* actress Shannon Elizabeth, who professed to using identical techniques to manage her own bad publicity.

If Allison has actual fans, they are by no means as active or engaged as the haters. Her tweets are typically answered by *RBD* commenters rather than admirers. She infrequently blogs these days, but when she does, there are only a few comments on each page. Whitney Phillips is an academic who studies trolls. She coined the term "pageview principle" to describe the phenomenon where negative comments are more common than positive comments online, and told me, "People are more likely to take the time to respond if they feel REALLY strongly, either positive or negative. It just so happens that online, negative emotions are often easier to generate."[52] The proprietors of *RBD* claim that Julia has e-mailed them "anonymous" tips about her dating life and other personal information, while simultaneously trying to have the hater sites shut down. If this is true, Allison is engaging with her community (of anti-fans) to increase traffic and interest even as she publicly decries the hate sites. Phillips cites several people who create outrageous online claims and personalities precisely to get attention: to these personas, even negative attention is better than no attention at all. This approach would be similar to the tactics employed by Paris Hilton, who staged a variety of absurd, over-the-top, and tasteless events in order to get press coverage.[53]

Social media celebrities are supposed to be authentic and responsive; popular rhetoric paints internet fame as "democratic" in that everyday people can become famous by virtue of their unique skills and talents.[54] Allison's persona does not fit this mold. She courts the attention of the traditionally famous; she is not modest; and she emphasizes her appearance. An article on the website of social media consultant Brian Solis listed the ways that Allison is doing micro-celebrity "wrong." She gave up her core competency of writing, she does not chat with her fans, and she has not built a strong community around her. In other words, Allison violates the norms of how a micro-celebrity is supposed to act, which are remarkably similar to the guidelines of self-branding that I discuss in Chapter 4. That is, even our newest social media tools arrive with signs of wear, full of social norms that can seem baffling (think of the pressure that Web 2.0 users feel to make a "useful" blog or "interesting" Twitter feed) until we trace them back to their point of origin, the Northern California technology scene.

Allison seems to crave the trappings of traditional celebrity like fashion shows, celebrity friends, and television appearances, but her use of the internet makes it difficult to achieve them because the norms of each type of celebrity are different. For instance, while starlets can get away with a certain degree of artifice, Allison feels that she cannot: "I'm honest, I can't get away with anything—I can't get away with anything! . . . If I get—like, I have [hair] extensions, I have to say it. Otherwise I get called out for it. . . . Every negative point I have, I have to be honest about. And it's brutal . . . on the other hand, ostensibly I'm doing what I love for a living." She straddles the exhibitionist world of the internet, which values transparency and openness, and the traditional media business, which is far more guarded. She pointed out to me in our interview that she cannot tweet about industry meetings or sponsorship opportunities without violating professional agreements, but is then criticized online for purportedly fabricating job opportunities. Because as a micro-celebrity Allison is supposed to be open, she is repeatedly attacked on *RBD* for withholding information while she struggles to gain a foothold in the mainstream media world. We often think of the traditional media business as wildly open, but in reality it is governed by contracts, publicists who carefully regulate access to their clients, and collectively generated artifice, such as the unspoken agreements within the entertainment industry not to "out" gay celebrities. Allison's inability to navigate these two sets of norms illuminates both how information is regulated within mainstream celebrity culture and how deep the ideal of "transparency" in Web 2.0 culture runs. She reveals far more personal information than many mainstream celebrities, but this does not satisfy her detractors; instead it opens her up for detailed scrutiny and criticism.

Jacy maintains that the dislike of Allison is a reaction to the saturation of celebrity culture and the attention economy of social media:

> I believe the reaction is a cultural backlash of some sort. We have been inundated with these types of "fame junkies" for what, a decade now? I think people are tired of it. This generation gets their entertainment online, and JA has courted attention on the Internet, solicited fans and followers, desperately tried to get people to pay attention to her antics, tried for years to get a reality show so she could achieve broader fame. She's been successful in getting online fame, to be sure. But it isn't the kind of fame she wanted.

Similarly, Wendy Atterberry wrote on the popular women's blog *The Frisky*, "Julia represents so much of what is icky about blogging and social networking. She is shamelessly narcissistic and vain, having posted thousands of photos of herself over the years and staging incredible, over-the-top 'photo shoots' simply to post on her blog . . . She's utterly obnoxious." Perhaps Allison represents the apotheosis of self-focused participatory content, but she has faced intense hatred for not "deserving" her fame. Owen Thomas described how he sees Allison:

> Julia is arguing the Julia Allison point. She is arguing the case for herself. And she doesn't have to actually believe it. She is arguing that she is a good editor, which she's not. She is arguing that she is a successful businesswoman, which she's not. She's arguing that she's a caring individual, which she's not. But, you know, it doesn't matter that all these things aren't true and that she may not actually believe them herself because she can argue the point. And that's all

that matters to her—arguing the point . . . And then you start defending the image rather than the authentic self. And . . . that is especially important when there is no authentic self.

Thomas is deeply critical of Julia's lack of authenticity and suggests that her online image is all artifice. To Thomas, and much of the tech sector, fame is something a person is just supposed to have, rather than something to which people should directly aspire.

Whether or not Allison is a good person is beside the point, as is whether her statements to me were "truthful" or not. If she were a movie star, she would not be expected to reveal an authentic self to her public, and she would have layers of handlers hiding her faults and protecting her artifice from the public. Although Allison receives the same type of online scrutiny as a "real" celebrity, she lacks the protections available to an actress or model. She does not have a bodyguard, a press agent, or a stylist. She summarized: "I can't react like celebrities do—but I have the same problems." As more and more people put more and more of their lives online, we might ask whether it is moral and appropriate to besiege them with negative attention because they do not fit our mold of how a celebrity should look or act.

———

Given the negative consequences, it is worth asking why people seek micro-celebrity. I gave a talk on the subject at SXSW 2010. My first question was from a young girl wearing punk clothes with a shaved head, her stubble dyed purple. She asked, "Why do people do this if they're not making money?" For her, becoming internet famous was a means to an end: a way to achieve traditional celebrity (and, presumably, wealth). But many of my informants found that their notoriety did not translate into more money; there was no equivalence between micro-celebrity status and income. For others, micro-celebrity was a way to advance their careers. The cultural logic of celebrity has infiltrated so many occupations that blatant self-promotion is now stock in trade not only for up-and-coming rap stars and actresses, but also for software developers, journalists, and academics. Creating a public presence has become a required part of securing and maintaining a job. Sarah Lacy described this as work: "When people are buying your book and the base of fans is making you a brand, I think there's your responsibility to give back to that . . . it's very draining, but that's kind of the fun part of it." Similarly, some social media firms will not hire people without blogs or Facebook profiles, which become signs of cultural participation.

But "micro-celebrity" and "high status" do not necessarily go hand in hand. Although Julia Allison and Nick Starr are both well-known in their respective communities, neither is well-regarded. Perhaps this is because they are both up-front about their desire for attention. In the San Francisco tech community, where people often claimed that status was based on an accomplishment like building a successful company or inventing a useful technology, "famewhoring" was considered distasteful and gauche. But in other communities, like the teen-targeted entertainment site Buzznet, the relentless self-promotion of self-styled models like Audrey Kitching and Raquel Reed was a normal and acceptable practice. The boundaries of micro-celebrity practice are very much contextualized by the scene that the person originates from, and can easily backfire. Moreover, there are plenty of high-status individuals, such as Mark Zuckerberg or Chris Messina, who no longer seek the spotlight. It is also worth keeping in mind that even if Allison is poorly regarded among technologists, she does reap the benefits of high status in other communities: she attends New York Fashion Week, wears designer clothes, and was hired by Sony to serve as a web spokesperson for the brand due to her network and influence.

Several informants described the changes that micro-celebrity brought about in people. An ex-girlfriend of an internet entrepreneur spoke wonderingly of his newfound predilection for expensive clothes and trendy restaurants, saying that she could no longer recognize in him the person she dated. Melissa Gira Grant described such men as "bubble hotties": entrepreneurs who had gotten rich without developing the necessary social skills to handle it. Indeed, the attention and admiration that many micro-celebrities receive can be both validating and transformative. In *Fame: The Psychology of Stardom*, Andrew Evans and Glenn Wilson describe the difficulties of adjusting to newfound fame and how frequent positive feedback can lead to self-absorption, narcissism, and grandiosity, as well as a resentment of public scrutiny.[55] While micro-celebrity exists on a much smaller scale than, say, film stardom, it is possible that the increased attention has similar effects. But mainstream celebrities have access to systems of attention brokerage, such as bodyguards, drivers, PR specialists, agents, and managers, while micro-celebrities rarely do. The nearly constant negative attention given to many micro-celebrities, particularly the critiques of appearance and sexuality targeted at women, requires a very thick skin.

This brings us back to the question: if being a micro-celebrity is so draining and uncomfortable, why would anyone attempt to become one? The primary motivator for pursuing micro-celebrity seems to be attention and status. While Adam Jackson wanted to increase his access and influence within the tech scene, Julia Allison wanted to attain a more conventional type of celebrity. Whatever the social context, celebrity culture is considered high status, and so will probably always draw those interested in improving their status within their particular communities.

## 4

# SELF-BRANDING

---

## The (Safe for Work) Self

Laura Fitton was a working mom with a floundering home business when she discovered Twitter. As one of the service's earliest adopters, she rocketed to fame in 2007, garnering more than fifty thousand followers at a time when having a thousand was impressive. Known as @pistachio, Fitton used the service to follow Web 2.0 celebrities she had only read about on blogs. "It was such a fast, rapid, effective way to start meeting people," she told me. "I felt like the people I was interacting with on Twitter were co-workers." Fitton quickly found out that "all the American heavyweights" she followed on the service were going to a conference, called LeWeb, in Paris. There, Fitton would cement her reputation as a Twitter consultant.

Guy Kawasaki was an early Apple employee turned Silicon Valley venture capitalist who had become a popular blogger and fixture on the tech scene circuit. Fitton, excited by her newfound Twitter friends, encouraged him to use the service, and he took avidly to the new platform, becoming one of the most followed people in the tech scene. Kawasaki recommended her for speaking gigs and conferences, and she quickly became a go-to authority on the service, writing the popular book *Twitter for Dummies*. She appeared on the "best-attended panels at prestigious conferences and is surrounded by the most people when the talk ends," one interviewer wrote. But Fitton was unable to convert this social prestige to actual capital, and she found herself deep in credit card debt and struggling to pay bills. In 2009, Fitton founded a company called OneForty. Originally conceived as an app store for Twitter, it morphed into a social media guide for business. Attracting clients such as Virgin and CitiBank, OneForty raised more than $2 million in venture capital.

Fitton's is the ultimate Web 2.0 success story: a driven entrepreneur achieves financial independence solely through her use of social media. Self-branding functions as a culmination of all the dynamics discussed in this book: the production of knowledge as a commodity, the belief that status is something better achieved than ascribed by the group, and the idea that micro-celebrity is something better ascribed than achieved. Fitton's knowledge consisted of knowing who "mattered" and where they would be gathered. Her status was achieved through her accomplishments: not only enormous numbers of Twitter followers, but also publications, speaking gigs, and her own successfully funded company. And her micro-celebrity was ascribed and legitimized with a public stamp of approval from celebrities like Kawasaki, who boasted significant business experience. Fitton's persona-brand, Pistachio, was literally a "thing" separate from her everyday understanding of herself.

Fitton's story is extremely unusual, but Web 2.0 experts and self-branding consultants attest that it is consummately achievable. The key element? Self-branding. The idea of turning yourself into a brand is now presented as an essential Web 2.0 strategy, and is firmly instilled in modern business culture. Self-branding has become popular at a time when brand creation is championed as a solution to all sorts of business problems, such as a lack of competitiveness, a failure to stay up-to-date, and ineffective communication.

As a result, a wide swath of social organizations—including countries, ethnic groups, and the military—have adopted branding techniques.[1] The personal brand extends to individuals the philosophy and tactics of contemporary "promotional culture," in which information, economics, and persuasion are inextricably linked.[2]

## What Is Self-Branding?

In August 1997, on the cusp of the dot-com boom, Tom Peters wrote an article for internet-gold-rush magazine *Fast Company* called "The Brand Called You." Apart from Peters's mention of his new CD-ROM, the article reads as if it was written in 2009 or 2011.

> The main chance is becoming a free agent in an economy of free agents, looking to have the best season you can imagine in your field, looking to do your best work and chalk up a remarkable track record, and looking to establish your own micro equivalent of the Nike swoosh. Because if you do, you'll not only reach out toward every opportunity within arm's (or laptop's) length, you'll not only make a noteworthy contribution to your team's success—you'll also put yourself in a great bargaining position for next season's free-agency market. The good news—and it is largely good news—is that everyone has a chance to stand out. Everyone has a chance to learn, improve, and build up their skills. Everyone has a chance to be a brand worthy of remark.[3]

This concept was a response to several social changes: the success of huge corporate brands, the rise of project-based work cultures and entrepreneurial labor models, and the gradual popularization of the internet. As Peters explained, the web made it possible for anyone to have a website, and brands distinguished mediocrity from quality. He advised readers to identify their distinguishing characteristics and write a fifteen-word statement differentiating themselves from their peers. He told workers to think of their skills using the "feature-benefit" model of major corporate brands: every feature generates a corresponding benefit for the customer, the employer. Peters instructed readers to ask themselves: "What do I want to be famous for? That's right—famous!"

This article spawned a slew of personal branding books—*Me 2.0, The 10Ks of Personal Branding, Authentic Personal Branding*—by new personal branding experts. Technology meetups continue to hold sessions on self-branding, and entire conferences, such as Brand Camp University and Brand Camp NYC, are devoted to the topic. Dan Schawbel, a personal branding guru, launched *Personal Branding* magazine in 2008. It comes out quarterly in PDF format and contains interviews with personalities like Vanna White and M. C. Hammer. In the wake of the 2008 economic recession, personal branding transcended white-collar consulting and technology, and became a popular career strategy for people in all industries.

Self-branding is primarily a series of marketing strategies applied to the individual. It is a set of practices and a mindset, a way of thinking about the self as a salable commodity that can tempt a potential employer. Self-branding, the strategic creation of an identity to be promoted and sold to others, has moved beyond its origins— the modern culture of creative, entrepreneurial labor in Silicon Valley and an association with the dot-com boom—to become a staple of career counseling and employment advice.[4] Self-branding, which would be impossible without the affordable means of information distribution that the internet provides, is intrinsically linked to the features of social media technologies that make self-promotion on a wide scale possible.

While founding a company or working independently certainly can be creatively fulfilling, this option isn't available to everyone. The most successful self-branders are white-collar professionals with creative or engineering capacities, or people selling goods and services over the internet. In other words, the Web 2.0 workers I interviewed function as the "proof" that self-branding, and entrepreneurial governance in general, works, but only in exceptional cases. Championing self-branding as a universal solution for economic woes demonstrates the disconnect between neoliberal ideals of identity—which emphasize self-improvement, responsibility for skill acquisition, and self-surveillance—and the reality of day-to-day life.

Most academics are quite disparaging of self-branding. They argue that practitioners remake themselves as products to be sold to large corporations, that they rely on an imaginary sense of what employers might want, and that they sully personal feelings and relationships with market forces.[5] Self-branding, while widely taken up in the tech scene, is inherently contradictory. It promotes both "authenticity" and business-targeted self-presentation. This incongruity creates tension and stress for practitioners, who must engage in emotional labor and self-surveillance to ensure an appropriate branded persona. The experiences of a young man named Ben, whom I met in line for a taco truck while outside a networking event at the San Francisco club Mighty, are illustrative. Ben told me that he struggled with self-branding strategies, because he was at an early stage of his career and hadn't figured out his main interests. He was barraged by advice to market himself and found it useless, but the continual emphasis on self-branding drowned out any other useful guidance.

Others told me that they disliked personal branding's emphasis on audience. Caroline McCarthy, a former C|Net tech journalist who by 2012 had thirty thousand Twitter followers, said "Honestly, for me, it's kind of scary because I don't want to be a brand pusher. I don't want everybody listening, but they are." Even in 2009 the term was such a cliché that when I interviewed Rdio employee April Buchert (now Walters) about her experience volunteering at an "unconference" called LaidOffCamp, she said, "A lot of personal branding [workshops] in the afternoon, which is one of the reasons I was so happy to be in the coat check. Because it was like 'Ahh, no thanks.'"

Bombastic blogger Stowe Boyd also had no problem criticizing the self-branding idea, which he compared to Freudian psychology and multitasking, two widely accepted ideas that in his opinion were invalid:

> The self-branding thing, the thing that you're treating yourself like you are a product, is a relatively new meaning that's only been around about 15 years. But, it's so embedded now into the American psyche. I mean, it's like Freudian psychology in the '50s. It's like you couldn't argue against it even though there was absolutely no evidence to suggest that it was true, that Freudian psychology had any therapeutic benefits. Self-branding is like that now. It's commonplace, you can't convince people that it's an un-useful metaphor because everyone takes it for granted.

Boyd's intelligence, hubris, and self-confidence come through in his easy dismissal of Freudian psychology and personal branding. He felt that the complete inundation of self-branding into his social milieu was an instance of the "emperor has no clothes." Stowe explained further on his personal blog:

> I don't buy the personal branding metaphor. Remember that metaphors are not "true" or "false": [they're] inductive. If the listener doesn't get it, or buy into it, a metaphor fails. For me, objectifying ourselves as products just rubs me the wrong way. I am not a product I am trying to sell. I am a person, and I want to be respected, listened to, influential. As I wrote earlier this week, it is ok to want to make a difference in the world, to influence others, and to take actions that make that more likely . . . It's only natural. But we can simply talk about reputation, authority, and influence, and drop the '90s personal branding mumbo-jumbo, now.[6]

Boyd thought the tech scene's wide acceptance of self-branding rhetoric was ridiculous. Not only did he believe it to be ineffective; he found the idea of self-commodification distasteful. But he recognized that these ideas had wide currency in the tech scene.

Such insider critiques are rare, perhaps because the industry is already saturated in the primacy of business language and philosophy. Overwhelmingly, San Francisco technology workers during the period I studied looked to self-branding as a powerful and necessary strategy. But self-branding should not go uncriticized; rather, it needs to be analyzed on both an individual and community-based level. That analysis should include an understanding of how the social becomes economic and vice versa. It should question how people describe the fantasy of personal branding, and how market-centered practices fulfill or neglect self-branders' needs. We must understand the concrete effects of self-branding—a neoliberal technology of subjectivity—on the practitioners themselves.

## Modeling the Self-Brand

Self-branding fits within technology culture's strong autodidactic tradition. Self-taught coding, hacking, or networking skills demonstrate inquisitiveness, drive, and intelligence. But in Web 2.0 culture, entrepreneurs rather than programmers provide models for social media success; building businesses, rather than software, is important.[7] As such, people have created entire careers by teaching entrepreneurial techniques to technology enthusiasts. Two examples are Gary Vaynerchuk and Tim Ferriss, independent entrepreneurs who thumb their noses at the status quo way of doing things while emphasizing self-branding and marketing. Vaynerchuk's and Ferriss's popularity in the tech sector—and they are very popular—derives significantly from their embodiment of the entrepreneurial ideal. Neither are programmers; instead, they are proficient at social media like online video, Twitter, and blogs. While both men are selling their personal approach to professional success to similar people, they resemble competing corporate brands.

Vaynerchuk is the founder of an online liquor store called WineLibrary.tv and a social media consulting company called Vaynermedia. He's written two best-selling business books, *Crush It!* and *The Thank You Economy;* has almost a million Twitter followers; and is a fixture on the conference circuit. Ferriss is a martial-arts champion, former CEO of an herbal supplement company, and author of three number-one *New York Times* bestsellers: *The 4-Hour Work Week, The 4-Hour Body,* and *The 4-Hour Chef.*[8] Both men have successfully positioned themselves as maverick self-starters who use lectures and books to teach others how to be successful financially and personally using social media. If Vaynerchuk is Pepsi, Ferriss is Coke.

Neither Vaynerchuk nor Ferriss are technologists, but their advice is targeted directly at the technology community. Ferriss said in an interview with blogger Derek Sivers: "I went after the audiences that read a handful of tech blogs in Silicon Valley. That was the niche I wanted because I knew that even though they represent a small number of people geographically, they are the loudest and most prolific online. By winning a fan base of 100 technophiles that spend most of their time online, then if people attack me online, . . . I would have other people defending it."[9] Ferriss strategically targets his work to members of the tech scene because they have online influence far beyond their actual numbers. The self-help techniques that Ferriss and Vaynerchuk advocate use social media invented in Northern California (Twitter, YouTube, Facebook) and reinforce concepts like meritocracy, independence, and entrepreneurship, which are highly valued within the tech scene and its global fan base. Ferriss and Vaynerchuk are self-improvement gurus in the tradition of Oprah, televangelists, and Landmark Forum facilitators, but they emphasize the technolibertarianism of Silicon Valley rather than therapeutic, Christian, or New Age principles.

Both Vaynerchuk and Ferriss teach readers to present an identity divorced from interpersonal relationships and social ties. Instead, the self exists in a competitive, insecure business environment, and acts primarily through social media.

## Gary Vaynerchuk

Everyone—EVERYONE—needs to start thinking of themselves as a brand. It is no longer an option; it is a necessity.

—Gary Vaynerchuk[10]

Gary Vaynerchuk's career began as a liquor store owner. Vaynerchuk, known throughout the tech industry as Garyvee, inherited Shopper's Discount Liquors from his father, and claims that he increased the store's yearly revenue from four to fifty million dollars in eight years.[11] To promote his business, Gary created a series of five-minute wine review videos called WineLibrary.tv, which concluded in 2011 after a thousand episodes. He pinpoints the video series as the start of "building his personal brand." The success of this series, along with his blog and Twitter stream, made Garyvee a sought-after speaker, owner of a social media consulting firm, and best-selling author (he received a million dollar advance on his seven-book deal with Harpers). He is known for his hyper, excitable stage presence and frequent use of profanity ("Social media doesn't mean jack shit").[12] He also claims to respond to anyone who e-mails or @ replies him.[13]

Gary is personable and charismatic and his aggressive methods have gained him many fans among aspiring entrepreneurs. He has almost 900,000 Twitter followers and was named by *BusinessWeek* someone "every entrepreneur should follow." *Crush It!*, the book that teaches the Garyvee method of success, debuted at number two on the *New York Times* bestseller list; despite tepid reviews (*Publishers Weekly* noted that "his unappealing swagger—repeated stories of how he crushed it and dominated grate particularly—gives his story more the tone of adolescent peacocking than of worthwhile and sober business advice"), it has a four-and-a-half-star rating on Amazon with 520 reviews. Vaynerchuk followed *Crush It!* with *The*

*Thank You Economy*, targeted at business owners. He crowd-sourced the cover design.

*Crush It!* is a slim book with large type (it's only 142 pages long). The book claims that great financial rewards will come to anyone who follows his or her passion and uses social media to broadcast about it. To Gary, a "passion" is what someone cares about the most, whether that be tortilla chips, worms, or marketing, all of which Gary advises turning into a personal brand and leveraging across all forms of social media including Twitter, Facebook, Tumblr, and YouTube. Vaynerchuk claims that anyone who creates outstanding content, about anything, will benefit accordingly, whether by commanding enormous speaking fees, getting paid for blog advertisements, or landing television interviews. He himself serves as a walking billboard that this method works.

Vaynerchuk doesn't advocate promoting a company, a product, or a service. He advocates promoting the individual; what the individual actually produces or does is secondary to his or her self-promotional skills. Unlike most self-branding guides, Vaynerchuk does not guide the reader through exercises or worksheets. Rather, he maintains that success will come if you work hard enough. While Gary has three maxims (love your family, work superhard [*sic*], and live your passion), the book focuses on the latter two, since he advocates working pretty much all the time:

> Live your passion. What does that mean, anyway? It means that when you get up for work every morning, every single morning, you are pumped because you get to talk about or work with or do the thing that interests you the most in the world. You don't live for vacations because you don't need a break from what you're doing—working, playing, and relaxing are one and the same. You don't even pay attention to how many hours you're working because to you, it's not really work. You're making money, but you'd do whatever it is you're doing for free.[14]

In the last quarter of the book, Vaynerchuk outlines a thirteen-point program that anyone can follow to achieve financial success. The reader should begin by choosing a passion and learning everything he or she can about it, "absorbing every single resource you can find." Like most personal branding gurus, Vaynerchuk advises buying a domain name and registering the same username at every social media site. He then tells readers to "start pumping out content."[15] "Content" is an industry term for what used to be called "writing" or "articles," but now includes blog entries, tweets, videos, audio, podcasts, and even profiles on social network sites. Once the reader has written a blog post or made a video, Garyvee tells them to spend hours on other blogs and on Twitter posting links to it. Vaynerchuk says "if that sounds tedious or repetitive, just close this book and go do your best to enjoy the life you've got because you're not cut out for this."[16] With all his talk of loving life and living with passion, Vaynerchuk is primarily advocating that self-branders create linkspam.

There's also the detail of actually making money. Vaynerchuk claims that with this method the "big fish will be jumping straight into your hands."[17] He suggests putting ads on your blog, getting on the lecture circuit, selling products, using affiliate links, writing articles, holding seminars, and "consulting." The chapter devoted to money-making is short (ten pages) and vague; Vaynerchuk earnestly explains that the best content will rise to the top and opportunities will somehow appear for anyone who uses this method. He believes that his own success story is easily replicated, and he cites celebrity blogger Perez Hilton and comedian Andy Samberg as role models—even though neither used these techniques.

It's debatable whether vague promises of financial opportunities are worth eliminating one's work-life balance. Vaynerchuk suggests that every social opportunity, including picnics and weddings, is a networking opportunity; tells readers to work at home between 7 P.M. and 2 A.M. after their regular eight to five job; and advocates focusing on the "hustle" over spending time with friends and family.

Anything insane has a price. If you're serious about building your personal brand, there will be no time for Wii. There will be no time for Scrabble or book club or poker or hockey. There will be time for meals, and catching up with your significant other, and playing with the kids, and otherwise you will be in front of your computer until 3:00 A.M. every night. If you're employed or retired and have all day to work, maybe you knock off at midnight instead. Expect this to be all consuming.[18]

Although Vaynerchuk repeats "love your family" as an essential part of success, time with loved ones is sandwiched between long stretches of time on Twitter. This also assumes, of course, that the person crushing it has someone else to do housework; isn't a primary caregiver for kids or aging relatives; doesn't go to the gym or therapy or AA meetings; has the stamina to subsist on minimal sleep; and doesn't value interests outside of work. Being your best, in Vaynerchuk's world, is being a marketable version of yourself twenty-four hours a day.

Ultimately, *Crush It!* suggests that if you aren't a success after doing all this late-night hustling, it is simply because you aren't working hard enough. Vaynerchuk warns, "Someone with less passion and talent and poorer content can totally beat you if they're willing to work longer and harder than you are."[19] Balancing "life" with "work," in Vaynerchuk's eyes, is simply laziness. He writes: "No matter how successful you get, you cannot slack off or the grass is going to grow, the paint is going to peel, and the roads will start to crumble. Stop hustling, and everything you learn here will be useless. Your success is entirely up to you."[20] This rhetoric places the onus of responsibility on the individual for financial success or failure. *Crush It!* tells readers that one's failure to achieve prosperity is never due to structural equality, a lousy economy, or stagnating wages; instead, it is the worker's fault. When taken to its logical conclusion, such rhetoric justifies the elimination of social services like unemployment benefits and welfare, if the only people who use them are lazy. The "Crush It" method also equates financial success with meritocracy. The affluent are so because they are better than everyone else. Unfortunately, neither of these presuppositions is supported by empirical evidence. Web 2.0's emphasis on pull-yourself-up-by-the-bootstraps entrepreneurialism is simply a rehash of conservative and libertarian sloganeering.

In reality, even if Garyvee's methods do generate wealth for some people, they are unsustainable for most. Vaynerchuk doesn't mention that "crushing it" requires, at minimum, a white-collar job and technical skills. Gary himself has unusual charisma and entrepreneurial spirit, and a multi-million dollar family business to fall back on. *Crush It!*'s methods systematically exclude women (who are the majority of caregivers), single parents, people with disabilities, and a whole host of others from "succeeding" using these tactics. (Does this mean they are just lazy?) Gary's extraordinary success has yet to be replicated by the legion of followers attempting to "Crush It" through homemade videos about accounting and real estate, most of which imitate Vaynerchuk's brash spirit. Gary's followers seem mostly to work in technology and marketing; it's apparently harder to "monetize" a passion for secretarial work, social justice, or community gardening than a passion for wine, entrepreneurship, or real estate.

Vaynerchuk renders the self an "it," a "passion," implying that "crushing it" is both fun and compulsive, that the worker has no choice but to "live" his or her passion. The worker's relentless self-promotional labor is thus naturalized and made invisible through the language of desire. The phantasm of "crushing it" is the latest in a long line of American fantasies of self-realization, from Dianetics to *The Secret*. What's new is the social media wrinkle. In Vaynerchuk's world, social media provides the means to broadcast one's self-promotion far and wide. Like most social media evangelists, Gary derides the one-to-many model of media and emphasizes talking to customers and networking with others. But in many ways these are just good public relations strategies, reworked to adhere to the norms of social media. There is no true collaborative, networked, or open-source culture to crushing it. Instead, social media becomes a way for frustrated white-collar workers to support themselves while working eighty-hour weeks. But his ideas are tremendously popular. This fantasy is clearly one that people want to buy into.

### Tim Ferriss: The 4-Hour Guru

I believe that life exists to be enjoyed, and that the most important thing is to feel good about yourself.

—Tim Ferriss[21]

*The 4-Hour Work Week*'s author, Timothy Ferriss, is the type of guy who brags about winning a gold medal in Chinese kickboxing by pushing his opponents off an elevated platform. Ferriss is an infamous self-promoter and a consummate personal brander (*Wired* named him the top self-promoter of 2008, which he promptly added to his official bio.) His first book, *The 4-Hour Work Week*, has been a bestseller since its publication, and his second book, *The 4-Hour Body*, debuted at number one on the *New York Times* bestseller list. (He also received a million-dollar advance from Amazon's new publishing imprint for *The 4-Hour Chef*, a cookbook/self-help amalgam published in late 2012 that describes Ferriss as a cross between Jason Bourne and Julia Child.) Ferriss's version of "hacking"—which he defines as getting the biggest result for the smallest amount of work—focuses on entrepreneurship, travel, and self-experimentation. His first book introduced the concept of the "muse," a product that generates plenty of income but requires little supervision, giving one enough time to pursue his or her passions: wakeboarding, visiting Asia, or learning gourmet cooking; in short, living the life of the "new rich." His *4-Hour Body* diet is popular among the technorati and endorses "body hacks" like nutritional supplements, ice packs on the back of the neck, and calorie-rich "cheat days" over regular exercise and a careful diet. He is an angel investor in a number of popular startups like Twitter and ReputationDefender, speaks frequently at conferences like Foo Camp and TED, and regularly appears in the media. He has a sporadic online video show with Digg founder Kevin Rose, where they discuss the minutia of everyday life.[22] Ferriss is currently promoting an exclusive, $10,000-ticket marketing conference called "Opening the Kimono" where he will reveal the secrets of his success.

Unlike Gary Vaynerchuk, who focuses on working more, Ferriss focuses on working *less*. The "4-Hour" in the titles of his books refers to the amount of time working, or working out, to achieve financial or corporeal success. His get-rich- and get-thin-quick techniques are tremendously popular online; he has more than 300,000 Twitter followers and 100,000 "likes" on Facebook, and he claims a million blog visitors a month. The *New York Times* followed him through South by Southwest and wrote, somewhat bemusedly, that "at nearly every turn, young bespectacled men with Silicon Valley dreams approach."[23] Each post on *Tim Ferriss's Blog* has more than a hundred comments from his (primarily male) supporters, like "I may be an expert but from Tim Ferriss there's always a new angle to learn from!" and "I'm going to see how I can assimilate your body language and style in general to public events." While his readers use him as a role model, Tim uses his blog community as a test market; he explained that his readers function as "open-source clinical trials to test the diets and the workouts."[24] He frequently asks for feedback and solicits testimonials from his fans. While his three books are quite different, the common threads are self-experimentation, "hacking," challenging conventional wisdom, and improving oneself.

*The 4-Hour Work Week* is replete with exercises and worksheets for the potential entrepreneur. Ferriss advocates living like a millionaire, making just enough money to take "mini-retirements," which involve trips to foreign places to wholeheartedly pursue hobbies and activities. He also advocates a process called "dreamlining," which involves brainstorming goals like the adolescently masculine "own an Aston Martin DB9" and "find smart and gorgeous girlfriend," and coming up with concrete plans to achieve them, which involves determining how much money these goals would cost. To pay for all this, Ferriss suggests leaving traditional employment and choosing a muse. In practice, his disciples tend to sell "information products" like weight loss e-books or DVDs about real estate speculation. The muse can only be self-sufficient with copious use of outsourced and freelance labor to answer customer e-mails, manufacture products, make websites, and do personal errands.

The book's emphasis on entrepreneurship is a reaction to modern anxieties over the rapid business transitions brought about by new technologies. Ferriss provides step-by-step guides to tools like Google AdWords, automated sales templates, search engine optimization, online shopping carts, and print-on-demand services so that readers can determine, test, and launch their muses. He describes people who take advantage of these tools to work remotely or start their own businesses as the "new rich" with control over "what you do, when you do it, where you do it, and with whom you do it," which he refers to as the "freedom multiplier."[25]

*The 4-Hour Work Week* is also a response to social anxiety over outsourcing and the loss of American competitiveness in the global economy. Rather than worrying whether one's job will be outsourced to Bangalore, Ferriss teaches readers to use virtual personal assistants (VPAs), workers in India who do errands and research for four to twenty dollars an hour, to deal with research tasks, customer service, and even relationships—Ferriss retells a writer's account of using a VPA to apologize to his wife. The affordability of these services is only possible due to the exchange rate and labor differentials between the United States and developing countries like India. Similarly, Ferriss encourages his readers to travel for extended periods of time to countries where the cost of living is significantly lower, like Argentina and Thailand. He writes, "If you can free your time and location, your money is automatically worth 3–10 times as much."[26]

The second step of Ferriss's plan, "E is for Elimination," is full of tricks to decrease workload, like eradicating small talk, refusing to attend meetings, answering e-mail only once or twice a day, and maintaining an "information-poor diet" by ignoring blogs and news sources to boost productivity to the point where the reader can actually work a "four hour work week." Obviously, the reader must have a white-collar desk job in management, marketing, or business, with plenty of phone calls, meetings, and e-mails to answer. His techniques are not so useful for people in service industries, manufacturing, or labor.

Instead of spending time on work, Ferriss believes in a life of constant self-improvement. While Ferriss does recommend splurging on a few big-ticket items that the reader really wants, he also advocates paring down personal property to simplify travel. He exemplifies the lifehacking philosophy "to live is to learn" and recommends that the new rich spend their time traveling, learning new languages and skills (he mentions martial arts, a variety of athletics, ballroom dancing, and Irish flute), doing service work, and volunteering.[27] This fantasy lifestyle of "continual learning and service" represents the idealism of technology workers—who emphasize experience, intelligence, and travel—taken to the logical extreme.[28] Notably, Ferriss does not account for romantic or family relationships; he assumes that the reader is single with a lifestyle unencumbered by a partner, children, or friends.

Ferriss's second book, *The 4-Hour Body,* is a mishmash of advice on corporeal activities like weight loss, sex, weightlifting, and recovery from injury. Ferriss's emphasis mirrors the tech industry enthusiasm for endurance athletics like marathons, triathlons, and long-distance bicycle rides, but he highlights body hacks and self-quantification, not typical fitness regimes of diet and exercise. While his slow-carb diet does eliminate junk food in favor of lean proteins and vegetables, Ferriss advocates that readers only work out for about an hour a week, put Saigon Cinnamon in their coffee, and take a daily "supplement stack" called PAGG made up of policosanol, alpha-lipoic acid, green tea flavanols, and garlic extract. In a scathing and very funny review, the *New York Times* wrote, "*The 4-Hour Body* reads as if *The New England Journal of Medicine* had been hijacked by the editors of the *SkyMall* catalog. Some of this junk might actually work, but you're going to be embarrassed doing it or admitting to your friends that you're trying it."[29]

Most of *4-Hour Body* is harmless, if ridiculous, but its ideas about women are problematic. Like a pick-up artist or member of the online "seduction community," Ferriss treats women as objects or trophies, every now and then tossing a bone to his female readers ("to the ladies, for whom peanut butter seems to be like crack, the tablespoon scoop should be no more than a small mound"). Other mentions of women are not so magnanimous:

> I met "The Kiwi" in Buenos Aires, Argentina . . . his obses-sion started when he saw a professional samba dancer in Brazil balance tequila shots on top of each butt cheek in a dance club. Lamenting the lack of similar scenes in his own country, he set off on a mission to isolate the best exercises to create buttocks worthy of tequila shots . . . In four weeks, he took his then-girlfriend, an ethnic Chinese with a surf-boardlike profile, to being voted one of the top 10 sexiest girls out of 39,000 students at the University of Auckland.[30]

This attitude—that women are the grateful subjects of male expert attention—is made the most explicit in a chapter entitled "The 15-Minute Female Orgasm." While most people's prurient interest would be aroused by the idea of a fifteen-minute-long orgasm, Ferriss really means that he is able to bring a woman to orgasm within fifteen minutes. He confides solemnly, "I was able to facilitate or-gasms in every woman who acted as a test subject."[31] The book includes detailed diagrams of a fully-clothed man kneeling over a half-naked woman, clinically rubbing her clitoris. Ferriss explains, "I'll explain this from the standpoint of a man, as that's what I am, meng."[32]

This example points to a much larger problem with Ferriss's approach; he universalizes a wealthy, white man's experience as a workable method for others. Certainly life would be easier for many people if they were wealthy, white, and male, but Ferriss does not even seem to recognize, let alone account for, his own privilege.

Thus Ferriss reinscribes white normativity and heterosexual male privilege into his instructions. He encourages social media enthusiasts to adopt a subjectivity that's very specific, very limited, and very privileged. To Ferriss, like Vaynerchuk, the self is also an "it," an attainable fantasy of life. The labor of self-improvement is made invisible by framing it as excavating a newer, better self.

## Learning a Neoliberal Ideal

Both *Crush It!* and *The 4-Hour Work Week* are instruction manuals for surviving without an economic safety net. Ferriss and Vaynerchuk assume that the changes that the internet has wreaked on industries like journalism and music are prescient of larger shifts in the American economy. They strongly advocate independence from corporate structures by encouraging people to start their own businesses. Both use the motivational language common to both neoliberalism and American self-help culture, extolling readers to imagine and bring about an ideal life. While in Vaynerchuk's world work is a passion and everyone can be an entrepreneur, Ferriss believes that constant self-improvement should be one's passion, with work existing only to pay for it. Since both Gary Vaynerchuk and Timothy Ferriss have legions of supporters who follow their instructions to the letter—their blogs contain hundreds of comments and video testimonials from grateful readers who found success using their methods—these techniques clearly work for some people. But both books present a fantasy life as realistic and desirable, and position strategic self-presentation within a commodity-based culture as the way to achieve it.

Moreover, both men present the professional male experience as normal, and anything else as an aberration, to the extent of describing tasks like childcare or dating as wastes of time. Vaynerchuk's advocacy of nonstop work is simply not realistic for people who want to live full lives. Derek Overby, for example, described how his nonstop use of social media created problems at home:

My wife came out and just said, "What are you doing? You're losing a connection with me and, more importantly, your kids." I was like, "Wow." That was eye-opening, like having to go to rehab or something. [Laughs.] Social media rehab. So I just kind of took a good look at it and said, "Maybe I'm going a little overboard." I was really trying to establish my-self within the circles, so I just toned it down a lot. So now I go home and I'll maybe stay up until 9:30 or 10:00, then I just shut it off and say, "I've got to have a real life, too."

Unlike many, Overby could rely on his partner to take care of their children so he could work late hours. Even with this support, the lack of separation between work and the rest of life, a common Silicon Valley ideal, alienated Overby from the people most important to him—his family. His compromise, working until 10 P.M., still makes it challenging to equitably participate in childcare or household duties. The unspoken assumption of *Crush It!* is that to have a family, a subservient partner is needed to do all that work. Ferriss does not even address family or relationships: instead he promotes a male fantasy of travel, ripped abs, and frequent casual sex.

Ferriss and Vaynerchuk may be easy targets, but they are superstars in the Web 2.0 world. If these are the type of men who are held up as icons, what does that say about the culture of the technology industry? I think Vaynerchuk and Ferriss are successful for two reasons. First, they uphold the values of the tech community by emphasizing passion, business success, self-improvement, and meritocracy. They do not criticize or interrogate anything that the tech community holds dear. Second, they evangelize tools developed by the tech community like blogs, Twitter, YouTube, online advertising, and so forth. Overall, both men emphasize Web 2.0's revolutionary impact on business, employment, the self, and even the body. This reinforces the Web 2.0 scene's sense of itself as uniquely special, smart, and socially revolutionary.

But the ideals furthered by Ferriss and Vaynerchuck are not revolutionary. While a worker is busy creating a self-brand, building an entrepreneurial self, monitoring Google Alerts, building a website, writing free articles for newspapers, giving free seminars, and doing various other forms of free labor, who benefits from her unpaid labor? In Ferriss's case, the get-rich-quick techniques he advocates can only be pursued by a few people before becoming unsustainable; not everyone can game Google AdWords.[33] The class position that these books assume, and with it assumptions about gender, race, and sexuality, go unmentioned in both *Crush It!* and *The 4-Hour Work Week* but are reinforced in *The 4-Hour Body.*

Regardless of how realistic or specific self-branding and self-commodification techniques are, they have been taken up enthusiastically by people in the technology industry and the distributed network of people who want to be in the technology industry. These ideas have trickled down and are being played out in interpersonal interactions both on and offline.

## Self-Branding and Web 2.0

It is no coincidence that self-branding is contemporaneous with the Web. Internet technologies have made it possible for people to apply sophisticated branding strategies used by modern multinational companies to themselves, and social media in particular has allowed individuals with internet access to broadcast to the world in an affordable way.[34] Perhaps due to its origins in the dot-com boom, self-branding has had a remarkably wide reach within the technology industry.

"I've kind of self-branded myself as a digital anthropologist," Ariel Waldman told me, "because a lot of what I do, and what I get paid to do, is [to] be actively involved in online interactions." Waldman had worked in several different areas of the technology industry, and the term "digital anthropologist" captured well her job skills, giving her a distinctive but easily understood title with which to market herself to potential employers. Similarly, I met a man at a conference who called himself a "change agent," which is similar to

WordPress employee Marianne Masculino's formal business title of "happiness engineer." These terms use advertising and marketing terminology to describe aggressively a set of skills and tasks in a catchy and appealing way that is easily consumable by potential employers.

Even people with more traditional job titles used self-branding strategies. Tara Hunt described herself as "an author, speaker, consultant, and marketing strategist, with a heavy focus on online strategy," as did Anu Nigam, who called himself a "serial entrepreneur and an angel investor." Both used enterprise language to mark themselves as modern workers in the high-technology sector. Hunt positioned herself above the average marketing drone by describing herself as an author, speaker, and consultant. Similarly, while Nigam called himself a "serial entrepreneur," a high-status term for someone who launches several successful startups, he had worked as a rank-and-file engineer for many of his former employers. These techniques—coining slogans to describe oneself and emphasizing the positive—are key parts of self-branding.

Because websites are affordable compared to television or newspaper advertisements, which are prohibitively expensive for most individuals, many tech enthusiasts have recognized them as a way to participate more effectively in an attention economy. Tantek Çelik explained why he owns www.tantek.com: "You're basically putting yourself on the same footing as a company. So that's status, right? Like companies have URLs. Well, I have my own URL. I don't need to have my Facebook or whatever, I have my domain." To Tantek, his dot-com domain let him occupy an online position equivalent to, yet independent from, a major consumer brand. Leah Culver agreed. "So if you can own your name, in that your first name associated with being a person is you, that's pretty good, right? Matt Mullenweg is really proud of this. He owns the top search results for Matt. His business card says go to Google, type in Matt, and press 'I'm feeling lucky.'" As self-branding expert Dan Schawbel writes:

As more people tune into media online, you have more of an opportunity to broadcast your brand and command exposure for your personal niche. That is not to say that if you appear on TV, the radio, or in print magazines, your brand won't gain exposure, but these expensive options are out of reach for most personal brands. The internet, by far the cheapest medium you can use to build an audience, is leveling the playing field.[35]

During the period of my study, Web 2.0 workers, well aware of the significance of global technology brands, used internet technology to reconfigure themselves into brands with the same potential significance as those produced by corporations.

People in technology agreed with self-branding consultants that a successful personal brand involves a distinct username (like garyvee or, in my case, alicetiara), multiple social media accounts, the distribution of content using the internet, and the promotion of this content using social media.[36] My informants concurred that potential personal branders should at least have a central web presence. Leah Culver summarized, "So the personal branding includes your domain name and your blog and if you do projects, a list of projects that you worked on and here's the link to my projects." Julia Allison gave a workshop on personal branding at the Learning Annex in which she laid out a website structure including sections called Meet Me, Work with Me, E-mail Me, Social Media Links, Blog, Articles, Videos, Press, Recommendations, and Best Of.[37]

The internet makes it possible to disseminate this personal information on an exponentially greater scale than in the past. Online, average Americans can distribute content globally, instantly, and cheaply. Before the internet, a prospective self-brander was limited to putting up fliers at grocery stores, knocking on neighbors' doors, buying advertisements in the local paper, or attending potentially inaccessible industry-only events. None of these techniques could reach more than a limited local audience. Self-branding books still advise people to create traditional self-promotional material like resumes, portfolios, and newsletters, but the internet makes distribution of this content inexpensive and simple. Self-branding involves not only creating an image of oneself, but also making that image visible to others. Even if their content is only viewed by a handful of people, self-branders argue that their potential audience is in the millions.

This networked visibility promises practitioners fame and wealth on a global scale. Venture capitalist Anu Nigam explained the process by which people used Twitter and blogging to advance their careers:

> There's a lot of people out there trying to get attention and trying to be famous. And that's just what's happening as technology enters the mainstream and now it's become a worldwide thing where the brand matters. Actually, that's what blogging has done. In general, if you write a book too, it's brand identity and people are paying for your brand now. They're paying for you to write. They're paying for you to join, when they hire you there, they want your skillset and they also want to tell everyone.

My informants agreed that self-branding was a career-benefiting move. When the financial software company Intuit hired Tara Hunt, who had built a strong reputation using Twitter and her blog *HorsePigCow*, they accessed her extended network of fans and followers, and made themselves look savvy for hiring a well-known social media user.[38] For freelancers, contractors, or consultants, self-promotion was necessary to find a steady stream of clients.

Creating and distributing online content was seen as way to create expertise without holding a professional job in a desired field. I asked Veronica Belmont how she would advise someone to make it big in San Francisco. She responded:

> Looking for a job in your industry, whether it's podcasting or blogging, I always suggest that people start their own

podcast or start their own blog, and just write about the things that they are really passionate about and that they really love. That way there is something to fall back to, when they put their resume out there, they can say, "Look, I've been covering the subject for two years now in my personal blog and I'm obviously versed on the subject." I think that goes a long way on getting jobs and with getting your name out there.

Belmont mirrors the language of "passion" when describing her job. In practice, this method could work out, as social media presence can substitute for a job title or company affiliation (although this is not necessarily the case outside of Silicon Valley). Megan McCarthy explained:

Silicon Valley is very forgiving of strangers who just show up at the doorstep. I mean, you can have any hook whatsoever that gets you in. The company you work for can do that like if you're with a hot startup, like if someone is like, "Oh, I work for Digg." You instantly say, "OK, that's that type of person." It sort of gives you entrance or a membership in a tribe, almost, but you can also create your own legitimacy. You can just start blogging every day, like "Hi, oh, I'm Megan. I write for My Blog," and then suddenly it's like, "Oh, OK, that's great. You're a blogger," and that makes sense to people.

As previously mentioned, McCarthy began her career blogging about tech parties on *Valleywag* for a few hundred dollars a month and is now a full-fledged technology journalist and editor despite her lack of formal training. McCarthy's affiliation with a well-known technology brand opened doors for her, but this legitimization can also be done with a personal blog.[39]

The technical features of social media reward attention, making the potential audience clearly visible to the user by turning ephemeral status or reputation information into quantifiable metrics, such as blog analytics, number of Facebook friends, or Twitter followers. Comments, references, Facebook "Likes," and Twitter @replies indicate the user's value, rewarding the ability to provoke the awareness of others. Within self-branding ideology, success intrinsically involves the actions of others, thus marking status through visibility and attention. These metrics for "success" differentiate self-branding from business-oriented self-help guides like Dale Carnegie's *How to Win Friends and Influence People,* published in 1934. Self-branding presumes that the broadcasting and connective capacities of Web 2.0 technologies make the subject available and intelligible to others. It is both this visibility and the presence of a network that make self-branding seem possible.

### In the Scene

Beyond social media, successful Web 2.0 entrepreneurs had to promote and maintain their personal brands in everyday interactions as well. The culture of personal branding was reinforced and replicated in these moments, further cementing the necessity of the strategy. Sarah Lacy, a technology journalist whose first book, *Once You're Lucky, Twice You're Good,* was about 2.0 culture, explained: "I think being Sarah Lacy the reporter is blogging, is doing my show, you know, going out and reporting, going to dinners. I think having to be Sarah Lacy the brand is being on TV, being on radio, giving speeches, going to parties, being visible, being out there." In practice, there is little discernible difference between self-branding and self-promotion. Lacy saw self-branding as distinct from actual work, which she understood to be "writing and creating content." She promoted "Sarah Lacy the brand" by speaking at conferences, networking, and doing media appearances to get plum assignments and drive book sales. This tactic is explicitly advocated by self-branding experts like Garyvee. For instance, Dan Schawbel's *Me 2.0* advocates writing personal press releases "to announce one's brand to the world," inculcating personal relationships with bloggers to encourage link-backs, and contributing to publications to reinforce an image as an expert.

In person, the most widely practiced self-branding skill was networking. Networking was ever-present during my time in San Francisco; each week brought a flurry of tech industry events with the primary goal of meeting other industry workers.[40] At these events, "everyone talks about work, not personal stuff," I was told at a Lunch 2.0 event. Networking requires comfort with small talk, the ability to chat with anyone, and the talent to connect people with others whom they might want to meet. The typical networking interaction takes place between two people. The opening gambit is often "Who are you with?" meaning "What company do you work for?" This triggers the "pitch," a summary of one's business in thirty seconds or so, which ends with an action item like "we're looking for funding," or PR, or engineers. (People were remarkably candid about looking for venture capital.) Each person pitches the other, and the two spend a few minutes identifying and discussing commonalities, followed by exchanging cards and often ending the interaction by brokering an introduction to someone else.

The self-branding angle comes with the ability to successfully pitch to other people. Pitching "off book" (with a memorized "hook") was absolutely necessary to network successfully. Here are some examples of pitches I heard:

> We create a social mesh where people feel connected to each other with similar taste.

> My job is to help people find interesting stuff on the Internet with very little effort.

> It's like Twitter, but for video. We have a launch event next month.

These pitches came from the founders of tiny startups; for entrepreneurs, the personal brand was aligned with their small company. For freelancers, the pitch statement was the personal brand. I had to learn my own pitch to be comfortable in networking environments. Without a pitch, conversation doesn't flow smoothly, determining commonalities is impossible, and the other person often becomes uncomfortable. My pitch went something like "I'm a Ph.D. student studying how people use social media to increase their status. I'm investigating self-branding, micro-celebrity, and lifestreaming, and I'm looking for people in the industry to interview." Creating this pitch took four or five months of practice.

Business cards are a physical instantiation of the personal brand. At networking events, people exchanged cards if there was even the slightest chance that they might be mutually useful (I returned from fieldwork with several hundred business cards). Business cards sometimes carried fanciful titles like "Director of Awesome" or "Mac Daddy," but many people gave out personal cards designed to work with their brand identity. For example, one business card contained links to an individual's website; Twitter, Facebook, and Skype accounts; e-mail; phone; and address, all using the same internet nickname. I was given a card at South by Southwest 2008 that read: "Hello, my name is Kathryn Finney, aka "The Budget Fashionista," aka "America's Best Shopper," aka "The girl with the cool shoes." I write a blog, which led to a book, which led to lots of TV, which led to a blog network. Email me at [e-mail address] or visit thebudgetfashionista.com. Happy Shopping." The card is hot pink with a simple sans-serif font, succinctly conveying Finney's brand: a friendly, frugal fashion guru with a budding media empire.

A final necessary component of self-branding was brand monitoring. Some people set up Google Alerts that e-mailed them whenever their name popped up online, or used Twitter and third-party software like TweetDeck to track how often they were @replied or re-tweeted. Others spent hours on Facebook, Flickr, or Google tracking search results for their name. Glenda Bautista, then head of product for video at AOL, describes this process: "Your personal brand is being affected by—your online identity is being developed by people around you. And again like it kind of touches on the point where I say, you know, 'it's not really within your control.' You constantly have to police yourself. You constantly have to police other people, police your friends. Like nag them to take photos down. It's exhausting." This brand monitoring becomes a form of labor that can be both emotional and taxing. It requires continually imagining oneself through the eyes of others, creating a "dual gaze" of internalized surveillance. Because most individuals developing a personal brand are connected to a networked audience in which their friends and family interact with their online presence, informants had to check on their friends' activities, like tagging photos on Flickr, TwitPic, Google Plus, or Facebook, to make sure that nothing they did in a social context showed up in more professional contexts.[41] This caused conflicts when better-known people felt that others were using them for increased brand recognition through affiliation, a process that Bautista called "flooding": peppering content streams with mentions of high-status individuals even if they were not really close friends. In following the advice of Garyvee and other branding experts, people would push to demonstrate relational ties between themselves and their audience, even when genuine intimacy and interest were lacking. Interpersonal relationships were intertwined with self-branding efforts, and the two often clashed.

### Maintaining the Edited Self

Social media technologies allow people to self-consciously construct images of themselves—the young executive, lauded entrepreneur, or glamorous television host. But the collaborative, networked audience of social media requires people to engage in unpaid labor to keep their brand image "pure." As Bautista noted, "People are in marketing here, whether they like it or not."

There are two points of view about how this came about. The first perspective, the technologically determinist view, implies that the technology itself dictates this type of self-presentation. It suggests some inherent property of contemporary social media technologies that promotes this enterprise view of the self. This view ignores the context in which technology is used; it is also empirically false since early social media like IRC (internet relay chat),

MUDs (multi-user dungeons), and Usenet allowed for similar interactions, but marketable self-presentations were largely absent. Instead, a sense of play and identity experimentation abounded in pre-Web internet spaces—something that is in short supply on sites like Facebook and strongly discouraged by self-branding.[42]

A second viewpoint, and one that is closer to my perspective, is that social media enables many different self-presentation strategies, and due to current social circumstances, many people choose self-branding. The Web 2.0 culture is responsible for the behaviors we see, not the technology. Self-presentation involves using advertising and marketing strategies to sell the self, and since internet media are accessible in a way that television or radio advertising is not, social media allows for a level of strategic, business-focused identity construction that would be otherwise impossible. It's true that technologies like Facebook and Google Plus systematically discourage identity play by linking a single, presumably authentic self to a body of verifiable information, creating a persistent identity. But in technologies like Twitter, which can be used for all types of self-presentation, having a good reputation, and being trustworthy and authentic, play such an important role in self-branding theory that Web 2.0 aficionados use it to construct a single constructed identity leveraged across multiple media types. This self is "authentic" (in that it is not openly false), marketable (in that it fits safely into current business culture), and in line with the values of "enterprise culture," which associates those skills most useful to modern business as positive moral values: that is, it rewards those who are entrepreneurial, positive, self-motivated, and who provide information-rich content.

In other words, social media allows people to strategically construct an identity in ways that are deeply rooted in contemporary ideas that the self is autonomous and constantly improving.[43] But it is Web 2.0 culture that encourages this behavior by advancing a particularly neoliberal conception of the "enterprising self," one that advocates the use of technology for identity creation and presentation. In social media applications and Web 2.0 culture, identity can be constructed, managed, and changed. Technologies let people choose strategically how they present themselves, from carefully selecting favorite artists for a Facebook profile to re-tweeting certain celebrities.[44] People imagine a self or a life and use social media technologies to bring this self into being. Want to be a cookbook author? Julia Child attended Le Cordon Bleu culinary school in Paris, taught students from her homes in France and Washington, D.C., and spent years testing recipes before attempting to write a book. *Mastering the Art of French Cooking* was rejected by Houghton Mifflin for being too long, and Child took several years to edit and revise the manuscript before submitting it to Knopf. Promotion did not begin until the book was finished.[45] Today, promotion, not cooking, is most important: start a food blog, make cooking videos and post them to YouTube, correspond with other food bloggers on Twitter, write newspaper and magazine articles, appear on television, and sign a book contract to write a cookbook.

In practice, most self-branding books and seminars begin with a series of exercises to define the personal brand, suggesting that everyone has an easily monetizable passion that needs only to be uncovered. Dan Schawbel in *Me 2.0* provides a "Personal Discovery Assistant" that helps readers "learn more about yourself, where you are right now, and where you want to be in the future."[46] In *Make a Name for Yourself,* Robin Fisher Roffer outlines a "Developing Your Brand Description" worksheet, which encourages readers to fill in the statement "I'm [my brand] because [justification]" as a way of identifying their core values, passions, and talents within the context of a brand description.[47] These exercises imply that the reader is excavating a true, authentic self to present to an audience. Of course, the reader is "uncovering" only potentially profitable interests.

The second stage of self-branding is goal-setting. Ferriss calls this "dream-lining," "an exercise in reversing repression" whereby the reader lists five things he or she dreams of having, being, and doing.[48] Roffer agrees, saying that "every respected brand has very specific objectives" while Catherine Kaputa of SelfBRAND LLC claims that "without a tactical plan your success is left to chance."[49] Like Pepsi or Microsoft, self-branders should set concrete goals.

Finally, readers are told to connect these two steps by strategically creating an audience-targeted identity. The blog *The Art of Self-Branding* suggests asking close friends and relatives to describe you in three words.[50] Julia Allison told her audience to prepare five documents:

1. Full bio: Write as if someone was writing a profile of you
2. One page: Narrow down; three or four paragraphs; who you are, what is your brand
3. Elevator pitch: 30 seconds
4. 140 characters: Appropriate for Twitter
5. Tag line: 2–3 words, e.g., Joe Blow, celebrity architect

Self-branding practitioners identify their strengths and goals and use advertising and marketing techniques to frame themselves for a potentially lucrative audience. Drawing from slogans, celebrity profiles, and public relations material, people are told to choose certain traits and experiences to show the public. Personal brand advocates advise acolytes to use social media to promote this newly created personal brand to potential clients, employers, and fans. Schawbel writes that people get "discovered" every day on social media; this is echoed by Gary Vaynerchuk who claims that the "best" expert in any field will be recognized and legitimated by mainstream media. Not only is this self the most easily marketed; it is strategically edited to appeal to potential customers and clients.

### Laboring, Emotionally

While Web 2.0 ideology promises that self-branding is a means to find personal fulfillment and economic success, it explicitly instructs people to create and project a self-conscious persona—one that makes the world think they are entrepreneurial, knowledgeable, positive, and self-motivated—using tools drawn from commercial advertising. I call this persona the "edited self." The edited self requires real work to maintain. This edited self must remain business-friendly and carefully monitored, despite social media culture's advocacy of transparency and openness. The edited self is an entrepreneur whose product is a neatly packaged, performed identity. When people use social media to self-brand, they are encouraged to regulate themselves along the well-trod paths of enterprise culture, regardless of how much unpaid time this effort might require.[51]

In one way, this type of labor evolved from a long line of other types of unpaid work. The term "fan labor" was first used in cultural studies to discuss the myriad of activities undertaken by fans of shows like *Star Trek*, which included discussing episodes online, organizing conventions, and producing feature-length films.[52] Theories of fan labor extended the idea of an "active audience" to show how fans engage in productive activities that financially and culturally benefit the creators of the original film, book, or television series. Following fan labor is "immaterial labor," a concept framed by Marxist-influenced cultural historians. Maurizio Lazzarato defined the term as "the kinds of activities involved in defining and fixing cultural and artistic standards, fashions, tastes, consumer norms and . . . public opinion."[53] This definition of "labor" would include tagging Facebook photographs, posting status updates on Twitter, and contributing to Wikipedia. Related is "affective labor," the positive benefits that people derive from these acts within a community, whether these are increased social status, intimacy, reputation, prestige, or self-satisfaction.[54] Others think of participation in social media frameworks, particularly commercial frameworks, as another kind of labor: through participation, the value of these sites is created and extracted, in the form of user data, viewings of advertisements, or click-throughs.[55] Many scholars consider this exchange uneven, and view "user-generated content" or "participatory culture" as a form of exploitation by the social software and culture industries.[56]

While free labor has become a mainstay of digital communities, it is important to look at how this manifests in social software as "emotional labor." In her book *The Managed Heart*, Arlie Hochschild defined emotional labor as that which "requires one to induce or suppress feelings in order to sustain the outward countenance that produces the proper state of mind in others."[57] Emotional labor is a type of performance integrated into the nature of the job itself. For example, a hostess at a gourmet restaurant must, with her mannerisms, facial expressions, and the tone of her voice, embody the overall image of the chef and the food as well as extend seemingly genuine care to her customers. This type of forced behavior for a desired emotional affect occurs in varying degrees down the food chain of service work, as Deborah Cameron describes in her study of call center workers, who are required to evoke "smiling," sincerity, and confidence while on the telephone with customers.[58]

Web 2.0 enthusiasts engage in both immaterial and emotional labor to boost their popularity. This work requires revealing personal information, sometimes to the point of extreme discomfort or vulnerability; feigning and successfully performing interpersonal interactions; and creating a self that is simultaneously authentic and carefully edited. This self is immaterial in that it is digital, and emotional in that it involves using real emotional affect when presenting oneself and interacting with others. Self-branding, for instance, necessitates the careful construction of an edited yet authentic self, which demands ongoing self-monitoring, a thick skin, and an ongoing awareness and evaluation of the audience.

Many informants told me that there were significant negative emotional costs to self-branding, including anxiety, information overload, lack of time, and hurt feelings due to audience comments and interactions. Constantly monitoring one's actions and maintaining a "dual gaze" was often exhausting and time consuming. Keeping up with the sheer amount of work that self-branding requires means neglecting other aspects of life. I asked Overby how he managed information overload:

> Not very well. I do what I can do . . . I used to be so worried about it that I didn't get back to people. There're still people

that I haven't contacted since I got back from South By. And I feel really bad about that but I still have a job that I have to do and my side projects. I have to put my priorities in line. I have a family. I have two young children. So I have to do what I do. I spend a lot of nights up until midnight or 1:00 in the morning. So I don't get a lot of sleep. But I try to do as much as I can and then at the end of the day, you just have to hope that people understand that you're only one person.

Lacy admitted that she worked all the time, which differentiated her from her peer group of reporters. "For me, this is my entire life and I am fine with it being my entire life. I don't have any balance and there are just very few people who are willing to do that." Hunt agreed: "One [requirement for success] is a super-drive. Focus on that thing and focus on that thing only. You can't be all over the place. You are focused and obsessed with that one thing. You start up your idea so you can work 14 hours a day. You deny yourself sleep and a social life, and all that stuff. And you just focus on it." These comments reflect Garyvee's ideal of the constant hustler, a neoliberal subjectivity through which people organize themselves and their lives according to market principles. Interestingly, both Ferriss and Vaynerchuk use emotional, affective language to evangelize particular types of labor: think of "following your passion" or "crushing it." Just as one's peers determine what makes an interesting Twitter feed and *Valleywag* polices the right type of micro-celebrity, self-help gurus script what the "right" sort of affect looks like for social media users looking to capitalize on self-branding. The net effect of this policing is that self-branding, which requires both immaterial and emotional labor, has been both naturalized and gendered.

Several informants confessed that negative comments or e-mail "flames" from audience members had upset them or even made them cry. Even people who claimed that negative comments didn't affect them had developed coping mechanisms. Adam Jackson said: "I announced after that I'm going to start tagging negative comments and I'm going to turn it into a blog one day. So I did a hash tag,

'#Dick.' So from now on, when I get just a really asinine comment I'll re-tweet it and hash tag it '#Dick.' So now when someone says, 'why are you so bitter over Twitter?' I'll just send them that to that hash tag and they can see all of that negative crap I get." Ariel Waldman turned to her friends who had gone through similar things to ask for help. "[Sex blogger Violet Blue] just goes through a lot of shit online and so she's become kind of this veteran of . . . whenever I'm going through, I guess, drama online of any sort, I kind of look up to her because she's somehow weathered it." People also found ongoing self-surveillance to be anxiety provoking, because they were engaged in a continuous loop of measuring themselves against an audience. As Glenda Bautista said, "A lot of my own anxieties have been developed by online judgments."

Authenticity, as it is described in self-branding culture, is something absolute that can be found through self-examination, or perhaps through filling out workbook exercises. Authenticity is viewed as real, unqualified, and biological or even genetic. Vaynerchuk says: "Your DNA dictates your passion—whatever it is that you were born to do; being authentic, and being perceived as such by your audience, relies on your ability to ensure that every decision you make when it comes to your business is rooted in being true to yourself."[59] This suggests that each person has an intrinsic value based on their possession of a singular, intrinsic, and moreover, marketable skill; it also implies that success is wrapped up in a sense of the "authentic self"—which, as discussed elsewhere, is a social construct. Putting it all together, this suggests that what is truthful or authentic is what is good for business. These are not values that are somehow inherent in internet technologies; rather, they are traditional market values that have been mapped over a new application: social media.

The myth that the personal brand represents the authentic self is belied by the need for constant monitoring. While micro-celebrities are supposed to reveal personal information to seem authentic, self-branders are encouraged to edit private moments in the name of brand consistency. Many people have been fired from their jobs for truly authentic actions that they broadcast through social media—such as drinking alcohol, doing drugs, talking about politics, or having sex—because these actions do not fit a "businesslike" image. Thus personal branding books simultaneously tell people to "be themselves" while setting up a framework in which self-presentation is regulated and surveyed. Julia Allison advised her seminar audience that "if your brand doesn't match up with who you really are, people will smell it"; she feels that she must disclose her use of hair extensions and plastic surgery or her audience will criticize her for being "fake." At the same time, Allison bemoans that other people have labeled her an "oversharer" and a "famewhore" because she did not define herself well enough. Even while trumpeting authenticity, Web 2.0 enthusiasts generally accept the idea that one should self-censor online.

Thus self-branding contains a paradox: if one's projected self is both "authentic" and "businesslike," the assumption becomes that people never do anything that would be considered unbusinesslike, illegal, or controversial in any way. As Tantek Çelik summarizes: "For so long, there's been this conservative assumption of authority. In other words, if you have authority or are in authority, you must be socially conservative, which is . . . merely a consensual assumption. There is no actual reason for it to be true at all." Self-branding is not a reflection of actual life. It is about constructing a strategic self-image to appeal to a particular audience and furthering that image through every online and offline action. Clearly, there are a few occasions when the "authentic" self will be entirely acceptable as a business self; this is because we still have clear distinctions between acceptable behavior in social life and acceptable behavior in the workplace. If the Web 2.0 self is one that must be both entirely transparent and entirely business-oriented, that self cannot logically exist. Furthermore, this elimination of long-standing divisions between corporate life and social or home life is a myth—but even trying to blend the two requires a great deal of time, effort, and affective output. Those struggling to make it happen often feel discouraged from engaging in any nonbusinesslike behavior so they can minimize the amount of intrigue or labor that is required. They try to avoid "not safe for work" situations all of the time, to the detriment of their real-life relationships and emotional health.

I observed two other serious drawbacks to self-branding and online promotion. The first was the risk of being fired by a more traditional company for engaging in self-branding. Although self-branding advocates maintain that everyone will need to engage in self-branding in the future, at many companies the interests of the entrepreneurial self do not line up with the interests of the enterprise. One acquaintance was fired for doing freelance work on the side, which her company considered "spreading herself too thin." Ariel Waldman left a job after the organization asked her to stop talking about personal things in her Twitter stream, which she also used to promote company business. And in 2010, entrepreneur Jason Calacanis posted a diatribe against hiring "job-hoppers," who exemplify the freelance, self-interested worker. He instead argued that startups should hire people willing to work for low salaries and long hours with the promise of equity.[60] It seems from these examples that there is an instability in the relationship between personal branding philosophies and corporate America. The ideal of having all workers be independent actors who can flourish without ties to larger corporations is a mythic element of neoliberalism rather than a reality. Even so, the economic downturn, with its mass firings, has made it difficult to generate the kind of company loyalty that Calacanis would require.

The second danger is coming off as too self-promotional and therefore narcissistic or uninterested in others. There is a sense, especially with regard to technologies like Twitter, that the service's "proper" use is to share personal information with others. Using the channel as a one-to-many method of broadcast advertising is viewed as bad form and an indicator of low status.[61] As mentioned in the discussion of ascribed versus achieved celebrity, while tech insiders may look down on people using Twitter to unashamedly spread content, the ability to amass huge numbers of followers does open doors (or at least it did while I was doing research). Additionally, many people enthusiastically follow the teachings of Vaynerchuk, Ferriss, and their ilk, and support each other in achieving their goals. To those people, having large follower accounts and success-fully self-promoting is a worthwhile goal. But to high-status mem-bers of the tech community, blatant self-promotion is déclassé and very uncool.

Although the social media scene is highly capitalist and involves an immense blurring of the lines between work and self, the com-munity's adherence to self-branding mechanisms is not a wholesale acceptance of status quo economics. Rather, the valorization of independence and entrepreneurialism documented in self-branding literature was used by my participants not to embrace life as entre-preneurs within the enterprise, but to reject the enterprise in favor of freelance, consulting, or startup work cultures.

Indeed, much of this self-production of the neoliberal subject is pleasurable for the subject; it would not be so widespread if it wasn't. During the dot-com era, Michael Goldhaber gave a speech at a Harvard conference on digital economies in which he stated that "having attention means having recognition, identity, and meaning in the eyes of those around you. It provides sustenance to spirit, mind and body, in just about any form."[62] The pleasure involved in pursuing self-branding strategies comes partially from having peo-ple pay attention: being read, getting @replies, and receiving con-ference invites have real affective benefits. Moreover, the exhilarating pursuit of self-realization is the new American Dream of indepen-dence from a boss or an office. The dot-com era's emphasis on cre-ative workplaces, while partially a rhetorical and strategic move to justify long hours and low benefits, still created physical spaces and workers that differed from those that had come from the top-down management strategies of the 1960s. In the social media scene, working for any large company, even an "enlightened" one like Google, is lower status than self-employment; the ideal neoliberal subject is decoupled from multinational corporations. For many of my infor-mants, the freelance lifestyle did create real satisfaction (and financial success), particularly when coupled with small business ownership.

It is a mistake to see a critique of self-branding as a value or moral judgment on capitalism overall.

Many contemporary critiques of neoliberalism stem from Marxist beliefs in the alienation inherent in industrial labor models. In this model, the worker is alienated from the products of her labor, and the work itself lacks a "sense of meaning."[63] But according to Marxist traditions, what defines humanity is the "capacity for creative labor."[64] Although the neoliberal, freelance model of the independent agent has its drawbacks—lack of job security, benefits, and stability—it provides many practitioners with a sense of agency and creativity. And even though the self-branding ideology oversells the ability for most people to engage in this type of work, it is a mistake to presume that it never provides self-actualization.

My informants were perhaps the people most positioned to find neoliberalism pleasurable. They—and others like them—have been championed by local governments as a solution to economic troubles and held up as role models. President Barack Obama tweeted, "This is a country that's always been on the cutting edge—and the reason is that America's always had the most daring entrepreneurs." New York City mayor Michael Bloomberg has poured enormous resources into encouraging entrepreneurship to benefit the local economy. But self-branding gurus advocate techniques that are inapplicable to factory workers, people in service positions, or simply people without access to technical skills and sophisticated personal networks. While Ferriss, Schawbel, Roffer, and Vaynerchuk claim that their strategies can be used by anybody, they are deeply rooted in white-collar professional culture. At Allison's personal branding seminar, I received the following card from a fashionably dressed woman:

> Makeup with MICHELLE
> Everybody has STAR Power!
> Michelle E. Thompson
> Design YOUR Best Face!!!
> ALL over Town . . .

TV, Film, Print, Stage, Brides & Private.
www.michelleinthecity@tumblr.com: BLOG [@ crossed out]
www.makeupwithmichelle.biz
[e-mail address, crossed out]
Text: [phone number]

Michelle Thompson had clearly followed the instructions in personal branding books to the letter: she had a Tumblr blog (advocated by many self-branding gurus since it is free and simple to use), but had printed her URL and e-mail address incorrectly on her business cards. Thompson's attempt to use social media as she had been directed made her seem amateurish. At the same time that personal branding is posited as an economic solution, it shifts the burden of stability, financial success, and advancement to the worker. Anyone who fails to achieve these things can be blamed for not "wanting it enough" or not working hard. But self-branding entails considerable work. The strategy spills into all parts of life more than does a forty-hour-a-week job, due to the overwhelmingly frequent need for maintenance and monitoring. And the anxiety, distress, and uncertainty felt by many of my informants have not been reported in the self-branding literature.

The use of social media to create a branded self is an example of enterprise self-regulation, or a "technology of subjectivity."[65] While Web 2.0 ideology advocates self-branding as a way to find personal fulfillment and economic success, successfully creating an "edited self" means trying to bridge the inherent contradictions between one's real-life behavior and the more restrained behavior required by workplaces. In other words, it requires engaging in immaterial emotional labor to maintain a business-friendly self-presentation while feigning an "authentic" self. It is not productive to criticize self-branding's emphasis on commodification just because it feels distasteful. As Adam Arvidsson writes in the preface to his book *Brands,* "to be critical of brands per se is about as fruitful as it is to be critical of factories or bureaucracies."[66] The problem is that self-branding, as a practical technique, is limited and will only be successful for a slim sliver of the population, yet it is being advocated as a universal solution to the economic downturn that can be adopted by anyone. Moreover, although my informants often found freelance project-based culture to be creatively fulfilling, they also were burdened by the stress of continuous self-monitoring—a burden that demonstrates the dissonance between neoliberal ideals and the reality of day-to-day life.

# LIFESTREAMING

---

## We Live in Public

The 2009 documentary *We Live in Public* told the story of Josh Harris, a late-1990s dot-com millionaire who funneled his considerable fortune into what he considered the future: people broadcasting their lives via internet-enabled closed-circuit television. Harris founded an internet television network with channels like "88 Hip Hop" and "Cherrybomb," but the technology was limited and only allowed for choppy, frame-by-frame video. When that venture failed, he built an underground bunker in Manhattan, filled it with television screens and cameras, and invited a collection of scenesters and technologists to move in. The bunker also included a shooting range, random cross-examination of participants, and plenty of recreational substances. (This experiment quickly devolved; the combination of drugs, alcohol, guns, and CIA-influenced interrogation techniques did not produce positive results.) Finally, Harris and his girlfriend fitted out their apartment with cameras, including one in the toilet, that broadcast to the web twenty-four hours a day, seven days a week. The website weliveinpublic.com included a forum where viewers could weigh in on the couple's activities and arguments. The relationship, unsurprisingly, did not last.[1]

Smith was eccentric, but his vision of the future has come to pass for a sliver of the population, especially in tech culture. Reality television, Skype, FaceTime, Twitter, Nike+, GPS-enabled cellphones, Instagram, Facebook, Spotify, YouTube, and hundreds of other media have popularized the capturing and broadcasting of personal information to large, networked audiences. While most of us don't live in apartments with bathroom cams, many of us have tablets or smartphones that make it simple to upload photos and micro-blog entries. The Pew Internet and American Life Project found that 88 percent of American adults own cell phones, and of those who do, more than half use their phone to go online. Of the 44 percent of adults with a smartphone, 90 percent access the mobile internet.[2] The influence of always-on internet has been rapid and significant. Texting, Facebook, and Twitter are used by teens to remain in nearly constant contact with friends, creating strong bonds of intimacy and togetherness.[3] Celebrities use Twitter to stay in touch with fans by strategically revealing insider information.[4] Web 2.0 folks intentionally reach out to followers to increase their visibility and social capital in the scene.

In the Introduction, I argued that social software may, inadvertently, promote inequality rather than countering it. In Chapter 2, I considered how metrics facilitate this process by rendering status into something that can be quantified, qualified, and publicized. In this chapter, I want to demonstrate how the process of "digital instantiation" likewise works toward quantification, qualification, and publicity by rendering users' lives in piecemeal fashion, unintentionally creating a whole that is larger than the sum of its parts. Social media tools digitize formerly ephemeral pieces of information, like what one had for breakfast, making it possible to create a bigger picture of a person or community's actions. Once "breakfast" is captured in a Foursquare check-in or Instagram photo, it can be combined, searched, or aggregated with other pieces of information to create mental models of actions, beliefs, and activities. Within this context, social surveillance, or the monitoring of friends' and peers' digital information, becomes normal.[5] While there are plenty of affective benefits to lifestreaming, there are also costs. Lifestreamers must see themselves through the gaze of others, altering their behavior as needed to maintain their desired self-presentation. This constant monitoring against the backdrop of a networked audience creates anxiety and encourages jockeying for status, even as it brings forth new forms of social information.

Looking at lifestreaming as a community property makes it possible to evaluate information disclosure beyond platitudes about privacy. If the authentic self of micro-celebrity is the self that discloses in the name of knowledge production, and the authentic self of self-branding is the one that edits in the name of knowledge consistency, how do individuals balance these competing notions of authenticity, avoid harsh social policing, and gain status for themselves within an information economy? Lifestreaming is worth studying because this is the terrain on which questions of authenticity and disclosure are currently playing out.

Framing lifestreaming in this way makes it easier to understand the prevalence of information disclosure within a social context where it is expected by peers. Rather than looking at social media use as an intrinsic privacy violation, lifestreaming needs to be understood as an act of publicity. Lifestreaming can be used to publicize knowledge; to gain emotional benefits, social capital, and information; or to shore up support in an argument, but it is rarely used as a way to disregard or eliminate privacy. Most lifestreamers have sophisticated understandings of what they would or would not share online. They balance their need for publicity with their desire to control their own online image. The necessity of presenting an edited self to the world requires a careful understanding of the risks and benefits of information sharing.

## Always On, Always Tracking

Awesomesauce is on tap for today: Venice casa hunting, Doomies
(omfg!!), Jumbo's (hello ladies), Coraline (ArcLight I <3 u)

At Seed for the second day in a row, repeating a
southwest burger. So good.

I dont want to jinx it but me and @seanbonner are 85% getting
the most amazing place right on the beach in
Venice #goaheadbejealoussuckas

Doomies was deelish. I hope he can raise $$ to re-open in a
good location

Off to ArcLight for Coraline. Jealous of everyone at the Grammy's!

Coraline was excellent. Moar 3D movies please!

—Partial Twitter lifestream from Tara Brown, 2/8/09

Lifestreaming is the ongoing sharing of personal information to
a networked audience, the creation of a digital portrait of one's ac-
tions and thoughts. People who lifestream use software like Twit-
ter, Facebook, and Foursquare to track information about themselves
and make it available to others. By networked audience, I mean the
real and potential audience for digital content, made up of people
who are connected both to the user and each other. Lifestreaming is
the "always-on" aspect of social media, the constant pings and alerts
that make smartphones so hard to ignore.

The term "lifestream" was coined by David Gelernter, a com-
puter science professor at Yale University. In a 1994 *Washington Post*
article suggesting possible future uses for the "information super-
highway," he wrote:

Your "lifestream" captures your whole life, in terms of chunks
of information: letters, documents, bills, bank statements,
video footage of your son's first birthday party, a database,

anything. Imagine a queue of documents laid out neatly on (say) the living room floor—only the queue might be tens of thousands of documents long, and it exists only as chunks floating in the void.[6]

A few years later, one of Gelernter's graduate students, Eric T. Freeman, developed software that organized files chronologically, creating a "time-ordered stream of documents."[7] Gelernter and Freeman envisioned a private, personal filing system that would help people organize their lives and memories.

Gelernter's vision of organized receipts and work documents has been realized in part, but contemporary lifestreaming is more expansive. Everyone who uses the internet has a detailed, persistent "digital footprint," created knowingly or unknowingly, actively or passively. Posting video footage of a child's birthday party to YouTube is active, while Google's tracking of every site its users visit without user input is passive.[8] Lifestreaming involves two processes, tracking personal information and broadcasting it to an audience, and most social media sites are designed to facilitate both aspects. Large sites like Facebook and Twitter serve as aggregators for niche sites like Spotify (music), Runkeeper (fitness), and GoodReads (book reviews), encouraging users to share data. Last.fm, for instance, has a plug-in for iTunes and Spotify that logs every song played, creating charts of top tracks and artists that can be displayed on Facebook, Tumblr, or personal blogs. Smartphone apps further assist users in tracking while on the go, often sharing information automatically.

The tracking aspect of lifestreaming is also called self-quantification, or "personal informatics." Self-tracking junkies monitor every aspect of their lives, from moods to sex life to temperature, often with the help of gadgets like the Withings scale (which tweets out your weight every week), the Fitbit pedometer (which wirelessly uploads your daily steps), and the Nike Fuel band (which tracks athletic output). There are a plethora of online tools for personal informatics, like Curetogether.com, which lets people compare their symptoms and find possible causes, and BedPosted.com, which encourages users to track their sexual activities. This data can be aggregated and analyzed using customizable online tools like Daytum, which can track anything from "rides to work" to "types of coffee consumed."[9] The *Quantified Self* blog collects information about this movement and holds meetups in seventy cities in twenty-six countries.

Many personal informatics enthusiasts are devoted to the idea of optimizing themselves and their environments for maximum happiness; in other words, applying engineering practices to everyday life. Self-trackers believe that self-monitoring and regulating one's behavior accordingly are conducive to self-improvement. The research psychologist Seth Roberts, for instance, has popularized self-experimentation as he tracks his own weight, sleep, and mood to formulate theories on weight loss and depression.[10] Others use digital media to create a personal archive, such as taking a self-portrait or writing in a journal every day.[11] These projects echo the work of artists like Eleanor Antin, whose 1972 *Carving: A Traditional Sculpture* displays four photos a day of her thirty-six-day weight loss, and Linda Montano, whose "living art" works can last up to seven years. Such work, however, never expressly tied quantification to monetization, whereas personal informatics frequently are connected to broader economic goals.

Tracking one's personal information is not a new concept. Diarist Samuel Pepys recorded details of his daily life for ten years. Samuel Johnson and Benjamin Franklin were both compulsive self-trackers: Franklin kept a chart chronicling his daily adherence to thirteen self-identified virtues such as frugality, chastity, and humility.[12] Keeping a diary, even a very detailed one, is a fairly common practice today. Former Senator Bob Graham, for instance, keeps color-coded daily logs of his activities that are so meticulous that they were admissible as evidence in government investigations.[13] And tracking food and exercise, or simply counting calories, is a common precept of weight-loss programs. What makes

the lifestream different from its paper predecessors is that lifestreamers use the internet to make this information widely readable.[14]

## Writing into Digital Being

Lifestreaming requires the digital instantiation of formerly ephemeral pieces of information. For instance, what Jim had for breakfast
is ephemeral. There is no permanent record of his cornflakes. Few of
us remember what we ate for breakfast last week, let alone years
ago. But once Jim digitizes this information by tweeting about it,
posting a picture of his cereal bowl, or carefully tracking his caloric
intake, his breakfast is written into (digital) being. Similarly, defining a relationship as "it's complicated" on Facebook categorizes and
codifies what may be a complex interpersonal interaction. The act of
classification is political and ideological.[15] The social digitization
encouraged by social media converts all sorts of nuanced interactions into cut-and-dried bits and bytes.

Lifestreaming is the sum of a person's digital parts, aggregated
and monitored by others. The "digital self" that results is composed
of particular types of information; it is a type of funhouse mirror,
casting certain aspects of life into sharp relief but obscuring others.
Lifestreamers can attempt to manage this self to create particular
impressions, but the presence of a networked audience makes this
challenging. Like self-branding, this management, if done "correctly," requires frequent, ongoing emotional labor. The lifestream is
not a direct reflection of a person, but a strategic, edited simula-
crum, one specifically configured to be viewed by an audience.

## The Networked Audience

The audience is a crucial element of lifestreaming, because lifestreaming without an audience is simply tracking. Lifestreaming
involves broadcasting personal data to other people, whether anyone with an internet connection or a subgroup of readers defined by
a privacy filter. In a social group of lifestreamers, people place

themselves as part of a networked audience in which participants are both sender and receiver.[16] Looking at the collective lifestreams of a group shows that players constantly reference each other, revealing a coherent picture of social actions and connections within a community. Furthermore, almost all members of the tech scene contribute to their own lifestream. These lifestreams make up the Twitter stream of people one follows, or the Facebook News Feed of one's friends. Thus as each person lifestreams a piece of content, they are simultaneously reading the content of others, commenting on it, and adding it to their mental picture of the scene. Audience members watch each other's actions by consuming their content, and by doing so formulate a view of what is normal, accepted, or unaccepted in the community. This understanding of audience creates an internalized gaze that reflects community norms. Members of the tech scene imagine how the audience will view their own lifestreamed self-presentation, and alter it accordingly. Monitoring of oneself and others thus becomes an expected and normative part of this social interaction.

I use the term audience rather than the public when describing viewers of a piece of digital content. The term "audience" can refer to the imagined audience, the actual audience, or the potential audience for one's content. But while "potential audience" resembles the vernacular sense of "public," I use "audience" here to mean the actual audience, the people interested in a piece of information who actually view it. Just as media professionals do not use the term "public" for people watching a movie or TV show, we should not use it for digital content. The use of audience also implies performance, because a lot of digital content is created with impression management in mind. While it is never possible to determine who exactly has or has not viewed something online, because the actual audience may be very different from what a creator imagines, keeping in mind the difference between publicity done for an audience and information made public will help us to understand some of the social dynamics described in this chapter.

The networked audience is distinct from the broadcast audience in that the networked audience is connected. The tech scene is a superlative example of the networked audience, because the social element is articulated both on and offline. Unlike many online communities where a small percentage of people create most of the content, people in the tech scene act as both content producers and consumers to maintain status and intimate ties with the community. Lifestreamers read others' lifestreams and create content with their audience in mind. Their online and offline lives are intrinsically interwoven, meaning that nonparticipation has real social costs.

The networked audience is distinct from the networked public, which danah boyd defines as the social space created by technologies like social network sites and the imagined community that thrives in this space.[17] While it is possible to describe a single site like Twitter as a networked public (although I would not do so), I think the term networked audience is more appropriate for lifestreaming. "Networked public" implies a set of people communicating through a single technology (MySpace, Usenet, and so on), while the networked audience moves across sites. Moreover, the concept of audience as explained earlier implies a specific set of people interested enough to view digital content rather than an amorphous mass of potential readers. Given these properties, what does lifestreaming look like in a social group that uses social media intensively?

## Lifestreaming in Practice

Lifestreaming is a normal part of the technology scene. People expect their friends to be familiar with the latest social media applications and to connect and engage using blogs, Twitter, and Facebook. As Auren Hoffman, CEO of the reputation management firm RapLeaf, stated in our interview: "If you were an employer, and someone applied and they didn't have any activity on social networks and that person was 23 years old, you'd think they were the Unabomber. You would be really scared to meet this person without even a bodyguard. I don't even know if that person exists." To people like Hoffman who are intimately familiar with Web 2.0 technology, not using social media marked unsophistication and backwardness. In Hoffman's view, the relationship of employer and worker requires the familiarity of common social ties and community involvement; nonparticipation would not only make it difficult to contribute to social and technological conversations, but also potentially limit one's economic mobility. Consequently most people I knew during this period used microblogging technologies, such as Facebook, Pownce, Twitter, and FriendFeed, to lifestream media consumption, location, digital pictures and videos, and the flotsam and jetsam of everyday life.[18] The availability of these streams to an audience varied by individual and service, from entirely publicly accessible Twitter accounts to password-protected digital files. Lifestreaming ranged from piecemeal aggregation like FriendFeed, a trendy piece of software that pulled in dozens of data streams to create a semi-comprehensive picture of what friends were doing across the internet, to personal blogs that dynamically aggregated day-to-day doings.[19] While I did meet people in the technology scene who used social media specifically to track personal data for self-improvement, they were a minority.

Proponents say this type of networked lifestreaming facilitates connections to others, deepens relationships, and creates a source of real-time information. Sharing information through services like Twitter creates an "ambient awareness" of others, a sense of what friends and acquaintances are doing or thinking that builds up over a long period of time.[20] This ambient awareness is akin to a sense of co-presence, even if the participants are not geographically proximate. At the same time, networked lifestreaming often creates anxieties about creating and maintaining one's social identity in front of an audience, and the extra layers of social information can result in intense social conflicts and arguments colloquially referred to as "drama."[21] Drama is "performative, interpersonal conflict that takes place in front of an active, engaged audience, often on social media."[22]

Drama can be a form of norm policing, where social media is used to call out community members who violate explicit or implicit social norms. While this definition of drama was formulated during a large-scale study of teenagers, it applies equally to other social milieus that display the same networked audience effects. Inferences and implications made visible by social media can reveal connections and actions that are usually tucked away from each other. These difficulties have given rise to a variety of different ways of conceptualizing the "public" and the "private" and of managing how information flows between different entities, websites, and users. This delicate balancing act is made even more difficult in a community where virtually everyone lifestreams.

## Benefits of Lifestreaming

Jessica Mullen experimented with lifestreaming for her master's thesis in fine arts, which led to "The Lifestreamer's Manifesto: A Life Design Methodology." It states:

> Utopian lifestreaming embraces living life in public. Utopian lifestreaming fills your needs by creating a life support system to guide the daily decisions that add up to form your life.
>
> 1. I will document my daily activities to work towards my goals, even when I fail to meet them.
> 2. I will gauge my health and resources with online tools instead of burying my head in the sand.
> 3. I will share my experiences with my community for feedback and accountability. I will observe the experiences of others and help where I can.
> 4. As my lifestream grows, my reputation and confidence will do the same.
> 5. I will find the invisible patterns and systems holding me back and publicly eliminate them from my life. I will profitably share my hard earned knowledge.[23]

Mullen's manifesto frames self-regulation as entirely positive, while people in other social contexts might view it as rigid or strange. This manifesto focuses more on the benefits of self-tracking than the public aspects of living, but two of Mullen's points are worth investigating. When she writes "As my lifestream grows, my reputation will do the same," she shows that lifestreaming contributes significantly to status. Her statement "I will profitably share my hard earned knowledge" points to the material and immaterial benefits of the lifestream. While some people have managed to profit directly from online self-presentation through advertising, sponsors, or sales, others use lifestreaming to build up the identifiable online persona that is a crucial part of micro-celebrity and self-branding. But lifestreamers identify many other benefits that are largely due to the involvement of the networked audience.

One of the most important benefits is the previously mentioned ambient awareness of others, or the development of "digital intimacy."[24] While Twitter is frequently characterized as a chattering stream of irrelevant pieces of information, these pieces of information, gossip, small talk, and trivia serve to create and maintain emotional connections between members of the networked audience. A study by Gina Masullo Chen found that the more time people spent on Twitter, the more they felt a sense of camaraderie and connection with other users.[25] Kate Crawford, in her valuable piece on Twitter and intimacy, writes: "The communicative modes of Twitter, and others like it, operate as disclosing spaces. The 'confidences' relayed in these spaces create relationships with an audience of friends and strangers, irrespective of their veracity. They build camaraderie over distance through the dynamic and ongoing practice of disclosing the everyday."[26] Crawford argues that it is the "small details and daily events" that give "a sense of the rhythms and flows of another's life."[27] Regardless of whether the details given are significant or even truthful, Twitter streams feel like listening to a voice. Crawford conceptualizes Twitter as a place where people listen to others' disclosures, in an exchange that creates a sense of intimacy.[28] While most Twitter messages are not substantive in and of themselves, Vincent

Miller argues that they serve as phatic communication—as small talk that has the explicit purpose of "expressing sociability and maintaining connections or bonds."[29] This intimacy resembles the "telecocooning" observed among Japanese teenagers who form strong emotional bonds with others using only the cellphone.[30]

Participants told me that Twitter enabled them to stay in touch with faraway friends and deepened relational bonds with people they knew in person. Individual items from the lifestream, such as what music someone is listening to or where they are eating, probably have little or no intrinsic value to the audience. But each tidbit aggregates with other pieces of personal information to form a larger picture and reinforce a social bond. This experience was almost unanimously echoed by informants and was the most frequently cited benefit of Twitter. Kevin Cheng, a former product manager at Twitter, explained:

> Do you ever talk to someone you haven't talked to a long time and say, "What's new?" Say you give the update on your job. You give the update on your marital status. You give the update on whether you've moved or things like that. And then conversation kind of stalls for a while. And that seems counterintuitive to the fact that [with] the person you see every day, you can carry on with conversations for an hour or hours at a time . . . you've been gone so long that you feel like the events that are worth discussing have to be of significance. You're not going to say like, "My God I haven't seen you in a year. What's new?" "Well, I saw 'Forgetting Sarah Marshall' yesterday." What lifestreaming is giving us is that ability to keep up with the minutia.

Cheng identifies one of the difficulties of living in an environment where people expect to stay in touch. Social network sites like Facebook have created a semi-permanent address book of former coworkers, high school friends, ex-boyfriends and girlfriends, distant family members, and other acquaintances whom users may rarely see. Twitter allows people to have an ongoing connection by sharing small pieces of information about the day-to-day experience that provide conversation starters and closeness. Andrew Mager, a former ZDNet employee who now works at Spotify, told me that Twitter enabled him to have personal interactions with one of his firm's executives, whom he could now ask about golfing and movies. To my informants, "intimacy" was a process of sharing knowledge about one another.

In addition to connecting faraway friends and acquaintances, lifestreaming helped people in the scene feel closer to each other. By scrolling through the day's Twitter updates or Facebook feed, people could see what others were doing. Video blogger Veronica Belmont, a self-described homebody, said, "I feel very connected to the community still because I know the minutiae of their lives through Twitter, through FriendFeed and Facebook. So you still have that sense of familiarity every time you run into them." Others said they became better friends with acquaintances after following them on Twitter. The virtual discussions and short messages reinforced in-person friendships. This was especially important for shy people who found online socializing easier, or were intimidated by the bustling social life of the technology community. Lifestreaming made it easy for people to mediate their friendships through the computer. Social media was also used to announce major life events, such as marriage, divorce, pregnancy, job changes, or family trouble. During my fieldwork, two couples in the scene announced their engagement on Twitter, while a single mother revealed her pregnancy and expressed gratitude for her followers' positive responses.

Others used lifestreaming to create accountability. Personal informatics enthusiasts used technology to record and monitor personal data, often using the internet to broadcast weight loss or health progress. For many, knowing that people were watching their data streams created a sense of obligation to an audience, much in the way that groups such as Weight Watchers or Alcoholics Anonymous use peer accountability to help members maintain desired behaviors. Similar principles applied to social obligations. Actions like wishing people "happy birthday" and attending events were done in view of others, encouraging people to hew to social norms. And people who violated social rules in significant ways could be taken to task publicly (which often caused "drama").

## Drawbacks of Lifestreaming

While social media's advantages have been chronicled extensively, so have claims of negative consequences. Social media has been linked to narcissism, as it is said to reward shallow social connections, vanity, and self-promotion.[31] Others state that social media is addictive, or creates information overload and attention deficit disorder-like symptoms that diminish long-term concentration.[32] None of these linkages have been proven, but they are frequently mentioned in scare stories about technology. While some of these negative effects were mentioned by informants, the most frequently discussed downsides to social media use were those relating to the extra layer of social information that the lifestream provides.

## Somebody's Watching Me: Social Surveillance

Before the internet, people would learn about parties or romantic relationships by gossiping or asking friends. This type of knowledge wasn't secret, but it wasn't available to everyone and was rarely written down. Today, any member of the networked audience can peruse a Facebook invite to see who was or wasn't invited, or look at Foursquare check-ins to see who is spending time together. Social information is digitized and aggregated through the lifestream to create a layer of relational data that lays over the ordinary social graph. While this information facilitated bonding and personal connection, it also magnified gossip, suspicion, and uncertainty. A friend, "Jill," suspected that her boyfriend was having drinks with "Jane," whom she strongly disliked. Jill first noticed that her boyfriend's Twitter feed had been silent for several hours. She then saw Jane use Dodgeball to check-in to a bar on his street and subsequently tweet out a photo of the bar. Jill interpreted this information to mean that the two were together, and was convinced that Jane intended her to know about it. Combining information from both people's lifestreams created a larger social picture that was interpreted through a lens of suspicion. In retaliation, Jill tweeted a message about trustworthiness without naming either party.

Social surveillance is the process by which social technologies like Facebook, Foursquare, and Twitter let users gather social information about their friends and acquaintances.[33] As Christina Nippert-Eng writes, "Humans are constantly scanning, constantly receptive to and looking for whatever they can perceive about each other, for whatever is put out there."[34] Eavesdropping is a very human action, and people are resourceful at combining information from disparate sources to create a "bigger picture" of social activities.[35] This picture is augmented by information provided on social media sites like Twitter or Flickr. Social media has a dual nature whereby information is both consumed and produced, which creates a symmetrical model of surveillance in which watchers expect, and desire, to be watched themselves. The presence of the networked audience not only enables connection, it encourages performances of intimacy and conflict to elicit reactions from others. Social media creates a context in which people are constantly monitoring themselves against the expectations of others—a context that can provoke anxiety and paranoia.

In the absence of face-to-face cues, people will extrapolate identity and relational material from any available digital information. Jennifer Gibbs and her colleagues found that online personal ads were constructed with a hyper-aware self-consciousness because users knew that misspellings, cultural references, and even time stamps were likely to be scrutinized by potential suitors.[36] Similarly, in textual sociable media like IRC or MUDs, people would infer identity information from e-mail addresses, nicknames, signatures, spelling, and grammar.[37] Digital traces and nuances are often interpreted incorrectly, but the act of interpreting becomes normal. Privacy scholar Helen Nissenbaum writes that the value of aggregation is in extracting "descriptive and predictive meanings from information that goes well beyond its literal boundaries."[38] Social media users are practiced in the extraction of nuance through ongoing analysis of the lifestream. While each piece of information by itself may not mean much, it creates a larger picture when combined with others. For example, knowing that Julie visited a local bar on Tuesday night is not, in isolation, particularly interesting. The bar is publicly accessible, Julie can expect to be seen there, and she will probably tell her friends where she is. If she tracks, codifies, and broadcasts this information using social media, however, the information can undergo a transformation. If analysis of the lifestream reveals that Julie's best friend's ex-boyfriend was also at the bar, and this is the third night in a row that they have been in the same place, a new picture emerges. The accessibility and persistence of personal information tracked and broadcast through social media create an extra layer of relational data that is not easily explained by the dichotomy of "public" or "private." It is very complicated to manage self-impressions and relationships with others when faced with this phenomenon.

People in the scene recognized these complexities and shared strategies on how to handle them. For example, two Digg employees, Aubrey Sabala and Joe Stump, proposed a (rejected) panel at South by Southwest called "Is the internet killing your game?" which described how relationships were affected by the lifestream. Digital pictures posted on Twitter, Facebook, or Flickr were open to interpretation, meaning that someone who wasn't present when the picture was taken could jump to the wrong conclusion. As shown in the earlier example, "radio silence," or "dropping off the Twitterverse" for a day was noticeable and questionable. They also mentioned what they called the "right hand vs. left hand problem," which described situations where "not everyone knows not to Twitter something out." This occurs when a group of people have different information boundaries, and someone lifestreams something that other group members want to keep private. These practices reveal intensive attention to detail and monitoring of other people's lifestreams, which from my observation was common among members of the scene.

All of this extra information, and the additional meanings it sometimes implied, made the people I spoke to anxious. Since it was possible to keep close tabs on virtually anyone with a lifestream, people in my study spoke of trying, and failing, to resist the temptation to monitor ex-boyfriends and girlfriends, rivals, or partners. Some people installed browser software that blocked them from looking at specific Facebook profiles or Twitter feeds so that they would not be tempted to "cyber-stalk" exes or their new partners. But nothing was foolproof. If someone they wished to avoid was connected to the networked audience, their username or picture would pop up in retweets, @replies, and other people's Facebook messages. This created endless social conflicts, and I frequently saw someone get upset because they saw a picture of their ex in their Flickr stream, or noticed when a trusted friend checked in with a sworn enemy. Because the networked audience includes indirect connections (for example, someone connected to a friend or friend-of-friend), it makes visible those interactions that one could otherwise avoid.

### Drama

The presence of the networked audience not only encourages the self-conscious performance of identity; it enables others to weigh in on social norm violations. In October 2008, for instance, Nick Starr and Tara Brown engaged in a public argument over allegedly stolen iPhones. The incident was so charged with drama that it is hard to tell exactly what happened; not only have the principal players written contradictory accounts, but these have been augmented by blog posts, Facebook status updates, and Twitter messages. Tara Brown, a former program manager at Microsoft and TopSpin media, is well known in the scene. She got engaged on Twitter to Sean Bonner, a similarly well-connected technologist based in Los Angeles (they have since married and had a son, whose baby shower was livestreamed). One evening, Brown used a Facebook invite to organize a *Rock Band* party at her house.[39] Nick Starr came to the party with a date, Ben. The next morning, Brown realized her iPhone was missing, and asked people on Twitter if they had seen it.

> And my day gets even better . . . my iPhone is nowhere to be found since last night 1:12 P.M. Oct 17th

> Calling AT&T to report my phone stolen. I'm so sad to think it was stolen from my house. :( 2:33 P.M. Oct 17th

Starr also tweeted that he had lost his phone at the party:

> Crap I think I left my iPhone at that Rock Band party @ekai or @msmelodi can you get me the number of whose place it was? 10:24 A.M. Oct 17th

Starr called Brown and found that her phone was missing as well, at which point he posted:

> WTF I thought I left my iPhone at @tarabrown's place but she said it wasn't there and her iPhone is gone too . . . wtf??? 1:15 P.M. Oct 17th

> Well it is official, my iPhone is gone, stolen, and/or missing. That effen sucks b/c I really don't want to spend the money for a new one. 2:15 P.M. Oct 17th

At this point the two stories diverge. After several e-mails, Facebook messages, and phone calls, Brown accused Starr's date, Ben, of stealing the phones, which Starr denied. She then accused Starr of stealing her phone. The conflict turned into an online argument. Both parties posted long blog posts telling their side of the story and called each other names on Twitter. In her personal blog, Brown wrote:

> So in my mind I was thinking about 3 possible scenarious [*sic*]: 1) Ben took it and Nick knew about it. 2) Nick took it

3) Ben took it and Nick didn't know. Either way, Nick brought this guy into my house and I as far as I'm concerned, needs to get my phone back or pay to replace it. A lot of other emails, IMs, tweets, etc. occurred throughout the day. I spoke to my Dad who is a Private Investigator and he said that the first email that Nick sent me was very suspicious. I went to the Mission Police Department to report this crime and they said the same thing.[40]

Brown's friends began posting messages on Twitter accusing Starr of theft:

Jpdefillippo: @nickstarr you are a stupid little shit who needs the snot beat out of you and next time I see you I will ablige. Bet on it.

DieLaughing: @NickStarr Actually it's time to move out of San Francisco. Saying 'Fuck @tarabrown' was the last straw. You are not local. Leave soon.

Starr responded with an equally long post responding to these tweets and refuting each of Brown's points (calling her a "lying cunt" and a "manipulative liar") and concluded:

I'm done . . . this whole mess is just too much . . . and guess what . . . IT'S ALL OVER A GOD DAMN PHONE! Tara lost her phone . . . so did I. Not one person seems to remember that my phone is gone too. I don't care what other people are going to say . . . I know the truth and the truth is that I'm as much a victim as Tara Brown is. If you have my phone, please return it. Thank you.[41]

Brown's phone was returned after a complicated series of events (an unidentified person in a hoodie left it outside her house; she, of course, believed this person was Starr), while Starr claimed that his was still missing.

When the dust cleared, both players were criticized by people in the scene for handling the situation publicly, with some characterizing the situation as having a "mob mentality" or as being "like high school." While Starr was not a particularly popular member of the community, some believed that Brown had abused the power of her audience (she had 1,205 followers, which was a relatively large number at the time). One informant told me:

> I made a cheesy Spiderman quote. And was like, "With great power comes great responsibility" and when you have that much power online with the number of followers and things like that, you have to be . . . you should be very responsible of what you . . . what accusations you make in public, right? That's like going on a loud speaker. It's a gigantic loud speaker especially with Sean [Bonner], as well, combined. And then not only to do that, but to make physical threats, um, yeah.

Both Brown and Starr portrayed the incident and their involvement in it in such a way as to gain the maximum sympathy from friends, followers, and people in the scene. Having over a thousand Twitter followers amplified Brown's accusations, bringing other people into the drama, but Starr had more than two thousand followers. It is likely that some of Brown and Starr's followers overlapped, but this is the nature of the networked audience. The networked audience is intrinsically involved in any event publicized over social media, and are able to use their own Twitter accounts, blog comments, or Facebook walls to add their opinions and thereby become an ever-present member of the conversation. Unlike the broadcast audience, the networked audience is connected through the lifestream, which allows for active participation beyond simply reading digital messages. The incident was debated both online and in-person, and the amplification ability of social media created a wider set of stakeholders in its outcome. Conflicts like these are dramatized as they play out in public, and serve as entertainment for the audience.

Further, while audience involvement can be seen as promoting accountability, social media also amplifies the amount of drama and conflict as other people besides the original two players become involved in the argument, chiming in much as gossip blog readers weigh in on the latest celebrity divorce or feud.

## FOMO

Location-based social software like Dodgeball, Foursquare, and BrightKite were especially anxiety-provoking to my interviewees. People use these applications to "check in" to a place and broadcast their location to friends, making it possible to see where friends and acquaintances are at all times. If ten friends checked into a bar, the eleventh friend would wonder why she hadn't been invited. This feeling is recognized by many in the tech scene as FOMO, or "fear of missing out."[42] Deciding to have a quiet night in doing laundry can seem like the wrong decision when faced with pictures and tweets from friends doing something that looks more fun. Megan McCarthy explained:

> I mean, there are people that I care about that I'm really interested to know what they're up to. There have been situations where I've seen people that are going out and doing stuff and it's like "Hey, they're right in my neighborhood. Let's go hang out," so I like that. Do I see it as like a status thing? I guess. When you see a lot of people who are all like "Hey, I'm at this party. Hey, I'm at this party" and you're not, it's like "Why am I not at her party?"

Services like Dodgeball, the SMS-based predecessor to Foursquare, were developed with the ideal of facilitating spontaneous connections with friends.[43] While many tech scenesters told me that they loved that aspect of location-based social software, its popularity in the scene created a set of expectations and social pressure. Kevin Cheng told me that Dodgeball had inspired him to go out so much that he wasn't getting his work, or his laundry, done. Cheng turned Dodgeball off to avoid FOMO. Location-based social software sits at the intersection of online and face-to-face socializing, and shows the importance of in-person interactions for cementing one's status in the scene. Notably, social software is explicitly designed for this; as Williams and Dourish write, "Dodgeball.com assumes discretionary mobility and leisure time. The service expects users to be able to switch locations effortlessly to socialize with friends, who are, naturally, available to socialize at about the same time."[44] In other words, services like Dodgeball and Foursquare are designed precisely for young, urban people like those in the tech scene.[45] But it was just this geographic proximity of people connected through always-on internet services that gave rise to a feeling that there was always something better to do.

Lifestreaming created other anxieties. People worried about their status in the community and whether they were participating appropriately. They fretted over what information should be revealed and what should be concealed. They regretted certain remarks they had made over social media and debated the appropriateness of others. Some even found the concept of an audience paralyzing in itself. Adrian Chan, an intense, cerebral interaction designer, said, "I'm hypersensitive, [I'm] unable to write or post tweets because I'm afraid they'll sound stupid, or people will read into their possible meaning, read things into it." While some people enjoyed performing for an audience, the potential public eyes made it hard for Chan to engage at all.

## Overloading on Information

Many participants believed that lifestreaming created information overload. Some adopted techniques for managing it, such as sampling a little at a time. Dale Larson, an executive coach, explained, "There's too much good stuff to read out there. But if I just plug in to the noise for a little bit, dip my toe in it and get back out, I'll have a good sense for what's going on at a high level. And I'll know if there's something I want to actively go after." In the scene, staying on top of current issues is a mark of status. Events like gadget launches, tech controversies, breaking news stories, and funny memes spread quickly through the networked audience, and people used Twitter to announce and discuss them. By reading a small sample of his tweets, Larson believed he could stay up on issues that were being talked about and thus maintain status and connection to the scene. Andrew Mager, who seemed comfortable with the San Francisco hyper-tech culture, told me:

> I almost say that the people are futuristic. They're from the future. They're like, "Oh, did you just, did you Twitter that? Did you Twitter this?" They just seem so up to date. Twitter is a phenomenon inside itself, but people are just so up to date. Even for me, when I first started here, it was very intimidating. Now, I kind of feel like I've caught up. But, for someone new jumping in, they would be totally bombarded and overwhelmed with it.

Plenty of people told me that they blocked Twitter during the day to boost their productivity. Others checked it only at certain times, or installed add-ons that helped them use the service more "efficiently." For informants with several hundred friends, Twitter would update every few seconds, creating a constant distraction. While the long-term effects of internet access on attention span are debated heatedly in the media, I found anecdotal evidence that the always-on, constantly updated nature of Twitter was both distracting and addictive.[46] It is impossible, however, to conclude from this whether Twitter, let alone the internet as a whole, causes behavioral or emotional changes. My informants consumed huge amounts of information from many different on and offline sources, including television, books, and newspapers.

The realization that people were using Twitter extensively, and were very closely monitoring their tweets, reinforced the strategic posturing and performance aspects of relationships that were being maintained through social media. Although monitoring was framed positively, as a way for people to build social ties with others and remain connected to the network, it also engendered anxiety and suspicion. Given these downsides, why did people share so much personal information? How did people navigate privacy in this culture of sharing and surveillance? I found that most people in the scene framed this information sharing not as a disregard for privacy, but as a shift to publicity.

### Privacy versus Publicity

Issues of information disclosure in social network sites are usually framed within a discourse of privacy.[47] For example, the introduction to *Privacy Online: Perspectives on Privacy and Self-Disclosure in the Social Web* summarizes:

> Communications and personal information that are posted online are usually accessible to a vast number of people. Yet when personal data exist online, they may be searched, reproduced and mined by advertisers, merchants, service providers or even stalkers. Many users know what may happen to their information, while at the same time they act as though their data are private or intimate. They expect their privacy will not be infringed while they willingly share personal information with the world via social network sites, blogs, and in online communities.[48]

This discourse maintains that social media users are credulous about their information disclosure, expecting privacy but unknowingly revealing personal data and making themselves vulnerable. Many studies confuse "information disclosure" with "lack of regard for privacy," but others have found no correlation between the two.[49] This inconsistency becomes more clearly understood when evaluating information disclosure online through a lens not of losing privacy, but of gaining publicity. My informants chose to reveal information for political reasons, for self-promotion, and to participate in the social life of the scene, but they all maintained carefully considered boundaries between information they would and would not publicize online.

There is a difference between making information public and publicizing it. "Public" implies democracy, freedom, participation, and inclusion, while "publicity" suggests openness, visibility, attention, status, and spectacle.[50] Information that is public can, in theory, be accessed by virtually anyone, but in practice will probably only be seen by a few. In contrast, information that is publicized is strategically made visible to a greater audience through three dimensions: the effort it takes to find information, the ease of locating that information, and the interest in that information.[51] For instance, imagine that the records of an acrimonious celebrity divorce are made public. To read them, one must drive to a California courthouse, find the court records department, request them from an archivist, and wait for the records to be found. The requestor may be able, at best, to make a photocopy to take home.[52] These steps are significant barriers to obtaining the information, and so place it in a state of what law scholars call "practical obscurity."[53] But once a tabloid reporter goes through this process, scans the documents, puts them on the tabloid website, and adds an enormous headline, the records are publicized, or "hyper-disseminated."[54] Publicizing information is thus an effort to make it more interesting (by placing it on a tabloid site with a large headline), easier to find (through Google or other indexes), and easier to obtain (once it is online).[55]

The status element of lifestreaming, that is, the way that people share personal information with others in exchange for inclusion and intimacy within the technology scene, encourages publicity. Publicity is a crucial element of micro-celebrity and self-branding strategies. It is the strategic promotion of self-provided information. In *PR: A Social History of Spin*, Stuart Ewen writes, "The ability to publicize—self, product, concept, issue, or institution—is a basic survival skill in contemporary life, and field-tested publicity strategies are everywhere to be found."[56] These public relations strategies are drawn from celebrity culture and product marketing and applied to social media, which incorporates status metrics that encourage people to publicize themselves to gain status, visibility, and audience. As Ernest Sternberg writes, "At every economic level, the ability to present oneself has become a critical economic asset . . . within any industry, corporation or profession, the aspirant reaches the economic apex when she becomes a celebrity, a human icon."[57] This is only possible with publicity. While I documented several distinct groups of attitudes about information disclosure, no one I met dismissed the need for privacy. Indeed, they were primarily motivated by publicity.

## Publicity as Freedom

For many people I talked to, living a "public life" was a physical instantiation of the open and participatory ideals of Web 2.0, which holds that transparency is highly valued for its contribution to accountability and freedom. For instance, WikiLeaks, a website that hosts leaked documents implicating corporations and governments in various shady activities, claims that transparency is a check on power and injustice:

> We believe that transparency in government activities leads to reduced corruption, better government and stronger democracies. All governments can benefit from increased scrutiny by the world community, as well as their own people. We believe this scrutiny requires information. . . . But with technological advances—the internet, and cryptography—the risks of conveying important information can be lowered . . . Today, with authoritarian governments in power around much of the world, increasing authoritarian tendencies in democratic governments, and increasing amounts of power vested in unaccountable corporations, the need for openness and transparency is greater than ever.[58]

The Freedom of Information Act makes many U.S. government documents available by request, reinforcing the idea that the people have a "right to know." The internet creates new opportunities for transparency by facilitating cheap and easy document publishing, widespread feedback, and increased communication between governments and constituents or corporations and customers. Yochai Benkler writes in *The Wealth of Networks* that increased transparency in corporate decisions, such as Google's use of a link to the Chilling Effects website to explain why certain search results for "Scientology" were removed, invites reflection about the meaning of culture and thus encourages "writable," or participatory, culture.[59] (Google's actions could also be considered a public relations strategy designed to appeal to an audience that values transparency.) Similarly, in *Code 2.0*, Lawrence Lessig argues that "open code is a foundation to an open society" and compares open code to public lawmaking.[60] In Chapter 1, I discussed how ideals of openness and transparency were realized in the organizational structure of activist groups and in the licenses of free and open-source software. In this context, self-disclosure is framed as a way to embrace and enact the principles of openness in everyday life.

There is a distinction between openness and transparency: openness is about making all information available, whereas transparency happens when there is a policy of making useful and relevant information available.[61] For example, when asked for climatology statistics, an environmental agency might make hundreds of thousands of pages of raw data available. This act of openness is neither useful nor readable. Creating and disseminating a top-level summary document that can be consumed easily, however, is both useful and readable and represents transparency. Similarly, true openness in one's personal life means allowing everything to "hang out" in a nonselective way, whereas transparency provides useful and meaningful information. When considering personal information, what is "meaningful" is a normative judgment that may vary widely among members of the audience. But the distinction between revealing everything and selective divulgence is important.

When the ideals of openness and transparency are applied to one's personal life, they may involve disclosing drug use, sexual habits, or emotional vulnerabilities via the internet. This type of "public living" was heralded by some as signifying a new era of greater freedom in which people can be authentic without judgment or prosecution. This mindset holds that society is inevitably moving toward greater transparency, as demonstrated by the increased visibility of previously hidden subcultures and increased respect for minority rights. "Gay rights" were often offered as an example, with "coming out" framed as a brave, political act.[62] According to this view, until this larger social shift takes place, people must courageously pioneer the principles of openness. If everyone reveals enough personal information, nobody can be discriminated against and culture will change for the better. Dale Larson stated:

> At the point where critical mass is reached of everybody exposing enough private information, it becomes too honest for anybody to pay attention to it all and try to discriminate on it. At the point where everybody really is out there with whatever their little weird thing is, that's the point at which you stop, when you say, "Oh, you know what, a fact with humanity, is that all of us have some weird freaky thing we fantasize about, or some weird freaky thing that we're afraid of, or some weird freaky thing that, I don't know, that's what's normal!" There's no such thing as a weird freaky thing. But until that critical mass happens, it's an act of courage to put that picture up on your Facebook . . . and it's an act of courage that, you know, very much comes with some tradeoffs.

According to this viewpoint, weathering the drama caused by publicizing formerly private acts is the downside of living one's life truthfully and authentically. Larson acknowledges the possible negative consequences and that "public living" requires emotional effort and bravery, but he believes that the eventual social benefits are more important. He also suggests a version of "authenticity" that implies the full disclosure of what may be very personal habits. Authenticity is thus defined as publicity, not simply a lack of artifice.

Computer scientist Tantek Çelik further claimed that "living in public" exemplifies Western ideals of democracy and freedom for the rest of the world:

> And, you know, if that means I sacrifice some amount of opportunities whatever, then I think that's good because it opens the door for more people to feel free to do that. And the more people do that, it's like eventually the flood gates break open. It's unstoppable . . . if you want to talk about making a difference in the world, I think that's one of the things that is probably one of the most important things any of us can be doing. Like okay, we have the privilege of a free society, how come we're not using it. As opposed to a lot of theocracies, it's like they don't have that choice, right? So, the more you can set a better example for people in the world as a whole and even if you make them jealous that you have an open, free society and want . . . to change.

This position follows conservative political ideologies that position American society as a global model of freedom and democracy.[63] Çelik expressed frustration with what he saw as the status quo notion that authority figures are expected to live conservative lives. He believes that he can combat this viewpoint and challenge authority by simultaneously being a leader in the technology community and living in public. Thus openness online becomes a political act.

Idealizing openness implies that there should be no difference in self-presentation regardless of circumstance. Under this particular definition of authenticity, an honest and forthright person will be who they "really are" consistently, regardless of who is listening. But this view does not reflect the realities of how people differ in the ways they use gesture, language, and tone to manage impressions face-to-face.[64] The idea of a single, "authentic" self, although it carries a great deal of currency in contemporary American culture, is a social construction, one at odds with actual social practice.

Promoting transparency also implies that privacy is only necessary for people who have "something to hide." Eric Schmidt, CEO of Google, told CNBC that "if you have something that you don't want anyone to know, maybe you shouldn't be doing it in the first place" (he later claimed he was joking).[65] The idea that privacy is only necessary for those engaging in illegal activities is, unfortunately, widespread in the general U.S. population, yet it does not hold up under scrutiny. Virtually everyone who advocates openness in their personal lives is talking about being selective in what they reveal rather than making everything about themselves available: I do not believe Schmidt would want his credit card number or a naked photo of himself appearing in the *New York Times*. This presumption was tested when tech news outlet C|Net Googled Schmidt and posted personal information about him online. Schmidt did not talk to the technology news outlet for several months afterward, allegedly in retaliation.[66]

Privacy theorists Daniel Solove, Priscilla Regan, and Helen Nissenbaum all argue that conceptualizing privacy as secrecy ignores the myriad of other reasons that privacy is necessary.[67] Solove writes: "Even surveillance of legal activities can inhibit people from engaging in them. The value of protecting against chilling effects is not measured simply by focusing on the particular individuals who are deterred from exercising their rights. Chilling effects harm society because, among other things, they reduce the range of viewpoints expressed and the degree of freedom with which to engage in political activity."[68] Allowing absolute electronic surveillance limits government and corporate accountability, creates an imbalance of power, and, overall, compromises social freedom. When Çelik or Larson idealize living in public, they are not talking about complete disclosure of personal information, but instead transparency along specific lines, namely drug use and sexuality. The belief that these aspects of life should be publicized, however, has an ideological function.

Promoting absolute openness disregards the privilege of most people in the tech scene. It is one thing for a wealthy, white male programmer to admit that he sometimes smokes pot. It is another for an undocumented worker to publicize his immigration status, or for a woman escaping a domestic violence situation to reveal her home address. Advocating "openness" ignores the very circumstances that may make self-disclosure dangerous. Furthermore, upholding personal transparency as an ideal supports the business models of social software, which profit from information disclosure. Mark Zuckerberg said in a 2010 interview:

> And then in the last 5 or 6 years, blogging has taken off in a huge way and all these different services that have people sharing all this information. People have really gotten comfortable not only sharing more information and different kinds, but more openly and with more people. That social norm is just something that has evolved over time . . . We view it as our role in the system to constantly be innovating and be updating what our system is to reflect what the current social norms are.[69]

Zuckerberg echoes the belief that society is becoming more open, claiming that Facebook is changing its privacy settings to reflect this. But Facebook has a huge vested interest in encouraging people to publicize personal information, since they make money by selling user data and "eyeballs" to marketing firms, data aggregators, and advertisers. The more people depend on Twitter, Foursquare, or Facebook to learn about their friends, the more money their parent companies make. Zuckerberg's interpretation of "openness" does not cover corporate openness—Facebook and Apple are notoriously tight-lipped—but only personal openness. While people like Larson and Çelik are well intentioned, selectively revealing information to a targeted audience is not the same as, say, coming out as gay in Iraq. They frame openness as socially beneficial, but the tools and culture of Web 2.0 have evolved to promote a particular kind of openness and transparency because it drives profit to social media companies, not because it furthers freedom and democracy.

## Privacy through Disclosure

I also encountered the belief that strategically publicizing personal information was a way to maintain privacy. Melissa Gira Grant told me:

> In terms of the public/private divide, I think people think I have no private life. Because I talk about a lot of very intimate things but I use that strategically. [But] there are a lot of private things that I would never even think to talk about and people don't even know; they can't even conceive. They think that because I'm talking about sexuality or activism or things I'm very passionate about that they must know everything about me, which is a marvelous way to have a private life. Because people think they already know your dirty secrets.

Grant is a blogger, author, and sex-work activist who was romantically involved with former *Valleywag* blogger Nick Douglas during the period of my fieldwork; the two had a tumultuous relationship with a visible online component. She posted a lot of personal information online, including nude pictures, stories about her sex life, and arguments with her partners. But Grant had clearly defined boundaries around personal information sharing. She believed that sharing more than most people online (for example, her fervent writing about sexuality) allowed the rest of her private life to fly under the radar. While Grant reveals more online than many people do—she is contemplating a project that would document her sexual encounters—she is playing a character, the feminist performance artist known for her forthrightness, rather than living her entire life in public. It is precisely through revealing more that she attempts to conceal what she wants to keep most private; she is still presenting an edited self.

Grant's position also reveals the extent to which "public living," and therefore publicity, is necessary for a successful member of the tech scene. For Grant to maintain her freelance career, she needed a visible public persona. Much of her work involved advising nonprofits on social media use, so it was vital for her to demonstrate proficiency with the technologies. And as a sex writer and activist, she was expected to blog and tweet about sex, relationships, and intimacy. Her strategy to reveal the very personal was not only a way for her to keep some topics to herself; it also enabled her to attract an audience and to interest freelance clients. She was able to use this audience interaction to build her career further; in 2010, she and a partner used Kickstarter, a "crowdfunding" site that solicits donations for creative projects, to raise more than $17,000 to print an anthology of sex writing.

### Publicity as Strategy

The third viewpoint that I encountered had to do with traditional publicity, or the revealing of information to maintain one's personal brand or to boost micro-celebrity. While extensive use of social media is necessary for many technological careers, this can create conflicts with employers, as Ariel Waldman explained:

> It really bothered [the company] that there was any entity online where it was me, meaning all of me and not divided. Like they didn't want to have my title associated with stuff I did personally. They're like, "Can't you create a different account, to separate them?" I'm like "This is my name" . . . they were saying things to me like, "The way you live your life online is an obvious detriment for your career," and I was like, "No, it's not," and they got really pissed. It was two different languages because they couldn't understand that I wouldn't have a career if I didn't live my life online the way I was.

To Waldman, the publicity gained through lifestreaming was necessary to cement her reputation as a social media expert. She maintained that any account under her name needed to be "all of me and not divided," with anything she came into contact with being fair game for Twitter. Rather than keeping her accounts highly edited, Waldman aimed to build a strong brand that would transcend a single client. This reveals the intrinsic conflict between self-branding and corporate employment, since what may be best for the company is not always in the self-brander's self-interest. To Waldman, showing facility with social media was more important than the needs of one client. Moreover, because authenticity is so highly valued in the technology community, discussing both personal and professional topics on social media helps build ties with an audience and deepen intimacy, strengthening the brand or increasing micro-celebrity status. But although Waldman used pieces of personal information to build emotional ties with her audience, she withheld many things from social media. While disclosing personal details is valued as a marker of authenticity, strategic self-presenters tactically manage and limit self-disclosure.

Looking at information disclosure as the desire for *publicity* reveals the complex negotiations that lifestreamers face between disclosure and reservation. While many people have looked at the problems created by shifting notions of private and public on social networks, there is little work on the impact of publicity, openness, and audience on communities that constitute networked audiences. That these issues create problems is widely acknowledged, but there is no agreement on how to handle them. Since revealing personal information online has both benefits and drawbacks, choosing how much to share and with whom is approached differently. Within the scene there are numerous degrees of public-ness, from people who graphically document their sex lives to those who adhere to a strictly professional self-presentation. On one end of the spectrum, Nick Starr tweets about sexual activities, homelessness, his HIV status, and plastic surgery. On the other, Julia Allison, who is considered very public, does not lifestream meetings with potential clients or famous friends so as not to compromise her business dealings. Still others choose not to speak publicly about their children or their relationships, but carefully dole out other pieces of personal information to appear authentic to their audiences. These choices are affected by the software that people use, their motivations, and complex webs of obligations to others. But even people who reveal a great deal of personal information online do this thoughtfully.

### Managing the Lifestream

Because lifestreaming has emotional and personal drawbacks, people employ many creative strategies to manage online presence and impressions. An enormous amount of work goes into maintaining "the edited self." Deciding what information should be private and which should be public is labor. Tara Hunt explains the drawbacks of "open living":

> The only sort of drawback is that I can't cuss, purely or literally let my hair down in a certain way anymore privately, . . . because everything I do has to reflect the public image that I need to keep up. That's the irony of openness, because it's not so open, right? It's a manufactured openness in that way, that it's always filtered. It's kind of like open source; anybody can take the code and mess around with it but there's a very structured way of doing it. And you check in and you check out and you sign your name to it. And you have to go through certain meritocratic levels to work on the kernel. It's not like people can just take the code and just fly with it and open living is the same way. It's ironic because it's ultimately less open, in a lot of ways, personally, that's my experience.

Hunt is open about many aspects of her life; she tweeted that her son had run up a $1,051 phone bill texting his friends in the United

States, and asked for advice on how to manage the problem. But Hunt has defined a set of acceptable boundaries for information disclosure—she generally avoids talking about relationships or dating—and strictly manages her self-presentation. This management requires self-monitoring, seeing herself through the gaze of others and altering her actions accordingly. As a result, Hunt is constantly working to produce and edit her desired image.

Others decrease their involvement in social media to reduce anxiety or drama. People in the scene often cycled through phases of social media use, from intense to mild. Glenda Bautista told me that people often scaled back their information disclosure after one particular incident. In her case, Bautista began the difficult process of "locking down" her online presence after a recruiter referred to her personal blog and boyfriend in a job interview.

Because the lifestream exists among a networked social graph, people must monitor both their own information disclosure and that of their friends. Bautista recognized that her desire to be less public online was a losing battle:

> I remember once, just to keep my name out of Google, or just to not have anything track back to me, I tried to redo my last name, so that it wouldn't be attributed to me. That didn't go well, because some people . . . It's not that they have big mouths, it's just that they don't know where my line is . . . some people literally do not have the boundaries. And it takes too much policing, too much energy to literally be like, "Take that down, put that up . . ." I mean, it's exhausting.

People frequently reveal information about others, deliberately or inadvertently, through the lifestream. Someone without a Twitter account can be referenced in a tweet. A person who chooses not to check in at a bar can still be photographed by another patron. Someone can be tagged in a photo on Facebook even if they do not have a Facebook account. Two users who are not directly connected through social media site may appear in each other's streams through mutual friends. The previously mentioned problem of "right hand, left hand," where people at an event have different informational norms, can create conflicts. For example, "John" may not want "Mike" to know that he is having dinner with Mike's rival "Chris." But Mike may learn this anyway if Chris tweets or blogs about his dinner with John. John can ask Chris to keep the dinner secret, but ultimately he cannot control how private this information will be. Andrew Mager elaborated: "It's almost like you're too transparent. I was sitting with the editor of ZDNet last night, Larry Dignan, and he is like a top writer, and he is like, 'I'm scared of Facebook, because all my middle school friends are going and scanning photos,' and he is like 'I don't want all that.' Almost now we're at the point when we don't have control over what people publish about us." Dignan is a professional who presumably does not want his online reputation sullied by unflattering childhood photos. Even sans tags, online photos can be misinterpreted. A friend once asked me to remove a picture of him hugging a female friend from my Flickr stream, because he did not want his notoriously jealous girlfriend to misinterpret it. As Glenda Bautista said, monitoring can be "exhausting," a form of emotional labor. It may also be impossible, because new tools and sites are constantly being developed.

Contrary to the utopian theories of transparency and openness promoted in Web 2.0 discourse, and the moral panics around lack of privacy online, lifestreaming is not an unvarnished digital stream of someone's online actions. Instead it is a carefully edited, purposeful construction of self. Lifestreamers choose what to reveal and conceal: they monitor their own and other's actions, publicizing certain aspects of their lives while keeping other parts to themselves, and they may even exaggerate or falsify information to produce a desired effect. The resulting lifestream is an attempt to inculcate a particular version of oneself that appeals to others in the networked audience. This should not surprise anyone familiar with the intricacies of face-to-face communication. People vary their self-presentations based on context and audience; we present ourselves differently in a job interview than we do in a bar with our friends. Social media technologies are distinct from face-to-face interactions, however, in that they frequently demonstrate "context collapse," where every relationship has equal balance and widely variable social contexts are "collapsed" into one.[70] On Facebook or Twitter, where it is very tricky to vary self-presentation, both potential employees and friends could be part of the same audience. But there are flagrant contradictions between the ideals of transparent, public living and the realities of lifestreaming in a community where virtually everyone lifestreams. Lifestreaming creates an additional layer of social information: by digitizing previously unrecorded things and forming, in the aggregate, a whole that reveals more than the sum of its parts, it becomes part of a digital mirror held up to the scene that often reveals more than the participants intended. The arguments, contradictions, and dramas that play out as a result cause people to hold back, restrict, and manage their lifestream. The lifestream becomes a portrayal of a formal, edited self. Even those who pride themselves on their risqué or boundary-pushing public life make careful choices about how much to reveal or conceal. Unfortunately, self-presentation in the lifestream is not wholly self-dependent. The tagged photos, @reply references, and Foursquare check-ins provided by others can be monitored, but rarely changed.

Social media applications encourage people to provide personal information as part of their business model, but often, putting personal information online is interpreted by researchers and the media alike as a lack of concern for privacy. This ignores the fact that participating in social information-sharing has many benefits, including intimacy, friendship, and status. There are strong social pressures to participate in social media in the technology scene. Nonparticipation marks one as an outsider and a Luddite, and limits how far one can go in the community, and perhaps professionally as well. Rather than expecting theories about privacy in the public sphere to explain these behaviors, we can understand information disclosure as an act of publicizing the self to a networked audience.

The value of visibility and access motivates people to share with each other, resulting in affective benefits. The inclusion of many members of the scene in the lifestream both enables these benefits and creates emotional and social drawbacks.

I found no correlation between how much someone cares about privacy and the amount of information they put online. For instance, Melissa Gira Grant reveals a great deal about her sex life, but is very protective of what she chooses not to share. Frequent tweeters are upset if a friend's tweet publicizes something they did not want disclosed. These findings are supported by other empirical studies showing that information disclosure does not imply a lack of concern for privacy.[71] People employ strategies like withholding certain pieces of information, monitoring their friends' use of social media, adopting varying definitions of privacy, and editing their own lifestream in order to maintain a level of privacy they are comfortable with. Due to the imprecision of these controls and the new levels of inference possible with aggregated social information, however, it is often impossible to avoid drama in a community where social life exists both on and offline, and where information sharing is a normative behavior. Further, while the Web 2.0 culture may frame this sharing within a discourse of freedom and democracy, we must remember that the profit models of social media depend on user-contributed information. Perhaps not surprisingly then, the models of openness idealized by Web 2.0 both ignore the negative consequences of transparency and promote a particular type of transparency that privileges the kinds of information sharing that benefit corporations more than individuals.

# 6

# DESIGNED IN CALIFORNIA

---

## Entrepreneurship and the Myths of Web 2.0

Well, there's this view here that it's like you deserved to get rich.
—C-level tech executive

I think in Silicon Valley folks want to believe it's a lot more of a
meritocracy than it actually is.
—Tristan Walker, Foursquare

I began this book by arguing that social software may inadvertently do more to promote inequality than to counter it. While Web 2.0's complex history bestows social media with radical, transformative power, it has ended up prioritizing entrepreneurialism, commodification, and independence. This combination has played out in complex and contradictory ways; for example, the tech scene values self-made status over ascribed status, but looks down on individuals who actively court attention rather than "earning it" for their accomplishments. Many of the assumptions about "correct" behavior that stem from these values are shaped and reinforced by technical features of social media, such as quantifiable metrics and digital instantiation of social information. To participate in the tech scene, and to attempt to rise to the top of its economic hierarchy, people must negotiate these inconsistencies in their most personal understandings of themselves: what they reveal, what they conceal, and to whom they connect. For all my informants' talk of passionate, revolutionary lives, they paid a price—having a peanut gallery of spectators evaluating and judging their every movement.

In a cultural context where idealists have linked social media to democracy, egalitarianism, and participation, the tech scene in San Francisco considers itself to be exceptional. Supporters speak glowingly of a singularly meritocratic environment where innovative entrepreneurs disrupt fusty old industries and facilitate sweeping social change. In this chapter, I look at how the tech scene thinks about itself. Even those people who privately acknowledge problems and difficulties offer platitudes about participation when asked about San Francisco. But if the tech scene is really a meritocracy, why are so many of its key players, from Mark Zuckerberg to Steve Jobs to Gary Vaynerchuk, white men? If entrepreneurs are born, not made, why are there so many programs attempting to create entrepreneurs? If the most successful people in tech are authentic, why do people feel so much distress around revealing and concealing information? If tech is truly game-changing, why are old-fashioned capitalism and the commodification of personal information never truly questioned?

These myths—authenticity, meritocracy, and entrepreneurialism—have some basis in fact. But they are powerful because they reinforce ideals of the tech scene that shore up its power structures and privileges. Believing that the tech scene is a meritocracy implies that those who obtain great wealth deserve it, and that those who don't succeed do not. The undue emphasis placed on entrepreneurship, combined with a limited view of who "counts" as an entrepreneur, function to exclude entire categories of people from ascending to the upper echelon of the industry. And the ideal of authenticity privileges a particular type of self-presentation that encourages people to strategically apply business logics to the way they see themselves and others.

Taken as a whole, these themes of authenticity, meritocracy, and entrepreneurialism reinforce both a closed system of privilege and one centered almost entirely around the core beliefs of neoliberal capitalism. This does not make technology intrinsically better or worse than any other American business; I'd certainly rather socialize with tech people than bankers. But it does reveal the threadbare nature of digital exceptionalism. People in tech repeatedly portray San Francisco and Silicon Valley as places where the smartest, most motivated people from around the globe are changing the world for the better, and this rhetoric has been taken up and repeated often by traditional media outlets. Unlike, say, community activists, public schoolteachers, social workers, or health care providers, technologists are ultimately focused on a small slice of the population, and they are primarily looking for ideas that will prove profitable. These entrepreneurs may have a passion for better audio streaming or e-mail, but to say that such pursuits are world-changing is a bit disingenuous.

This chapter closes with a lengthy analysis of how these myths contribute to continued male dominance in the tech industry. (I could have written a similar chapter about race or sexual preference.) The egregious gender problem has been the subject of much public controversy, with more organizations and resources than ever before focused on solving it, such as Women 2.0 and Girls in Tech, Etsy's "Hacker Grants," which pay for women to attend an elite programming summer camp, and New York's Change the Ratio, which is dedicated to increasing the number of women speakers at tech conferences.[1] Ultimately improving this problem will be very difficult, because the issue of gender is intimately woven into Silicon Valley's view of itself and its highest-status members. It even manifests itself in seemingly unrelated issues, like the ideal of authentic content.

## Striving Toward Authenticity

Ideally, online content created by individuals is more authentic than its mass-media counterpart. After all, it has been influenced by the DIY ideals of early internet culture and media activists, who maintained that consolidated media were producing homogenized, soulless products that failed to capture the experience of many Americans. Small media like zines, blogs, and personal homepages created opportunities for people to earnestly and honestly discuss their experiences with work, parenting, illness, politics, and other intimate topics. Implicitly, media activists believed that mass media's dependence on advertisers, which necessitated promoting products and consumerism, prevented the presentation of non-mainstream life choices and any critical discussion of neoliberal capitalism. Early homepage culture, as detailed in the first chapter, had a strong alternative bent, featuring discussions of punk rock, anarchism, feminism, libertarianism, and other philosophies of living that rarely appear on *Modern Family* or in the *Wall Street Journal*.

As the web has become more mainstream, authenticity has become an axiom that primarily differentiates user-generated brands from each other. For example, at a fashion blogger conference that I attended in 2011, blogger after blogger spoke earnestly of the importance of authenticity in attracting an audience. They felt that it was important to be "authentic" in order to attract and maintain a large audience of readers who would interest those large fashion and beauty brands that might advertise on, or sponsor, one's blog. In other words, authenticity was a content strategy carried out to gain readers and differentiate oneself both from one's peers and from mainstream fashion magazines. Operationally, this meant that fashion bloggers worked very hard on their "personal style," but were careful not to present content that would alienate themselves from potential advertisers—unless distancing themselves from certain brands was a way to inculcate authenticity. One Washington, D.C., blogger frequently rallied against Ugg boots and Vera Bradley bags; Ugg reached out and offered free products and a tour of the factory, but she primly declined. I do think she honestly hated Uggs (it would be hard not to), but she also needed to maintain a consistency in her brand so not as to alienate her similarly Ugg-hating followers.

This begs the question of what authenticity means in this context. As we have seen, the tech scene considers it possible to be "authentic" while engaging in self-editing and self-censorship. In Carl Elliott's *Better Than Well*, he discusses "the notion of authenticity as a moral ideal: the idea that we each have a way of living that is uniquely our own, and that we are each called to live in our own way rather than that of someone else."[2] But "authenticity" is a social construct that is always defined against something else; it is a slippery concept that is impossible to pin down. As David Grazian writes,

> Although it remains a figment of our collective imagination, we still continue to employ the concept of authenticity as an organizing principle for evaluating our experiences in everyday life, and that makes it significantly meaningful and, in many ways, *real*. In this manner, authenticity shares a similar place in our hearts as love or beauty; it is an old wives' tale we tell ourselves over and over again until we believe it to be true, and as a result it gains a certain kind of power over us.[3]

In contemporary American culture, this concept of "authenticity" is evident in self-help literature that emphasizes the importance of "being true to yourself" or "following your passion"—as we saw with Gary Vaynerchuk's books. Contestants on cheesy reality television shows face the camera and recite similar platitudes, using them to justify poor choices. In the beauty and weight-loss industries, the true self is often framed as hiding inside the less svelte, less adorned, frumpier body.[4] This authentic self can—and must—be excavated to live one's "best life."

While the technology industry piously positions itself above such (feminized) dreck, it is as susceptible to trends and platitudes as any other aspect of popular culture. The ideal of authenticity runs very deep, and although it manifests itself differently in Tim Ferriss's books than it does on *The Biggest Loser*, it is still taken quite seriously. Despite the harping on authenticity in tech, there is little discussion of what this actually means, and people were often taken a bit aback when I asked them. Notably, authenticity is inevitably tied to the business logic of the tech scene.

Tristan Walker explains what he sees as inauthentic:

> Let's say Foursquare started to take off or raise a new round of money or something like that . . . and I could help sway a decision. Only then would they [inauthentic people] start following me on Twitter, becoming my best friend, other things . . . [When] they don't get what they wanted, [they] unfollow me and do stupid shit like that . . . I appreciate it more when people are truly transparent and say, "Hey Tristan, here's what I want. Can you help me with it?" As opposed to folks going a roundabout way, and me figuring it out after the fact.

To Walker, authenticity is about being honest and transparent with intentions rather than sneakily attempting to curry favor. Because Walker worked for the hot startup Foursquare when I interviewed him, he was privy to a great deal of obsequiousness. Obviously, flattery and sycophancy come hand in hand with business dealings, but it was difficult for any potential investor to disguise his intentions given sites like CrunchBase and AngelList, which provide detailed biographical information about tech people. Walker's definition of authenticity made sense given the realities of startup investment.

A more common concept of authenticity involved self-promotion. People widely accepted self-promotion, with the caveat that one should only shill for things that they honestly, authentically liked. Stowe Boyd said, "I use [Twitter] to promote things all the time. But I do it in a way that is constant with people's perception of me." Similarly, I frequently heard businesses promoting "authentic" connections with their customers. Kelly Williams, who worked on the Facebook gaming platform, explained at a social games meetup: "We discourage incentivizing notification. We want a really genuine, authentic 'hey check this out.'" Rather than awarding game players for promoting the game, Williams wanted true word-of-mouth marketing in which people promoted games not for money but because they honestly liked them. Notably, this ethic of authenticity was not one in which consumption or business ethics were separated from interpersonal relationships. Instead, people took this integration for granted but expected that people would be honest in their recommendations to others.

Another definition of authenticity involved the creation and promotion of intimate knowledge. Rather than simply tweeting about business, people expected each other to reveal something about themselves, even if that something was mundane. Earlier in the book, Walker used the goofy sneakers he was wearing during our interview as an example of personal information that he'd be comfortable sharing with the audience. Soraya Darabi, former social media strategist for the *New York Times,* described this approach as strategic: "Say you're an author, a book aficionado. Most [of your followers] have tagged music as a passion. You might want to throw them a bone about your favorite song. There are a lot of Venn diagram overlaps in this community. It's to your advantage to be as much as part of a community as possible which means engaging with people's interests." In other words, sharing personal information was a branding strategy in that it humanized businesspeople and allowed for a greater connection with their audience. This was, of course, assuming that what one shared was consistent with his or her brand-image. Neither the type of sneakers one wears nor the music one listens to is a notably controversial piece of personal information, but tech scene insiders saw it as a way to strategically engage with their audiences and to maintain their popularity.

As discussed in Chapter 5, my informants had strict individual boundaries around what they considered appropriate to reveal online. People frequently filtered out discussions of family, relationships, body issues, or insecurities—not coincidentally, topics that are typically considered feminine. Those who talked too much about dating, sexuality, or non-tech interests were liable to find themselves losing status in the community as a result. For example, Nick Starr, mentioned previously, was notorious for his revealing blog entries and tweets about sex and plastic surgery. Starr spent a year living on the streets to save up money for liposuction, and discussed his weight loss and frequent hookups in detail online. I often heard him referred to as a "drama queen," "oversharer," or "attention whore."[5] Julia Allison's status in the scene plummeted partially due to her frequent sharing of insecurities and relationship dilemmas on Twitter. Anthony Hoffman's critical discourse analysis of media coverage about oversharing found that the term was overwhelmingly negative, applied primarily to women, and had "the effect of creating a devalued subclass of information sharing online," mostly comprised of "sex and romance, intimate relationships, parenthood and reproduction, and so on."[6] Allison's detractors demonstrate a similar pattern of normative judgment around information sharing. Her discussions of her dating life, desire to get married and *Sex and the City*–esque fantasies of urban life are labeled as "desperate" and "delusional" because these topics are constructed as silly or irrelevant. That these are historically, intrinsically feminine topics is not coincidental. Authenticity in my study was not about revealing one's true and complete self, but about constantly performing in an "authentic" way that met the needs of the audience while still being not too revealing and still "safe for work." This "authenticity" encourages people to filter their thoughts and feelings through a capitalist logic that frames only certain types of self-expression as acceptable. In the tech industry, these topics are often those deemed acceptable to men.

## Meritocracy

The mythology of Silicon Valley success holds that those who "make it" do so due to their excellent ideas and ability, because the tech scene is a meritocracy that rewards intelligence and hard work. Paulina Barsook writes: "Philosophical technolibertarianism gives one pause because it colors, deeply and widely and mostly unconsciously, a zillion personal and institutional decisions. The notion that because one is rich one must be smart, however fallacious, is deeply embedded: People can equate piles of money—or the promise of it—with good sense, wisdom, and savoir faire."[7] This meritocratic notion of wealth through accomplishment was often contrasted with an archaic view of the East Coast as peppered with prep schools and debutante balls. Anu Nigam said, "There's no past legacy like in the East Coast, or tradition. It's who you work with, who you know, what have you done." Sarah Lacy concurred: "When I hear 'social status' I think of like a very East Coast notion of it. I just think it's so different here. It's so wrapped up in achievement." Dan Nye, describing what made San Francisco unique, said, "On the East Coast you frequently start the conversation with what prep school, what college, where did you spend your summers—there's less of that out here."

Leaving aside the Whartonian notion that the East Coast is still governed by the norms of the Philadelphia Main Line or the Upper East Side, San Francisco is widely viewed as a meritocracy where what you do, not who you are, matters. There is some truth to this statement. To a certain extent, there is a lower barrier to entry in tech than in some other industries. Megan McCarthy, for instance, began her editorial career as a *Valleywag* party crasher while holding down a day job as a secretary. (She admits this but adds, "I think the myth of a meritocracy is that everything starts out fair to begin with, and that everyone sort of has a level playing field, and that's not true. There are people who have advantages.") Until fairly recently, engineers could be self-taught and did not need college degrees. (Google, among other companies, now requires a bachelor's degree in computer science, and virtually all tech companies recruit heavily from elite computer science schools like MIT, Carnegie Mellon, and Stanford.) Having a famous father or coming from an old money family would not necessarily be an asset as it might in banking, but it wouldn't necessarily hurt, either; Bill Gates came from a famously wealthy family. And certainly the highest status in the tech scene comes from one's job rather than family name, although wealth factors considerably into status.

The myth of meritocracy holds that anyone can come from anywhere and achieve great success in Silicon Valley if they are skilled. An anonymous technology executive said, "It's like the new version of the American Dream. It used to be get a good job, kind of just have a stable life but the good jobs aren't even that good anymore . . .

there's this feeling that anyone can do it. Anyone can come to America and have a good life or whatever and starting an internet company, it feels like anyone can do it and there's some truth to it. It aligns with American values." Hillary Hartley told me what she saw as a typical tech scene success story:

> Some kid starts playing with Ruby on Rails, and builds this kickass site, and then gets sucked in by TechCrunch. He's this 15-year-old kid that goes to all the Web 2.0 parties. He is one of those kinds of social climbers in this world. He gets his parents' permission; they drop him off at the party. In this last year, he made friendships with Gary Vaynerchuk and a couple other guys. So, he's in this world of hanging with the social media elite, but I don't know if he wants to finish high school. I don't know if he wants to go to college. He probably doesn't have to.

Hartley's story reveals that while it was the "kickass" Ruby on Rails site that got the young teen noticed, it is his networking skills that have elevated him to "elite" status. The always-caustic Owen Thomas agreed. "The ultimate story about the Valley is about a meritocracy. If you strip away everything else, that is the story," he noted, but in fact, San Francisco is "a place where personal connections rule." Such personal connections are necessary to attract venture capital, find a co-founder, set up a possible acquisition, and get noticed by tech blogs and technology journalists. These economic hierarchies are naturalized and made invisible by framing them as innocuous social ties. Kevin Rose, with a huge amount of social capital established by Digg, founded a startup called "Milk," which raised $1.5 million in an angel round from boldface names like Michael Arrington, Ron Conway, Tim Ferriss, Ashton Kutcher, and Matt Mullenweg. The startup launched one mobile app and was quickly scooped up for $15 million by Google, which kept the product team, including Rose, and fired everyone else.[8] Given that Digg was ultimately an unprofitable and unsuccessful startup, it is debatable whether these deals were based purely on Rose's merits as a product designer. Daniel Raffel, who was seeking funding for his startup when I talked to him, explained:

> People are shallow. The fat, ugly girl is not gonna get as many dates. She might be the most amazing person in the world, but, unfortunately, there's a lot of people [for whom] appearance is everything. I think for investors, you see a lot of stuff: someone who doesn't have a specific track record, who has a name that's foreign-sounding, or who has worked at places that they've never heard of. These are the fat, ugly girls. And it's sad, and there's just a lot of marketing and hype, I think, to create value. Unfortunately, I think the things that are really apparent to me at this stage [are] that there's definitely a bias towards people who are younger. There's definitely a bias towards people who have a certain pedigree.

I heard this metaphor dozens of times; the saying "everyone wants to take the pretty girl to the dance," refers to the tendency venture capitalists have to cluster around popular deals. (The prevalence of this phrase is very revealing of who is in these meetings.) In reality, everyone wants to be in business with young, white, male entrepreneurs with connections to high-status people, a pedigree from certain companies, a well-known mentor, and perhaps a Stanford degree. In a *TechCrunch* article by Harvard professor Vivek Wadhwa, Sharon Vosneck, the CEO of nonprofit Astia, which helps fund women entrepreneurs, identified "systematic and hidden biases" in technology funding:

> VCs [venture capitalists] hold clear stereotypes of successful CEOs (they call it pattern recognition, but in other industries they call it profiling or stereotyping.) John Doerr [a venture capitalist] publicly stated that his most successful investments—and the no-brainer pattern for future investments—were in founders who were white, male, under

30, nerds, with no social life who dropped out of Harvard or Stanford.[9]

This formula certainly filters out enormous numbers of people who may be equally skilled.

The myth of meritocracy also ignores the level of privilege that participation in the tech scene involves, as *i09* editor Annalee Newitz points out:

> Let's say that most people can have access to computers sometimes but only some people can have access to computers all the time, and then an even smaller group can have access to the net while they're just out wandering around doing Twitter, right? They're like, I have my phone and I can say things while I'm walking around where somebody else has to actually go home, to their one computer that they own. So the more that you want to participate in this network of wealth and entrepreneurialism, the more stuff you have to have to participate in it. So there [are] these levels of participation that are enabled by either being wealthier or having the free time to participate.

Certainly, a level of material wealth is necessary to participate in San Francisco tech culture. Nick Douglas was one of the few people I met who pointed to the elephant in the room of assumed wealth. "People behave as if we all make kind of the same. Which is weird because I had about half a year where I wasn't really doing much of anything and so I was almost always broke. And meanwhile a few friends are like, oh, you should go rock-climbing with us . . . I wanted to. I just couldn't fucking afford it." To forge the type of social connections necessary to move into the upper echelons of the tech scene requires being able to take part in group activities, travel to conferences, and work on personal projects. This requires middle- to upper-class wealth, which filters out most people.

The mythology of meritocracy has several ideological effects. It denies the role of personal connections, wealth, background, gender, race, or education in an individual's success. If, for example, women (or people of color, or gay people) are not getting venture-capital funding at the same rate as men, the myth maintains, it is due to their lack of ability rather than institutional sexism. It also justifies immense wealth as the worthy spoils of the smartest and best. This libertarian bent may explain why wealthy technology workers are far less philanthropic than their "high society" counterparts; the mythology certainly implies that those mired in poverty are similarly deserving of their lowly status.[10] The myth of the entrepreneur goes hand in hand with the myth of meritocracy, setting entrepreneurs apart as a rare, visionary breed who uniquely deserve their success.

### Entrepreneurship

Throughout this book we have seen that the entrepreneur occupies the highest-status position in the tech scene. Entrepreneurs personify individualism, technological innovation, creativity, and intelligence—all characteristics that reinforce the myth of meritocracy. When I asked Tristan Walker of Foursquare whom he considered high status, he explained:

> I'm still jealous of a lot of folks in the valley, just out of respect. Because they've gone out and started their own companies and done things. I've been fortunate to work at two of the hottest tech companies ever. But I didn't start them. There's a kind of inherent sexiness about that, and it's a drive that I'll always have. It's like eventually at some point, be it 50 years down the road or 100, I'd like to start my own company. I think that's kind of the pinnacle; not only do it on your own but do it well, in a way that really fundamentally changes the way people interact in the world.

Here Walker reinforces the ideas that being an employee of even a "hot" company is not as cool as being an entrepreneur and that the best entrepreneurs create significant social change. Entrepreneurs almost never claim that they founded a company to get rich; instead, they usually cloak their ambitions in idealistic language. This rhetorical move justifies the extremely high status of people who sold companies for millions of dollars: members of the tech community claim that their drive and intelligence are impressive, not their wealth. Yelp founder Jeremy Stoppelman said, "That's really the competition, whose startup is more revolutionary and impactful in driving the industry forward, is more interesting than just who has the most money or who has the fancy corporate jets or who drives the fancy cars."

Technology journalist Kara Swisher disagrees: "Money is the most important factor. They would deny it up and down, but you know, stock options, who is in on a hot company, who gets the stock options, what kind of stock options they get, how they are paid. I think the people at Google suddenly became the smartest people in the universe, because, you know, they are, but they aren't. And the minute that stock went down, they definitely lost status." Similarly, former *Valleywag* editor and professional cynic Owen Thomas scoffs: "Well, when you really dig down into OK, 'What are your personal goals, where do you see yourself?' Like, they don't want to change the world really. They want to better their wallet, which is not that different from everyone else out there. And, you know, not that bad of a thing really, except they're trying to blow up like just living an ordinary life into something grandiose and, you know, into a cult." Membership in the "cult" of people like Steve Jobs or Mark Zuckerberg, as we will see, is highly coveted by young people.

Because entrepreneurs are so high status, there is an enormous industry focused on teaching and promoting entrepreneurship. Stanford, which has an outsized influence on the tech scene, has a Center for Entrepreneurial Studies at its business school, the Stanford Technology Ventures Program in the engineering school, and so many other groups devoted to entrepreneurship that there is an umbrella organization called the Stanford Entrepreneurship

Network that coordinates them all. The *Princeton Review* now ranks both graduate and undergraduate entrepreneurship programs. Global Entrepreneurship Week (GEW) holds activities in 115 countries and is supported by President Obama and dozens of other world leaders. (GEW describes its mission as "about unleashing ideas and doing what it takes to bring them to life—spotting opportunities, taking risks, solving problems, being creative, building connections and learning from both failure and success. It is about thinking big and making your mark on the world—doing good while doing well at the same time.") At the elite tech conference Google Zeitgeist, I met teenagers who were founding charitable non-profits and calling themselves "social entrepreneurs." Many of these non-profits were basically student organizations with a handful of participants, but "social entrepreneurship" sounded much sexier. When I asked Twitter co-founder Ev Williams why he thought young people were so focused on becoming entrepreneurs, he answered: "One is you can get rich, that's pretty good. But the newer part of it culturally seems to be that you're like a hero. Steve Jobs is the epitome. You're an artist. You're a visionary. You're a hero. You're a billionaire. You have tremendous amounts of power. Power is also probably a huge part of it. And it's like well what's more awesome than that. It's like the fame of a rock star, but more power and more money. It sounds pretty good." The glamour and wealth of young entrepreneurs, combined with the "halo effect" of beloved products, make it easy to see why such prospects, even if rare, are so attractive.

Another common myth about entrepreneurship was that it was an inherent personal attribute that could not be taught. As journalist Om Malik described, "You are a natural born entrepreneur. There is no other way, you know. Like, you have to be hustling from day one. Winners are those who just know one thing, basically. My favorite description of an entrepreneur is a person who cannot handle the status quo and who wants to rearrange the world basically in their own vision." In this case, entrepreneurs are like writers who cannot help but write: they cannot help but "change the world." In reality, both writing and entrepreneurship require a great deal of repetitive grunt work without which few will be successful. Moreover, the entrepreneurs who are successful are so at least partially due to luck. Many great products never gain a significant user base, and other ideas fail and are replaced with newer and trendier iterations. Most successful entrepreneurs fully acknowledge this. As Jeremy Stoppelman explains:

> We put a lot of stock in the heroics of the entrepreneur and the genius of the idea or whatever. But if you actually look at it, it's so rare, there [are] basically almost no examples of a great idea where there was just one team that figured it out magically. At the time, when we started Yelp, I was like, "We're super stealthy, nobody has this idea, we're such super geniuses." Then literally, like, a couple of weeks before we launched, somebody announced that [he] was doing almost the same thing. And like a month after we launched, somebody else comes out of the closet, doing the same thing. And we were all clustered so close together, which meant a bunch of technology lined up that people knew could potentially solve this issue of how you find a great little business, how you bring word of mouth to the web. There are some nuances to how do you get that right and how do you nail it, and how do you actually win, but it just goes to show that the idea itself is very rarely truly novel.

Scholarship on innovation backs up this perspective. It turns out that the entrepreneur as a "great man" falls into the myth of technical innovation in which individuals are responsible for progressive leaps in technology. Rather than a "great man" with a eureka moment who single-handedly invents something game-changing, most innovations involve parallel developments, uncredited contributors, failures and starts, and lengthy social histories, all of which make for a far less exciting narrative.

The myth of the entrepreneur is so popular because it aligns with core American values. Orvis Collins and David Moore write that the entrepreneur is a "heroic figure in American folklore akin perhaps, to Davy Crockett and other truly indigenous epic types—

stalwart independents who hewed forests, climbed over the mountains, built new communities, rose from nothing to something, and did all the things American heroes must have done to build a great nation."[11] American culture places a high value on the "self-made man" and the rags-to-riches story of Horatio Alger, both of which are still remarkably persistent tropes in popular discourse and business writing.[12] The image of the successful high-tech entrepreneur is surprisingly similar across twenty-five years of technology development: young, rich, famous, intrinsically risk-taking, innovative, and intelligent. This image has deep implications for the way the technology industry functions, particularly when it comes to gender.

## Gender and the Myths of Entrepreneurship and Meritocracy

Entrepreneurialism is a loaded concept that incorporates male-normative notions of behavior and success—and because entrepreneurs are so high status, this means that women have been systematically excluded from the highest levels of the technology scene. Scholars widely agree that the trope of the "entrepreneur" is white and male. John Ogbor writes that entrepreneurship "has sustained traditional dichotomies, oppositions and dualities—between male and female—where the male-oriented definition of reality is upheld as the legitimate world-view celebrating masculine concepts of control, competition, rationality, dominance, etc."[13] Similarly, studies of entrepreneurship discourse have repeatedly found that "entrepreneurs" are male-gendered, while "female entrepreneurs" are ignored, under-covered, and portrayed less favorably than men.[14] For instance, in her study of entrepreneurs, Helene Ahl found that in business discourse 70 percent of words used to describe entrepreneurs were male-gendered (these included self-reliant, assertive, forceful, risk-taking, self-sufficient, leader, competitive, and ambitious).[15] This skewed discourse has an ideological effect, namely, it discourages women from pursuing entrepreneurship by positioning it as a male enterprise, and by portraying "women entrepreneurs" as unusual.[16]

In Silicon Valley specifically, the image of the entrepreneur that has persisted through thirty years of boom-and-bust cycles is almost always young, white, and male. Back in the mid-1980s, in his book *The Big Score: The Billion Dollar Story of Silicon Valley,* Michael Shawn Malone described Silicon Valley denizens as "thirty year old tycoons in T-shirts, making their first hundred million before they buy their first pin-striped suit; secretaries worth millions thanks to a few dollars spent on stock options; garage inventors suddenly finding themselves on lists of the world's richest men."[17] In this portrayal, the "world's richest" inventors are men, while the "secretaries," presumably female, get rich through the almost-accidental purchasing of stock. This image of the industry as male-dominated, with women either irrelevant or playing the part of girlfriends or gold-diggers, persisted through the microelectronics era:

> Why there are few women in positions of responsibility in SV [Silicon Valley] is complex and puzzling . . . females have yet to enter the boardrooms or the executive suites of SV . . . [venture capitalists, scientists, finance people, startups—] these power brokers rely exclusively on their personal networks, passing information about job openings, possibilities for expansion, and promising companies to their friends— other men. Women are virtually absent from the power centers of SV corporations.[18]

To the dot-com era:

> Money doesn't impress. It's too ubiquitous to dazzle. And there are too many ways here to make a lucky bundle and never really have deserved it. Driving a Ferrari doesn't impress anyone but the heavy-on-the-eye-shadow secretaries perched on the bar stools at the Friday evening Black Angus happy hour.[19]

To the Web 2.0 era:

> By the time they had started the incubator, all three [company founders] had gotten hipster makeovers . . . add designer

jeans, Pumas, and a supply of tight-fitting T-shirts with witty sayings, and the geeks were now practically ladies' men. Add the bank accounts, and they definitely were. And don't forget the ultimate Web 2.0 accessory: puppies.[20]

In each segment, taken from a different book about Silicon Valley life, the movers and shakers are men, while women are secretaries or sex objects easily impressed by wealth or cute animals.

The same tropes run through more contemporary descriptions of the Web 2.0 scene. In 2008, *Details* magazine ran an article called "The Playboys of Tech." It profiled the wild-and-crazy lives of entrepreneurs Mark Zuckerberg (Facebook), Jakob Lodwick (CollegeHumor), Kevin Rose (Digg), David Karp (Tumblr), Charles Foreman (OMGPOP), and Pete Cashmore (*Mashable*). The story describes these men's extreme youth and wealth, and the women who fall all over them; while a few accomplished women like technology journalist Caroline McCarthy appear in the story, they are framed as romantic interests. The writer even includes the term "founder fetishism: when a woman goes only for men who have started high-tech companies."[21] During fieldwork, people joked about "Web 2.0 floozies" and "CE-ho's" to describe women who enter the tech scene just to sleep with founders. Clearly, these portrayals are deeply sexist and heterosexist, reducing women to playthings and trophies. But they also restrict women (and non-white men or gay men) to a secondary role, positioning the "entrepreneur" as something only white men can embody successfully.

While entrepreneurs are consistently portrayed in popular discourse as young, brash white men, this does not actually map to the reality of American entrepreneurship. No less than 40 percent of privately held businesses in the United States are owned by women.[22] And despite the attribution of entrepreneurial traits to men, studies have shown no significant differences between women and men who start companies in terms of education, technical background, or motivation.[23] In fact, by some metrics, women-owned companies outperform the average: women owners, on average, are more conservative about spending money, and are more likely to survive the transition from startup to established company.[24] Despite this, women are virtually absent from the upper echelons of technology. While venture-backed technology companies do not represent the majority of U.S. companies, they are given the highest status in Silicon Valley and are overwhelmingly run and funded by men. Only 8 percent of venture-backed startups are founded by women, and only 14 percent of venture capitalists are women; at the top technology venture-capital firms, only 8 percent of investment professionals are women.[25]

### The Influence of Myths about the Male Entrepreneur

These assumptions about women and entrepreneurship are reflected in individual-level discourse. While many members of the tech scene—both men and women—espoused equality and meritocracy during the period of my study, they simultaneously reenacted and reinforced sexist stereotypes about women in technology through their own talk and practice. Women's contributions to the scene were undervalued or attributed to men, women were systematically sexualized and judged on appearance, and structural sexism was denied. This lopsided description of women's roles discourages women's participation in entrepreneurial technology, creating fewer female role models and mentors for younger women and thus perpetuating the low rates of women in technology.

One informant who chose not to be named offered the following comment that demonstrates several recurring themes. The informant is discussing Tara Hunt and Chris Messina, two members of the social media scene who dated, worked on several projects together, and then broke up (I interviewed Hunt). Hunt is a marketer and author, while Messina is a technologist and developer.

> If you wanted a pivotal story about the difference between doing stuff that's real and matters, and doing stuff that's superficial and just social flurry, [look at] the whole relationship of Chris Messina and Tara Hunt . . . The divergence of those two people is dramatic. Chris is going to live to do

great things over the next 40 years. Tara, if she can keep her head above water, . . . is going to become a PR flak. She's going to have a PR agency and she's going to help people use social media. If she's sensible, she'll mature and figure out how to do it as a business. She'll exploit the brand that she has for that benefit, but it's not going to cure cancer.

This informant illustrated several patterns I observed when people discussed women in the scene. First, earlier in our conversation he called Hunt "one of those young beautiful people" as opposed to Messina, someone who has "done great things." The informant, like others in this scene, objectifies Hunt, evaluates her based on her looks, and ultimately dismisses her. (This is not solely something men do to women; some women in the scene engage in self-objectification, including posting flattering or risqué shots of themselves online, or find public discussion of their sexuality empowering.) Second, Hunt's accomplishments, including co-founding an agency, organizing several conferences, and writing a book, are attributed to her involvement with Messina. Third, her contributions to the scene are seen as insignificant compared to Messina's. Sadly, these motifs recurred throughout my fieldwork. Individual women in the tech scene were discussed in terms of appearance and sexuality, their accomplishments were attributed to their involvement with men, and their contributions to the scene were devalued—by both men and women.

These themes in individual discourse were picked up by the media. Megan McCarthy told me: "When you have a story about a female entrepreneur, their looks get mentioned, men's looks never do. They'll be described as like, a petite blonde. Would you ever say tall, dark-haired Kevin Rose or something? I mean come on, although actually Kevin did get called doughy, which was great." This account is consistent with studies showing that media portrayals of powerful women, whether lawyers, sports stars, or politicians, are often sexist and objectifying, but it is particularly ironic in the tech industry given its claims of exceptional egalitarianism.[26] For instance, a *BusinessWeek* story on Google executive Marissa Mayer described her as a "tall, striking blonde with blue eyes" while *Pop-Crunch* called Leah Culver "the hottest software engineer alive." These comments are often positive (one informant said "you've got the Ariel Waldmans of the world who are completely out there about everything that happens in their lives, and sexually and technically, who are really smart, really beautiful, and you scratch your head and go, 'And you can actually manage that?' And they do!"). But they still base a woman's worth on her looks rather than accomplishments, lessening women's contributions to the scene and positioning them as objects rather than actors. This constitutes a barrier to women's participation that is not in place for men, who are rarely, if ever, evaluated on their looks.

Mentoring and networking are common in technology. During the period of my study, events were held for the express purpose of networking, and mentorship, both formal and informal, was widespread. Adam Jackson, a newcomer to San Francisco and aspiring entrepreneur, was mentored by several older (male) technologists and spent time working with teenage (male) entrepreneurs. Studies show that mentorship is an important part of career mobility and longevity in business in general, but that women face more barriers than men in finding a mentor due to a lack of women in upper-level management and the belief that there is too little common ground between men and women in the field to make cross-gender mentor-protégé relationships work.[27] This mentoring problem is compounded in the technology industry since there are so few women in upper management.[28] I found that relationships that might have been characterized as "networking" or "mentoring" between men were sexualized if one member of the dyad was female. Leah Culver, for instance, had worked with several well-known technologists, but *Valleywag* consistently framed her involvement with these men as sexual and painted these collaborations as shameful. In an informal analysis of discourse around "hinted" affairs in media stories, *Awl* blogger Jane Hu wrote:

> The relative stories I found all contained one trend: ambitious and often "troublesome" women who profited professionally

by their involvement with established men of authority. Of course, had these stories involved the relationship between two men, one would always (well, almost always) have simply called it "networking." With women, networking was recast as a pejorative and manipulative working of the system. And because there were ladies involved, the articles . . . emphasized their sexual appeal and activities with the men in question.[29]

This is virtually identical to two dynamics I observed in gossip and talk around male-female friendship: mentoring and networking were sexualized, and any accomplishments of the women involved were attributed to men.

While there certainly were women and men within the scene who both dated and worked together, these relationships were described in terms like "gold-digging" or "sleeping her way to the top" regardless of whether they were romantic or not. Culver's founding of Pownce was attributed to her friendship with Kevin Rose or Twitter designer Daniel Burka. Owen Thomas wrote a lengthy blog post about Culver, which read, in part: "If she doesn't want to be famous, Culver might want to take a look at her relentless techno-sexuality, which more than hints at the acquisition of influence rather than intimacy as its goal. Is it sexist to point this out? Perhaps, but not nearly as sexist as touting technical skills while sleeping your way to the top."[30] I argued with Thomas about this interpretation in our interview, but he responded:

> I find the Leah Culver story fascinating because you actually have a woman who is very deliberately sleeping her way to the top. Like a classic, classic stereotype, almost a parody of how you might imagine that would be done. So, if you think that is something that is bad and should not be encouraged and falls outside the social norms that we would like to foster, what do you do? Do you say I'm not going to write about that because people might say, "Oh look, you know, there is this woman acting like a stereotype and we

don't want to encourage the existence of that stereotype"? Or do you say, "Well, no actually you want to say, 'Look, this is bad, don't do this, don't support this, don't tolerate this, don't remain silent about this.'"

From Thomas's point of view, Culver truly was "sleeping her way to the top," and it was his journalistic duty to point this out so that other women wouldn't follow the same path. This story was widely accepted; one informant, a self-professed feminist woman, said snidely, "Unfortunately for Leah, it's not that she's sleeping."[31]

Thomas's questionable logic becomes even more problematic when this portrayal of Culver is shown to be part of a pattern. In addition to Tara Hunt and Chris Messina, one informant told me that the career of Ariel Waldman, a social media consultant and blogger, had been launched when technologist Tantek Çelik "discovered" her. Blogger Penelope Trunk wrote a post calling business strategist Glenda Bautista a "gold-digger" for her relationship with WordPress founder Matt Mullenweg, although Mullenweg achieved his success only after he and Bautista began dating (Trunk backpedaled once Bautista's considerable professional accomplishments were pointed out).[32] In all these instances, women's accomplishments were attributed to their involvement with men; I did not witness a single instance of this with men who were mentored by other men.

This devaluation of women's accomplishments was systematic, reflecting the idea that women in the tech scene are overlooked or excluded because they are less worthy than men.[33] One informant, an investor, said some very questionable things about women in an interview. (He looked horrified when he realized what he had said on the record, and I promised to keep his identity secret.) In his words: "The basic conclusion we came to is like, women are just emotional and it reminds me—don't take this the wrong way—of a seven-year-old kid, or an eight-year-old kid who's struggling with emotions, doesn't know what's happening, they can't verbalize it, it happens to all of us, even men. And men can shut down, get angry, but we can logically do something. And women can't express it to the guy logically." Clearly, if a venture capitalist thinks that women are less logical and emotionally mature than men, this will make him less likely to fund women-run companies. One (male) informant told me:

> Ariel Waldman when she got hired as the Community Manager at Pownce she didn't really have a track record other than being a sex blogger, and now she is writing a book about social media and she is doing community management work for NASA. So Pownce was a failure, not because she failed but, if you look at her resume, it would appear that so far Ariel doesn't really have a track record still. So she is running off of, I guess fumes and she is doing a great job but if I was an analyst . . . I would say, I don't know how she got this job at NASA. She is a sex blogger who worked for a failed startup who is on Twitter. She has like 20,000 followers.

The informant implies that Waldman's success is unwarranted because she does not have the "track record" for it. While he admits she is doing a "great job," he undermines this statement by suggesting she isn't qualified. Similarly, another informant said about Tara Hunt: "It's very high school or college. It's like the sorority sisters, the great girls at school, that cadre of people who definitely were not the nerds, who were not the geeks . . . you know, the beautiful people. And so there's that, but it's paper-thin. No offense, I like Tara and she's a nice person, but if you sit down and actually talk to her, it's like two inches and a mile wide. There's no depth." After disclaiming that he means "no offense," this informant places Hunt in the category of the "beautiful people," stating that she is pretty, but has no intellectual depth. (I interviewed Bautista, Hunt, and Waldman and found each to be thoughtful, intelligent, and knowledgeable about their respective fields.) These quotes are troubling because they suggest the systematic gender discrimination that women in the scene must endure on their way to achieving success, discrimination that stems from the perception that they are less qualified than their male peers. As the former dean of MIT concluded after a lengthy study of gender discrimination and the status of women faculty members, "Once and for all we must recognize that the heart and soul of discrimination, the last refuge of the bigot, is to say that those who are discriminated against deserve it because they are less good."[34]

Significantly, these patterns are perpetrated by women as well as men. Some women capitalize on their looks, making their appearance a significant component of their online persona. In a social milieu where women are commonly objectified, self-objectification makes strategic sense, but it plays into the underlying problem that women are evaluated on appearance while men are not. It also spurs resentment from others who perceive that good-looking women have an unfair advantage in the scene. Just as many women as men have made judgmental comments to me about another woman's looks, dating prospects, or sexuality. Moreover, some women I spoke with dismissed sexism as a problem. Ariel Waldman said: "[Leah Culver] doesn't buy into the whole super feminist thing which I enjoy because I'm of the same mindset where, you know, it's like, we're working on cool stuff, we don't have this, I guess attitude of like, "We're a woman in tech." [Laughter] . . . and when I meet people who are like that, I don't know. It's sad but the first thing I think is like, are you actually good?" Waldman's statement emphasizes how widespread the myth of meritocracy is. Tokenism is widely denounced, and often women are accused of being tokens when they appear on a panel or achieve a professional accomplishment.

There are two major implications of this type of discourse. First, gender discrimination undermines claims that the tech industry is a meritocracy. Although even successful women in the scene will say they do not want to be a "woman in tech" but just a woman "in tech," their gender affects how people perceive their accomplishments. While the technology industry is supposedly egalitarian and democratic, it privileges the voices and experiences of men. For instance, at the 2009 Web 2.0 Summit, 80 percent of the speakers were men, while the 2009 "Future of Web Apps" conference boasted a single woman speaker and no people of color. A 2013 conference organized by Facebook, Google, and the *Financial Times* had not even one female speaker.[35] And the startup incubator Y Combinator came under attack for accepting only 14 women out of 450 participants.[36] The high status placed on the entrepreneur, a mantle that very few women can or do wear successfully, systematically excludes women from the upper echelons of social media culture.

The second has to do with the culture of production. While most of the people in Web 2.0 are not engineers per se—there are more entrepreneurs, marketers, business development people, and so on than developers—technology skills are valued most. Women in tech, however, generally work in marketing, public relations, project management, event planning, graphic design, or community management, all lower-status jobs than developers, engineers, venture capitalists, or entrepreneurs. The number of women in computer science is dismally low; according to the U.S. Bureau of Labor, women comprise 19 percent of hardware engineers, 21 percent of software engineers, and 22 percent of computer programmers. Computer and mathematical professions are, overall, 75 percent male.[37] Moreover, these numbers have actually decreased since the 1980s.[38] The issue of women in computer science and engineering is tremendously complicated. Researchers have identified a plethora of reasons for these numbers, including a masculine programming culture, low rates of female math and science students, a lack of role models, and few depictions of female programmers in the media.[39] The attitudes I identified are part of this problem, but it is difficult to identify which part. Certainly, systematic gender bias in the tech scene, whether conscious or unconscious, contributes to maintaining a male-dominated culture of production.[40] This suggests that women's perspectives are not being incorporated into technological products.

These problems are widely acknowledged by others. There are many organizations dedicated to supporting women in technology, such as Women 2.0, Change the Ratio, Astria, Girls in Tech, the Forum for Women's Entrepreneurs and Executives, and the National Center for Women and Information Technology. And there has been a flurry of attention paid to egregious sexist incidents at technology conferences and among nerd subcultures.[41] But complex problems have complex solutions. Unfortunately, the persistent idea that the technology industry is a meritocracy undermines these efforts, because it implies—incorrectly—that those who do not rise to the top are less capable than those who do.

# CONCLUSION

———

In September 2011, I flew to Scottsdale, Arizona, for a conference. After checking in at a luxury desert resort, I was shuttled to another luxury resort to eat lamb gyros and stuffed grape leaves in a Moroccan-style courtyard glittering with lights. Speakers like Newark mayor Cory Booker, Google's Eric Schmidt, and CNBC's Maria Bartiromo mingled with conference attendees and the winners of the Zeitgeist Young Minds contest, ten people between eighteen and twenty-four years old who were "changing the world." Over the next two days, we wined and dined, heard Sandra Day O'Connor and Robert Reich discuss the economy, saw the band OK Go play an intimate dinner concert, watched skateboarder Tony Hawk beat teen idol Justin Bieber's manager at the iPhone sensation Angry Birds, and received complimentary Google Chromebooks as a token of the company's appreciation.

This was Google Zeitgeist, Google's exclusive, all-expenses-paid attempt to bring together the "great minds of our time" for the benefit of the invited guests—mostly advertising executives, the bread and butter of Google's business model. I was one of perhaps five academics, but the entertainment industry and non-profits were well represented (I was very excited to meet Guy Oseary, Madonna's manager). The theme was "one of us, all of us," with a strong undercurrent of the buzzword du jour, social entrepreneurship. We heard repeatedly that the values of technology, Silicon Valley, and innovation could help solve the problems of society at large. As Schmidt said, "This model of investment, innovation, and overcoming failure is necessary. If we're going to achieve greatness in the twenty-first century, and I believe we will, we have to start with some Silicon Valley thinking." He stated that "ultimately, this world will be owned by an entrepreneur."

I was impressed by the calls for greater public investment in education, and enjoyed listening to talks by highly motivated people who had founded non-profits, made groundbreaking documentary films, and otherwise donated significant time and energy to social justice and social welfare causes. People called for doubling teacher salaries, for investing in primary and preventative care in poor neighborhoods, and for increasing public funding for foreign journalism. Rather than the libertarian philosophy often attributed to Northern California executives, Zeitgeist furthered a spirit of can-do philanthropic optimism similar to that espoused by Google's former chief rival Bill Gates, now at the Bill and Melinda Gates Foundation.

The event was dazzling, and I was dazzled. I felt like I had arrived as part of the digerati. Although my own occupation—postdoc at Microsoft Research and future university professor—did not impress anyone besides marketers who wanted to hear my insights on young people, I felt that I was in good company. Wealth cast a velvety comfort over the event, with Google showering us with gifts from Havaianas flip-flops to hardbound copies of speakers' books. The executives, who frequently slipped out of sessions to take calls or write e-mails, gave the event a feeling of busy importance. Everything about the event positioned the attendees as elites. The nice hotel rooms, delicious meals, intelligent speakers conversing on world issues, and being repeatedly told that we were the brightest and best all contributed to a pleasurable feeling of specialness.

Zeitgeist demonstrated the seductiveness of digital elitism. Being part of the digital elite is a heady feeling. It incorporates social consciousness and intellectual discussion. It is optimistic, in that technology is positioned as a solution to an array of difficult problems. At the same time, it inculcates an air of superiority and a universality of experience that truly only applies to a very small number of the world's most privileged individuals. The speakers were a diverse lot, but the attendees were primarily men, they were primarily white, and they were primarily middle-aged.

Digital elitism does not reconfigure power; it entrenches it. It provides justification for enormous gaps between rich and poor, for huge differences between average people and highly sought-after engineers who are paid large starting salaries and showered with benefits. It idealizes a "better class of rich people," as Kara Swisher put it, who evangelize philanthropy and social entrepreneurship, but it also promotes the idea that entrepreneurship is a catch-all solution, and that a startup culture is the best way to solve any problem. (The libertarian bent of tech culture, too, means that most tech people are not very philanthropic.) But as I've discussed extensively in this book, not everyone can work at a startup, and the business model of startups cannot be applied to all situations.

My original impetus behind this project was to look realistically at the influence of profit-driven business models on the use and development of social media applications. I wanted to provide a counterbalance to the notion that social media promoted some sort of ideal, egalitarian society. I knew from my years of working in dot-com companies that decisions about software were often based on what would make the most money, rather than what would be the most beneficial for the user or, even less realistically, what was more democratic or participatory. I also wished to test the theory that social media was providing new, meritocratic opportunities for visibility and success. There certainly are people who can attribute much of their professional success to tools like blogs and Twitter. In September 2008, I was squeezing through a crowded party for the social media blog *Mashable* when I met Stowe Boyd. Boyd, wearing a Kangol hat and a white beard, was a Silicon Valley veteran and blogger. In the first five minutes I met him, he told me that he had been blogging for ten years; had invented the term "social tool" and was the top Google result for the phrase; and had 90,000 visitors a month on his three blogs. Boyd, a consummate self-promoter and connector, despises the term "self-branding." Yet he's good at it. He exemplifies the entrepreneurial self, one who harnesses social media's broadcasting ability to its fullest extent. Boyd knew everyone in the scene, and during our interview gave me lengthy, detailed descriptions, and critiques, of its movers and shakers. His blog contains thoughtful commentary and analysis of social software; in another life, he might have been an academic. Yet his professional accomplishments did not include starting a company, garnering funding, or writing popular software. Boyd, through sheer force of will, successful networking, and strategic use of social media, had positioned himself as an expert and tech scene heavyweight, and those around him seemed happy to accept his take on things.

Boyd is a new breed of tech scene insider, one who has harnessed self-presentation techniques to successfully build a career. He is exactly the sort of person whom Gary Vaynerchuk might hold up as a role model, and who is poised to succeed in a de-centered, destabilized American economy. But Boyd's success is exceptional. He is able to talk about the "right" sort of things and have the "right" sort of people pay attention. There are far more people who have tried, and failed, to make this work, because they find the discomfort and conflict that comes with an internet presence too difficult; because the information they broadcast is too feminine, raw, or "uninteresting"; or simply because they exist outside of the tightly wound networks of power and capital that make up Silicon Valley.

Social media applies contradictory ideals of counterculture and capitalism to the self, friendships, intimate relationships, and interpersonal interactions. People can spread ideas and creations to a formerly inconceivable mass audience, but only bounded and influenced by the restraints of modern neoliberal capitalism. As sociolinguist Crispin Thurlow writes, "The line between commerce and the rest of life is often blurred—and, indeed, strategically blurred—in the rhetoric of social media."[1] The strategies I've documented involve reconceptualizing and repositioning oneself into the familiar limits of a commodity: the brand or the celebrity. But they are not exactly the same. The micro-celebrity is held to a different set of standards than the movie star; in particular, the micro-celebrity is expected to be available and transparent, in line with the exhibitionist internet, rather than carefully guarded and assisted by a network of managers like the movie star. Because the self-brand is a person underneath his or her shiny exterior, with the attendant imperfections and mistakes, creating and maintaining a consistent image involves real labor, which is exchanged for the relational and personal benefits provided by social media, such as support, intimacy, and connection. This labor value is also converted into literal capital by social media companies like Facebook, YouTube, and Twitter, which profit from personal disclosure and its attraction of users to their products. This series of exchanges thus commodifies identity, emotion, and relationships within a digital context.

The self-branded, micro-celebrity ideal also invites a normalization of surveillance that threatens individual agency. When social technologies emerged, pundits and journalists hailed YouTube, Flickr, and Wikipedia as a way for individuals to fully participate in the creation and dissemination of culture and knowledge. But what is acceptable to create and disseminate has been increasingly circumscribed by what is safe: that is, what is acceptable to be publicly judged, permanently recorded, and viewed by all manner of people, from one's family to one's future employer. Even in contexts that are largely permissive about acceptable behavior, thinking of oneself as a product means sharing strategically rather than honestly. The "edited self" is one constructed with a particular group of people in mind, and one that people expect will be scrutinized. In fact, for decades, the Northern California tech community has celebrated the white, male entrepreneur, and the further one's public presentation drifts from this normative ideal, the more one is subject to public judgment.

The care with which people create their "edited self" is at odds with the stated ideals of equality, meritocracy, and collaboration that permeate the tech scene. Although it is normal, even socially necessary, for technology workers to create a visible presence online and participate fully in social media, members do this with a critical eye as to how their actions will be received. Since women in the scene are subject to scrutiny for their appearance, information-sharing, and relationships in a way that men are not, there is a stark gender imbalance in the way user-created content is perceived and judged.[2]

Social technology, like other forms of mass media, teaches us about ourselves and how to be in the world. In *The Celluloid Closet*, a documentary about portrayals of gays and lesbians in film, narrator Lily Tomlin says that people learn gender and sexuality from watching reflections of femininity, masculinity, heterosexuality, and homosexuality in the movies.[3] Modern Americans learn to be proper citizens not only from each other, but also from reality television, self-help books, talk shows, novels, magazines, and films. All of these media teach viewers how their homes should look, how they should dress, and how pets and kids should behave; equally important, they provide models of inappropriate behavior. Although most social media technologies allow a broad range of self-presentation strategies, users look to friends and peers to learn appropriate use of these technologies, and alter their online identities accordingly. Not everyone is subject to the harsh scrutiny with which *Reblogging Donk* criticizes Julia Allison, but sites like *Lamebook.com*, a blog that mocks inappropriate Facebook actions, demonstrate the collective policing and judgment of online behavior. For instance, on the site someone had posted a screen capture of an exchange that occurred when a teenager, Emily, complained on Facebook that she "wants to get a place with someone, and b on hur own finally . . . and when I do I'm gunna party allday and night, stay out as long as I want and I wont have a dumb curfue and wont have to worry about any parents. HA!!!" Her mother, Polly, read her status update and responded: "If you get a place with someone, you won't be on your own. You only have a curfew because I need to go to bed and don't have a key to the deadbolt. Remember, when you don't have 'to worry about any parents,' you won't have parents to worry about you either. Just saying." This site, and the many others like it, is only funny because of the unwritten norms around social network sites; in this case, don't forget that you're friends with your mother. Readers of *Lamebook.com*, which may include Emily herself, learn that "successful" social media use requires self-monitoring and censorship—one must always be mindful of the internet audience.

The norms of social media are deeply influenced by the Northern California technology scene. Although this scene incorporates many of the countercultural, radical presuppositions of activist movements—that media consolidation limits diversity of opinions, that government should be transparent, that corporations should be responsible to their communities and customers, and so forth—it does so in a way that prioritizes personal reforms over structural change. The famous slogan of the second-wave feminist movement, "the personal is political," emphasized that gender roles and discrimination played out in micro-interactions and personal choices, what Michel Foucault calls "capillaries of power."[4] When applied to the inward focus and self-monitoring encouraged by social media, the personal is antithetical to the type of large-scale structural change that these activist groups originally advocated. This shift fits within a larger history whereby corporate discourse has incorporated radical principles and diluted them in the process—consider advertising executives' use of counterculture individualism to sell soda or personal computer manufacturers' parroting of the idealism of hackers and phone phreaks.[5]

In fact, the values promoted by users of social media are those of the enterprise business culture. Although the top-down, hierarchical management style of the 1950s and 1960s was replaced in the dotcom era with one that emphasized the leveling of hierarchies in the workplace, creative self-expression through labor, and independent workers, this has not significantly improved the lot of the individual worker.[6] If anything, the free-agent culture of enterprise labor justifies neoliberal policies, which dismantle socioeconomic protections like pension plans and employer-sponsored health insurance, and so both provide less protection to workers and normalize instability. These changes are not always experienced negatively. Many people in the tech scene love the independence and self-actualization that small business ownership or freelancing brings them, and a sense of bubbling creativity was palpable among many of the technologists I interviewed. People like Stowe Boyd, and the tech scene as a whole, prove that this model is viable, and successful freelance developers and two-person startups are lauded as an ideal to which all others must aspire. But this business model is generally limited to a very small percentage of the population: namely, white-collar creative professionals with advanced technology skills, high levels of education, and self-motivation. That is, not everyone can be an entrepreneur, even though in neoliberal philosophy, everyone should be. Self-help gurus like Tim Ferriss and Gary Vaynerchuk reinforce this idea by suggesting that if one doesn't find success, one isn't working hard enough.

The strategies and tactics observed among members of the technology scene have trickled down to other social contexts. Certainly, researchers have chronicled micro-celebrity practice among different groups of young people; the word "micro-celebrity" was coined by Theresa Senft in a study of camgirls, not technology professionals.[7] While these tactics will look different when adopted by hip-hop artists, teenage Tumblr celebrities, food bloggers, or Pinterest enthusiasts, what remains common is how social media has rapidly and enthusiastically become bound up in market rhetoric. While working on this book, I began a study of online conspicuous consumption, looking at fashion bloggers. Traditionally, conspicuous consumption has referred to the physical display of high-status goods in face-to-face contexts; you won't want to keep up with the Joneses if you don't know that they have a Mercedes SLK or an in-ground pool. Fashion bloggers take pictures of their outfits and post them online, but they've also fully integrated the values of social media metrics, which position blog readership, number of comments, and so forth as indications of self-worth. Fashion bloggers try to present images of "authentic" style and fashion to engage their readers (and set them apart from traditional, presumably inauthentic fashion magazines), and moreover to appeal to potential advertisers and brands, who flood the successful bloggers with free clothes and invites to fashion shows. Online self-expression becomes valuable insofar as it is an instrument of attention.

When this project began, the economy was soaring and Web 2.0 was hyped not only as a social revolution but also as a potential source for immense wealth. The social revolution claim has since been tempered by nuanced critiques of the culture, commerce, and impacts of social software, while the wealth hype has been softened somewhat by the economic downturn (at the last South by Southwest I attended, a friend and I kept track of how often the phrase "in these troubling economic times" was repeated during presentations).[8] Yet although I conceived this project as a way to critique an over-the-top rhetoric that has been dampened by circumstance and harsh reality, the critique still stands. The status-seeking techniques that I found to be prevalent in the Northern California technology scene—lifestreaming, self-branding, and micro-celebrity—reflect many aspects of contemporary American culture: obsession with celebrity, fame, and publicity; fleeting job security; widespread belief in personal authenticity and the "American Dream"; and the increasing popularity of social media. Web 2.0 technologies represent a significant shift in how people record, track, and disseminate personal information, with potentially troubling effects. In addition to shaping our views of social status, privacy, and community, these technologies have enabled the infiltration of neoliberal, market-driven values and ethics into day-to-day relationships with others and even into ways that we, as users of social media, think about ourselves.

# CAST OF CHARACTERS

—

The following people are mentioned in this book. Due to the fluctuating nature of internet careers, many of them have since moved on to bigger and better things.

| | |
|---|---|
| Allison, Julia | Writer, television personality |
| Barcelona, Jim | Engineer, formerly at Dogster.com |
| Bautista, Glenda | Online advertising project manager and strategist |
| Beale, Scott | Founder of Laughingsquid.com; blogger and photographer |
| Belmont, Veronica | Video blogger and host |
| Benveniste, Gabriel | Founder of SonicLiving |
| Boyd, Stowe | Technology blogger |
| Brown, Tara "Tiger" | Founder of LA Makerspace; former Microsoft project manager; |

| | |
|---|---|
| Camp, Garrett | Co-founder of Stumbleupon and Uber |
| Çelik, Tantek | Former Chief Technologist at Technorati; micro-formats advocate |
| Chan, Adrian | User experience and social interaction designer |
| Cheng, Kevin | Founder of Incredible Labs; formerly at Twitter and Raptr |
| Codel, Eddie | Co-founder of Webzine; livestream video producer |
| Crowley, Dennis | Co-founder of Dodgeball and Foursquare |
| Culver, Leah | Engineer; co-founder of Pownce.com |
| Douglas, Nick | Former editor of *Valleywag*; internet humorist |
| Fake, Caterina | Co-founder of Flickr and Hunch |
| Fitton, Laura | a.k.a. Pistachio; Twitter marketing expert |
| Grant, Melissa Gira | Former *Valleywag* writer; writer and activist |
| Hartley, Hillary | Government 2.0 advocate |
| Hoffman, Auren | CEO of Rapleaf.com |
| Horowitz, Ben | Venture capitalist at Andreesson Horowitz |
| Hunt, Tara | Marketing blogger and writer; founder of Buyosphere |
| Jackson, Adam | Startup and Twitter enthusiast currently living in New Hampshire |
| Junell, Ryan | Co-founder of Webzine; director and documentarian |
| Kelly, Kevin | Founding editor of *Wired*; co-founder of Quantified Self meetups |
| Lacy, Sarah | Technology writer |
| Larson, Dale | Startup coach |
| Mager, Andrew | Former employee at C\|Net; currently Hacker Advocate at Spotify |
| Malik, Om | Journalist and blogger; founder of GigaOM.com |

| Masculino, Marianne | Former happiness engineer at Wordpress .com |
| McCarthy, Caroline | Former C\|Net tech blogger |
| McCarthy, Megan | Former *Valleywag* writer; technology journalist |
| Muller, Thor | Co-founder of Get Satisfaction; writer |
| Musk, Elon | Founder of Tesla Motors; formerly at PayPal |
| Newitz, Annalee | Writer and journalist; editor of i09.com |
| Nigam, Anu | Serial entrepreneur and venture capitalist |
| Nye, Dan | Former CEO of LinkedIn |
| Overby, Derek | Former director of social media marketing at Roost.com |
| Raffel, Daniel | Co-founder of Yahoo! Pipes; CEO of HeavyBits |
| Rose, Kevin | Co-founder of Digg and co-host of Diggnation |
| Russiangirl, Jacy | Julia Allison anti-fan |
| Starr, Nick | Blogger; Twitter enthusiast; provocateur |
| Steenson, Molly | Co-founder of Maxi; writer and academic |
| Stoppelman, Jeremy | CEO of Yelp.com |
| Swisher, Kara | Technology journalist at AllThingsD.com |
| Thomas, Owen | Former editor of *Valleywag*; technology journalist |
| Waldman, Ariel | Digital anthropologist and founder of Spacehack.org |
| Walker, Tristan | Former director of business development at Foursquare |
| Walters, April | Former community manager at Next New Networks; community manager at Foodspotting |
| Williams, Ev | Co-founder of Twitter |

# ACKNOWLEDGMENTS

———

I've been working on this project for more than five years, since I woke up one morning in San Francisco and thought, "I should write about status in social media!" (The idea of status came from my obsession with counterfeit luxury goods at the time. I believe I immediately took to Twitter to find out what people thought about this idea.) To write a dissertation, and then to return to that material and rewrite all of it into a book for an entirely different audience, requires both fortitude and a lot of people willing to contribute time and energy to your selfish cause.

Much of this book was written during my postdoc at Microsoft Research New England in the Social Media Collective. Extra special thanks go to the founder of SMC and my mentor, danah boyd. Danah is my biggest champion and my most productive collaborator, and even when we want to strangle each other (too many days spent together in the field, or in Israel, Redmond, D.C., or . . . ),

I love her very much and am very thankful for our robust scholarly partnership. MSRNE-SMC is a truly superlative group of scholars, and the warmest and most supportive intellectual environment possible was created by Mike Ananny, Nancy Baym, Kate Crawford, Mary Gray, and Andrés Monroy-Hernández while I was there. Thanks to frequent visitors Margy Avery, Beth Coleman, Nicole Ellison, and Eszter Hargittai for giving me career/publishing/negotiation/job-talk advice, as well as for modeling superior scholarship. Our research assistants and interns, particularly Alex Leavitt, Laura Norén, Jessa Lingel, Germaine Halegoua, Jazmin González-Rivero, Shawn Walker, and Heather Casteel, were inspiring in their enthusiasm, creativity, and intellectual breadth. Thanks must also go to Jennifer Chayes and Christian Borgs for supporting the SMC when we followed various crazy, meandering paths. And I very much appreciate Microsoft's commitment to basic research, as well as its support toward my progress on this book.

Yale University Press has been a wonderful home for this project, largely because of my editor, Joseph Calamia, who was a pleasure to work with throughout the process (and always very understanding when my deadlines slipped). Joe's thoughtful, detailed commentary on every word—several times!—is reflected on every page of this project. Thanks also to the anonymous reviewers of the proposal and manuscript, who took the time to write carefully considered critical feedback. My former editor, Alison MacKeen, also deserves credit for taking a chance on this book. I called in a lot of favors during the writing process that must be acknowledged. Terri Senft and Annette Markham provided detailed feedback on the micro-celebrity chapter and gave me brilliant critical feedback throughout. Warm thanks to my manuscript editor, Julie Carlson, who was a pleasure to work with. Laura Portwood-Stacer, Alex Leavitt, Molly Wright Steenson, Jed Brubaker, and Ann Friedman all generously read various drafts and chapters.

I had the privilege to work with a fantastic committee at New York University's Department of Media, Culture and Communication. My adviser, Marita Sturken, who read every word of my rambling five-hundred-page dissertation, has been an amazing source of pragmatic advice and intellectual commentary. My dissertation— and thus this project—could not have been completed without her. Helen Nissenbaum deeply influenced my thinking on privacy (and surveillance, and technological determinism, and value-embedded design) and provided me with wonderful examples for the life-streaming chapter. Biella Coleman pushed me to complicate my ideas and provided a solid anthropological grounding. All three women exemplify forward-thinking research and supportive collegiality. Thanks as well to Fred Turner, who was an outside reader for the dissertation and whose fantastic work on the California technical community served as a great inspiration for the history chapter. I also want to thank my graduate cohort, particularly Wazhmah Osman and Rachelle Sussman Rumph, for sticking with me through many ups and downs, including an extremely contentious graduate student strike during our first semester. My former adviser, Siva Vaidhyanathan, has been there for me since I was a prospective student. And while working toward my master's degree at the University of Washington, I was lucky enough to work with three terrific and inspiring scholars, Crispin Thurlow, David Silver, and Beth Kolko. I hope our paths continue to cross.

Fieldwork is very hard. I will repeat: it is very hard. I was fortunate to have wonderful friends who, in addition to providing background info on the scene and helpful insights into San Francisco, provided a much-needed break from tech meetups and interviews. My roommate, Aubrey Sabala, was an endless fount of information, juicy gossip, and support. My great friends Ali Berman, Fred Blau, Carla Borsoi, Corey Denis, Stephanie Dub, Sean Kelly, Ryan King, Manlio Lo Conte, Willo O'Brien, Jess Owens, Micah Saul, Mike Sharon, April and Cameron Walters, and Rick Webb all deserve special mention.

Without my informants, this project would have been impossible. Thank you to various anonymous individuals, as well as Adam Jackson, Adrian Chan, Andrew Mager, Annalee Newitz, Anu Nigam, April Buchart, Ariel Waldman, Auren Hoffman, Jim "Barce"

Barcelona, Ben Horowitz, Caroline McCarthy, Caterina Fake, Dale Larson, Dan Nye, Daniel Raffel, Derek Overby, Eddie Codel, Ev Williams, Gabriel Benveniste, Garrett Camp, Glenda Bautista, Hillary Hartley, Kara Swisher, Kevin Cheng, Kevin Kelly, Kevin Rose, Jeremy Stoppelman, Julia Allison, Laura Fitton, Leah Culver, Marianne Masculino, Megan McCarthy, Melissa Gira Grant, Molly Steenson, Nick Douglas, Om Malik, Owen Thomas, Ryan Junell, Sarah Lacy, Scott Beale, Stowe Boyd, Tantek Çelik, Tara Hunt, Thor Muller, Tristan Walker, and Veronica Belmont for their generosity of spirit and willingness to take time helping with this project. Thank you as well to the many other San Francisco and Silicon Valley denizens who spoke to me at events, parties, in coffee shops, and on the street. I also appreciate their counterparts in the New York tech scene who welcomed me with open arms.

Parts of this project were presented at the Berkman Center for Internet and Society, the Consortium for the Science of Sociotechnical Systems Summer Research Institute, the Oxford Internet Institute Summer Doctoral Program, the Privacy Research Group at NYU, the Cybersurveillance in Everyday Life workshop, and conferences for the Society of Social Studies of Science and the Association of Internet Researchers. Thank you to everyone who provided thoughtful feedback. I am privileged to be part of a great community of internet and technology scholars including Geoffrey Bowker, Jean Burgess, Kathleen Fitzpatrick, Tarleton Gillespie, Bernie Hogan, Phillip Howard, Nathan Jurgenson, Liz Lawley, Amanda Lenhart, Gilad Lotan, Larisa Mann, Adrienne Massanari, Lisa Nakamura, Gina Neff, Katy Pearce, David Phillips, Kate Raynes-Goldie, P. J. Rey, Christian Sandvig, Clay Shirky, Christopher Soghoian, Fred Stutzman, T. L. Taylor, Zeynep Tufekci, Janet Vertesi, Michael Zimmer, and many others. I look forward to seeing them at conferences, chatting with them on Twitter, and continuing to work together for many years to come.

Thank you to my welcoming colleagues in the Department of Communication and Media Studies at Fordham University, particularly Amy Aronson, Margaret Schwartz, and Jenny Clark, and my wonderful undergraduate students who remind me every day why I chose this profession.

I am lucky enough to have fabulous friends in New York. Grace Kang is my bad-movie-going, Gchatting, and cute-animal-link-sharing buddy. Thanks to my girls Taha Ebrahimi, Camille Fournier, Jocelyn Malheiro, Misha Doubrovkine-Paskar, Catrin Morgan and Marci DeLozier Haas. Much love to the Beachaus crew: Dens Crowley and Chelsa Skees, Brooke Moreland and Joe Weisenthal, Lockhart Steele and Lindsey Green, Alli Mooney, Meg Robertson, Ashley Granata, and Katie Welch. Thanks to my friends in Boston, especially Greta Merhy and Emma Welles, for keeping me sane during my long time away from home.

Thank you to my family for never asking me "Aren't you done with school yet?" or "Aren't you done with that book yet?" My awesome brother, Dave, who was a shoulder to cry on while in San Francisco, is always a wonderful dinner partner, hilarious conversationalist, and solid proof that you can be BFFs with your sibling. Huge thanks to my mom, Ann Marwick, and stepdad, Gordon Russell, for their open hearts and home. Thanks to my father, the original Dr. Marwick, for his always spot-on career advice and commentary, and my step-mother, Ilene Avery.

And of course, the most effusive thanks to my boyfriend-fiancé-husband-partner, Harry, without whom this project literally would never have been completed. Harry read early drafts, discussed every element of the project with me, and lived vicariously through coursework, exams, the proposal, fieldwork, dissertation writing, the defense, the postdoc, the job search, my first assistant professor-ship, and six or so moves (and counting). I love you.

# NOTES

---

## Introduction

1. Helft, "Yahoo Layoffs Today May Not Be the Last."

2. Bajaj and Grynbaum, "For Stocks, Worst Single-Day Drop in Two Decades."

3. Fickensher, "Not Much Life Left in the Party."

4. Taylor, "Facebook Has 955 Million Active Users—Still Shy of a Billion"; Foster, "How Many Users on Facebook?"; Sengupta, "Facebook Moves to Aid Its Shares."

5. Madden and Zickuhr, *65% of Online Adults Use Social Networking Sites;* Brenner, "Pew Internet: Teens."

6. A few years later, similar claims were made about Boxee and other digital media centers that allowed people to "cut the cable" and access internet content on their television. See also Marwick, "The People's Republic of YouTube?"

7. Joseph, "Social Media, Political Change, and Human Rights."

8. Benkler, *Wealth of Networks;* Shirky, *Here Comes Everybody;* Jenkins, *Convergence Culture.*

9. Quoted in Miller and Wortham, "In Silicon Valley, a Lack of Engineers."

10. Pricewaterhousecooper and National Venture Capital Association, *MoneyTree™ Report: Venture Capital Investments Q1 1995–Q2 2012 Investments by Region.*

11. An incubator is a program in which people are provided funding and business support to develop new startups, with the expectation that the funders will own equity in the startup if it is successful. The most famous is Y Combinator, which launched hot startups like Dropbox and AirBnB.

12. Calderon, "U.S. Students' Entrepreneurial Energy Waiting to Be Tapped."

13. The strangest thing that happened to me while working on this project was watching my own status rise. Not only did my interviews build social capital, as did my frequent collaboration with the well-known danah boyd, but while I was finishing fieldwork, my then-boyfriend (now husband) became the first employee at a startup called Foursquare. The service quickly grew from a few thousand users to 25 million and became exactly the kind of trendy, hot company I had spent fieldwork dissecting and criticizing. Foursquare became the cornerstone of the burgeoning New York City startup scene and I watched as the founders posed for Gap and VitaminWater ads and appeared on magazine covers. The New York City tech scene became my primary social outlet and I found myself participating as an insider rather than an observer. (I realized I had lost all perspective after agonizing over what to wear in front of the step-and-repeat at an event called "the Webutante Ball.") This somewhat surreal set of developments has complicated my own position and perspective in relation to the technology industry. On one hand, it is very difficult to accurately write about the technology industry without the deep knowledge that comes from participation. I needed significant social capital to gain access to many of my more prominent subjects and to truly understand some of the complex processes that I chronicle in this book. And as a critical internet scholar with insider access, I think I have a responsibility to use that access in the service of scholarship. On the other hand, there is the very real possibility that I have lost the ability to write critically from the fear of hurting someone's feelings, or even to observe clearly. As Raymond Madden writes, "The ethnographic manner of being with people is to find a way to get close, but not so close one can't step back again . . . One acculturates and socializes to the point of being comfortable with representing the ethnographic context, but one doesn't give over totally to the cultural and social immersion" (Madden, *Being Ethnographic,* 79). It has been easier to maintain that "step back" with

regard to the San Francisco tech scene, which is the focus of this book. The bits and pieces of the New York tech scene that have leaked into this book are written with an attempt at objectivity, but no expectation of success.

14. A social graph can also be described as a publicly articulated social network for a particular person. The term was coined by Facebook founder Mark Zuckerberg, and has been adopted by social network site researchers (Farber, "Facebook's Zuckerberg Uncorks the Social Graph"; Fitzpatrick, "Brad's Thoughts on the Social Graph").

15. Zittrain, *Future of the Internet.*

16. Anderson, *Imagined Communities.*

17. The Sidekick was a proto-smartphone that emphasized texting and web browsing. It was popular with teenagers and celebrities like Paris Hilton.

18. Hayes, *Behind the Silicon Curtain;* English-Lueck, *Cultures@Silicon Valley;* Saxenian, *New Argonauts.*

19. The word "meetups" comes from Meetup.com, a site that facilitates meetings based on common events. Although people used other sites to organize events, including Facebook, Eventbrite, and Upcoming, the word is a general term used for interest-based gatherings. "Drinkups" are meetups held at a bar. "Tweetups" are meetups organized through Twitter or about Twitter.

20. Co-working is when two or more people with flexible jobs, usually freelancers, meet at a common location to work side-by-side on their laptops on separate projects. There are formal co-working spaces set up to provide the camaraderie of the workplace that is missing from freelance life. Most, for a nominal fee, will rent desks and provide coffee, office supplies, phone lines, internet access, and a printer.

21. This participation included actively monitoring my followers; when I started my fieldwork, I had 447, but by the time I left San Francisco in May 2009, I had over a thousand. At the time of this writing I have something like 3,100, but most of them want to sell me erectile dysfunction remedies.

22. Data collection from Facebook presented an ethical conundrum. I was "friends" with many informants and tech scene members, but these links had been forged without any kind of disclosure on my part about possible data collection. Using my personal account was out. I briefly considered setting up a second research account and awkwardly re-friending people, but maintaining multiple accounts is against the Facebook terms of service. Multiple inquiries to Facebook regarding data collection were ignored. As a result, I decided against systematically collecting data from Facebook. The blogs and Flickr accounts of most of my informants were public, so I judged them allowable for data collection.

23. For a detailed discussion of the research methods involved in this project, please see Marwick, "Status Update."

24. In the past few years, many scholars have investigated the relationship between internet communication and in-person social interaction. For examples, see Coleman, "Ethnographic Approaches to New Media"; boyd, "Why Youth (Heart) Social Network Sites"; Gray, *Out in the Country;* Kelty, *Two Bits.*

25. Marwick and Ellison, " 'There Isn't Wifi in Heaven!' Negotiating Visibility on Facebook Memorial Pages."

26. The term "neoliberalism" originated with economists affiliated with the German Freiburg school in the years after World War II. Theorists like Rüstow, Eucken, Röpke, and Müller-Armack sought to decouple from laissez-faire economic policy a classical liberal position, namely that market competition brings prosperity (Tribe, "Political Economy of Modernity"). The Freiburg school saw monopolies and cartels as a threat, and advocated humanistic, social values. In other words, "neo" liberals were attempting to make positive improvements to classical liberalism; they saw an unfettered faith in the free market as out of date, and pejoratively classified those who believed in it as "paleo-liberals" (Boas and Gans-Morse, "Neoliberalism"). Economic theories that Progressives would today characterize as neoliberal were taken up by Chilean economists trained according to the Chicago school who admired the "German Miracle" post–World War II. These economists studied under Milton Friedman and Friedrich Hayek, and implemented "rapid and extensive privatization, deregulation, and reductions in trade barriers" when they returned to Chile (Boas and Gans-Morse, "Neoliberalism," 15). While these practices differed greatly from the original normative ideology advocated by the Freiburg school, they took its name and became the first wave of a major reorganization of governments and political markets that would characterize the 1980s, 1990s, and 2000s.

27. Juris, *Networking Futures.*

28. McChesney, "Introduction," 7.

29. Boas and Gans-Morse, "Neoliberalism."

30. Read, "Genealogy of Homo-Economicus"; Foucault et al., *Technologies of the Self.*

31. Foucault et al., *Technologies of the Self,* 19.

32. Ong, *Neoliberalism as Exception,* 4.

33. Rose, *Inventing Our Selves.*

34. Callahan, *Education and the Cult of Efficiency.*

35. Mayer, *Union Membership Trends in the United States.*

36. Levy and Kochan, "Addressing the Problem of Stagnant Wages"; Censky, "How the Middle Class Became the Underclass."

37. Davidson, "Making It in America"; David, Dorn, and Hanson, *China Syndrome.*

38. Sender, "Queens for a Day"; McCarthy, "Reality Television."

39. McMurria, "Desperate Citizens and Good Samaritans."

40. Read, "Genealogy of Homo-Economicus," 28.

41. Ong, *Neoliberalism as Exception.*

42. Gershon, *Breakup 2.0.*

43. For an excellent example of how these norms affect non-elite users, see Burrell, *Invisible Users.*

44. Silver and Massanari, *Critical Cyberculture Studies;* Lovink, *Zero Comments;* Nakamura, *Digitizing Race;* Zimmer, "Preface: Critical Perspectives on Web 2.0"; Hindman, *Myth of Digital Democracy;* Morozov, *Net Delusion;* Lanier, *You Are Not a Gadget.*

## Chapter One. A Cultural History of Web 2.0

1. Ken Spencer Brown, "Web 2.0, Wikis, Commercial Open Source All Came of Age."

2. Rothenberg, "Power to YouTube's People."

3. Granick, "Saving Democracy with Web 2.0."

4. Change Congress, "Who We Are."

5. Robinson, "Cory Doctorow."

6. Barbrook and Cameron, "Californian Ideology."

7. Fairclough, *Analysing Discourse.*

8. boyd, "Social Network Sites as Networked Publics."

9. Wynn and Katz, "Hyperbole over Cyberspace"; Gomez et al., "Disembodiment and Cyberspace."

10. Turkle, *Life on the Screen;* Stone, *War of Desire and Technology.*

11. Wu, *Master Switch,* 5.

12. Smith and Marx, *Does Technology Drive History?*

13. Eisenstein, *The Printing Press as an Agent of Change,* 137.

14. Ito, Okabe, and Anderson, "Portable Objects in Three Global Cities."

15. Carr, *The Shallows.*

16. Lanier, *You Are Not a Gadget.*

17. Keen, *Cult of the Amateur.*

18. This is not to say that valid criticisms of Web 2.0 discourse do not exist. Among popular books, Evgeny Morozov's *Net Delusion* critiques the "Google Doctrine," which holds that the internet can induce democracy in authoritarian governments. Morozov pokes holes in popular narratives of the Iranian Green Revolution (his book was written before the Arab Spring) and compares Western enthusiasm over Twitter to the theory that the

USSR fell due to U.S.-provided pamphlets and photocopiers. While Moro-zov dismisses much legitimate net activism, his work provides a needed check on the worst excesses of the mainstream press (although I think he is unfair to cyber-activist groups). Eli Pariser's *Filter Bubble* argues that per-sonalized content risks filtering out unpopular and unusual opinions, main-taining the status quo for online media surfers and encouraging homophily. Both men provide counterpoints to utopian Web 2.0 discourse, and they engage fully with the rhetoric and tropes of their counterparts.

19. Quoted in Clarke, "Roger Clarke's 'Information Wants to Be Free . . .'"

20. Coleman and Golub, "Hacker Practice"; Nissenbaum, "Hackers and the Contested Ontology of Cyberspace."

21. Levy, *Hackers;* Coleman and Golub, "Hacker Practice."

22. Raymond, "Hack"; Wikipedia Contributors, "Life Hack."

23. Coleman, "Code Is Speech"; Coleman and Golub, "Hacker Practice."

24. Thomas, *Hacker Culture.*

25. Levy, *Hackers,* 140; Markoff, *What the Dormouse Said.*

26. Levy, *Hackers,* 218.

27. Coleman, "Code Is Speech"; Thomas, *Hacker Culture.*

28. Levy, *Hackers,* 7.

29. Coleman, *Coding Freedom,* 17.

30. Turner, *From Counterculture to Cyberculture.*

31. Levy, *Hackers.*

32. Quoted in Markoff, *What the Dormouse Said,* 285.

33. Quoted in Levy, *Hackers,* 232.

34. Quoted in Turner, *From Counterculture to Cyberculture,* 137.

35. Levy, *Hackers;* Kelty, *Two Bits.*

36. Coleman and Golub, "Hacker Practice," 261. Italics mine.

37. Kelty, *Two Bits,* 191.

38. Quoted in Coleman and Golub, "Hacker Practice," 261.

39. Quoted in Coleman and Hill, "How Free Became Open."

40. Jordan, *Hacking,* chap. 5.

41. Kelty, *Two Bits,* 97.

42. Jordan, *Hacking.*

43. Kelty, *Two Bits,* x. Italics mine.

44. Wikipedia Contributors, "Wikipedia."

45. OpenCourseWare Consortium, "About Us."

46. Budapest Open Access Initiative, "Budapest Open Access Initia-tive, Frequently Asked Questions."

47. Benkler, *Wealth of Networks.*

48. Lessig, *Free Culture.*

49. Electronic Frontier Foundation, "Innovation."

50. Katz, "Age of Paine."

51. Wright, "From Zines to Ezines." *Teenage Gang Debs* is devoted to the *Brady Bunch*. Some well-known personal zines are *Dishwasher, Doris,* and *Cometbus.*

52. Duncombe, *Notes from Underground*, 2.

53. Book Your Own Fucking Life is now online at http://www.byofl.com.

54. Sinker, *We Owe You Nothing*, 10.

55. Moore, "Friends Don't Let Friends Listen to Corporate Rock."

56. Hence the origin of the term "indie rock."

57. Scott, "Statement_."

58. There is a lot of controversy in the zine world about the difference between a zine, an e-zine, a webzine, and an online magazine, as well as the origins of these terms (see Wright, "From Zines to Ezines" for a comprehensive overview). For the purposes of clarity, I use "zine" to refer to a paper zine and "e-zine" to refer to any zine published online, including webzines. Since publishers of both e-zines and paper zines referred to themselves as "zinesters," I use this nomenclature also.

59. Duncombe, *Notes from Underground.*

60. Labovitz, "E-zine List of Electronic Zines."

61. Wright, "From Zines to Ezines."

62. Rauch, "Hands-on Communication."

63. Comstock, "Grrrl Zine Networks," 399.

64. Junell, "15 Megs of Fame."

65. Ibid.

66. Junell, "Independent Publishing on the Internet."

67. Piepmeier, *Girl Zines.*

68. Ngô and Stinson, "Introduction."

69. Scott, "Girls Need Modems!"; Comstock, "Grrrl Zine Networks."

70. Ganahl, "Chief Chick of ChickClick."

71. Janelle Brown, "What Happened to the Women's Web?"

72. Ibid.

73. Freedman, "Zines Are Not Blogs."

74. Kahn and Kellner, "New Media and Internet Activism"; Jackie Smith, "Globalizing Resistance"; Juris, "New Digital Media and Activist Networking Within Anti-corporate Globalization Movements."

75. Klein, *No Logo;* Schlosser, *Fast Food Nation.* See also *The Corporation* (2003), *Super Size Me* (2004), *Adbusters* (1989–present), *Stay Free!* (1992–2007) and *The Baffler* (1988–present).

76. Juris, *Networking Futures,* 9.

77. Jenkins and Thorburn, "Introduction," 4.

78. Pickard, "United Yet Autonomous," 317.

79. Pickard, "Assessing the Radical Democracy of Indymedia," 20.

80. Smith, "Globalizing Resistance," 10.

81. Pickard, "Assessing the Radical Democracy of Indymedia," 27.

82. Ibid., 25–26.

83. Ibid., 36.

84. Bennett, Lawrence, and Livingston, *When the Press Fails;* McChesney, *Rich Media, Poor Democracy;* Klinenberg, *Fighting for Air.*

85. Bennett, Lawrence, and Livingston, *When the Press Fails.*

86. Kahn and Kellner, "New Media and Internet Activism," 92.

87. Rosenberg, *Say Everything,* 144–146.

88. Gillmor, *We the Media;* Raymond, "The Cathedral and the Bazaar."

89. Herring et al., "Women and Children Last."

90. Rosenberg, *Say Everything,* 79.

91. Herring et al., "Women and Children Last."

92. Siles, "From Online Filter to Web Format."

93. Lovink, *Zero Comments.*

94. Deuze, "Corporate Appropriation of Participatory Culture"; Kahn and Kellner, "New Media and Internet Activism"; Kim and Hamilton, "Capitulation to Capital?"

95. Other scholars have argued that while bloggers are more likely to link to and engage with like-minded bloggers, engagement does exist across ideological lines. The idea that the internet increases political isolation is similarly refuted (Hargittai, Gallo, and Kane, "Cross-Ideological Discussions Among Conservative and Liberal Bloggers"). More persuasive is Eli Pariser's argument that algorithms for search and automatic content creation allow people to simply avoid opinions that disagree with their own (Pariser, *Filter Bubble*).

96. Lawrence, Sides, and Farrell, "Self-Segregation or Deliberation?"; Hargittai, Gallo, and Kane, "Cross-Ideological Discussions Among Conservative and Liberal Bloggers."

97. Keen, *Cult of the Amateur.*

98. Cammaerts, "Critiques on the Participatory Potentials of Web 2.0."

99. Pickard, "Assessing the Radical Democracy of Indymedia," 35.

100. Castells, *Internet Galaxy,* 37.

101. Rogers and Larsen, *Silicon Valley Fever,* 26.

102. Lécuyer, *Making Silicon Valley,* 2.

103. Ibid.; Saxenian, *Regional Advantage.*

104. Bronson, *Nudist on the Late Shift,* 215.

105. English-Lueck, *Cultures@Silicon Valley,* 19.

106. Borsook, *Cyberselfish;* ibid.; Bronson, *Nudist on the Late Shift;* Rogers and Larsen, *Silicon Valley Fever.*

107. Iacono and Kling, "Computerization Movement and Tales of Technological Utopianism."

108. Barbrook and Cameron, "Californian Ideology," 3.

109. Ibid.; Borsook, *Cyberselfish.*

110. Hayes, *Behind the Silicon Curtain.*

111. Pellow and Park, *Silicon Valley of Dreams,* 1–2.

112. Harvey, *Brief History of Neoliberalism,* 2.

113. Dawson, "Siliconia"; Wikipedia Contributors, "List of Places with 'Silicon' Names."

114. Rossetto, "To: Mutoids (Re: The Californian Ideology)."

115. Pearce, "Californian Ideology: An Insider's View."

116. Turner, *From Counterculture to Cyberculture.*

117. Rushkoff, *Cyberia,* 3.

118. Rucker, Sirius, and Mu, *Mondo 2000;* Wikipedia Contributors, "Cyberdelic"; Rothstein, "Connections"; Dery, *Escape Velocity,* 22.

119. Rucker, Sirius, and Mu, *Mondo 2000,* 10.

120. Cool, "Communities of Innovation."

121. Behlendorf, "A Little of That Ol' VISION Thang."

122. Cool, "Communities of Innovation," 152.

123. Cool and Hall, "Manifesto."

124. Goodell, "Jonathan 'Dr. Cheeze' Makes His Million-Dollar Cyborganic."

125. This appreciation of Macintosh computers is deeply ironic given that Apple had shifted to highly proprietary, non-configurable software, and is generally a very secretive company. They are aesthetically aligned with the principles of technology culture, but do not adhere to them. For in-depth discussions of these contradictions, see Wu, *Master Switch;* Zittrain, *The Future of the Internet.*

126. Cool, "Communities of Innovation," 171.

127. Dery, *Escape Velocity;* Beale, "Interview with Scott Beale"; Brill, "What Is Burning Man? Early Years."

128. Black Rock City LLC, "What Is Burning Man? Early Years, 1986–1996."

129. Black Rock City LLC, "What Is Burning Man? Ten Principles."

130. Turner, "Burning Man at Google."

131. Google Inc., "Doodle 4 Google."

132. Quoted in Turner, "Burning Man at Google," 83.

133. Quoted in Terdiman, "Tech Carries a Torch for Burning Man."

134. Turner, "Burning Man at Google," 86.

135. Ibid., 81.

136. Cassidy, *Dot.con*, 155.

137. Quoted in Lacy, *Once You're Lucky, Twice You're Good*, 11.

138. Schwartz and Leyden, "Long Boom."

139. Cassidy, *Dot.con*, 292.

140. Johnson, "The Place for the Aspiring Dot Com."

141. Peters, "The Brand Called You."

142. Neff, Wissinger, and Zukin, "Entrepreneurial Labor Among Cultural Producers."

143. Ibid., 309–310; Turner, "Burning Man at Google."

144. Ross, *No-Collar*, 37.

145. Ibid., 39.

146. Florida, *Rise of the Creative Class*, 8.

147. Ross, *No-Collar*, 12.

148. Lacy, *Once You're Lucky, Twice You're Good*, 13.

149. Cassidy, *Dot.con*, 316.

150. Lacy, *Once You're Lucky, Twice You're Good*.

151. O'Reilly, "What Is Web 2.0"; Allen, "What Was Web 2.0?"

152. MediaLive International and O'Reilly Media, "Web 2.0 Conference Speakers."

153. Rivlin, "Silicon Valley (Version 2.0) Has Hopes Rising for Economic Rebound."

154. O'Reilly, "What Is Web 2.0."

155. Matthew Allen points out that Web 2.0 was the "principal way in which the *then-current* web was described rather than being a term which looked towards an as-yet unreached future." See Allen, "What Was Web 2.0?"

156. Graham, "Web 2.0."

157. Lessig, *Free Culture*.

158. Lessig, *Web 2.0 Conference*.

159. Quoted in Shelton, "Ted Shelton."

160. MacManus, "Tim O'Reilly Interview, Part 1."

161. Allen, "What Was Web 2.0?"

162. Kopytoff, "Internet Bigwigs Upbeat."

163. Williams, "Live from Web 2.0."

164. MacManus, "Tim O'Reilly Interview, Part 1."

165. Levy, "Farewell Web 1.0!"

166. Olsen, "Mark Cuban Raises Specter of Dot-com Redux."

167. Rupley, "Web Snap(s) Search and Rebounds."

168. Levy, *Hackers*; Markoff, *What the Dormouse Said*; Kelty, *Two Bits*; Coleman, "The Hacker Conference."

169. Progrium, "SuperHappyDevHouse 2 at SuperHappyFunHouse."

170. Çelik, "Remembering the Idea of BarCamp."

171. Barcamp, "BarCamp / FrontPage."

172. Barcamp, "BarCamp / BarCampNewsArchive2009."

173. Ingram, "Ingram: Web 2.0 Report Card."

174. Although MySpace is now a punch line, at the time it was an enormous juggernaut that inspired countless copycat sites and a huge secondary market of startups that only built plug-ins and "codes" for MySpace.

175. Anderson, *The Long Tail;* Surowiecki, *Wisdom of Crowds.*

176. Lanier, *You Are Not a Gadget,* 17.

## Chapter Two. Leaders and Followers

1. Note that this hierarchy does not have to be perceived the same way by all members of a group. While my informants roughly agreed on who was high and low status, there were significant degrees of disagreement. So to a certain extent, status is in the eye of the beholder. As one becomes inculcated into the community, one's understanding of status will sharpen (as we see in the case study of Adam Jackson in Chapter 3).

2. De Botton, *Status Anxiety,* vii.

3. Turner, *Status;* Huberman, Loch, and Önçüler, "Status as a Valued Resource"; Ridgeway and Walker, "Status Structures."

4. Anderson et al., "Who Attains Social Status?"; Hogan and Hogan, "Personality and Status"; Barkow, "Prestige and Culture"; Turner, *Status.*

5. Ridgeway and Walker, "Status Structures"; Anderson et al., "Who Attains Social Status?"; Marmot, *Status Syndrome;* Belliveau, O'Reilly, and Wade, "Social Capital at the Top."

6. Huberman, Loch, and Önçüler, "Status as a Valued Resource."

7. Christofides, Muise, and Desmarais, "Information Disclosure and Control on Facebook."

8. Baym, *Tune In, Log On.*

9. Glott, Schmidt, and Ghosh, *Wikipedia Survey.*

10. Reagle, "DRAFT: 'Free as in Sexist?'"

11. Linton, *Study of Man.*

12. Although I did not conduct individual interviews with current employees of every technology mentioned in this chapter, my informants include creators and employees at a wide range of social media companies including Yelp, Flickr, Twitter, Quora, Digg, Foursquare, and WordPress, as well as Google, Yahoo! and so forth.

13. English-Lueck, *Cultures@Silicon Valley,* 25.

14. Ibid., 22–23.

15. Girls in Tech was an organization that supported women in technology.

16. English-Lueck, *Cultures@Silicon Valley*, 30.

17. Although Thailand often symbolizes the sex trade, that was not the reason behind its popularity; instead, informants often talked about scuba diving, rock climbing, hiking to remote places, and so on.

18. Bronson, *Nudist on the Late Shift*.

19. Tocci, "Well-Dressed Geek."

20. Clarke, *Tupperware*, 64.

21. Coleman, "The Hacker Conference," 52.

22. O'Dell, "SXSW 2010 for Web Celeb Stalkers."

23. Lorek, "Where the Geeks Are."

24. Taulli, "How Angel Investing Works."

25. Marwick and boyd, "To See and Be Seen."

26. Milner, *Freaks, Geeks, and Cool Kids*.

27. Marwick and boyd, "I Tweet Honestly, I Tweet Passionately."

28. Boyd, Golder, and Lotan, "Tweet, Tweet, Retweet," 1.

29. Ibid.

30. Honeycutt and Herring, "Beyond Microblogging."

31. Ibid.

32. Boyd, Golder, and Lotan, "Tweet, Tweet, Retweet," 2.

33. Henshaw, "Origin of the @reply."

34. Dickey, "Ten Commandments of Twitter."

35. Ives, "Are We at Advertising Age a Bunch of Twitter Snobs?"

36. Ferriss, "How to Use Twitter Without Twitter Owning You."

37. Gershon, *Breakup 2.0*.

38. Fono and Raynes-Goldie, "Hyperfriendship and Beyond."

39. Benkler, *Wealth of Networks*.

40. Klout, Inc., "Understanding the Influence Metric."

41. Peterson, "Tumblr Posts Analytics Platform with Union Metrics."

42. Obviously there are female tech bloggers, but the technology space is dominated by men.


## Chapter Three. The Fabulous Lives of Micro-Celebrities

1. As of March 2013, Kevin has 1.4 million Twitter followers.

2. I am indebted to Annette Markham for providing this frame for thinking through authenticity.

3. Senft, *Camgirls*, 25.

4. Braudy, *Frenzy of Renown;* Inglis, *Short History of Celebrity.*

5. Brown, "How to Become an Internet Rockstar."

6. "Tron Guy" is a pudgy middle-aged man who dresses in a homemade skin-tight costume from the 1982 film *Tron;* the Numa Numa kid released a video of himself enthusiastically lip-syncing to the europop hit. See Feuer and George, "Internet Fame Is Cruel Mistress for a Dancer of the Numa Numa."

7. Milner, "Celebrity Culture as a Status System."

8. Sternberg, "Phantasmagoric Labor," 3.

9. This strategic self-presentation has been observed among many internet populations. See Ellison, Heino, and Gibbs, "Managing Impressions Online"; Papacharissi, "The Presentation of Self in Virtual Life"; Marwick and boyd, "I Tweet Honestly, I Tweet Passionately"; Liu, "Social Network Profiles as Taste Performances."

10. Horton and Wohl, "Mass Communication and Para-Social Interaction."

11. Marwick and boyd, "To See and Be Seen."

12. "Whuffie" was coined by Cory Doctorow in his novel *Down and Out in the Magic Kingdom* (Tor Books, 2003) and appears in his short story "Truncat."

13. Hunt, *Whuffie Factor,* 49.

14. Grazian, *Blue Chicago.*

15. Trilling, *Sincerity and Authenticity.*

16. Elliott, *Better Than Well;* Banet-Weiser, *Authentic TM.*

17. Welch, "Luxury Gets More Affordable."

18. Thomas, *Deluxe;* Twitchell, *Living It Up.*

19. Sorgatz, "The Microfame Game."

20. Milner, "Celebrity Culture as a Status System."

21. "Fanboy" describes an opinionated and ardent male fan. It is considered pejorative and originated in comic book fandom. "Fangirl" has a slightly different connotation that implies romantic interest. While "fanboy" is deeply gendered, I found that most global Web 2.0 enthusiasts were, indeed, male.

22. The quotation is from my interview; for more information on this project, see Nevius, "Lessons from That Tenderloin Camera Web Site."

23. Jackson, "Thank You Roger Ebert."

24. Leo Laporte is a prominent podcaster. Merlin Mann blogs for *43 Folders.*

25. Kurzman, "Celebrity Status," 356.

26. After *Valleywag,* Thomas wrote for the gossipy New York blog *Silicon Valley Insider* and is now a founding editor at the tech blog *ReadWrite;*

see Wikipedia Contributors, "Valleywag." On reviving the blog, see Shontell, "Nick Denton Is Resurrecting *Valleywag.*"

27. Hempel, "Silicon Valley Confidential."

28. Ibid.

29. Quoted in Sorkin, "Memo: Valleywag Gets down to Business."

30. Feasey, "Reading Heat."

31. Quoted in Angwin, *Stealing MySpace.*

32. Wikipedia Contributors, "Valleywag."

33. Thomas wrote a number of articles at *Valleywag* skewering Musk, and when he left, deputized replacement editor Ryan Tate to do the same. *Gawker* has been equally critical of Musk. See Thomas, "Is Elon Musk Aiming to Take over Tesla?"; Thomas, "Ze'ev Drori Out, Elon Musk in as Tesla CEO"; Tate, "This Man Founded Everything (And So Did You)."

34. Arrington, "When Will We Have Our First Valleywag Suicide?"

35. Hempel, "Silicon Valley Confidential."

36. Lovink, *Zero Comments.*

37. I am again indebted to Annette Markham for this phrasing.

38. Yeung, "So Open It Hurts."

39. Gray, "New Audiences, New Textualities."

40. Click, "Untidy."

41. Julia had 15,000 followers in May 2012, 55,000 that June, and 133,000 in October. These spikes are probably due to promotion for *Miss Advised.*

42. The original name of the blog was *Reblogging Julia Allison.* When Julia co-founded the site Non-Society, the name of the blog was changed to *Reblogging Non-Society,* or *RBNS.* The current name of the blog is *Reblogging Donk,* based on the writers' nickname for Julia. The site's various moves and name changes are purportedly due to threats of legal action by Julia's father.

43. Juliaspublicist, "Apparently We Hurt Julia Allison's Feelings"; Partypants, "yoohoooo! Kelly Cutrone!!!!!!! Over Here!"

44. Lawson, "A Reblogger Speaks"; Lawson, "Into the Internet's Ninth Circle of Hell."

45. Henderson, "A Social Media Game Plan from the Internet's Self-Promotion Princess."

46. I am tempted to write a lengthy rebuttal particularly to the difference between ethnographic research and investigative reporting, but I will instead simply comment that the point of ethnographic interviews is not to determine the veracity of an informant's statements but to examine how they understand and portray their experiences and the world around them.

47. A former founder, Alice Wright Walker, who goes by the name PartyPants, left *RBD* and founded a blog called "Get Off My Internets" where she makes fun of fashion, lifestyle, and mommy bloggers. She also has a webcam. She declined to be interviewed for this book.

48. Gray, "Antifandom and the Moral Text," 849.

49. http://rebloggingdonk.com/2012/04/26/codename-donkey-is-coming-up-people.

50. http://rebloggingdonk.com/2012/04/25/codename-donkey-more-dispatches-from-the-donk-side.

51. Pinkowitz, "Rabid Fans That Take [Twilight] Much Too Seriously."

52. Phillips, "Re: Yo Haters."

53. Sconce, "Vacancy at the Paris Hilton."

54. Marwick, "The People's Republic of YouTube?"

55. Evans and Wilson, *Fame*, 134–136.

## Chapter Four. Self-Branding

1. Aronczyk and Powers, *Blowing Up the Brand*.

2. Wernick, *Promotional Culture*.

3. Peters, "The Brand Called You."

4. Neff, Wissinger, and Zukin, "Entrepreneurial Labor Among Cultural Producers."

5. Self-branding is largely celebrated in marketing literature, but has been heavily criticized in media studies, sociology, and cultural studies for its encouragement of blatant self-commodification, which Hearn argues is a false consciousness primarily benefiting employers rather than practitioners (Hearn, "Meat, Mask, Burden"). Lair et al. see personal branding as unethical because it promotes an unequal system and distorts social relations, emphasizes "political maneuvering, competition, and cynicism," and furthers alienation (Lair, Sullivan, and Cheney, "Marketization and the Recasting of the Professional Self"). They emphasize self-branding's inability to transcend systematic inequalities in work environments that break down along lines of age, class, and gender. Wee and Brooks argue that self-branding is an example of "symbolic domination," whereby governments and companies are allowed to shift the responsibility for the problems of late capitalism to the individual subject (Wee and Brooks, "Personal Branding and the Commodification of Reflexivity").

6. Boyd, "Sarah Lacey."

7. Entrepreneurial skills are also "softer" than programming skills, which can be judged more or less objectively.

8. *The 4-Hour Chef* was published by Amazon.com and subsequently boycotted by Barnes and Noble, affecting its placement on the bestseller lists. Ferriss has been openly critical of the methodology of bestseller lists, particularly in relation to digital downloads and e-books. See Ferriss, "The 4-Hour Chef Is a NYT, WSJ, and USA Today Bestseller!"

9. Sivers, "Tim Ferriss Interview."

10. Vaynerchuk, *Crush It!*, 9.

11. Ibid., 2.

12. Collins, "Affiliate Summit West 2009 Keynote Address by Gary Vaynerchuk."

13. The *New Yorker* lampooned this claim in a Talk of the Town piece, snarking that "a relationship with Gary V means an ironclad guarantee that he'll reply to your email within four months, with at least a 'thx' or a 'mwaa'" (Friend, "V-va-va-voom!"). But when I emailed Gary asking for sales figures for *Crush It!*, he did reply, forwarding me to his publisher (who then refused). He also found a one-star review I wrote of *Crush It!* on GoodReads .com and directly responded, very politely.

14. Vaynerchuk, *Crush It!*, 3.

15. Ibid., 105.

16. Ibid., 107.

17. Ibid., 109.

18. Ibid., 89.

19. Ibid., 88.

20. Ibid., 13.

21. Ferriss, *4-Hour Workweek, Expanded and Updated*, 294.

22. A recent "NSFW" (not safe for work) episode of *The Random Show* showed the two at a luxury resort in Cabo, discussing anti-oxidants and tech IPOs while a topless girl in a bikini appeared in the background.

23. Rosenbloom, "Tim Ferriss, the 4-Hour Guru."

24. Romaniello, "Tim Ferriss Interview—AskMen."

25. Ferriss, *4-Hour Workweek, Expanded and Updated*, 22.

26. Ibid.

27. Ibid., 294.

28. Ibid., 293.

29. Garner, "Timothy Ferriss—'The 4-Hour Body'—Review."

30. Ferriss, *4-Hour Body*, 161.

31. Ibid., 228.

32. "Meng," or more commonly "mang," is racist slang mimicking a supposedly Latino pronunciation of "man" or "men." Al Pacino's Tony Montana in *Scarface* epitomizes. Thanks to my Twitter followers and Urban Dictionary for decoding this.

33. Much of search engine optimization involves "tricking" services like Google into ranking one's content higher than it warrants.

34. This of course cuts out more than 60 percent of the world's population, who lack internet access. Fast broadband and technical competency are even rarer.

35. Schawbel, *Me 2.0,* 156.

36. There is a lot of debate in the Twitter marketing world about whether one should use a "real" name or what is often referred to as an "avatar," or internet nickname. (For more about internet nicknames, see Donath, "Identity and Deception in the Virtual Community"; Bechar-Israeli, "From <Bonehead> to <cLoNehEAd>.") Recently, some companies, notably Facebook, are deprecating internet nicknames in favor of "real names." (Gaming company Blizzard's attempt to require "real names" on their forums was overwhelmingly rejected by users, causing the company to reverse their position—see Shiels, "Blizzard Backs Down over Gamers Using Real Names.") The popularity of Facebook Connect, which allows companies to use Facebook for identity authentication in lieu of their own logins, is hastening this transformation. I wrote about this shift in my master's thesis, linking it to the need for companies to track individuals across website lines and monetize their interests and social networks. See Marwick, "Selling Your Self."

37. Note that the "best" technology for self-branding changes frequently; at the time of my fieldwork it was Twitter, a few years before that it was blogs, and in a few years it will be something else.

38. Hunt left Intuit after four months to return to her native Canada, where she founded her own startup, Buyosphere.

39. Note that in that case, the personal blog has to be successful; I ran into many cases of people with blogs that were poorly designed, badly written, or unread, which made their proprietors seem like amateurs.

40. For instance, during the week of July 25, 2011, there were sixty-eight tech-related events in the San Francisco/Silicon Valley area, twenty-three of which were free. They included "Gamification: Business Models, Traction and Investment Trends," a personal branding workshop for women in tech, a salsa dance for tech workers, a hack day at social media company LinkedIn, and a party at a venture capital office.

41. Marwick and boyd, "I Tweet Honestly, I Tweet Passionately."

42. Dibbell, "A Rape in Cyberspace"; Nakamura, "Race In/For Cyberspace"; Donath, "Identity and Deception in the Virtual Community"; Bechar-Israeli, "From <Bonehead> to <cLoNehEAd>."

43. Rose, *Inventing Our Selves;* McGee, *Self-Help, Inc.*

44. Ellison, Heino, and Gibbs, "Managing Impressions Online"; Liu, "Social Network Profiles as Taste Performances."

45. Child and Prud'homme, *My Life in France*.

46. Schawbel, *Me 2.0*, 86–87.

47. Roffer, *Make a Name for Yourself*, 37–38.

48. Ferriss, *4-Hour Workweek, Expanded and Updated*, 57.

49. Roffer, *Make a Name for Yourself*; Kaputa, "10 Self-Branding Strategies for Career Success."

50. Alcantara, "Art of Self-Branding: Part One."

51. Ong, *Neoliberalism as Exception*.

52. Jenkins, *Textual Poachers*; Baym, *Tune in, Log on*; Andrejevic, "Watching Television Without Pity"; Gregg, "Learning to (Love) Labour"; Milner, "Working for the Text."

53. Lazzarato, "Immaterial Labor."

54. Gregg, "Learning to (Love) Labour."

55. Terranova, "Free Labor"; Andrejevic, "Watching Television Without Pity"; Milner, "Working for the Text"; Van Dijck, "Users Like You?"

56. Galloway and Alsina, "We Are the Gold Farmers"; Jarrett, "Interactivity Is Evil!"; Scholz, "Market Ideology and the Myths of Web 2.0."

57. Hochschild, *Managed Heart*, 7.

58. Cameron, "Styling the Worker," 332.

59. Vaynerchuk, *Crush It!*, 85.

60. Calacanis, "Red, Jackson, Gen Y and Loyalty."

61. Marwick and boyd, "I Tweet Honestly, I Tweet Passionately."

62. Goldhaber, "Attention Economy and the Net."

63. Du Gay, *Consumption and Identity at Work*, 11.

64. Ibid., 12.

65. Ong, *Neoliberalism as Exception*.

66. Arvidsson, *Brands*, vii.

## Chapter Five. Lifestreaming

1. Timoner, *We Live in Public*.

2. Aaron Smith, *Cell Internet Use 2012*.

3. Ito and Okabe, "Intimate Connections"; boyd, "Why Youth (Heart) Social Network Sites."

4. Marwick and boyd, "To See and Be Seen."

5. Marwick, "The Public Domain."

6. Gelernter, "The Cyber-Road Not Taken."

7. Freeman, "Lifestreams Project Home Page"; Freeman, "The Lifestreams Software Architecture."

8. Madden et al., "Digital Footprints."

9. Brophy-Warren, "The New Examined Life"; Bielski, "My So-Called Life."

10. Roberts, "Self-Experimentation as a Source of New Ideas."

11. These processes are becoming automatized through services like Timehop and MemoMail, which send a daily email including Foursquare check-ins, Facebook messages, tweets, and Flickr pictures from that day years ago.

12. Rubin, *Happiness Project.*

13. Mullen, "Lifestreaming as a Life Design Methodology."

14. It is a fallacy to assume that printed diaries were always personal and intended to be private. Van Dijck, in her "Composing the Self," argues that the diary is always written for an audience, whether or not that audience ever reads the diary. She disregards the categorization of diaries into "public" and "private": all diaries are written to an addressee. Also see Lee Humphreys's piece "Historicizing Microblogging," which compares microblogging to historical diaries.

15. Bowker and Star, *Sorting Things Out.*

16. Marwick and boyd, "I Tweet Honestly, I Tweet Passionately."

17. boyd, "Social Network Sites as Networked Publics."

18. As with the rest of this book, many of these technologies are now obsolete because my fieldwork took place from 2007 to 2010.

19. See busterbenson.com and Julia Allison's lifecast on Julia.nonsociety.com for examples.

20. Thompson, "Brave New World of Digital Intimacy."

21. Fono and Raynes-Goldie, "Hyperfriendship and Beyond"; Marwick and boyd, "It's Just Drama."

22. Marwick and boyd, "It's Just Drama."

23. Mullen, "Lifestreaming as a Life Design Methodology," 54.

24. Thompson, "Brave New World of Digital Intimacy."

25. Chen, "Tweet This."

26. Crawford, "These Foolish Things," 252.

27. Ibid., 259.

28. Ibid., 262.

29. V. Miller, "New Media, Networking and Phatic Culture," 394.

30. Habuchi, "Accelerating Reflexivity."

31. Buffardi and Campbell, "Narcissism and Social Networking Web Sites"; LaPorta, "Twitter and YouTube." Much of this linkage is often sensationalized (see, for example, Twenge and Campbell, *Narcissism Epidemic*).

Buffardi and Campbell do not claim that social network site use promotes narcissism, but they do point out that the personality traits exhibited by narcissists are rewarded by social network sites, so narcissists may be over-represented there.

32. Carr, "Is Google Making Us Stupid?"; Richtel, "Hooked on Gadgets, and Paying a Mental Price"; Richtel, "Silicon Valley Worries About Addiction to Devices."

33. Marwick, "The Public Domain."

34. Nippert-Eng, *Islands of Privacy,* 8.

35. Locke, *Eavesdropping.*

36. Gibbs, Ellison, and Heino, "Self-Presentation in Online Personals."

37. Bechar-Israeli, "From <Bonehead> to <cLoNehEAd>"; Donath, "Identity and Deception in the Virtual Community"; Reid, "Hierarchy and Power."

38. Nissenbaum, *Privacy in Context,* 42.

39. *Rock Band* is a popular video game.

40. Tara Brown, "Has Anyone Seen My iPhone?"

41. Starr, "And Now You Know."

42. The term "FOMO" did not exist during fieldwork, but it precisely describes the "feeling" expressed by interview participants. See Wortham, "How Social Media Can Induce Feelings of 'Missing Out.'"

43. Humphreys, "Mobile Social Networks and Social Practice"; Humphreys, "Mobile Social Networks and Urban Public Space."

44. Williams and Dourish, "Imagining the City," 40.

45. Dennis Crowley, who founded and created both Dodgeball and Foursquare, has openly stated that the services were designed for people like his friends, young New York City professionals.

46. Carr, "Is Google Making Us Stupid?"; Carr, *The Shallows;* Pinker, "Mind over Mass Media"; Richtel, "Hooked on Gadgets."

47. Trepte and Reinecke, *Privacy Online;* Barnes, "A Privacy Paradox"; Abril, "A (My) Space of One's Own."

48. Trepte and Reinecke, *Privacy Online.*

49. Tufekci, "Can You See Me Now?"

50. Dean, *Publicity's Secret,* 2.

51. boyd, "Making Sense of Privacy and Publicity."

52. Conley et al., "Sustaining Both Privacy and Open Justice in the Transition from Local to Online Access to Court Records."

53. Davis, "Electronic Access to Information and the Privacy Paradox"; Bepko, "Public Availability or Practical Obscurity."

54. Nissenbaum, *Privacy in Context.*

55. I am indebted to conversations with Helen Nissenbaum, and her "Online Court Records, Privacy, and Contextual Integrity" project with Amanda Conley, for this example and the vocabulary used.

56. Ewen, *PR! A Social History of Spin*, 27.

57. Sternberg, "Phantasmagoric Labor," 420.

58. WikiLeaks contributors, "WikiLeaks."

59. Benkler, *Wealth of Networks*, 292–293.

60. Lessig, *Code*, 153.

61. Nissenbaum, "Defining Transparency."

62. During my fieldwork for this book, the debate over California's Proposition 8 was heated, and increased tolerance for gay, lesbian, transgender and bisexual people, particularly marriage equality, was frequently cited as evidence of a move toward a more equal society. This being San Francisco, other locally prominent minorities such as polyamorous people, the leather/BDSM community, and drug users were also often discussed.

63. The libertarian political tradition of Silicon Valley celebrates capitalism and government non-interference and idealizes its own culture as a model for the rest of the world. For example, during the economic collapse of 2008, many Silicon Valley denizens bragged that the technology/computer companies of Silicon Valley did not need an economic bailout like the banking or auto industries. There was a sense of pride in the self-sufficiency of the technology industry and a belief that they do not take any kinds of government support.

64. Banaji and Prentice, "The Self in Social Contexts."

65. Schneier, "My Reaction to Eric Schmidt."

66. See Elinor Mills's series for CNET about this incident. She writes, "We Googled some personal information about Schmidt and wrote about what we found. He didn't like it, and News.com was on the receiving end of a very stern corporate silent treatment from Google for nearly two months." Mills, "My Stunted Interview with Google's Eric Schmidt"; Mills, "Google Balances Privacy, Reach."

67. Solove, "'I've Got Nothing to Hide' and Other Misunderstandings of Privacy"; Regan, *Legislating Privacy;* Nissenbaum, *Privacy in Context.*

68. Solove, "'I've Got Nothing to Hide' and Other Misunderstandings of Privacy," 765.

69. Kirkpatrick, "Facebook's Zuckerberg Says the Age of Privacy Is Over."

70. Marwick and boyd, "I Tweet Honestly, I Tweet Passionately"; Marwick and Ellison, "There Isn't Wifi in Heaven!"

71. Tufekci, "Can You See Me Now?"; Hoofnagle et al., *How Different Are Young Adults from Older Adults When It Comes to Information Privacy Attitudes and Policies?*

## Chapter Six. Designed in California

1. Goldstein, "How to Fix the Gender Gap in Technology."

2. Elliott, *Better Than Well,* 29.

3. Grazian, *Blue Chicago,* 16.

4. Marwick, "There's a Beautiful Girl under All of This."

5. Nick and I attempted to schedule an interview several times, but I was ultimately unable to meet with him.

6. Hoffman, "Oversharing," 71.

7. Borsook, *Cyberselfish,* 22.

8. Lacy, "Milk Completes $1.5 Million Angel Round, Packed with Valley Names"; Tsotsis, "Winning a Bidding War with Facebook, Google Picks up the Milk Product Team."

9. Quoted in Wadhwa, "Silicon Valley."

10. Talbot, "How Much Tech Can One City Take?"

11. Collins and Moore, *The Enterprising Man.*

12. Ogbor, "Mythicizing and Reification in Entrepreneurial Discourse."

13. Ibid., 620.

14. Baker, Aldrich, and Liou, "Invisible Entrepreneurs"; Ahl, "The Making of the Female Entrepreneur"; Bruni, Gherardi, and Poggio, "Doing Gender, Doing Entrepreneurship"; Achtenhagen and Welter, "Media Discourse in Entrepreneurship Research."

15. Ahl, "Why Research on Women Entrepreneurs Needs New Directions."

16. Ogbor, "Mythicizing and Reification in Entrepreneurial Discourse."

17. Malone, *Big Score.*

18. Rogers and Larsen, *Silicon Valley Fever,* 142.

19. Bronson, *Nudist on the Late Shift,* 219.

20. Lacy, *Once You're Lucky, Twice You're Good,* 39.

21. Chaplin, "Playboys of Tech."

22. Center for Women's Business Research, "Key Facts About Women-owned Businesses."

23. Wadhwa et al., "Anatomy of an Entrepreneur"; Cohoon, Wadhwa, and Mitchell, *Are Successful Women Entrepreneurs Different from Men?*

24. Miller, "Out of the Loop in Silicon Valley"; Padnos, *High Performance Entrepreneurs.*

25. Miller, "Out of the Loop in Silicon Valley"; Bradshaw, "How Women Are Getting Left Out of the Venture Capital Game"; Brush et al., *Gatekeepers of Venture Growth.*

26. Chase, "Lawyers and Popular Culture"; Faludi, *Backlash;* Koivula, "Gender Stereotyping in Televised Media Sport Coverage."

27. Noe, "Women and Mentoring"; Scandura, "Mentorship and Career Mobility."

28. Claire Cain Miller, "Out of the Loop in Silicon Valley."

29. Hu, "Ambitious, Difficult Women."

30. Thomas, "Temptress of Silicon Valley Shuts Down Useless Site."

31. To her credit, Culver herself was remarkably thick-skinned. She told me she was happy if she showed up on *Valleywag* because it helped promote her site and increased her visibility (as a model of a woman developer). At a Girls in Tech event, she said, "I'm not worse [at coding] than any dude. Calling me stupid, that really hurts. Petty, from dudes who never did anything. It wasn't about me being the best coder in the world. I took risks doing what I wanted to do and not caring if I failed. I don't care about failing. I don't care about comments on my appearance, about who I'm dating."

32. Trunk, "Gold Digging Web 2.0 Style."

33. Sullivan, "Woman in Technology."

34. Massachusetts Institute of Technology, "Study on the Status of Women Faculty in Science at MIT."

35. Andrews, "Diversity in Tech."

36. Harris, "Harris: Startup Boot Camp Illustrates Dearth of Women in Tech."

37. National Center for Women and Information Technology, *NCWIT Scorecard, 2007;* Dines, "Why You Should Care About Having a Diverse IT Ops Department."

38. Ashcraft and Blithe, *Women in IT;* Misa, *Gender Codes.*

39. Spertus, *Why Are There so Few Female Computer Scientists?;* Margolis and Fisher, *Unlocking the Clubhouse;* Misa, *Gender Codes.*

40. Gürer and Camp, "An ACM-W Literature Review on Women in Computing"; Margolis and Fisher, *Unlocking the Clubhouse;* Ashcraft and Blithe, *Women in IT.*

41. O'Leary, "Sexual Harassment in Online Gaming Stirs Anger."

## Conclusion

1. Thurlow, "Fakebook."

2. Naturally, this differs in other social contexts, but it would surprise me if there are many online social contexts where normative judgments do

not break down along traditional lines such as sexuality, class, race, education, or a host of other status markers and differentiating factors.

3. Epstein and Friedman, *Celluloid Closet*.

4. Foucault, "Governmentality."

5. Pfaffenberger, "The Social Meaning of the Personal Computer"; Frank, *Conquest of Cool*.

6. Neff, "Risk Relations"; Ross, *No-Collar*.

7. Senft, *Camgirls*.

8. Silver and Massanari, *Critical Cyberculture Studies;* Lovink, *Zero Comments;* Nakamura, *Digitizing Race;* Zimmer, "Preface"; Hindman, *Myth of Digital Democracy;* Morozov, *The Net Delusion*.

# BIBLIOGRAPHY

Abril, P. S. "A (My) Space of One's Own: On Privacy and Online Social Networks." *Northwestern Journal of Technology and Intellectual Property* 6, no. 1 (2008): 73.

Achtenhagen, L., and F. Welter. "Media Discourse in Entrepreneurship Research." In *Handbook of Qualitative Research Methods in Entrepreneurship,* edited by H. Neergaard and J. P. Ulhoi, 193–215. Cheltenham, UK: Edward Elgar, 2006.

Ahl, H. J. "The Making of the Female Entrepreneur: A Discourse Analysis of Research Texts on Women's Entrepreneurship." Ph.D. diss., Jönköping International Business School, 2002. http://his.diva-portal.org/smash/get/diva2:3890/FULLTEXT01.

———. "Why Research on Women Entrepreneurs Needs New Directions." *Entrepreneurship Theory and Practice* 30, no. 5 (2006): 595–621.

Alcantara, Lea. "The Art of Self-Branding: Part One." *Lealea Design,* 2008. http://www.lealea.net/blog/comments/the-art-of-self-branding-part-one.

Allen, Matthew. "What Was Web 2.0? Versions and the Politics of Internet History." Oxford, Eng.: Oxford Internet Institute, 2011. http://www.netcrit.net/wp-content/uploads/whatwasweb20.pdf.

Anderson, Benedict. *Imagined Communities: Reflections on the Origin and Spread of Nationalism*. London: Verso, 1983.

Anderson, C., O. P. John, D. Keltner, and A. M. Kring. "Who Attains Social Status? Effects of Personality and Physical Attractiveness in Social Groups." *Journal of Personality and Social Psychology* 81, no. 1 (2001): 116–132.

Anderson, Chris. *The Long Tail: Why the Future of Business Is Selling Less of More*. New York: Hyperion, 2006.

Andrejevic, Mark. "Watching Television Without Pity: The Productivity of Online Fans." *Television & New Media* 9, no. 1 (January 1, 2008): 24–46.

Andrews, Matt. "Diversity in Tech: Still an Issue in 2013?" *Three Chords*, January 3, 2013. http://www.threechords.org/blog/diversity-in-tech-still -an-issue-2013.

Angwin, Julia. *Stealing MySpace: The Battle to Control the Most Popular Website in America*. New York: Random House, 2009.

Aronczyk, Melissa, and Devon Powers. *Blowing Up the Brand: Critical Perspectives on Promotional Culture*. New York: Peter Lang, 2010.

Arrington, Michael. "When Will We Have Our First Valleywag Suicide?" *TechCrunch*, March 2, 2008. http://techcrunch.com/2008/03/02/when -will-we-have-our-first-valleywag-suicide.

Arvidsson, Adam. *Brands*. New York: Routledge, 2006.

Ashcraft, C., and S. Blithe. *Women in IT: The Facts*. National Center for Women and Information Technology, April 2010. http://www.ncwit.org /pdf/NCWIT_TheFacts_rev2010.pdf.

Bajaj, Vikas, and Michael M. Grynbaum. "For Stocks, Worst Single-Day Drop in Two Decades." *New York Times*, September 29, 2008, sec. Business Day. http://www.nytimes.com/2008/09/30/business/30markets.html.

Baker, T., H. E. Aldrich, and N. Liou. "Invisible Entrepreneurs: The Neglect of Women Business Owners by Mass Media and Scholarly Journals in the USA." *Entrepreneurship & Regional Development* 9, no. 3 (1997): 221–238.

Banaji, M. R., and D. A. Prentice. "The Self in Social Contexts." *Annual Review of Psychology* 45, no. 1 (1994): 297–332.

Banet-Weiser, Sarah. *Authentic TM: The Politics of Ambivalence in a Brand Culture*. New York: NYU Press, 2012.

Barbrook, R., and A. Cameron. "The Californian Ideology." *Science as Culture* 6, no. 1 (1996): 44–72.

BarCamp. "BarCamp / BarCampNewsArchive2009," 2010. http://barcamp .org/BarCampNewsArchive2009.

———. "BarCamp / FrontPage." Barcamp.org, 2010. http://barcamp.org.

Barkow, J. H. "Prestige and Culture: A Biosocial Interpretation." *Current Anthropology* 16 (1975): 553–572.

Barnes, Susan. "A Privacy Paradox: Social Networking in the United States." *First Monday* 11, no. 9 (September 4, 2006). http://firstmonday .org/htbin/cgiwrap/bin/ojs/index.php/fm/article/view/1394.

Baym, N. K. *Tune in, Log on: Soaps, Fandom, and Online Community.* London: Sage, 2000.

Bechar-Israeli, Haya. "From <Bonehead> to <cLoNehEAd>: Nicknames, Play, and Identity on Internet Relay Chat." *Journal of Computer-Mediated Communication* 1, no. 2 (1996). http://jcmc.indiana.edu/vol1/issue2/bechar .html.

Behlendorf, Brian. "A Little of That Ol' VISION Thang." *SFRaves,* July 2, 1993. http://hyperreal.org/raves/spirit/connecting/SFR_visionthang.html.

Belliveau, Maura A., Charles A. O'Reilly, and James B. Wade. "Social Capital at the Top: Effects of Social Similarity and Status on CEO Compensation." *Academy of Management Journal* 39, no. 6 (December 1996): 1568–1593.

Benkler, Yochai. *The Wealth of Networks.* New Haven, CT: Yale University Press, 2006.

Bennett, W. Lance, Regina G. Lawrence, and Steven Livingston. *When the Press Fails.* Chicago: University of Chicago Press, 2007.

Bepko, A. B. "Public Availability or Practical Obscurity: The Debate over Public Access to Court Records on the Internet." *New York Law School Law Review* 49 (2004): 967–991.

Bielski, Zosia. "My So-Called Life." *Globe and Mail,* February 19, 2009. http://www.theglobeandmail.com/life/article972670.ece.

Black Rock City LLC. "What Is Burning Man? Early Years, 1986–1996." Burningman.com, 2003. http://www.burningman.com/whatisburning man/1986_1996.

———. "What Is Burning Man? Ten Principles." Burningman.com, 2003. http://www.burningman.com/whatisburningman/about_burningman /principles.html.

Boas, T. C., and J. Gans-Morse. "Neoliberalism: From New Liberal Philosophy to Anti-Liberal Slogan." *Studies in Comparative International Development (SCID)* 44, no. 2 (2009): 137–161.

Borsook, Paulina. *Cyberselfish.* New York: PublicAffairs, 2001.

Bowker, G. C., and S. L. Star. *Sorting Things Out: Classification and Its Consequences.* Cambridge, MA: MIT Press, 2000.

boyd, d. "Making Sense of Privacy and Publicity." Presented at the South by Southwest Interactive Conference, Austin, TX, March 13, 2010. http:// www.danah.org/papers/talks/2010/SXSW2010.html.

———. "Social Network Sites as Networked Publics: Affordances, Dynamics, and Implications." In *A Networked Self: Identity, Community, and*

*Culture on Social Network Sites,* edited by Z. Papacharissi, 39–58. New York: Routledge, 2010.

———. "Why Youth (Heart) Social Network Sites: The Role of Networked Publics." In *Youth, Identity and Digital Media,* edited by D. Buckingham, 119–142. Cambridge, MA: MIT Press, 2007.

boyd, danah, S. Golder, and G. Lotan. "Tweet, Tweet, Retweet: Conversational Aspects of Retweeting on Twitter." In *Proceedings of the Forty-Third Hawai'i International Conference on System Sciences (HICSS-43),* 1–10. Kauai, HI: IEEE Computer Society, 2010.

Boyd, Stowe. "Sarah Lacey: Beyond Branding." Stoweboyd.com, January 3, 2009. http://stoweboyd.com/post/827973673/sarah-lacey-beyond-branding.

Bradshaw, Leslie. "How Women Are Getting Left Out of the Venture Capital Game." *Forbes,* January 10, 2012. http://www.forbes.com/sites /lesliebradshaw/2012/01/10/how-women-are-getting-left-out-of-the -venture-capital-game.

Braudy, Leo. *The Frenzy of Renown.* New York: Oxford University Press, 1986.

Brenner, Joanna. "Pew Internet: Teens." *Pew Internet & American Life Project,* April 27, 2012. http://pewinternet.org/Commentary/2012/April/Pew -Internet-Teens.aspx.

Brill, Louis. "What Is Burning Man? Early Years." Burningman.com, 2003. http://www.burningman.com/whatisburningman/1986_1996/firstyears .html.

Bronson, Po. *The Nudist on the Late Shift.* New York: Broadway Books, 2000.

Brophy-Warren, Jamin. "The New Examined Life." *Wall Street Journal,* December 6, 2008, sec. W.

Brown, Ben. "How to Become an Internet Rockstar." *Uber,* May 22, 2000. http://uber.nu/2000/05/22.

Brown, Janelle. "What Happened to the Women's Web?" Salon.com, August 25, 2000. http://www.salon.com/2000/08/25/womens_web/singleton.

Brown, Ken Spencer. "Web 2.0, Wikis, Commercial Open Source All Came of Age; Year Found Service-Oriented Architecture and Desktop Search Also Emerging Fast." *Investor's Business Daily,* January 3, 2006, sec. A.

Brown, Tara. "Has Anyone Seen My iPhone?" *Tara (Tiger) Brown,* October 18, 2008. http://tarabrown.wordpress.com/2008/10/18/has-anyone-seen -my-iphone.

Bruni, A., S. Gherardi, and B. Poggio. "Doing Gender, Doing Entrepreneurship: An Ethnographic Account of Intertwined Practices." *Gender, Work and Organization* 11, no. 4 (July 2004): 406–429.

Brush, Candida G., Nancy Carter, Elizabeth Gatewood, Patricia Greene, and Myra Hart. *Gatekeepers of Venture Growth: A Diana Project Report on the Role and Participation of Women in the Venture Capital Industry*. The Diana Project. Kansas City, MO: Ewing Marion Kauffman Foundation, 2004.

Budapest Open Access Initiative. "Budapest Open Access Initiative, Frequently Asked Questions." *Budapest Open Access Initiative*, July 1, 2010. http://www.earlham.edu/~peters/fos/boaifaq.htm.

Buffardi, L. E., and W. K. Campbell. "Narcissism and Social Networking Web Sites." *Personality and Social Psychology Bulletin* 34, no. 10 (2008): 1303.

Burrell, J. *Invisible Users: Youth in the Internet Cafes of Urban Ghana*. Cambridge, MA: MIT Press, 2012.

Calacanis, Jason. "Red, Jackson, Gen Y & Loyalty." *Calacanis.com*, April 26, 2010. http://calacanis.com/2010/04/27/red-jackson-gen-y-loyalty.

Calderon, Valerie. "U.S. Students' Entrepreneurial Energy Waiting to Be Tapped." *Gallup.com*, October 13, 2011. http://www.gallup.com/poll /150077/Students-Entrepreneurial-Energy-Waiting-Tapped.aspx.

Callahan, Raymond E. *Education and the Cult of Efficiency: A Study of the Social Forces That Have Shaped the Administration of the Public Schools*. Chicago: University of Chicago Press, 1962.

Cameron, D. "Styling the Worker: Gender and the Commodification of Language in the Globalized Service Economy." *Journal of Sociolinguistics* 4, no. 3 (2000): 323–347.

Cammaerts, Bart. "Critiques on the Participatory Potentials of Web 2.0." *Communication, Culture & Critique* 1, no. 4 (December 2008): 358–377.

Carr, Nicholas. "Is Google Making Us Stupid?" *Atlantic*, August 2008. http://www.theatlantic.com/magazine/archive/2008/07/is-google-making -us-stupid/6868.

———. *The Shallows: What the Internet Is Doing to Our Brains*. New York: W. W. Norton, 2010.

Cassidy, John. *Dot.con*. New York: HarperCollins, 2003.

Castells, Manuel. *The Internet Galaxy: Reflections on the Internet, Business, and Society*. New York: Oxford University Press, 2001.

Çelik, Tantek. "Remembering the Idea of BarCamp." *Tantek's Thoughts*, July 10, 2006. http://www.tantek.com/log/2006/07.html#d10t0805.

Censky, Annalyn. "How the Middle Class Became the Underclass." *CNN Money*, February 16, 2011. http://money.cnn.com/2011/02/16/news/econ omy/middle_class/index.htm.

Center for Women's Business Research. "Key Facts About Women-Owned Businesses." Women's Research Business Center, 2010. http://www.womensbusinessresearchcenter.org/research/keyfacts/.

Change Congress. "Who We Are." Change-congress.org, 2009. http://change-congress.org/who.

Chaplin, Heather. "The Playboys of Tech." *Details,* November 2008. http://www.details.com/sex-relationships/dating-and-cheating/200809/the-tech-stars-behind-tumblr-digg-are-hungry-for-fame.

Chase, A. "Lawyers and Popular Culture: A Review of Mass Media Portrayals of American Attorneys." *American Bar Foundation Research Journal* 11, no. 2 (1986): 281–300.

Chen, G. M. "Tweet This: A Uses and Gratifications Perspective on How Active Twitter Use Gratifies a Need to Connect with Others." *Computers in Human Behavior* 27, no. 2 (2011): 755–762.

Child, Julia, and Alex Prud'homme. *My Life in France.* New York: Random House, 2009.

Christofides, E., A. Muise, and S. Desmarais. "Information Disclosure and Control on Facebook: Are They Two Sides of the Same Coin or Two Different Processes?" *CyberPsychology & Behavior* 12, no. 3 (2009): 341–345.

Clarke, A. *Tupperware: The Promise of Plastic in 1950's America.* Washington, DC: The Smithsonian Institution Press, 1999.

Clarke, R. "Roger Clarke's 'Information Wants to Be Free . . .'" Rogerclarke.com, August 28, 2001. http://www.rogerclarke.com/II/IWtbF.html.

Click, M. A. "Untidy: Fan Response to the Soiling of Martha Stewart's Spotless Image." In *Fandom: Identities and Communities in a Mediated World,* edited by Jonathan Gray, Cornel Sandvoss, and C. Lee Harrington, 301–315. New York: New York University Press, 2007.

Cohoon, J. M. G., Vivek Wadhwa, and L. Mitchell. *Are Successful Women Entrepreneurs Different from Men?* Kansas City, MO: Ewing Marion Kauffman Foundation, 2010. http://www.kauffman.org/uploadedFiles/successful_women_entrepreneurs_5–10.pdf.

Coleman, E. G. "Code Is Speech: Legal Tinkering, Expertise, and Protest Among Free and Open Source Software Developers." *Cultural Anthropology* 24, no. 3 (2009): 420–454.

———. *Coding Freedom: The Ethics and Aesthetics of Hacking.* Princeton, NJ: Princeton University Press, 2012.

———. "Ethnographic Approaches to New Media." *Annual Review of Anthropology* 39 (October 2010). http://arjournals.annualreviews.org/doi/abs/10.1146/annurev.anthro.012809.104945.

———. "The Hacker Conference: A Ritual Condensation and Celebration of a Lifeworld." *Anthropological Quarterly* 83, no. 1 (2010): 47–74.

Coleman, E. G., and A. Golub. "Hacker Practice: Moral Genres and the Cultural Articulation of Liberalism." *Anthropological Theory* 8, no. 3 (2008): 255.

Coleman, E. G., and M. Hill. "How Free Became Open and Everything Else Under the Sun." *M/C: A Journal of Media and Culture* 7, no. 3 (2004).

Collins, Orvis F., and David G. Moore. *The Enterprising Man.* East Lansing: Michigan State University Press, 1964.

Collins, Shawn. "Affiliate Summit West 2009 Keynote Address by Gary Vaynerchuk [transcript]." FeedFront.com, February 19, 2009. http://feedfront.com/archives/article001707.

Comstock, M. "Grrrl Zine Networks: Re-Composing Spaces of Authority, Gender, and Culture." *Journal of Advanced Composition* 21, no. 2 (2001): 383–410.

Conley, A., A. Datta, H. Nissenbaum, and D. Sharma. "Sustaining Both Privacy and Open Justice in the Transition from Local to Online Access to Court Records: A Multidisciplinary Inquiry." *Maryland Law Review* (2012): 772–847.

Cool, Jennifer C. "Communities of Innovation: Cyborganic and the Birth of Networked Social Media." Ph.D. diss., University of Southern California, 2008. http://www.cool.org/chapterguide/.

Cool, Jenny, and Justin Hall. "Manifesto: What Is Cyborganic?" Cool.org, 1995. http://www.cool.org/portfolio/manifesto.html.

Crawford, Kate. "These Foolish Things: On Intimacy and Insignificance in Mobile Media." In *Mobile Technologies: From Telecommunications to Media,* edited by Gerard Goggin and Larissa Hjorth, 252–266. New York: Routledge, 2009.

David, H., D. Dorn, and G. H. Hanson. *The China Syndrome: Local Labor Market Effects of Import Competition in the United States.* NBER Working Paper. Cambridge, MA: National Bureau of Economic Research, 2012. http://www.nber.org/papers/w18054.

Davidson, Adam. "Making It in America." *Atlantic,* February 2012. http://www.theatlantic.com/magazine/archive/2012/01/making-it-in-america/308844/.

Davis, C. N. "Electronic Access to Information and the Privacy Paradox: Rethinking Practical Obscurity and Its Impact on Electronic Freedom of Information." *Social Science Computer Review* 21, no. 1 (2003): 15–25.

Dawson, Keith. "Siliconia." *Tasty Bites from the Technology Frontier,* June 24, 2001. http://tbtf.com/siliconia.html.

Dean, Jodi. *Publicity's Secret.* Ithaca, NY: Cornell University Press, 2002.

De Botton, A. *Status Anxiety*. New York: Vintage, 2005.

Dery, Mark. *Escape Velocity*. New York: Grove Press, 1997.

Deuze, M. "Corporate Appropriation of Participatory Culture." In *Participation and Media Production: Critical Reflections on Content Creation*, edited by N. Carpentier and S. Livingstone, 27–40. Newcastle upon Tyne, Eng.: Cambridge Scholars Publishers, 2008.

Dibbell, J. "A Rape in Cyberspace; or How an Evil Clown, a Haitian Trickster Spirit, Two Wizards, and a Cast of Dozens Turned a Database into a Society." *New York University Annual Survey of American Law* (1994): 471.

Dickey, James R. "The Ten Commandments of Twitter." *James R. Dickey.com*, December 15, 2008. http://jamesrdickey.com/2008/12/the-ten-commandments-of-twitter/.

Dines, R. "Why You Should Care About Having a Diverse IT Ops Department." *Forrester Blogs*, October 23, 2009. http://blogs.forrester.com/rachel_dines/09–10–23-why_you_should_care_about_having_diverse_it_ops_department.

Donath, Judith. "Identity and Deception in the Virtual Community." In *Communities in Cyberspace*, edited by Peter Kollock and Marc Smith, 29–59. London: Routledge, 1999.

Du Gay, P. *Consumption and Identity at Work*. Thousand Oaks, CA: Sage, 1996.

Duncombe, S. *Notes from Underground: Zines and the Politics of Alternative Culture*. New York: Verso Books, 1997.

Eisenstein, E. L. *The Printing Press as an Agent of Change*. Cambridge, Eng.: Cambridge University Press, 1980.

Electronic Frontier Foundation. "Innovation." *Eff.org*, 2010. http://www.eff.org/issues/innovation.

Elliott, C. *Better Than Well: American Medicine Meets the American Dream*. New York: W. W. Norton & Company, 2004.

Ellison, N., R. D Heino, and J. L Gibbs. "Managing Impressions Online: Self-Presentation Processes in the Online Dating Environment." *Journal of Computer-Mediated Communication* 11, no. 2 (2006): article 2.

English-Lueck, June Anne. *Cultures@Silicon Valley*. Palo Alto, CA: Stanford University Press, 2002.

Epstein, Rob, and Jeffrey Friedman. *The Celluloid Closet*. Documentary. Sony Pictures Classics, 1996.

Evans, A., and G. D. Wilson. *Fame: The Psychology of Stardom*. London: Vision Paperbacks, 2001.

Ewen, Stuart. *PR! A Social History of Spin*. New York: Basic Books, 1996.

Fairclough, Norman. *Analysing Discourse: Textual Analysis for Social Research*. New York: Routledge, 2003.

Faludi, S. *Backlash: The Undeclared War Against American Women*. New York: Crown Publishing, 1991.

Farber, Dan. "Facebook's Zuckerberg Uncorks the Social Graph." *ZDNet*, May 24, 2007. http://www.zdnet.com/blog/btl/facebooks-zuckerberg -uncorks-the-social-graph/5156.

Feasey, R. "Reading Heat: The Meanings and Pleasures of Star Fashions and Celebrity Gossip." *Continuum: Journal of Media & Cultural Studies* 22, no. 5 (2008): 687–699.

Ferriss, Timothy. *The 4-Hour Body: An Uncommon Guide to Rapid Fat-Loss, Incredible Sex, and Becoming Superhuman*. 1st ed. New York: Crown Archetype, 2010.

———. "The 4-Hour Chef Is a NYT, WSJ, and USA Today Bestseller! But There Is Mystery and Intrigue. . . ." *4-Hour Work Week*, November 30, 2012. http://www.fourhourworkweek.com/blog/2012/11/30/the-4-hour -chef-bestseller/.

———. *The 4-Hour Workweek: Expanded and Updated, with over 100 New Pages of Cutting-Edge Content*. New York: Crown, 2009.

———. "How to Use Twitter Without Twitter Owning You: 5 Tips." Blog. *4-Hour Work Week*, February 25, 2009. http://www.fourhourworkweek .com/blog/2009/02/25/how-to-use-twitter-without-twitter-owning-you -5-tips/#more-1263.

Feuer, Alan, and Jason George. "Internet Fame Is Cruel Mistress for a Dancer of the Numa Numa." *New York Times*, February 26, 2005, sec. New York Region. http://www.nytimes.com/2005/02/26/nyregion/26video .html?_r=1.

Fickensher, Lisa. "Not Much Life Left in the Party." *Crain's New York Business.com*, November 1, 2009. http://www.crainsnewyork.com/article /20091101/SMALLBIZ/311019960.

Fitzpatrick, Brad. "Brad's Thoughts on the Social Graph." *Bradfitz.com*, August 17, 2007. http://bradfitz.com/social-graph-problem/.

Florida, Richard L. *The Rise of the Creative Class*. New York: Basic Books, 2002.

Fono, D., and K. Raynes-Goldie. "Hyperfriendship and Beyond: Friendship and Social Norms on Livejournal." In *Internet Research Annual*, vol. 4: *Selected Papers from the Association of Internet Researchers Conference*. New York: Peter Lang, 2005.

Foster, Ben. "How Many Users on Facebook?" *Ben Foster on Digital Strategy, Social Media, and the Corner Office,* July 26, 2012. http://www.benphoster.com/facebook-user-growth-chart-2004–2010.

Foucault, Michel. "Governmentality." In *The Essential Foucault,* edited by P. Rabinow and N. Rose, 229–245. New York: The New Press, 2004.

Foucault, Michel, Luther H. Martin, Huck Gutman, and Patrick H. Hutton. *Technologies of the Self: A Seminar with Michel Foucault.* Amherst: University of Massachusetts Press, 1988.

Frank, Thomas. *The Conquest of Cool.* Chicago: University of Chicago Press, 1998.

Freedman, Jenna. "Zines Are Not Blogs." *Counterpoise,* Summer 2005.

Freeman, E. T. "Lifestreams Project Home Page." Yale University Computer Science Department, 1996. http://cs-www.cs.yale.edu/homes/freeman/lifestreams.html.

———. "The Lifestreams Software Architecture." Ph.D. diss., Yale University, 1997. http://www.cs.yale.edu/homes/freeman/dissertation/etf.pdf.

Friend, Tad. "V-va-va-voom!" *The New Yorker,* June 7, 2010.

Galloway, Alexander R., and Paul Alsina. "We Are the Gold Farmers," September 12, 2007. http://cultureandcommunication.org/galloway/interview_barcelona_sept07.txt.

Ganahl, Jane. "The Chief Chick of ChickClick: Spinning a Web for the Anti-Cosmo-Girl." *San Francisco Chronicle,* December 24, 1998. http://www.sfgate.com/cgi-bin/article.cgi?f=/e/a/1998/12/24/STYLE8833.dtl.

Garner, Dwight. "Timothy Ferriss—'The 4-Hour Body'—Review." *New York Times,* January 6, 2011, sec. Books. http://www.nytimes.com/2011/01/07/books/07book.html.

Gelernter, David. "The Cyber-Road Not Taken: Lost on the Info-highway? Here's Some Stuff That Could Really Change Your Life." *Washington Post,* April 3, 1994.

Gershon, I. *The Breakup 2.0: Disconnecting over New Media.* Ithaca, NY: Cornell University Press, 2010.

Gibbs, J. L., N. Ellison, and R. D. Heino. "Self-Presentation in Online Personals: The Role of Anticipated Future Interaction, Self-Disclosure, and Perceived Success in Internet Dating." *Communication Research* 33, no. 2 (2006): 152.

Gillmor, D. *We the Media: Grassroots Journalism by the People, for the People.* Sebastopol, CA: O'Reilly Media, 2006.

Glott, R., P. Schmidt, and R. Ghosh. *Wikipedia Survey—Overview of Results.* First survey of Wikipedians. Maastricht, Neth.: United Nations University Collaborative Creativity Group, 2010. http://wikipediasurvey .org/docs/Wikipedia_Overview_15March2010-FINAL.pdf.

Goldhaber, M. H. "The Attention Economy and the Net." *First Monday* 2, nos. 4–7 (April 1997). http://firstmonday.org/htbin/cgiwrap/bin/ojs/index .php/fm/article/view/519/440.

Goldstein, Dana. "How to Fix the Gender Gap in Technology." *Slate,* June 7, 2012. http://www.slate.com/articles/technology/future_tense/2012 /06/gender_gap_in_technology_and_silicon_valley_.html.

Gomez, G., et al. "Disembodiment and Cyberspace: Gendered Discourses in Female Teenagers' Personal Information Disclosure." *Discourse & Society* 21, no. 2 (2010): 135.

Goodell, Jeff. "Jonathan 'Dr. Cheeze' Makes His Million-Dollar Cyborganic." *Rolling Stone,* November 30, 1995.

Google Inc. "Doodle 4 Google." *Google.com,* 2010. http://www.google.com /doodle4google/history.html.

Graham, Paul. "Web 2.0." *Paulgraham.com,* November 2005. http://www .paulgraham.com/web20.html.

Granick, Jennifer. "Saving Democracy with Web 2.0." *Wired,* October 25, 2006. http://www.wired.com/software/webservices/commentary/circuit court/2006/10/72001?currentPage=all.

Gray, Jonathan. "Antifandom and the Moral Text: Television Without Pity and Textual Dislike." *American Behavioral Scientist* 48, no. 7 (March 1, 2005): 840–858.

———. "New Audiences, New Textualities: Anti-Fans and Non-Fans." *International Journal of Cultural Studies* 6, no. 1 (March 1, 2003): 64–81.

Gray, Mary L. *Out in the Country: Youth, Media, and Queer Visibility in Rural America.* New York: NYU Press, 2009.

Grazian, D. *Blue Chicago: The Search for Authenticity in Urban Blues Clubs.* Chicago: University of Chicago Press, 2003.

Gregg, Melissa. "Learning to (Love) Labour: Production Cultures and the Affective Turn." *Communication and Critical/Cultural Studies* 6, no. 2 (2009): 209–214.

Gürer, D., and T. Camp. "An ACM-W Literature Review on Women in Computing." *ACM SIGCSE Bulletin* 34, no. 2 (2002): 121–127.

Habuchi, Ichiyo. "Accelerating Reflexivity." In *Personal, Portable, Pedestrian: Mobile Phones in Japanese Life,* edited by Mitzuko Ito, D. Okabe, and Misa Matsuda. Cambridge, MA: MIT Press, 2005.

Hargittai, E., J. Gallo, and M. Kane. "Cross-Ideological Discussions Among Conservative and Liberal Bloggers." *Public Choice* 134, no. 1 (2008): 67–86.

Harris, S. D. "Harris: Startup Boot Camp Illustrates Dearth of Women in Tech." *Silicon Valley Mercury News*, July 19, 2010. http://www.mercurynews .com/ci_15517047?nclick_check=1.

Harvey, David. *A Brief History of Neoliberalism*. Oxford, Eng.: Oxford University Press, 2007.

Hayes, Dennis. *Behind the Silicon Curtain: The Seductions of Work in a Lonely Era*. Boston: South End Press, 1989.

Hearn, A. "Meat, Mask, Burden: Probing the Contours of the Branded Self." *Journal of Consumer Culture* 8, no. 2 (2008): 197–217.

Helft, Miguel. "Yahoo Layoffs Today May Not Be the Last." *New York Times Bits Blog*, December 10, 2008. http://bits.blogs.nytimes.com/2008 /12/10/yahoo-layoffs-today-may-not-be-last.

Hempel, Jessi. "Silicon Valley Confidential." *BusinessWeek*, April 17, 2006. http://www.businessweek.com/print/magazine/content/06_16/b398 0104.htm.

Henderson, J. Maureen. "A Social Media Game Plan from the Internet's Self-Promotion Princess." *The Ground Floor—Forbes*, July 13, 2011. http://blogs.forbes.com/jmaureenhenderson/2011/07/13/a-social-media -game-plan-from-the-internets-self-promotion-princess.

Henshaw, Evan. "Origin of the @reply—Digging Through Twitter's History." *Anarchogeek*, July 9, 2012. http://anarchogeek.com/2012/07/09/origin -of-the-reply-digging-through-twitters-history.

Herring, S. C., I. Kouper, L. A. Scheidt, and E. L. Wright. "Women and Children Last: The Discursive Construction of Weblogs." In *Into the Blogosphere: Rhetoric, Community, and Culture of Weblogs*, edited by L. J. Gurak, S. Antonijevic, L. Johnson, C. Ratliff, and J. Reyman, 2004. http:// blog.lib.umn.edu/blogosphere/women_and_children.html.

Hindman, Matthew Scott. *The Myth of Digital Democracy*. Princeton, NJ: Princeton University Press, 2009.

Hochschild, Arlie Russell. *The Managed Heart*. Berkeley: University of California Press, 1983.

Hoffman, Anthony. "Oversharing: A Critical Discourse Analysis." Master's thesis, Library and Information Science, University of Wisconsin-Milwaukee, 2009.

Hogan, R., and J. Hogan. "Personality and Status." In *Personality, Social Skills, and Psychopathology: An Individual Differences Approach*, edited by D. G. Gilbert and J. J. Connolly, 137–154. New York: Plenum Press, 1991.

Honeycutt, C., and S. Herring. "Beyond Microblogging: Conversation and Collaboration in Twitter." In *Proceedings of the Forty-Second Hawai'i International Conference on System Sciences (HICSS-42)*. Los Alamitos, CA: IEEE Computer Society, 2009.

Hoofnagle, C. J., J. King, S. Li, and J. Turow. *How Different Are Young Adults from Older Adults When It Comes to Information Privacy Attitudes and Policies?* Berkeley: University of California, Berkeley, April 14, 2010. http://papers.ssrn.com/sol3/papers.cfm?abstract_id=1589864.

Horton, D., and R. R. Wohl. "Mass Communication and Para-Social Interaction: Observations on Intimacy at a Distance." *Psychiatry* 19, no. 3 (1956): 215–229.

Hu, Jen. "Ambitious, Difficult Women: They May or May Not Be Pretty, Sleeping with Someone at Work." *The Awl*, July 26, 2010. http://www .theawl.com/2010/07/ambitious-difficult-women-they-may-or-may-not -be-pretty-sleeping-with-someone-at-work.

Huberman, B. A., C. H. Loch, and A. Önçüler. "Status as a Valued Resource." *Social Psychology Quarterly* 67, no. 1 (2004): 103–114.

Humphreys, Lee. "Historicizing Microblogging." In *Proceedings of CHI 2010 Workshop on Microblogging: What and How Can We Learn from It?* Atlanta, GA: ACM, 2010. http://www.cs.unc.edu/~julia/accepted-papers /Humphreys_HistoricizingTwitter.pdf.

———. "Mobile Social Networks and Social Practice: A Case Study of Dodgeball." *Journal of Computer-Mediated Communication* 13, no. 1 (2008): 341–360.

———. "Mobile Social Networks and Urban Public Space." *New Media & Society*, February 9, 2010. http://nms.sagepub.com/cgi/content/abstract /1461444809349578v1.

Hunt, T. *The Whuffie Factor: Using the Power of Social Networks to Build Your Business*. New York: Crown Publishing, 2009.

Iacono, S., and R. Kling. "Computerization Movement and Tales of Technological Utopianism." In *Computerization and Controversy: Value Conflicts and Social Choices*, edited by R. Kling, 85–105. 2nd ed. Orlando, FL: Academic Press, 1995.

Inglis, Fred. *A Short History of Celebrity*. 1st ed. Princeton, NJ: Princeton University Press, 2010.

Ingram, Mathew. "Ingram: Web 2.0 Report Card." *The Globe and Mail*, Toronto, December 27, 2005. http://www.globeinvestor.com/servlet/Arti cleNews/story/RTGAM/20051223/wmathyearend.

Ito, M., and D. Okabe. "Intimate Connections: Contextualizing Japanese Youth and Mobile Messaging." *The Inside Text* (2005): 127–145.

Ito, M., D. Okabe, and K. Anderson. "Portable Objects in Three Global Cities: The Personalization of Urban Places." In *The Reconstruction of Space and Time: Mobile Communication Practices*, edited by R. Ling and S. W. Campbell, 67–87. New Brunswick, NJ: Transaction Publishers, 2009.

Ives, Nat. "Are We at Advertising Age a Bunch of Twitter Snobs?" *Adage, Advertising Age*, June 2, 2009. http://adage.com/adages/post?article _id=137042.

Jackson, Adam. "Thank You Roger Ebert." *Adam-Jackson*, February 18, 2010. http://blog.adam-jackson.net/2010/02/18/thank-you-roger-ebert.

Jarrett, Kylie. "Interactivity Is Evil! A Critical Investigation of Web 2.0." *First Monday* 3, no. 3 (2008). http://firstmonday.org/htbin/cgiwrap/bin/ojs /index.php/fm/article/view/2140.

Jenkins, H. *Convergence Culture*. New York: New York University Press, 2006.

———. *Textual Poachers: Television Fans and Participatory Culture*. New York: Routledge, 1992.

Jenkins, H., and D. Thorburn. "Introduction: The Digital Revolution, the Informed Citizen, and the Culture of Democracy." In *Democracy and New Media*, edited by H. Jenkins and D. Thorburn, 1–20. Cambridge, MA: MIT Press, 2003.

Johnson, Kirk. "The Place for the Aspiring Dot Com; Internet Industry's Most Popular Address Is Manhattan." *New York Times*, September 30, 1997, sec. N.Y. / Region. http://www.nytimes.com/1997/09/30/nyregion /place-for-aspiring-dot-com-internet-industry-s-most-popular-address -manhattan.html.

Jordan, Tim. *Hacking*. Cambridge, Eng.: Polity, 2008.

Joseph, Sarah. "Social Media, Political Change, and Human Rights." *Boston College International and Comparative Law Review* 35, no. 1 (2012): 145–188.

Juliaspublicist. "Apparently We Hurt Julia Allison's Feelings." *Reblogging NonSociety*, March 22, 2010. http://rebloggingns.wordpress.com/2010 /03/22/apparently-we-hurt-julia-allisons-feelings/.

Junell, Ryan. "15 Megs of Fame." *TexasMonkey.com*, 2001. http://texasmonkey .com/15megs/.

———. "Independent Publishing on the Internet: Webzine and Fifteen Megs of Fame." In *Alternatives on Media Content, Journalism, and Regulation*, edited by S. P. Gangadharan, B. De Cleen, and N. Carpentier, 5–14. The Researching and Teaching Communication Series. Tartu,

Estonia: Tartu University Press, 2007. http://homepages.vub.ac.be/~ncarpent/grass/GrassEbook.pdf.

Juris, Jeffrey S. *Networking Futures*. Durham, NC: Duke University Press, 2008.

———. "The New Digital Media and Activist Networking Within Anti-Corporate Globalization Movements." *Annals of the American Academy of Political and Social Science* 597 (January 2005): 189–208.

Kahn, R., and D. Kellner. "New Media and Internet Activism: From the 'Battle of Seattle' to Blogging." *New Media & Society* 6, no. 1 (2004): 87–95.

Kaputa, Catherine. "10 Self-Branding Strategies for Career Success." *Self-BRAND*, 2008. http://web.mac.com/catherinekaputa/artofbranding/10_Self-Branding_.html.

Katz, Jon. "The Age of Paine." *Wired*, May 1995. http://www.wired.com/wired/archive/3.05/paine_pr.html.

Keen, A. *The Cult of the Amateur: How Today's Internet Is Killing Our Culture*. New York: Broadway Business, 2007.

Kelty, Christopher M. *Two Bits*. Durham, NC: Duke University Press, 2008.

Kim, E. G., and J. W. Hamilton. "Capitulation to Capital? OhmyNews as Alternative Media." *Media, Culture & Society* 28, no. 4 (2006): 541.

Kirkpatrick, Marshall. "Facebook's Zuckerberg Says the Age of Privacy Is Over." *Read Write Web*, January 9, 2010. http://www.readwriteweb.com/archives/facebooks_zuckerberg_says_the_age_of_privacy_is_ov.php.

Klein, N. *No Logo: Taking Aim at the Brand Bullies*. New York: Picador USA, 1999.

Klinenberg, Eric. *Fighting for Air*. New York: Macmillan, 2007.

Klout, Inc. "Understanding the Influence Metric: What Is the Klout Score?" *Klout*, 2012. http://klout.com/corp/kscore.

Koivula, N. "Gender Stereotyping in Televised Media Sport Coverage." *Sex Roles* 41, no. 7 (1999): 589–604.

Kopytoff, Verne. "Internet Bigwigs Upbeat: S.F. Meeting Brims with Optimism." *The San Francisco Chronicle*, October 8, 2004, sec. Business.

Kurzman, C., C. Anderson, C. Key, Y. O. Lee, M. Moloney, A. Silver, and M. W. Van Ryn. "Celebrity Status." *Sociological Theory* 25, no. 4 (2007): 347–367.

Labovitz, John. "E-zine List of Electronic Zines." *Alt.zines*, September 3, 1993. http://wiretap.area.com/Gopher/alt.etext/191.ezine.

Lacy, Sarah. "Milk Completes $1.5 Million Angel Round, Packed with Valley Names." *TechCrunch,* April 26, 2011. http://techcrunch.com/2011 /04/26/milk-completes-1–5-million-angel-round-packed-with-valley -names.

———. *Once You're Lucky, Twice You're Good.* New York: Penguin Group, 2008.

Lair, D. J., K. Sullivan, and G. Cheney. "Marketization and the Recasting of the Professional Self: The Rhetoric and Ethics of Personal Branding." *Management Communication Quarterly* 18, no. 3 (2005): 307–343.

Lanier, Jaron. *You Are Not a Gadget: A Manifesto.* 1st ed. New York: Knopf, 2010.

LaPorta, Lauren. "Twitter and YouTube: Unexpected Consequences of the Self-Esteem Movement?" *Psychiatric Times* 26, no. 11 (October 28, 2009).

Lawrence, Eric, John Sides, and Henry Farrell. "Self-Segregation or Deliberation? Blog Readership, Participation, and Polarization in American Politics." *Perspectives on Politics* 8, no. 01 (2010): 141–157.

Lawson, Richard. "Into the Internet's Ninth Circle of Hell: The Rebloggers." *Gawker,* January 7, 2010. http://gawker.com/5441578/into-the -internets-ninth-circle-of-hell-the-rebloggers.

———. "A Reblogger Speaks." *Gawker,* January 8, 2010. http://gawker.com /5443842/a-reblogger-speaks.

Lazzarato, M. "Immaterial Labor." In *Radical Thought in Italy: A Potential Politics,* edited by P. Virno and M. Hardt, 133–150. Minneapolis: University of Minnesota Press, 1996.

Lécuyer, Christophe. *Making Silicon Valley.* Cambridge, MA: MIT Press, 2006.

Lessig, Lawrence. *Code: Version 2.0.* New York: Basic Books, 2006. http:// codev2.cc/.

———. *Free Culture.* New York: Penguin Books, 2004.

———. *Web 2.0 Conference.* Mp3. ITConversations. San Francisco, 2004. http://itc.conversationsnetwork.org/shows/detail332.html.

Levy, Frank, and Thomas Kochan. "Addressing the Problem of Stagnant Wages." *Comparative Economic Studies* (August 16, 2012).

Levy, Steven. "Farewell Web 1.0! We Hardly Knew Ye." *Newsweek,* October 18, 2004. http://www.newsweek.com/id/55242.

———. *Hackers.* New York: Anchor Press/Doubleday, 1984.

Linton, R. *The Study of Man.* New York: Appleton-Century-Crofts, 1936.

Liu, H. "Social Network Profiles as Taste Performances." *Journal of Computer–Mediated Communication* 13, no. 1 (2007): article 13.

Locke, John L. *Eavesdropping: An Intimate History.* New York: Oxford University Press, USA, 2010.

Lorek, L. A. "Where the Geeks Are: Dispatches from the Largest SXSW Interactive Ever." *DailyFinance.com*, March 15, 2011. http://www.daily finance.com/2011/03/15/where-the-geeks-are-dispatches-from-the -largest-sxsw-interactiv.

Lovink, Geert. *Zero Comments: Blogging and Critical Internet Culture.* New York: Routledge, 2008.

MacManus, Richard. "Tim O'Reilly Interview, Part 1: Web 2.0." *ReadWriteWeb*, November 15, 2004. http://www.readwriteweb.com/archives /tim_oreilly_int.php.

Madden, Mary, S. Fox, Aaron Smith, and J. Vitak. "Digital Footprints: Online Identity Management and Search in the Age of Transparency." Pew Internet and American Life Project. Washington, DC: Pew Research Center, December 16, 2007. http://www.pewinternet.org/Reports /2007/Digital-Footprints.aspx.

Madden, Mary, and Kathryn Zickuhr. *65% of Online Adults Use Social Networking Sites.* Pew Internet and American Life Project. Washington, DC: Pew Research Center, August 26, 2011. http://pewinternet.org /Reports/2011/Social-Networking-Sites.aspx.

Madden, Raymond. *Being Ethnographic: A Guide to the Theory and Practice of Ethnography.* Thousand Oaks, CA: Sage, 2010.

Malone, Michael Shawn. *The Big Score: The Billion Dollar Story of Silicon Valley.* New York: Doubleday, 1985.

Margolis, Jane, and Allan Fisher. *Unlocking the Clubhouse: Women in Computing.* Cambridge, MA: MIT Press, 2003.

Markoff, John. *What the Dormouse Said.* New York: Penguin Books, 2005.

Marmot, Michael. *The Status Syndrome.* New York: Macmillan, 2005.

Marwick, Alice E. "The People's Republic of YouTube? Interrogating Rhetorics of Internet Democracy." Presented at Association of Internet Researchers 8.0, Vancouver, October 18–20, 2007. http://papers.ssrn.com /sol3/papers.cfm?abstract_id=1884349 .

———. "The Public Domain: Social Surveillance in Everyday Life." *Surveillance & Society* 9, no. 4 (2012). http://library.queensu.ca/ojs/index .php/surveillance-and-society/article/view/pub_dom.

———. "Selling Your Self: Online Identity in the Age of a Commodified Internet." Master's thesis, Department of Communication, University of Washington, 2005.

———. "Status Update: Celebrity, Publicity and Self-branding in Web 2.0." Ph.D. diss., New York University, 2010.

———. "There's a Beautiful Girl under All of This: Performing Hegemonic Femininity in Reality Television." *Critical Studies in Media Communication* 27, no. 3 (2010): 251–266.

Marwick, Alice E., and d. boyd. "'It's Just Drama': Teen Perspectives on Conflict and Aggression in a Networked Era." Microsoft Research Working Paper, 2012.

———. "I Tweet Honestly, I Tweet Passionately: Twitter Users, Context Collapse, and the Imagined Audience." *New Media & Society* 13, no. 1 (2011): 114–133.

———. "To See and Be Seen: Celebrity Practice on Twitter." *Convergence* 17, no. 2 (2011): 139–158.

Marwick, Alice E., and Nicole B. Ellison. "'There Isn't Wifi in Heaven!' Negotiating Visibility on Facebook Memorial Pages." *Journal of Broadcasting & Electronic Media* 56, no. 3.

Massachusetts Institute of Technology. "A Study on the Status of Women Faculty in Science at MIT." *The MIT Faculty Newsletter* 9, no. 4 (March 1999). http://web.mit.edu/fnl/women/women.html.

Mayer, G. *Union Membership Trends in the United States.* Congressional Research Service Report for Congress. Key Workplace Documents. Ithaca, NY: Cornell University ILR School, 2004. http://digitalcommons .ilr.cornell.edu/cgi/viewcontent.cgi?article=1176&context=key_work place.

McCarthy, A. "Reality Television: A Neoliberal Theater of Suffering." *Social Text* 25, no. 4 93 (December 2007): 17–42.

McChesney, Robert Waterman. "Introduction." In *Profit over People,* by Noam Chomsky, 7–18. New York: Seven Stories Press, 1999.

———. *Rich Media, Poor Democracy.* New York: New Press, 2000.

McGee, Micki. *Self-Help, Inc.* New York: Oxford University Press, 2005.

McMurria, J. "Desperate Citizens and Good Samaritans: Neoliberalism and Makeover Reality TV." *Television and New Media* 9, no. 4 (2008): 305.

MediaLive International and O'Reilly Media. "Web 2.0 Conference Speakers." *Web2con.com,* 2004. http://www.web2con.com/pub/w/32/speakers .html.

Miller, Claire Cain. "Out of the Loop in Silicon Valley." *New York Times,* April 16, 2010, sec. Technology. http://www.nytimes.com/2010/04/18 /technology/18women.html.

Miller, Claire Cain, and Jenna Wortham. "In Silicon Valley, a Lack of Engineers." *New York Times,* March 25, 2011, sec. Technology. http://www .nytimes.com/2011/03/26/technology/26recruit.html.

Miller, V. "New Media, Networking and Phatic Culture." *Convergence* 14, no. 4 (2008): 387.

Mills, Elinor. "Google Balances Privacy, Reach." *CNET News,* July 14, 2005. http://news.cnet.com/Google-balances-privacy,-reach/2100–1032 _3–5787483.html.

———. "My Stunted Interview with Google's Eric Schmidt." *News Blog— CNET News,* February 29, 2008. http://news.cnet.com/8301–10784 _3–9883410–7.html.

Milner, M. "Celebrity Culture as a Status System." *Hedgehog Review* 7, no. 1 (2005): 66–77.

———. *Freaks, Geeks, and Cool Kids: American Teenagers, Schools, and the Culture of Consumption.* New York: Routledge, 2004.

Milner, R. M. "Working for the Text: Fan Labor and the New Organization." *International Journal of Cultural Studies* 12, no. 5 (September 1, 2009): 491–508.

Misa, Thomas J., ed. *Gender Codes: Why Women Are Leaving Computing.* Hoboken, NJ: John Wiley and Sons, 2010.

Moore, R. "Friends Don't Let Friends Listen to Corporate Rock: Punk as a Field of Cultural Production." *Journal of Contemporary Ethnography* 36, no. 4 (2007): 438.

Morozov, Evgeny. *The Net Delusion: The Dark Side of Internet Freedom.* New York: PublicAffairs, 2011.

Mullen, Jessica. "Lifestreaming as a Life Design Methodology." Master's thesis, Fine Arts, University of Texas at Austin, 2010. http://posterous.com /getfile/files.posterous.com/jessicamullenmfa/565wvEahvgLsUh7oa SQeOHkhcqIOn08SFEUB5TM5cN5dC3uHcr8zS5BhOQs9/jmullen _thesis_final.pdf.

Nakamura, L. *Digitizing Race: Visual Cultures of the Internet.* Minneapolis: University of Minnesota Press, 2008.

———. "Race In/For Cyberspace: Identity Tourism and Racial Passing on the Internet." In *CyberReader,* edited by Victor Vitanza. Boston: Allyn and Bacon, 1999.

National Center for Women and Information Technology. *NCWIT Scorecard 2007: A Report on the Status of Women in Information Technology.* Boulder, CO: National Center for Women and Information Technology, 2007. http://www.ncwit.org/pdf/2007_Scorecard_Web.pdf.

Neff, G., E. Wissinger, and S. Zukin. "Entrepreneurial Labor Among Cultural Producers: 'Cool' Jobs in 'Hot' Industries." *Social Semiotics* 15, no. 3 (2005): 307–334.

Neff, G. "Risk Relations: The New Uncertainties of Work." *WorkingUSA* 5, no. 2 (2001): 59–68.

Nevius, C. W. "Lessons from That Tenderloin Camera Web Site." *SFGate .com*, December 13, 2008. http://www.sfgate.com/cgi-bin/article.cgi?f= /c/a/2008/12/12/BA7Q14N5S6.DTL.

Ngô, Fiona I. B., and Elizabeth A. Stinson. "Introduction: Threads and Omissions." *Women & Performance: A Journal of Feminist Theory* 22, nos. 2–3 (2012): 165–171.

Nippert-Eng, Christena E. *Islands of Privacy.* Chicago: University of Chicago Press, 2010.

Nissenbaum, H. "Defining Transparency." Presented at the workshop "Open Government: Defining, Designing, and Sustaining Transparency," Center for Open Technology Policy, Princeton University, January 21, 2010. http://citp.princeton.edu/open-government-workshop.

———. "Hackers and the Contested Ontology of Cyberspace." *New Media & Society* 6, no. 2 (2004): 195.

———. *Privacy in Context: Technology, Policy, and the Integrity of Social Life.* Palo Alto, CA: Stanford University Press, 2009.

Noe, Raymond A. "Women and Mentoring: A Review and Research Agenda." *Academy of Management Review* 13, no. 1 (January 1988): 65–78.

O'Dell, Jolie. "SXSW 2010 for Web Celeb Stalkers." *ReadWriteWeb*, March 9, 2010. http://www.readwriteweb.com/archives/sxsw_2010_for_web _celeb_stalkers.php.

Ogbor, J. O. "Mythicizing and Reification in Entrepreneurial Discourse: Ideology-Critique of Entrepreneurial Studies." *Journal of Management Studies* 37, no. 5 (2000): 605–635.

O'Leary, Amy. "Sexual Harassment in Online Gaming Stirs Anger." *New York Times*, August 1, 2012, sec. U.S. http://www.nytimes.com/2012/08 /02/us/sexual-harassment-in-online-gaming-stirs-anger.html.

Olsen, Stefanie. "Mark Cuban Raises Specter of Dot-com Redux." *C|Net News*, October 7, 2004. http://news.cnet.com/Mark-Cuban-prompts -dot-com-redux/2100–1026_3–5400029.html.

Ong, Aihwa. *Neoliberalism as Exception.* Durham, NC: Duke University Press, 2006.

OpenCourseWare Consortium. "About Us." *OpenCourseWare Consortium .org*, 2010. http://www.ocwconsortium.org/aboutus.

O'Reilly, Tim. "What Is Web 2.0." *O'Reilly.com*, September 30, 2005. http://oreilly.com/web2/archive/what-is-web-20.html.

Padnos, Cindy. *High Performance Entrepreneurs: Women in High Tech.* Oakland, CA: Illuminate Ventures, 2010. http://www.illuminate.com/whitepaper.

Papacharissi, Z. "The Presentation of Self in Virtual Life: Characteristics of Personal Home Pages." *Journalism and Mass Communication Quarterly* 79, no. 3 (2002): 643–660.

Pariser, Eli. *The Filter Bubble: What the Internet Is Hiding from You*. New York: Penguin, 2011.

Partypants. "ʏᴏᴏʜᴏᴏᴏ! Kelly Cutrone!!!!!!! Over Here!" *Reblogging Non-Society*, March 23, 2010. http://rebloggingns.wordpress.com/2010/03/23/yoohoooo-kelly-cutrone-over-here.

Pearce, Celia. "The Californian Ideology: An Insider's View." *Mute Magazine*, Winter/Spring 1996. http://www.metamute.org/en/The-Californian-Ideology-An-Insiders-View-Re-Californian-Ideology.

Pellow, David N., and Lisa Sun-Hee Park. *The Silicon Valley of Dreams*. New York: New York University Press, 2002.

Penley, Constance. *NASA/Trek: Popular Science and Sex in America*. Brooklyn, NY: Verso, 1997.

Peters, T. "The Brand Called You." *Fast Company*, 1997. http://www.fastcompany.com/magazine/10/brandyou.html.

Peterson, Tom. "Tumblr Posts Analytics Platform with Union Metrics." *Adweek*, October 4, 2012. http://www.adweek.com/news/technology/tumblr-posts-analytics-platform-union-metrics-144169.

Pfaffenberger, B. "The Social Meaning of the Personal Computer; or, Why the Personal Computer Revolution Was No Revolution." *Anthropological Quarterly* (1988): 39–47.

Phillips, Whitney. "Re: Yo Haters." April 27, 2012.

Pickard, V. W. "Assessing the Radical Democracy of Indymedia: Discursive, Technical, and Institutional Constructions." *Critical Studies in Media Communication* 23, no. 1 (2006): 19–38.

———. "United Yet Autonomous: Indymedia and the Struggle to Sustain a Radical Democratic Network." *Media, Culture & Society* 28, no. 3 (2006): 315.

Piepmeier, Alison. *Girl Zines: Making Media, Doing Feminism*. 1st edition. New York: NYU Press, 2009.

Pinker, Steven. "Mind over Mass Media." *New York Times*, June 10, 2010, sec. Opinion. http://www.nytimes.com/2010/06/11/opinion/11Pinker.html.

Pinkowitz, Jacqueline Marie. "'The Rabid Fans That Take [Twilight] Much Too Seriously': The Construction and Rejection of Excess in Twilight Antifandom." *Transformative Works and Cultures* 7 (September 20, 2010).

Pricewaterhousecooper and National Venture Capital Association. *Money-Tree™ Report: Venture Capital Investments Q1 1995–Q2 2012 Investments by Region*. Arlington, VA: National Venture Capital Association, July

20, 2012. http://www.nvca.org/index.php?option=com_docman&task =doc_download&gid=899.

Progrium. "SuperHappyDevHouse 2 at SuperHappyFunHouse (Saturday July 9, 2005)—Upcoming." *Upcoming.org,* June 17, 2005. http://upcoming .yahoo.com/event/22655/CA/San-Francisco-Bay-Area/SuperHappy DevHouse-2/SuperHappyFunHouse.

Rauch, J. "Hands-on Communication: Zine Circulation Rituals and the Interactive Limitations of Web Self-Publishing." *Popular Communication* 2, no. 3 (2004): 153–169.

Raymond, E. "The Cathedral and the Bazaar." *Knowledge, Technology & Policy* 12, no. 3 (1999): 23–49.

———. "Hack." *The Jargon File,* December 29, 2003. http://catb.org/jargon /html/H/hack.html.

Read, Jason. "A Genealogy of Homo-Economicus: Neoliberalism and the Production of Subjectivity." *Foucault Studies* 6 (February 25, 2009): 25–36.

Reagle, Joseph. "DRAFT: 'Free as in Sexist?': Free Culture and the Gender Gap," draft article, 2012. http://reagle.org/joseph/2012/05/free-as-in -sexist.html.

Regan, Priscilla M. *Legislating Privacy: Technology, Social Values, and Public Policy.* Durham: University of North Carolina Press, 1995.

Reid, Elizabeth. "Hierarchy and Power: Social Control in Cyberspace." In *Communities in Cyberspace,* edited by Peter Kollock and Marc A. Smith, 107–133. London: Routledge, 1999. http://www.sscnet.ucla.edu/soc/fac ulty/kollock/papers/communities_05.htm.

Richtel, Matt. "Hooked on Gadgets, and Paying a Mental Price." *New York Times,* June 6, 2010, sec. Technology. http://www.nytimes.com/2010/06 /07/technology/07brain.html.

———. "Silicon Valley Worries About Addiction to Devices." *New York Times,* July 23, 2012, sec. Technology. http://www.nytimes.com/2012 /07/24/technology/silicon-valley-worries-about-addiction-to-devices .html.

Ridgeway, C. L., and H. A. Walker. "Status Structures." In *Sociological Per- spectives on Social Psychology,* edited by K. Cook, G. Fine, and J. House, 281–310. New York: Allyn and Bacon, 1995.

Rivlin, Gary. "Silicon Valley (Version 2.0) Has Hopes Rising for Economic Rebound." *New York Times,* June 22, 2004, sec. C.

Roberts, S. "Self-Experimentation as a Source of New Ideas: Ten Examples About Sleep, Mood, Health, and Weight." *Behavioral and Brain Sciences* 27, no. 02 (2004): 227–262.

Robinson, Tanya. "Cory Doctorow." *The A.V. Club*, June 10, 2008. http://www.avclub.com/articles/cory-doctorow,14255.

Roffer, Robin Fisher. *Make a Name for Yourself.* New York: Random House, 2002.

Rogers, Everett M., and Judith K. Larsen. *Silicon Valley Fever.* New York: Basic Books, 1984.

Romaniello, John. "Tim Ferriss Interview—AskMen." *AskMen.com*, 2011. http://www.askmen.com/celebs/interview_400/493_tim-ferriss-interview.html.

Rose, Nikolas. *Inventing Our Selves: Psychology, Power, and Personhood.* New York: Cambridge University Press, 1996.

Rosenberg, S. *Say Everything: How Blogging Began, What It's Becoming, and Why It Matters.* New York: Crown Publishing, 2009.

Rosenbloom, Stephanie. "Tim Ferriss, the 4-Hour Guru." *New York Times*, March 25, 2011, sec. Fashion & Style. http://www.nytimes.com/2011/03/27/fashion/27Ferris.html.

Ross, A. *No-Collar: The Humane Workplace and Its Hidden Costs.* Philadelphia: Temple University Press, 2004.

Rossetto, Louis. "To: Mutoids (Re: The Californian Ideology)." *Mute Magazine*, Winter/Spring 1996. http://www.metamute.org/en/To-Mutoids-Re-The-Californian-Ideology.

Rothenberg, Randall. "Power to YouTube's People." *Los Angeles Times*, October 28, 2006.

Rothstein, Edward. "Connections: A Crunchy-Granola Path from Macramé and LSD to Wikipedia and Google." *New York Times*, September 25, 2006. http://www.nytimes.com/2006/09/25/arts/25conn.html.

Rubin, Gretchen. *The Happiness Project; or, Why I Spent a Year Trying to Sing in the Morning, Clean My Closets, Fight Right, Read Aristotle, and Generally Have More Fun.* New York: HarperCollins, 2009.

Rucker, Rudy von Bitter, R. U. Sirius, and Queen Mu. *Mondo 2000.* New York: HarperPerennial, 1992.

Rupley, Sebastian. "Web Snap(s) Search and Rebounds." *PCMag.com*, October 7, 2004. http://www.pcmag.com/article2/0,2817,1668298,00.asp.

Rushkoff, Douglas. *Cyberia.* New York: HarperSan Francisco, 1994.

Saxenian, AnnaLee. *The New Argonauts: Regional Advantage in a Global Economy.* Cambridge, MA: Harvard University Press, 2006.

———. *Regional Advantage.* Cambridge, MA: Harvard University Press, 1996.

Scandura, Terri A. "Mentorship and Career Mobility: An Empirical Investigation." *Journal of Organizational Behavior* 13, no. 2 (1992): 169–174.

Schawbel, Dan. *Me 2.0: Build a Powerful Brand to Achieve Career Success.* New York: Kaplan Publishing, 2009.

Schlosser, E. *Fast Food Nation: The Dark Side of the All-American Meal.* New York: Houghton Mifflin Harcourt, 2001.

Schneier, Bruce. "My Reaction to Eric Schmidt." *Schneier on Security,* December 9, 2009. http://www.schneier.com/blog/archives/2009/12/my_reaction_to.html.

Scholz, Trebor. "Market Ideology and the Myths of Web 2.0." *First Monday* 13, no. 3 (2008). http://firstmonday.org/htbin/cgiwrap/bin/ojs/index.php/fm/article/view/2138.

Schwartz, P., and P. Leyden. "The Long Boom: A History of the Future, 1980–2020." *Wired,* July 1997.

Sconce, J. "A Vacancy at the Paris Hilton." In *Fandom: Identities and Communities in a Mediated World,* edited by Jonathan Gray, Cornel Sandvoss, and C. Lee Harrington, 328–343. New York: New York University Press, 2007.

Scott, J. "Statement_." *T E X T F I L E S.* Accessed March 29, 2012. http://textfiles.com/statement.html.

Scott, Krista. "'Girls Need Modems!' Cyberculture and Women's Ezines." Master's thesis, Women's Studies, York University, 1998. http://www.stumptuous.com/mrp.html.

Sender, K. "Queens for a Day: Queer Eye for the Straight Guy and the Neoliberal Project." *Critical Studies in Media Communication* 23, no. 2 (2006): 131–151.

Senft, Theresa. *Camgirls: Celebrity and Community in the Age of Social Networks.* Digital Formations. New York: Peter Lang, 2008.

Sengupta, Somini. "Facebook Moves to Aid Its Shares." *New York Times,* September 4, 2012, sec. Technology. http://www.nytimes.com/2012/09/05/technology/facebook-moves-to-aid-its-shares.html.

Shelton, Edward. "Ted Shelton: Mitch Kapor at Web 2.0." *Ted Shelton,* October 7, 2004. http://tedshelton.blogspot.com/2004/10/mitch-kapor-at-web-20.html.

Shiels, Maggie. "Blizzard Backs Down over Gamers Using Real Names." *BBC News,* July 9, 2010. http://news.bbc.co.uk/2/hi/technology/8806623.stm.

Shirky, Clay. *Here Comes Everybody.* New York: Penguin Books, 2008.

Shontell, Allison. "Nick Denton Is Resurrecting *Valleywag.*" *Business Insider,* January 13, 2013. http://www.businessinsider.com/exclusive-nick-denton-is-resurrecting-valleywag-2013-1.

Siles, I. "From Online Filter to Web Format: Articulating Materiality and Meaning in the Early History of Blogs." *Social Studies of Science* 41, no. 5 (2011): 737–758.

Silver, David, and Adrienne Massanari. *Critical Cyberculture Studies.* New York: NYU Press, 2006.

Sinker, Daniel, ed. *We Owe You Nothing: Punk Planet: The Collected Interviews.* New York: Akashic Books, 2001.

Sivers, Derek. "Tim Ferriss Interview." *Sivers.org,* August 7, 2008. http://sivers.org/tim-ferriss.

Smith, Aaron. *Cell Internet Use 2012.* Internet & American Life Project. Washington, DC: Pew Research Center, June 26, 2012. http://pewinternet.org/Reports/2012/Cell-Internet-Use-2012.aspx.

Smith, Jackie. "Globalizing Resistance: The Battle of Seattle and the Future of Social Movements." *Mobilization: An International Quarterly* 6, no. 1 (March 1, 2001): 1–19.

Smith, M. R., and L. Marx. *Does Technology Drive History? The Dilemma of Technological Determinism.* Cambridge, MA: MIT Press, 1994.

Solove, Daniel J. "'I've Got Nothing to Hide' and Other Misunderstandings of Privacy." *San Diego Law Review* 44 (2007): 745.

Sorgatz, Rex. "The Microfame Game." *New York Magazine,* June 17, 2008. http://nymag.com/news/media/47958.

Sorkin, Andrew Ross. "Memo: Valleywag Gets Down to Business." *DealBook blog,* November 14, 2006. http://dealbook.blogs.nytimes.com/2006/11/14/memo-why-valleywag-sacked-its-editor/.

Spertus, E. *Why Are There so Few Female Computer Scientists?* AI Technical Reports. Cambridge, MA: Massachusetts Institute of Technology, 1991. http://dspace.mit.edu/handle/1721.1/7040.

Starr, Nick. "And Now You Know . . . the Rest of the Story." *Life As Nick Starr,* October 20, 2008. http://lifeasnickstarr.com/2008/10/20/and-now-you-know-the-rest-of-the-story.

Sternberg, Ernest. "Phantasmagoric Labor: The New Economics of Self-Presentation." *Futures* 30, no. 1 (January 1998): 3–21.

Stone, Allucquère Rosanne. *The War of Desire and Technology at the Close of the Mechanical Age.* Cambridge, MA: MIT Press, 1996.

Sullivan, Nicole. "Woman in Technology." *Stubbornella,* July 26, 2010. http://www.stubbornella.org/content/2010/07/26/woman-in-technology.

Surowiecki, James. *The Wisdom of Crowds.* New York: Anchor, 2005.

Talbot, David. "How Much Tech Can One City Take?" *San Francisco Magazine,* September 20, 2012. http://www.modernluxury.com/san-francisco/story/how-much-tech-can-one-city-take.

Tate, Ryan. "This Man Founded Everything (and So Did You)." *Gawker,* July 29, 2009. http://gawker.com/5325654/this-man-founded-everything-and-so-did-you.

Taulli, Tom. "How Angel Investing Works." *BusinessWeek*, October 10, 2008. http://www.businessweek.com/stories/2008–10–10/how-angel-investing-worksbusinessweek-business-news-stock-market-and-financial-advice.

Taylor, Chsi. "Facebook Has 955 Million Active Users—Still Shy of a Billion." *Mashable*, July 26, 2012. http://mashable.com/2012/07/26/facebook-955-million-users.

Terdiman, Daniel. "Tech Carries a Torch for Burning Man." *C|Net News*, August 28, 2006. http://news.cnet.com/Tech-carries-a-torch-for-Burning-Man/2100–1026_3–6109870.html.

Terranova, Tiziana. "Free Labor: Producing Culture for the Digital Economy." *Social Text* 18, no. 2 (2000): 33–58.

Thomas, Dana. *Deluxe: How Luxury Lost Its Luster.* New York: Penguin Group USA, 2007.

Thomas, Douglas. *Hacker Culture.* Minneapolis: University of Minnesota Press, 2002.

Thomas, Owen. "Is Elon Musk Aiming to Take over Tesla?" *Valleywag*, November 7, 2008. http://gawker.com/5079875/is-elon-musk-aiming-to-take-over-tesla.

———. "Temptress of Silicon Valley Shuts Down Useless Site." *Valleywag*, December 1, 2008. http://valleywag.gawker.com/5100552/temptress-of-silicon-valley-shuts-down-useless-site.

———. "Ze'ev Drori Out, Elon Musk in as Tesla CEO." *Valleywag*, October 15, 2008. http://gawker.com/5063557/zeev-drori-out-elon-musk-in-as-tesla-ceo.

Thompson, Clive. "Brave New World of Digital Intimacy." *New York Times*, September 7, 2008, sec. Magazine. http://www.nytimes.com/2008/09/07/magazine/07awareness-t.html.

Thurlow, C. "Fakebook: Synthetic Media, Pseudo-Sociality and the Rhetorics of Web 2.0." In *Discourse 2.0: Language and New Media*, edited by D. Tannen and A. Trester. Washington, DC: Georgetown University Press, 2013.

Timoner, O. *We Live in Public.* Documentary film. Pasadena, CA: Interloper Films, 2009.

Tocci, J. "The Well-Dressed Geek: Media Appropriation and Subcultural Style." Presented at "Media in Transition 5," Cambridge, MA, April 29, 2007.

Trepte, Sabine, and Leonard Reinecke. *Privacy Online: Perspectives on Privacy and Self-Disclosure in the Social Web.* New York: Springer, 2011.

Tribe, K. "The Political Economy of Modernity: Foucault's Collège de France Lectures of 1978 and 1979." *Economy and Society* 38, no. 4 (2009): 679–698.

Trilling, Lionel. *Sincerity and Authenticity*. Cambridge, MA: Harvard University Press, 1972.

Trunk, Penelope. "Gold Digging Web 2.0 Style." *Penelope Trunk Blog*, April 16, 2009. http://blog.penelopetrunk.com/2009/04/16/gold-digging-web -20-style.

Tsotsis, Alexa. "Winning a Bidding War with Facebook, Google Picks up the Milk Product Team." *TechCrunch*, March 15, 2012. http://techcrunch.com /2012/03/15/winning-a-bidding-war-with-facebook-google-picks-up -the-entire-milk-team.

Tufekci, Z. "Can You See Me Now? Audience and Disclosure Regulation in Online Social Network Sites." *Bulletin of Science, Technology & Society* 28, no. 1 (2008): 20.

Turkle, Sherry. *Life on the Screen: Identity in the Age of the Internet*. New York: Simon & Schuster, 1995.

Turner, Bryan S. *Status*. Minneapolis: University of Minnesota Press, 1989.

Turner, Fred. "Burning Man at Google: A Cultural Infrastructure for New Media Production." *New Media & Society* 11, nos. 1–2 (2009): 73.

———. *From Counterculture to Cyberculture*. Chicago: University of Chicago Press, 2006.

Twenge, Jean M., and W. Keith Campbell. *The Narcissism Epidemic: Living in the Age of Entitlement*. New York: Simon and Schuster, 2009.

Twitchell, J. B. *Living It Up: America's Love Affair with Luxury*. New York: Simon and Schuster, 2003.

Van Dijck, José. "Composing the Self: Of Diaries and Lifelogs." *Fibreculture* no. 3 (2004).

———. "Users Like You? Theorizing Agency in User-generated Content." *Media, Culture & Society* 31, no. 1 (2009): 41.

Vaynerchuk, Gary. *Crush It!* New York: HarperCollins, 2009.

Wadhwa, Vivek. "Silicon Valley: You and Some of Your VC's Have a Gender Problem." *TechCrunch*, February 7, 2010. http://techcrunch.com /2010/02/07/silicon-valley-you%E2%80%99ve-got-a-gender-problem -and-some-of-your-vc%E2%80%99s-still-live-in-the-past.

Wadhwa, Vivek, Krisztina Holly, Raj Aggarwal, and Alex Salkever. "Anatomy of an Entrepreneur: Family Background and Motivation." *SSRN eLibrary* (July 7, 2009). http://papers.ssrn.com/sol3/papers.cfm?abstract _id=1431263.

Wee, L., and A. Brooks. "Personal Branding and the Commodification of Reflexivity." *Cultural Sociology* 4, no. 1 (March 2010): 45–62.

Welch, David. "Luxury Gets More Affordable." *BusinessWeek,* April 22, 2002. http://www.businessweek.com/magazine/content/02_16/b3779608 .htm.

Wernick, A. *Promotional Culture: Advertising, Ideology and Symbolic Expression.* Thousand Oaks, CA: Sage, 1991.

WikiLeaks Contributors. "WikiLeaks: About." *WikiLeaks.org,* May 19, 2010. http://wikileaks.org/w/index.php?title=WikiLeaks:About&oldid=67599.

Wikipedia Contributors. "Cyberdelic." *Wikipedia: The Free Encyclopedia.* Wikimedia Foundation, January 24, 2010. http://en.wikipedia.org/w /index.php?title=Cyberdelic&oldid=339762925.

———. "Life Hack." *Wikipedia: The Free Encyclopedia.* Wikimedia Foundation, January 27, 2010. http://en.wikipedia.org/w/index.php?title=Life _hack&oldid=340297387.

———. "List of Places with 'Silicon' Names." *Wikipedia: The Free Encyclopedia.* Wikimedia Foundation, December 23, 2009. http://en.wikipedia .org/w/index.php?title=List_of_places_with_%22Silicon%22_names& oldid=333653398.

———. "Valleywag." *Wikipedia: The Free Encyclopedia.* Wikimedia Foundation, February 13, 2010. http://en.wikipedia.org/w/index.php ?title=Valleywag&oldid=343650851.

———. "Wikipedia." *Wikipedia: The Free Encyclopedia.* Wikimedia Foundation, July 12, 2010. http://en.wikipedia.org/w/index.php?title=Wikipedia &oldid=373092776.

Williams, A., and P. Dourish. "Imagining the City: The Cultural Dimensions of Urban Computing." *Computer* 39, no. 9 (2006): 38–43.

Williams, Evan. "Live from Web 2.0." *Evhead.com,* October 5, 2004. http:// evhead.com/2004/10/live-from-web-20.asp.

Wortham, Jenna. "How Social Media Can Induce Feelings of 'Missing Out.'" *New York Times,* April 9, 2011, sec. Business Day. http://www .nytimes.com/2011/04/10/business/10ping.html.

Wright, F. A. "From Zines to Ezines: Electronic Publishing and the Literary Underground." Ph.D. diss., Philosophy, Kent State University, 2001. http://www.zinebook.com/resource/wrightdissertation.pdf.

Wu, Tim. *The Master Switch: The Rise and Fall of Information Empires.* 1st ed. New York: Knopf, 2010.

Wynn, Eleanor, and James E. Katz. "Hyperbole over Cyberspace: Self-Presentation and Social Boundaries in Internet Home Pages and Discourse." *The Information Society* 13, no. 4 (December 1997): 297–327.

Yeung, Bernice. "So Open It Hurts." *San Francisco Magazine,* August 2008. http://www.sanfranmag.com/story/so-open-it-hurts.

Zimmer, Michael. "Preface: Critical Perspectives on Web 2.0." *First Monday* 13, no. 3 (March 3, 2008). http://firstmonday.org/htbin/cgiwrap/bin/ojs/index.php/fm/article/view/2137/1943.

Zittrain, Jonathan. *The Future of the Internet—And How to Stop It.* New Haven: Yale University Press, 2008.

# INDEX

―――

Accountability, 218
Achieved micro-celebrity, 116, 117,
    134–136
Achieved status, 76
Activism, 8, 27
Addressivity, 98
Affective labor, 195
Ahl, Helene, 261
Allen, Matthew, 302n155
Allen, Paul, 31
Allison, Julia: anti-fans of, 151–160,
    278; and authenticity, 252; and
    micro-celebrity, 113, 116, 122,
    139, 145, 146, 151–160; and
    publicity, 239–240; and self-
    branding, 185, 194, 199
Amazon.com, 45

Ambient awareness, 214
Anderson, Benedict, 7
Anderson, Chris, 70
Angel investment, 90
AngelList, 250
Anti-corporate activism, 43–48
Anti-fans, 151–160
Antin, Eleanor, 210
Anxiety, 226–227
Apache Software Foundation, 33,
    54
Apathy, 132
Apple, 29–30, 56
Arab Spring, 3, 297n18
Aragon, Maria, 15
Armstrong, Heather (Dooce), 116,
    121, 145

Arrington, Michael, 69, 107, 127, 133, 144

*The Art of Self-Branding* blog, 194

Arvidsson, Adam, 203

ASCII files, 37

Ascribed micro-celebrity, 114, 116, 134–136

Ascribed status, 76

AsianAve, 46

Aspirational production, 121–123

@replies, 95–100, 108

Attention economy, 143, 159

Atterberry, Wendy, 159

Audience for lifestreaming, 208, 211–213

Authenticity: as content strategy, 248; and lifestreaming, 233–234; and micro-celebrity, 114, 119–121, 160; myths of, 246, 247–252; and self-presentation, 17, 167, 198; and Web 2.0, 247–252

*Bamboo Girl* (zine), 40

Barbrook, Richard, 50, 51, 52

BarCamp, 67, 69

Barger, Jorn, 46

Barlow, John, 53

Barron, Jessica, 58

Barsook, Paulina, 252

Bartiromo, Maria, 273

BASIC programming language, 31

Battelle, John, 63, 64

Bautista, Glenda: on lifestreaming, 241, 242; and male entrepreneurship myth, 268; on metrics of status, 104, 105; and micro-celebrity, 135, 150, 151; and self-branding, 190, 191, 198

Baym, Nancy, 75

Beale, Scott, 58, 67, 69, 70, 123, 124, 126, 132

BedPosted.com, 210

Behlendorf, Brian, 54

Belmont, Veronica, 94, 96, 118–119, 186–187, 218

Beneviste, Gabe, 118

Benkler, Yochai, 3, 34, 70, 232

Bennett, Lance, 45

Berkeley People's Computer Club, 30

*Better than Well* (Elliott), 249

Bezos, Jeff, 63

Bieber, Justin, 14

*The Big Score: The Billion Dollar Story of Silicon Valley* (Malone), 262

Bill and Melinda Gates Foundation, 274

Black, Rebecca, 15

BlackPlanet, 46

Block, Ryan, 126, 127

Blogs: and independent media, 46–47; and self-branding, 185; and status, 93

Bloomberg, Michael, 202

Body hacks, 176

*Boing Boing*, 23, 38, 70

Bonner, Sean, 222

Booker, Cory, 273

Botton, Alain de, 74

boyd, danah, 25

Boyd, Stowe, 49–50, 103, 168–169, 250, 276

Brand, Stewart, 29, 32, 53

Brand Camp University, 166

*Brands* (Arvidsson), 203

Bronson, Po, 49

Brown, Ben, 116

Brown, Tara, 222–226

Bubble hotties, 161

Buchert, April, 167
Buffardi, L. E., 311–312n31
Burka, Daniel, 267
Burning Man festival, 24, 57–59, 87
Business cards, 190
*BusinessWeek:* on Mayer, 265–266; on New Economy, 60; on Rose, 113, 146; on Vaynerchuk, 171

Cacophony Society, 57
Calacanis, Jason, 65, 127, 200
Californian Ideology, 23–24, 48–52
Cameron, Andy, 50, 51, 52
Cameron, Deborah, 196
*Camgirls: Celebrity and Community in the Age of Social Networks* (Senft), 115
Cammaerts, Bart, 47
Camp, Garrett, 99
Campbell, W. K., 311–312n31
Capillaries of power, 279
Capitalism, 5, 23, 28, 110
Carnegie, Dale, 188
Carnegie Mellon University, 253
Carr, Andrew, 26
*Carving: A Traditional Sculpture* (Antin), 210
Cashmore, Pete, 263
Cassidy, John, 62
Castells, Manuel, 48
Çelik, Tantek: and BarCamp, 68, 69; as conference speaker, 39; on lifestreaming, 234; on metrics of status, 107; and micro-celebrity, 126; and self-branding, 184, 199; Waldman's success attributed to, 268
*The Celluloid Closet* documentary, 278
Chan, Adrian, 99, 227
Chance, Grayson, 14

Change Congress campaign, 23
Charice, 15
Chen, Gina Masullo, 216
Cheng, Kevin, 89, 90, 91, 217, 226–227
Chiang, Larry, 126
ChickClick, 41
Child, Julia, 193
Chomsky, Noam, 12
Citizen journalism, 24
CitizenSpace, 9
Clarke, Alison, 86
Coachella, 86
*Code 2.0* (Lessig), 232
Codel, Eddie, 39
Coleman, Biella, 32
Coleman, Gabriella, 87
Collins, Orvis, 260–261
Comstock, Michelle, 39, 41
Conferences, 39, 86–90. *See also specific conferences*
Consumer capitalism, 5
Content generation, 173
Cool, Jennifer, 55, 56, 57
Copyright, 23, 34
Counterculture, 4–5, 15, 24, 28
Co-working, 9, 295n20
Cox, Ana Marie, 67
*Craphound* (zine), 38
Crawford, Kate, 216
Creative Commons, 23, 34
Creative labor, 202
Creative nihilism, 47
Crowdsourcing, 22
CrunchBase, 90, 250
*Crush It!* (Vaynerchuk), 170, 171, 172, 174, 183
Cuban, Mark, 63
*Cult of the Amateur* (Keen), 26
*Cultures@SiliconValley* project, 77–78

Culver, Leah: as conference rock star, 89; laptop advertising sold by, 84; and male entrepreurship myth, 266, 267–268, 270, 315n31; and micro-celebrity, 136, 138, 143, 146, 149; and self-branding, 184, 185; on work-life balance, 81
Curetogether.com, 210
Cyberdelic culture, 28, 52–53
*Cyberia* (Rushkoff), 52
Cyborganic Corporation, 55–59
Cyprus 20, 146–147

Darabi, Soraya, 251
Denton, Nick, 137, 138, 139
Deregulation, 5, 11, 13, 51
*Details* magazine on tech industry playboys, 263
Diaryland, 46
Digg, 22, 112
Digital elitism, 16, 275
Digital exceptionalism, 4, 25, 247
Digital footprint, 209
Digital instantiation, 206, 211
Digital intimacy, 216
Digital self, 211
Dignan, Larry, 242
Disembodiment hypothesis, 25
Disney, 45
Doctorow, Cory, 23, 38, 63, 64, 70
Dodgeball, 122, 226–227
Doerr, L. John, 60
Domain names, 173, 185
Dooce. *See* Armstrong, Heather
Dorsey, Jack, 94
Dot-com boom, 39, 59–63
Douglas, Nick, 137–140, 144, 237, 256
Dourish, P., 227
Drama, 214–215, 222–226

Dreamlining, 177, 193
Duncombe, Stephen, 35–36
Dyson, Esther, 50, 65

Ebert, Roger, 129
Edited self, 191–195
Electronic Frontier Foundation, 34
Elites: access to, 90–92; digital elitism, 16; and micro-celebrity, 130–134
Elizabeth, Shannon, 157
Elliott, Carl, 249
Ellison, Nicole, 11
Emerging Technology (eTech) conference, 66
Emotional labor of self-branding, 194–204
Engineers, 108, 253, 271
English-Lueck, Jan, 49, 77–78, 81, 83–84
Entrepreneurship: and gender, 261–272; growth of, 3; myths of, 246, 257–272; and neoliberalism, 11; and self-branding, 170, 201; in social hierarchy, 80; and social media, 3
Estronet, 41
Etsy, 9
Evans, Andrew, 162
Ewen, Stuart, 230
E-zines, 28, 35–43, 299n58

Facebook: demographics of, 2, 295n22; employees, 1–2; friends as status metric, 188; Instagram acquired by, 80; for lifestreaming, 208, 214, 236; likes as status metric, 75; self-presentation management on, 243; social surveillance via, 220; and status, 93; as Web 2.0, 22

*Factsheet Five,* 38

Fake, Caterina, 38, 39, 71

*Fame: The Psychology of Stardom* (Evans & Wilson), 162

Famewhoring, 134, 146, 161

Fan labor, 195

Fashion bloggers, 280–281

*Fast Company* on self-branding, 165

*Fast Food Nation* (Schlosser), 43

Fauxparazzi, 122

Fear of missing out (FOMO), 8, 226–227

Feminism, 40, 42

Ferriss, Timothy, 101–102, 113, 169–170, 176–181, 197

*Filter Bubble* (Pariser), 298n18

Fitbit pedometer, 209

Fitton, Laura (Pistachio), 89, 117–118, 133, 163–164

Flickr, 2, 22

Flooding content streams, 191

Florida, Richard, 61–62

FOMO (Fear of missing out), 8, 226–227

Foo Camp, 68–69

Foreman, Charles, 263

Forum for Women Entrepreneurs and Executives, 272

FOSS. *See* Free and open-source software

Foucault, Michel, 11, 12, 13–14, 279

*The 4-Hour Body* (Ferriss), 170, 176, 179–180, 183

*The 4-Hour Chef* (Ferriss), 170, 176, 308n8

*The 4-Hour Work Week* (Ferriss), 170, 176, 183

Foursquare, 9, 67, 208, 220, 227

Franklin, Benjamin, 210

Free, Eris, 69

Free and open-source software (FOSS), 23, 28, 29–35, 45

*Free Culture* (Lessig), 34, 64

Free Culture Movement, 23

Freedman, Jenna, 42

Freedom multiplier, 178

Freedom of Information Act, 232

Freelance labor, 178, 202

Freeman, Eric T., 209

Free-market economics, 51

Free Software Foundation, 32

Freiburg school, 296n26

Freudian psychology, 168

Friedman, Milton, 11, 296n26

Friendfeed, 214

Gates, Bill, 31, 32, 85, 253, 274

Gawker Media, 136, 145

Gelernter, David, 208, 209

Gender: and entrepreneurship, 261–272; and meritocracy, 261–264; and self-branding, 180–181; and social hierarchy, 75; and status, 251–252; and tech industry, 247

Gershon, Ilana, 16

Gibbs, Jennifer, 220

Girls in Tech, 247, 272

Gladwell, Malcolm, 67

Global Entrepreneurship Week (GEW), 259

Globalization, 11

GNU project, 32

Goldhaber, Michael, 201

Golub, Alex, 32

GoodReads, 209

Google: employees, 3; and free and open-source software, 33; YouTube acquired by, 22, 70, 80
Google Zeitgeist, 259, 273–275
Graham, Bob, 210
Graham, Paul, 64
Gramsci, Antonio, 78
Grant, Melissa Gira: on access to elites, 92; on lifestreaming, 244; on micro-celebrity, 137, 140, 141, 143, 145, 146–147, 161; on privacy, 237
Grassroots media activists, 27, 47–48
Gray, Jonathan, 151, 154
Grazian, David, 249
Grossman, Lev, 21–22
Gunderloy, Mike, 38

Hacker culture, 29–35
Hall, Justin, 46, 56
Hammer, M. C., 166
Harris, Josh, 205–206
Hartley, Hillary, 88, 135, 254
Harvey, Larry, 57, 58
#hashtags, 100–101
Hayek, Friedrich, 11, 296n26
Hearn, A., 307n5
Henderson, Maureen, 153
Herring, Susan, 46, 98
Hewlett-Packard, 48
Hilton, Paris, 157
Hilton, Perez, 173
Hochschild, Arlie, 196
Hoefler, Don, 48
Hoffman, Anthony, 252
Hoffman, Auren, 213–214
Homebrew Computer Club, 30
Honeycutt, Courtenay, 98
HootSuite, 108
Horowitz, Andresson, 120

HorsePigCow blog, 186
Horton, D., 119
How to Win Friends and Influence People (Carnegie), 188
Hu, Jane, 266–267
Hunt, Tara: on access to elites, 91; on lifestreaming, 240–241; and micro-celebrity, 119, 133, 139, 149, 150, 151; and myth of male entrepreneurship, 264–265, 269; and self-branding, 184, 186, 197; on social hierarchy, 79, 80, 82

IBM, 48
Idealism, 84
Identity, 13–15, 192–193, 211. See also Self-presentation
Immaterial labor, 195
Independent media, 43–48
Independent Media Center (IMC, Indymedia), 44–45
Individualism, 18
Information overload, 227–229
Ingram, Mathew, 70
Innovation, 260
Insiders, 130–134. See also Elites
Instagram, 71, 80
Intel, 48
Internet famous, 115–116
Interoperability, 6
Intimacy, 216
Intuit, 186
Investor's Business Daily on user-contributed content, 22
iVillage, 41

Jackson, Adam, 103–105, 122–130, 197–198, 266
Jacy Russiangirl (pseudonym), 153–155, 156, 159

James, Jerry, 57

Jenkins, Henry, 3, 70

Jobs, Steve, 3, 259

Johnson, Samuel, 210

Juliaspublicist (pseudonym), 153–154, 155

Junell, Ryan, 39–40

Juris, Jeff, 43

Justin.tv, 124

Kahle, Brewster, 58

Kan, Justin, 124

Kapor, Mitch, 64, 70

Kaputa, Catherine, 193–194

Karp, David, 263

Katz, John, 35

Kawasaki, Guy, 97, 107, 163–164

Keen, Andrew, 26

Kelly, Kevin, 50, 56, 119

Kelty, Chris, 33

Kickstarter, 9, 238

King, Ryan, 68, 69

Kitching, Audrey, 161

Klein, Naomi, 43

Klinenberg, Eric, 45

Klout, 77, 105–106

Kurzman, Charles, 133

Kutcher, Ashton, 113

Lacy, Sarah, 150, 151, 161, 188, 197, 253

LaidOffCamp, 167

Lair, D. J., 307n5

*Lamebook.com*, 278–279

Lanier, Jaron, 26, 71–72

Laporte, Leo, 131

Larson, Dale, 227–228, 233

Last.fm, 2

Lazar, Shira, 113

Lazzarato, Maurizio, 195

Leary, Timothy, 53

Lessig, Larry, 23, 34, 63, 64, 70, 232

Levy, Steven, 30, 32, 65–66

LeWeb conference, 163–164

Libertarianism, 48–52, 313n63

"The Lifestreamer's Manifesto" (Mullen), 215–216

Lifestreaming, 205–244; audience for, 211–213; and authenticity, 233–234; benefits of, 215–219; defined, 208–211; and digital self, 211; and drama, 222–226; drawbacks of, 219; and fear of missing out, 226–227; and information overload, 227–229; management of, 240–244; and micro-celebrity, 124; in practice, 213–215; and privacy through disclosure, 237–238; and privacy vs. publicity, 229–231; and publicity as freedom, 207, 231–237; and publicity as strategy, 238–240; and social surveillance, 219–222; and status, 10, 16

Lillith Fair, 41

Linkspam, 173

Linux, 33

LiveJournal, 46

Lodwick, Jakob, 115, 132–133, 134, 263

*Los Angeles Times* on Google's acquisition of YouTube, 22

Lott, Trent, 46

Lovink, Geert, 47

MacManus, Richard, 65

Madden, Raymond, 294n13

Mager, Andrew, 106–107, 218, 228, 242

*Make a Name for Yourself* (Roffer), 193

Malik, Om, 63, 67, 107, 133, 259

Malone, Michael Shawn, 262

*The Managed Heart* (Hochschild), 196

Mann, Merlin, 131

Marketing strategies, 17, 184, 192

Marxism, 202

Masculino, Marianne, 106, 131, 184

*Mashable*, 8, 70, 132

*Mastering the Art of French Cooking* (Child), 193

Mayer, Marissa, 142, 265–266

McCarthy, Caroline, 91, 167, 263

McCarthy, Megan: on fear of missing out, 226; on gender and entrepreneurship, 265; on meritocracy, 253; on metrics of status, 104, 107; on micro-celebrity, 122, 133, 137, 139, 140–141; and self-branding, 187; on social network use, 99

McChesney, Robert, 12, 45

McGlynn, Nick, 122

M. C. Hammer, 166

McKenna, Terrence, 53

McLuhan, Marshall, 52

Media, 43–48

MediaLive International, 63

MemoMail, 311n11

Mentoring, 266

Meritocracy: and gender, 261–264; myths of, 246; and self-branding, 170; and status, 76; in tech scene, 18; and Web 2.0, 252–257

Messina, Chris, 67, 69, 139, 264–265

Metrics of status, 103–109, 187–188

*Me 2.0* (Schawbel), 188, 193

Microblogging, 214

Micro-celebrity, 112–162; achieved vs. ascribed, 134–136; and aspirational production, 121–123; and authenticity, 114, 119–121, 160; case study (Allison), 151–160; case study (Jackson), 123–130; creation of, 117–118; defined, 115–117; experiences of, 148–151; and fan interactions, 118–119; insiders vs. outsiders, 130–134; as learned status-seeking practice, 128; norms for, 158; persona creation for, 114, 117, 126–127; publicity as element of, 230; and social hierarchy, 280; and status, 10, 15; and *Valleywag*, 136–148

Microsoft, 31, 33, 45, 56

MiGente, 46

Miller, Vincent, 216–217

*Miss Advised* (reality show), 152, 155

MIT, 29, 33, 253, 270

Modeling of self-branding, 169–171

Montag, Heidi, 152

Montano, Linda, 210

Moore, David, 260–261

Morozov, Evgeny, 297n18

Mosaic web browser, 54

Mozilla, 33

Mullen, Jessica, 215–216

Mullenweg, Matt, 39, 67, 69, 131, 184, 254, 268

Muller, Thor, 88, 102, 121, 133

Multitasking, 168

Musk, Elon, 142, 306n33

MySpace, 22, 70

Narcissism, 219, 311–312n31

National Center for Women and Information Technology, 272

Neff, Gina, 61
Negroponte, Nicholas, 50
Neoliberalism, 5, 11–13, 51, 78, 181–183, 201, 296n26
*Net Delusion* (Morozov), 297n18
Net neutrality, 23
Networked audience, 211–213
Networking, 125–126, 128, 145, 173–174, 189–190, 266
New Communalist movement, 52, 55
New Economy, 60, 62
Newitz, Annalee, 103, 136, 256
New York City: as social media destination, 9; tech industry in, 61
New York Internet Week, 86
*New York Times:* on dot-com boom, 60; on Ferriss, 177, 179; on Web 2.0, 63
Nigam, Anu, 184, 186, 253
Nike Fuel band, 209
Nintendo, 45
Nippert-Eng, Christina, 220
Nissenbaum, Helen, 220, 235
"No-collar" labor model, 61
*No Logo* (Klein), 43
Nonparticipation, 243
Norms: for lifestreaming, 215; for micro-celebrity, 158; and self-presentation, 17; for Twitter, 100–101
Nye, Dan, 253

Obama, Barack, 202, 259
Occupy Wall Street, 43
O'Connor, Sandra Day, 273
Offline status, 109–111
Ogbor, John, 261
Omerosa, 154
OMGPOP, 71, 80

*Once You're Lucky, Twice You're Good* (Lacy), 188
OneForty, 164
*100 Interviews Project,* 131
Ong, Aiwa, 14
OpenCourseWare initiative, 33
Open-source culture, 6, 29–35. *See also* Free and open-source software (FOSS)
Opportunity, 78
O'Reilly, Tim, 63, 64
Organic intellectuals, 78
Outsiders, 130–134, 243
Outsourcing labor, 178
Overby, Derek, 96–97, 131, 135, 181–182, 196–197
Oxygen, 41

Page, Larry, 142
Pageview principle, 157
Para-social interaction, 119
Pariser, Eli, 298n18, 300n95
PariSoma, 9
Pearce, Celia, 52
Peer Index, 106
Peer-to-peer advocacy, 23
Penley, Constance, 151
Pepys, Samuel, 210
Peren, Bruce, 33
Persistence, 25, 221
*Personal Branding* magazine, 166
Personal informatics, 209–210
Peters, Tom, 165–166
Pew Internet and American Life Project, 206
PheltUp, 127–128
Philanthropy, 274
Phillips, Whitney, 157
*Phrack* (zine), 37–38

Pickard, Victor, 44, 47

Pinkowitz, Jacqueline M., 155

Pirillo, Chris, 39

Pistachio. *See* Fitton, Laura

Pitch statements, 189–190

Political power, 12

*PopCrunch,* 266

Pownce, 214, 267

*PR: A Social History of Spin* (Ewen), 230

Pratt, Spencer, 152

*Princeton Review* rankings of entrepreneurship programs, 259

Privacy: and lifestreaming, 229–231, 237–238; and micro-celebrity, 143–144

*Privacy Online: Perspectives on Privacy and Self-Disclosure in the Social Web* (Trepte & Reinecke), 229

Professor Camping (pseudonym), 153–154

*Profits over People* (Chomsky), 12

PROSkore, 106

Publicity: as freedom, 231–237; lifestreaming as, 207, 229–231; as strategy, 238–240

Punk rock, 36–37, 40

*Quantified Self* blog, 210

Quora, 109–110

Rabois, Keith, 3

*Radar* magazine on Allison, 153

Raffel, Daniel, 255

Rave culture, 52–59

Raymond, Eric, 33

Reagle, Joseph, 75

Reality television, 13, 16, 152, 206

*Reblogging Donk* (*RBD*), 153–154, 278

Reed, Racquel, 161

Regan, Priscilla, 235

Reich, Robert, 273

Replicability, 25

Reputation, 76

Re-tweets, 95–100, 108

Rheingold, Howard, 53, 56

Riot Grrrl, 40, 41

*The Rise of the Creative Class* (Florida), 62

Roberts, Seth, 210

Roffer, Robin Fisher, 193

Rose, Kevin: and Culver's founding of Pownce, 267; *Details* magazine profile of, 263; and meritocracy, 254–255; and micro-celebrity, 112–113, 116, 136, 143, 146, 150; as tech industry elite, 24, 89; Twitter use by, 101

Ross, Andrew, 61, 62

Rossetto, Louis, 51, 52

Rucker, Rudy, 53

Runkeeper, 209

Rushkoff, Douglas, 52–53

Sabala, Aubrey, 221

Samberg, Andy, 173

San Francisco: casual aesthetic of, 85–86; counterculture in, 4–5; dot-com crash in, 62; high-tech industry in, 3; tech scene in, 8, 246; Web 2.0 origins in, 23

Scalability, 25

Schawbel, Dan, 166, 184–185, 188, 193

Schlosser, Eric, 43

Schmidt, Eric, 142, 235, 273, 274

Scoble, Robert, 69, 89, 107

Scott, Jason, 37

Searchability, 25

Seattle, tech industry in, 45

Self-branding, 163–204; case study (Ferriss), 176–181; case study (Vaynerchuk), 171–176; defined, 165–169; and dot-com boom, 61; emotional labor of, 194–204, 277; limits of, 307n5; maintenance of edited self, 191–194; modeling, 169–171; and neoliberalism, 181–183; publicity as element of, 230; and status, 10, 16; in tech scene, 5, 188–191; and Web 2.0, 183–188

Self-censorship, 249

Self-employment, 201

Self-presentation, 5, 11, 17, 241. See also Lifestreaming; Micro-celebrity; Self-branding

Self-quantification, 209

Senft, Theresa, 115, 280

The Shallows (Carr), 26

Shirky, Clay, 3

Silicon Alley (New York), 61

Silicon Valley, 8, 24, 50. See also San Francisco

Silicon Valley Insider, 132

Sincerity and Authenticity (Trilling), 120

Singer, Daniel, 37

Sivers, Derek, 170

Slant (zine), 40

Slashdot, 75

Smith, Andy, 69

Social capital, 74, 254

Social entrepreneurship, 259

Social graphs, 5

Social hierarchy of tech scene, 4, 74, 77, 79–83, 280

Social inclusion, 99

Social media: and capitalism, 28; demographics of, 2; metrics of, 187–188; and self-branding, 170, 203; and status, 93–103; and Web 2.0, 7

Social surveillance, 207, 219–222, 277

Solis, Brian, 157–158

Solove, Daniel, 235

Sorgatz, Rex, 122

South by Southwest (SXSW), 66–67, 86, 88, 89–90, 112, 116

Spotify, 209

Stallman, Richard, 32, 33, 34

Stanford Artificial Intelligence Lab, 29

Stanford Entrepreneurship Network, 258–259

Stanford Research Institute, 29

Stanford Technology Ventures Program, 258

Stanford University, 49, 253, 258

Starr, Nick, 135, 222–226, 239, 251–252

State Department, 3

Status, 73–111; anxiety about, 227; and conferences, 86–90; and elite access, 90–92; and gender, 251–252; metrics of, 103–109; online vs. offline, 109–111; reasons for studying, 10–11; social hierarchy of tech scene, 79–83; and social media, 93–103; symbols of, 83–86; and Twitter, 7–8, 100–103

Status affordances, 75

Status Anxiety (Botton), 74

Steenson, Molly, 39
Sterling, Bruce, 67
Sternberg, Ernest, 117, 231
Steuer, Jonathan, 55
Stone, Sandy, 25
Stoppelman, Jeremy, 80, 82, 108, 134, 258, 260
Suicide Club, 57
Sundance festival, 86
Sunstein, Cass, 47
SuperHappyDevHouse, 67, 68
Survival Research Laboratories, 57
Swanson, Heidi, 41
Swisher, Kara, 85, 87, 107, 142, 258, 275
SXSW. *See* South by Southwest
Symbols of status, 83–86. *See also* Metrics of status

Tate, Ryan, 306n33
*TechCrunch*, 8, 70, 132, 144
Tech events, 124–125, 137. *See also* Conferences; *specific events*
Technical knowledge, 76, 107, 271
Technological determinism, 4, 6
Technology of subjectivity, 203
Technology of the self, 13–14
TED talks, 22, 86
Telecommunications Act of 1996, 45
*The Thank You Economy* (Vaynerchuk), 170, 171–172
Thomas, Owen: on Allison, 159–160; as conference speaker, 39; on Culver, 267–268; on metrics of status, 105; and micro-celebrity, 118, 136, 137, 140, 141, 143, 144, 306n33

Thurlow, Crispin, 277
Thurmond, Strom, 46
Timehop, 311n11
*Time* magazine on "You" as 2006 person of year, 3, 21
*TMI Weekly*, 152
Tomlin, Lily, 278
Transparency, 27, 75, 110, 159, 233, 235
Trilling, Lionel, 120
Trippi, Joe, 23
Trolls, 157
Trunk, Penelope, 268
Trust, 76
Tufts University, 33
Tumblr, 9
Turkle, Sherry, 25
Turner, Fred, 52, 58
TweetDeck, 108, 190
*2600: The Hacker Quarterly* (zine), 37–38
*Twilight* anti-fans, 155
Twitctionary, 100
Twitter: and Arab Spring uprisings, 3; @replies, 95–100, 108; followers as status metric, 75, 95, 108, 188; and information overload, 228; and intimacy, 216; and lifestreaming, 208, 214; and micro-celebrity, 125–126, 128; re-tweets, 95–100, 108; and self-branding, 186, 192, 200; self-presentation management on, 243; social surveillance via, 220; and status, 7–8, 77, 93–103; and SXSW, 67; as Web 2.0, 22
Twitterfall, 108
*Twitter for Dummies* (Fitton), 164
Twitter Grader, 106

Twitterholic, 95
Twitterrank, 95
Twittonary, 100

Unionized labor, 12
University of Washington,
    45
UNIX, 32
Usenet, 75
User-generated content, 22, 24
Usernames, 185, 309n36

*Valleywag,* 136–148
Vaynerchuk, Gary (Garyvee), 82,
    89, 116, 169–176, 194, 197–198
Venture capital, 3, 60, 255–256
Viacom, 45
Virtual personal assistants (VPAs),
    178
Vosneck, Sharon, 255

Wadhwa, Vivek, 255
Waldman, Ariel, 183, 198, 200,
    238–239, 268–270
Walker, Alice Wright, 307n47
Walker, Tristan: on access to elites,
    91; on authenticity, 120, 250, 251;
    on entrepreneurs, 257–258; on
    meritocracy, 245; on social
    hierarchy, 82, 133
Warren, Jim, 31–32
*Washington Post* on lifestreaming,
    208
*The Wealth of Networks* (Benkler),
    34, 232
Web 2.0, 21–72; and anti-corporate
    activism, 43–48; and authenticity,
    247–252; and Burning Man
    festival, 57–59; and Californian
    Ideology, 48–52; discourse of,

25–27; and dot-com boom, 59–63;
    and entrepreneurship, 257–272;
    and gender, 261–264; and hacker
    culture, 29–35; history of, 6–7;
    ideals of, 6; and independent
    media, 43–48; and meritocracy,
    252–257; myths of, 245–272; and
    open-source culture, 29–35;
    origins of, 27–29, 63–72; and rave
    culture, 52–59; and self-branding,
    183–188; and zines, 35–43
Web 2.0 Expo, 63–64, 66
Webrings, 40–41
Webzine conference, 39
*We Live in Public* documentary,
    205–206
WELL online community, 56
Where 2.0 conference, 66
White, Vanna, 166
*The Whuffie Factor* (Hunt), 119
WikiLeaks, 231
Wikipedia, 22, 33, 75
Williams, A., 227
Williams, Evan: on entrepreneur-
    ship, 259; as industry elite, 3, 24;
    on micro-celebrity, 136; and
    SXSW, 89; and Twitter, 94,
    95–96, 109; and Web 2.0 confer-
    ence, 65; as Webzine conference
    speaker, 39
Williams, Kelly, 250
Wilson, Glenn, 162
WineLibrary.tv, 170, 171
Winer, David, 46
*Wired* magazine on "Internet
    famous," 116, 146
Withings scale, 209
Wohl, R. R., 119
Work-life balance, 81–82, 173–174,
    181–182

World Trade Organization (WTO) protests (1999), 43, 44
Wu, Tim, 26

Xerox PARC, 29

Yahoo!, 2
Y Combinator, 271, 294n11

*You Are Not a Gadget* (Lanier), 26
YouTube, 3, 22, 70, 80

Zines, 28, 35–43, 299n58
Zuckerberg, Mark, 2, 3, 24, 139, 236, 263
Zynga, 80